TE MANA
TE KĀWANATANGA

The Politics of Māori
Self-Determination

I tāpaea tēnei pukapuka
ki a Meihana Te Rama, rāua ko Kahurautete
rātou ko te hunga kua wehe atu.

Nā rātou i whakato te kakano.

This book is dedicated to my

grandparents and earlier generations.

Their efforts have been the inspiration.

TE MANA
TE KĀWANATANGA

The Politics of Māori
Self-Determination

M. H. DURIE

Auckland

OXFORD UNIVERSITY PRESS

Oxford   Melbourne   New York

OXFORD UNIVERSITY PRESS NEW ZEALAND

Oxford New York

Athens Auckland Bangkok Bogota Bombay
Buenos Aires Calcutta Cape Town Dar es Salaam
Delhi Florence Hong Kong Istanbul Karachi
Kuala Lumpur Madras Madrid Melbourne
Mexico City Nairobi Paris Port Moresby
Singapore Taipei Tokyo Toronto Warsaw

and associated companies in
Berlin Ibadan

OXFORD is a trade mark of Oxford University Press

ISBN 0 19 558367 1

Edited by Simon Cauchi
Cover design by Sarah Maxey
Typeset by Archetype, Wellington
Printed through Bookpac Production Services,
Singapore
Published by Oxford University Press,
540 Great South Road, Greenlane,
PO Box 11-149, Auckland, New Zealand

Contents

TABLES

1

MANA MĀORI

DETERMINATION AND DEVELOPMENT

Ka maro te kakī o te kōtuku.[1]

INTRODUCTION

Two themes are interwoven in this book. One is about Māori autonomy and self-determination; the other explores Māori interaction with the state and the state's responses to Māori. Although both require some historical perspective, the book is not primarily a history about relationships between Māori and the state; instead, it is about events which have shaped the attitudes and accomplishments of both over the past decade or so as Māori have struggled to assert a greater measure of autonomy and control. Māori and the state are at times poles apart, at times more or less in agreement, and at times uncertain about their respective roles, obligations, and mutual expectations. However, the focus is not always on disagreements between Māori and the state, frequent though they are, or unilateral assertions of autonomy, or the arrogant imposition of unjust laws, or even disparities in standards of health, education and economic well-being that threaten to divide the country. For the most part this book is an analysis of Māori aspirations against the backdrop of a distinctive cultural identity, a changing national identity, and a worldwide assertion by indigenous peoples of the right to self-determination.

Consistent with the double focus, the book has Māori and English titles, *Te Mana Te Kāwanatanga* and *The Politics of Māori Self-Determination*. *Te Mana Te Kāwanatanga* incorporates two words which have come to symbolise much of the spirit of Māori determination to remain distinct and strong even when submission and assimilation were on the state's agenda. Of the two key Māori words, one, mana, is an old Māori word, the other, kāwanatanga, has been introduced from English.

Mana has several meanings. It was used in the Declaration of Independence to describe aspects of Māori sovereignty.[2] 'Ko te Kingitanga, ko te mana i te wenua o te wakaminenga o Nu Tireni, ka meatia nei kei nga tino Rangatira anake i to matou huihuinga, . . .' 'All sovereign power and authority within the territories of the United Tribes of New Zealand is hereby declared to reside entirely and exclusively in the hereditary chiefs and heads of tribes in their collective capacity, . . .' The word kingitanga had been coined by early missionaries. Because they could find no Māori word to describe an all-powerful federal sovereign, they simply used a transliteration of king—kingi—from which kingitanga (kingdom) is derived. It was a not uncommon practice when an appropriate equivalent could not be found in the source language.[3] Actually other words might well have been considered, including rangatiratanga and arikitanga.[4] But the notion of a supreme body politic, prescribed in the Declaration of Independence, appears to have been sufficiently novel in Aotearoa at that time to warrant a new word to capture, as it were, a new phase of political and constitutional development.[5] And it was new. The intention in 1835 was to create a Māori nation state, a departure from the exclusively tribal orientation which prevailed, and the introduction of a confederated approach to governance. Kingitanga signalled the new approach. Moreover, if there were doubts about the meaning of kingitanga, then the addition of an old Māori word—mana—alongside it, reduced the ambiguity. Mana has both worldly and ethereal meanings, but in the context of this book and as used in the Declaration of Independence it spells out authority and control.

Kāwanatanga forms the second part of the Māori title. The word is a transliteration of governance and was introduced by the missionaries in early biblical translations. Its use in the Treaty of Waitangi in 1840, however, is the reason for using it in this book. The phrase 'all the rights and powers of Sovereignty' is translated in the Treaty as 'te Kawanatanga katoa.'[6] As a translation for sovereignty, there are serious shortcomings since kāwanatanga (governance) has a lesser meaning than its weighty English equivalent, and in any event its meaning to Māori would have depended on their connecting it with some aspect of their own experience.[7] In 1840, any actual experience of a central type of government was limited to the few who had ventured overseas. Further, although in 1835 mana had been used to indicate sovereignty (or at least Māori sovereignty), in 1840 the word kāwanatanga had been selected. The choice remains puzzling, and may have been a deliberate deception.[8] Regardless, together mana and kāwanatanga form an apt doublet to convey the essence of this book—the relationship between Māori authority and control and the state's right to govern.

It will be obvious that the English title of this book, *The Politics of Māori Self-Determination*, is not a literal translation of *Te Mana Te Kāwanatanga*. In 1835 both control and authority were to be functions of the collective tribes, and governance would be the right of the chiefs, their representatives, acting independently of other nation states. Implicitly, the English title recognises that Māori aspirations for autonomy were no longer guaranteed after the signing of the Treaty of Waitangi. Indeed, the path of independence had the potential for conflict and collision when the courses charted by Māori or the Crown clashed or even strayed in opposite directions. A recurring theme in this book is the interface between Māori autonomy and the power of the state, but questions are also posed about the type of state within which Māori self-determination might best find expression. Even though they do not have identical meanings, however, the two titles are deliberately used to reflect the complexities and ambiguities surrounding the concepts of sovereignty, mana, self-determination, the state, and governance, within New Zealand.

Before the 1840 Treaty of Waitangi, New Zealand might well have entered the modern world as a Māori nation state. The Declaration of Independence, recognised in Britain and acknowledged by King William IV, proposed a Māori legislature, a Parliament made up of chiefs, to 'make laws and pass regulations' on behalf of the emerging nation as it prepared to bargain with other countries. Though a united tribal entity may have been Busby's fiction,[9] there is also a Māori oral history which suggests that the impetus for the Declaration came not from Busby but from a confederation of tribes, Te Whakaminenga.[10] Regardless, the difference from present times is that in 1835 Māori were themselves to form the government. Not only would the new nation join the international community as an independent state, but Nu Tirene (as New Zealand was described in the Declaration), was to be a state where Māori values, practices and aspirations would determine future directions. Māori self-determination was securely bound to collective Māori sovereignty.

In 1840 the Treaty of Waitangi countered the Declaration and removed the possibility of a Māori-led state. Because kāwanatanga (a transliteration of governance) and not mana was ceded in the Treaty, Māori understandings of self-determination do not always accept that control, and the mechanisms necessary for the exercise of control, have ever been abandoned. Yet even allowing for differences in meaning between the English and Māori versions of the Treaty and the debate about whether sovereignty was actually ceded or not, at the very least the Crown did obtain the right to govern. Subject to certain guarantees for the protection of Māori interests, the Treaty provided Britain with the necessary authority to shape and control the state as it applied to Aotearoa New Zealand. It is highly unlikely that the tribes fully understood the constitutional significance of the Treaty, especially the wide powers granted to the Crown in Article 1,[11] nor does it appear that the Crown fully understood its obligations to construct a state which would enhance the Māori interests it guaranteed to protect. By the end of the sovereignty wars some twenty-five years later, however, the tribes were left in little doubt that whatever else the Treaty promised, it had excluded them from active roles in the governance of their own country, or even their own tribal territories. [12]

Questions about the state, power, control and authority are important and reappear in several chapters of this book. There are other questions as well which are equally significant and probably more directly related to people in the day-to-day pursuit of their well-being, economic security, and enjoyment. What is self-determination? Why is it valued? Is it over-valued? How is it measured? What range of concerns does it cover, and how is it manifest at local and national levels? *Te Mana Te Kāwanatanga* does not provide answers to all those questions but it does explore many of the underlying issues as they pertain to resources, social and economic well-being, ratification of the Treaty of Waitangi, legal empowerment and self-governance. Moreover it concludes that the main aims of self-determination go well beyond academic discussion about constitutional arrangements or discourse on the hybridisation of peoples in a postmodern world, to embrace Māori people as they prepare for the next century and the well-being of their descendants.

THE GOALS OF SELF-DETERMINATION

While the politics of power between Māori and the state are critical for an understanding of self-determination, they are not synonymous with its fundamental aims and goals. Rather the aims of self-determination are practical and intimately bound to the aspirations and hopes within which contemporary Māori live. Essentially Māori self-determination is about the advancement of Māori people, as Māori, and the protection of the environment for future generations.

Advancement is not easy to define and because it is ongoing its outcomes may well defy measurement. In the context of self-determination, however, advancement encompasses three important dimensions. First, it signifies a commitment to strengthening economic standing, social well-being, and cultural identity, both individually and collectively. Second, it also touches on the dimension of power and control, again at individual and group levels. Māori advancement is about the better self-management of natural resources, greater productivity of Māori land, the active promotion by Māori of good health, a sound education, enhanced usage of Māori language, and decision-making that reflects Māori realities and aspirations. Third, advancement is also about change. Cultural fossilisation is not consistent with the spirit of development; and even though traditional values and knowledge have important lessons for today and offer some clues for the future, Māori self-determination is not about living in the past.

The aim of advancing as Māori—resolving to retain a Māori identity in the face of multiple pressures to join a paler mainstream—may well be the most challenging goal. As the world oscillates between the promotion of universal cultures and the fractionation of existing states and countries, as superpowers decide how nations should be formed only to be met by the determination of smaller powers to retain their own nationhood, and as international communities coalesce in Europe or in the Pacific while indigenous peoples seek to distance themselves from governments which still hold too many memories of colonial yesterdays, Māori in Aotearoa New Zealand want to remain Māori. They wish to advance as Māori into the next century. At the end of the nineteenth century there was every chance that genocide would run its full course. Depopulation was dramatic and simply staying alive became the goal confronting Māori.[13] Into the twentieth century, survival was no longer the central challenge but ethnocide, the loss of an ethnic identity, was a possibility. Now, at the threshold of the twenty-first century, self-determination is about being strong numerically, economically, and culturally—and rejecting any notion of passive assimilation into national or international conglomerates.

Nor should it be presumed that Māori are homogenous, even though they share many physical and cultural characteristics. Tribal identities and tribal management of resources remain vital for an understanding of contemporary Māori society. Some tribes, iwi, claim nation status for their tribe, insisting that attempts to describe Māori as if they were a single group are forced. Others are able to recognise the role and relevance of tribes but ascribe equal validity to a collective Māori identity or a single Māori nation. It should also be pointed out that not all Māori have active links with any tribe, even though they may be able to demonstrate tribal descent and even have shared interests in Māori land. As urbanisation has escalated, issues relating to Māori who are alienated from tribes have assumed greater importance, especially in urban New Zealand, and they have been further highlighted by the search for a formula for the distribution of assets such as those derived from Māori fishing quota.

The third aim of Māori self-determination is the protection of the environment for future generations. It goes without saying that survival is not possible in an environment contaminated and depleted by the appetites of an expanding materialistic population. Nor do Māori want their children and grandchildren to grow up in a world of concrete. Clean air, fresh water, access to traditional lands, forests, rivers, the sea, are all on the Māori agenda for tomorrow. Concerns about the environment often stem from the sense of grievance which comes from dispossession, but to an equal if not greater extent they are also about the retention of a cultural identity and the maintenance of a way of life. In expressing these concerns, Māori have often articulated the views of other New Zealanders, and, together, they have confronted the state. But at other times Māori views have been sidelined, especially when claims of ownership have challenged questions about conservation ethics or recreational access. If land and its alienation were the main point of contention between Māori and the state in the late nineteenth century, then the management and ownership of the environment and its natural resources has the potential for similar misunderstandings a hundred years later.

The broad aims of Māori self-determination and some of the component goals are shown in summary form in table 1.1.

Table 1.1 The Aims of Māori Self-Determination

The Aim of Māori Advancement	The Aim of Affirming a Māori Identity	The Aim of Environmental Protection for Future Generations
Economic self-sufficiency	Personal identity	Land and forests
Social equity	Whānau identity	Rivers and lakes
Cultural affirmation	Hapū identity	Harbours and the sea
Political strength	Iwi (tribal) identity	Air
	Identity as a Māori nation	Environmental links with humankind

MĀORI DEVELOPMENT

It has already been noted that self-determination has long been on the Māori agenda, but its re-emergence as an important aim for the twenty-first century owes something to the philosophy of Māori development. For more than a decade Māori advancement has been synonymous with Māori development, a term introduced to suggest a more positive approach to Māori policy. There are obvious similarities between the aims of self-determination and the aims of positive Māori development, although there is also a significant difference in emphasis. While both are concerned with social, cultural, and economic development, and Māori delivery systems, the aims of self-determination place more importance on Māori control over resources and greater independence from the state. The aims of positive Māori development, however, are not necessarily inconsistent with government policy and have not infrequently been initiated by government. While they inevitably promote discussion about Māori autonomy, essentially they are designed to be accommodated within a mainstream framework without challenging the authority of the state. In practice, however, the differences between self-determination and Māori development may be more apparent than real, especially at local levels. Certainly, since positive Māori development was launched as a preferred option for Māori, self-determination has been closer to realisation than at any other time this century.

Positive Māori development was heralded as a new policy initiative at the Hui Taumata, the Māori Economic Summit meeting held shortly after the fourth Labour Government took office in 1984.[14] Convened jointly by the Ministers of

Māori Affairs and Finance, and chaired by Professor Ngātata Love, the hui was well attended by Māori tribal and community representatives from a wide range of sector interests and had been motivated by the bleakness of the Māori economy and evidence of widening disparities between Māori and non-Māori.[15] At the opening session the Hon. K. T. Wetere encouraged participants to discuss four main objectives:

(a) to reach an understanding of the nature and extent of the economic problems facing New Zealand as they affect Māori people

(b) to examine the strengths and weaknesses of the Māori people in the current
position

(c) to discuss policies for Māori equality in the economic and social life of New
Zealand

(d) to obtain commitment to advancing Māori interests.[16]

Buoyed by the conciliatory approach of the new government and the desire that Māori policy should reflect the views of Māori leaders, the hui responded with enthusiasm and recommended several priorities for Māori cultural, social and economic development. Some of the initiatives which had emerged from earlier Hui Whakatauira were endorsed—the positive message of Tu Tangata, support for Kōhanga Reo[17]—and there was confirmation of the outcome from the Runanga o Waitangi (held at Turangawaewae in September 1984) that the Treaty was important to future Māori needs.[18] But the Hui Taumata also brought fresh approaches, emphasising greater commercial awareness and better resource utilisation, with active participation in education and the economy, nationally.

There was an expectation that Māori people could realise greater levels of economic self-sufficiency, improved social well-being and less dependency on the state if they took advantage of their own distinctive social institutions such as iwi and hapū and actively developed their own tribal resources.[19] Building on an earlier discussion paper, *Tirohanga Rangapū* (Partnership Perspectives),[20] a policy document, *Te Urupare Rangapū* was released by the Minister of Māori Affairs in 1988. It contained the vision and strategy which would guide Māori towards greater independence with reduced dependency on the state.[21] While not all goals were realised, the decade witnessed the emergence of innovative strategies in both the political and the economic fields and was associated with a renewed deter-mination by Māori to retain tribal structures and culture while at the same time embracing the challenges of a global economy.[22]

Arising out of the Hui Taumata, iwi (tribal) development became a preferred focus for Māori development and there was a devolution of several government functions to various tribal authorities. Matua Whāngai, Mana Enterprises and Maccess training programs were all premised on the belief that, given adequate resources, Māori were better placed to provide certain services to their own people than the state. Other programs, such as Māori language retention and revitalisation through early childhood education centres, kōhanga reo, arose from Māori initiatives and only later did they attract state support.

By the conclusion of the hui, the Decade of Māori Development had been prescribed and six themes, central to the philosophy of positive development, had emerged: the Treaty of Waitangi, tino rangatiratanga, iwi development, economic self-reliance, social equity, and cultural advancement. The six themes and their implications are shown in table 1.2.[23]

Table 1.2 Themes from the Decade of Māori Development

Theme	Implications
The Treaty of Waitangi	Māori–Crown relationships Settlement of claims Biculturalism
Tino rangatiratanga	Māori self-determination Constitutional review Māori mana motuhake
Iwi development	Tribal development as a vehicle for Māori advancement
Economic self-reliance	Development of a sound economic base Reduced state dependency Developmental funding
Social equity	Elimination of disparities Iwi social delivery systems Māori perspectives Iwi–state partnerships
Cultural advancement	Māori language Māori educational systems Marae focus

While these themes were not the only ones to emerge, they did so consistently enough to force major policy and legislative changes and to redirect Māori energies towards new visions based as much on old structures as on new economic imperatives. Having adapted awkwardly to life in urban surroundings, and being all too aware that the provision of social services was often inadequate to meet Māori needs, the new Māori call was for 'Māori solutions to Māori problems.' Both a lack of confidence in the capacity of the state to offer positive solutions and a desire to capitalise on existing Māori structures and values combined to inject a sense of independence and renewed commitment to alternative approaches. Positive funding rather than negative spending was the catch-cry and there was pressure on the government to move away from an exclusive focus on areas where disparities between Māori and non-Māori were evident (imprisonment, poor health, welfare benefits) and instead to accept some responsibility for assisting in a move towards positive development. Significantly, a sound economic base was seen as a crucial step towards achieving any real political autonomy or even cultural survival.

The Decade of Māori Development was punctuated by a change to a National government in 1990. Winston Peters, representing the Tauranga electorate, was appointed Minister of Māori Affairs and immediately set about redirecting Māori policy. A three-person working party produced a new document, *Ka Awatea (It is Dawn)*, heralded as an exciting new strategy for Māori development.[24] Some significant departures from the policies forged by Wetere were introduced. Importantly, there appeared to be less focus on iwi as a vehicle for Māori and a stronger emphasis on reducing disparities between Māori and non-Māori, largely through greater government responsibility—a reminder that the market by itself would not deliver for Māori.[25] Education, training, health and economic resource development were highlighted for special attention. Despite the differences, however, there was also a continuation of some of the directions contained in *Te Urupare Rangapū*—greater enhancement of the mainstream to meet Māori aspirations, reduced substantive program delivery from the new Māori ministry and, instead, a stronger policy and monitoring role. As well, *Ka Awatea* made a damning assessment of Labour's record on the settlement of Treaty claims.[26] Peters presented the policy to Māori leaders at a very public occasion in March 1991 and, although few had any chance to read its detail, the document was then delivered to the government as having wide Māori support.

Whether the government fully accepted *Ka Awatea* as Māori policy was never clear. Some parts were implemented: the Ministry of Māori Affairs and the Iwi Transition Agency were both disestablished and replaced by the single Ministry of Māori Development. And the priority areas of health, education, training, and economic resource development were recognised. But there was otherwise relative silence about the document as a comprehensive policy for Māori. By then conflict between the Minister and the government, especially the Prime Minister, had seriously intruded on the formulation of any policy and, after Peters departed from Cabinet and then from the National party, *Ka Awatea* was seldom mentioned. Six years later, however, when a coalition government had formed, it returned as the blueprint for Māori policy, now with a fresh Minister of Māori Affairs, Tau Henare, at the helm.

Two approaches to economic development had been launched during the Decade of Māori Development. In 1985 the Mana Enterprises Scheme was initiated. Its prime objective was to facilitate the entry of Māori into business, while a secondary aim was to reduce Māori unemployment. Loans were made available to potential businesses through Māori authorities, usually tribal but also urban, as well as the Māori Women's Welfare League and the Ratana church. Funds from government were allocated by the Department of Māori Affairs and were used for a wide variety of initiatives including rest homes, tourism, catering, agricultural contracting, fishing, and retailing. In 1988/89, Mana Enterprises had an allocation of $13.6 million, but by 1992 it was reduced to $9 million prior to being phased out and incorporated, along with other Māori-specific initiatives, into mainstream programs (in this case the Business Development Boards and Department of Labour). While there was considerable criticism of Mana, and many businesses failed, the record was probably no worse than for other small businesses at the time and, perhaps more importantly, through the scheme Māori had been encouraged to enter the commercial world.

A further initiative to promote Māori commercial enterprise was the Māori Development Corporation (MDC), established in 1987. Like Mana Enterprises it aimed to enhance business skills but also to provide financial resources for medium sized Māori businesses. The government invested $13 million in MDC and by 1990 130 loans, totaling $35.2 million, had been advanced. But when profits dramatically dropped from $1.5 million in 1989 to $193 000 in 1990, the focus of the corporation was changed to equity investment and financial restructuring. Problems over ownership and control also emerged. Shareholders from a Māori-owned ironsand company, Taharoa C, tried to take over the ailing corporation but were prevented from doing so. Then in 1993 government decided to sell its 49 per cent shareholding to other Māori shareholders, for a profit of $7.93 million. The government's decision to dispose of its shares without devising a method of ensuring that all tribes could benefit led to a Waitangi Tribunal claim in 1993 but did not stop the action. The claimants, Whatarangi Winiata and Te Aho Kotuku, argued that the Crown's contribution was in fact monies which would otherwise have been spent on Māori economic development and in that sense belonged to Māori generally, not to any one tribe or group.[27] Meanwhile in order to resolve protracted shareholding manoeuvrings, MDC bought out all the shareholders except the Tainui Māori Trust Board. As a result the Board became the sole owner of the Corporation so that by 1996 it was no longer a pan-Māori institution, even though Tainui did not discount fuller Māori participation some time in the future.[28] However, debate about the government's right to reclaim its $13 million plus profits continued and at a meeting of the Māori Congress in 1996 serious consideration was given by the tribes present to challenge the government's actions in the High Court.

THE WIDER CONTEXT FOR SELF-DETERMINATION

Neither the Hui Taumata nor the Decade of Māori Development took place in a vacuum. They occurred as episodes in the Māori voyage of survival, adaptation and change, and in that sense provided a link with the distant past as well as a signpost for the future. Many factors combined to influence the emerging principles, priorities, and goals. Demographic change by itself, for example, required the formulation of new strategies which could take into account the changing Māori population: urbanisation, fertility rates that were high at first and then (after 1960) sharply reduced, an increasing total Māori population, a predominantly youthful profile, increased life expectancy, and a likelihood of many more older people in the decades ahead.

But events outside Māori society also had implications for Māori development and the role Māori might play in shaping their own futures. In 1984, New Zealand embarked on a process of radical societal change, and the Māori Economic Summit occurred when the anticipated transformations were already gaining momentum. While Māori participants at the summit believed they were not only initiating a process of positive Māori development but also controlling its implementation, the government had its own agenda, which among other things included a reduction in the size and role of the state. Positive Māori development, with its focus on tribal responsibilities for health, education, welfare, economic progress, and greater autonomy, fitted quite comfortably with the free market philosophy of a minimal state, non-government provision of services, economic self-sufficiency, and privatisation.

There is no doubt that the Hui Taumata captured the attention of politicians but there was parallel concern that the Hui Taumata itself had been captured by the architects of a free market economy and the monetarist theories of the New Right.[29] Certainly, among the hui conclusions it was possible to discern some of the New Right values: encouragement of competition, open trading with deregulation, a reduced role for the state, a renewed spirit of enterprise, and greater individual freedom. Although there were substantial differences between the advocates of the free market and the champions of tino rangatiratanga, on the surface at least the differences were often blurred. Māori economic independence was caught rather uncomfortably in the wider political agenda of user pays, reduced government spending, lowered inflation rates, and a reduction in overseas borrowing. Devolution had become confused with partnership, iwi authorities were all too often indistinguishable from agencies of state, and sceptics argued that the whole exercise was a carefully orchestrated manoeuvre to rid the state of its ongoing financial obligations to Māori. Before long Māori development was seen by many Māori as little more than a restatement of the mainstream preoccupation with economic engineering at the expense of collective state responsibility.

At the time, though, Māori participants at the Hui Taumata recognised the dangers of continued Māori dependency on the state and the underdevelopment of their own physical and human resources. Economic self-sufficiency was not to be merely another name for abolition of state responsibilities; it was to be an opportunity for Māori to reach full potential on their own terms and for their own reasons. Whether or not it accorded with economic policies of the state currently in vogue was a secondary issue.

New Zealand's position in the world's market place also impacted on Māori development. The GATT agreement committed Māori as well as other New Zealanders to new directions and priorities; so did Agenda 21 and the global environmental challenges. Like other indigenous peoples, Māori were not always keen to embrace the philosophies and politics of the international arena. Importantly, however, a United Nations Working Group on Indigenous Populations (WGIP) provided a forum where many concerns could be raised and debated by indigenous peoples from around the world. The group has been developing a Declaration on the Rights of Indigenous Peoples and in that process Māori have been active participants. Completed at the eleventh session of the working group, the current draft contains 45 articles covering cultural, social, economic, political, and constitutional rights. Article 3 states: 'indigenous peoples have the right of self-determination. By virtue of that right they freely determine their political status and freely pursue their economic, social and cultural development.'[30]

Because of an interest in preserving territorial integrity, a principle adopted by the United Nations in the 1960 Declaration on the Granting of Independence to Colonial Territories and Countries and the 1970 Declaration on Principles of International Law concerning Friendly Relations and Co-operation among States, not all governments were able to support Article 3. To do so could imply agreement to aboriginal secession from the state with subsequent fragmentation and an undermining of the principle of territorial integrity. A distinction was therefore made between internal and external self-determination. Internal self-determination amounts to a form of internal self-government but within the framework of a unified state, whereas external self-determination implies a secession from the post-colonial state and the development of an independent indigenous nation-state. An aboriginal right to self-determination which does not threaten territorial integrity is more likely to be supported by governments.[31] On the other hand, it is unlikely that Māori, or other indigenous peoples, will readily accept such a narrow definition of self-determination even if they are not actively proposing to secede. Among other things they will be likely to argue that the capacity of states for shared sovereignty should not be discounted.

Indigenous developments elsewhere in the globe have attracted considerable Māori attention and, apart from WGIP, there are now well-worn tracks to (and from) Hawaii, mainland USA, Alaska, Canada, Norway, Australia, and Spain. Though the situations are not always comparable, common themes have been identified, self-determination among them. In some countries, such as the United States of America, different treatment has been afforded to different indigenous groups. Thus Indian bands are able to enjoy a measure of self-determination, even sovereignty, which is substantially more than that allowed native Hawaiians, whose position as the indigenous people of Hawaii is much less secure.[32] The inconsistency is not untypical of the ambivalence of states with regard to the right of indigenous peoples to control their own development and to do so in a manner which asserts traditional distinctive identities. For many indigenous peoples the ambivalent and non-compromising attitudes of the state remain barriers to the realisation of the aims of self-determination. It is also ample evidence that Māori development and self-determination are subject to many external forces, both at national and international levels. Table 1.3 summarises those factors.

Table 1.3 Māori Development and Māori Self-Determination: The Wider Context

Dimension	Consequences
Māori history	Survival Adaptation Change
Māori demography	Urbanisation Increased population Reduced fertility Youthfulness
National economic reform	Free market User pays Removal of state subsidies Competition
State restructuring	Reduced size of the state Devolution Privatisation of the state's commercial activities
Indigenous development	Declaration on the Rights of Indigenous Peoples Self-governance Shared sovereignty

NGĀ POU MANA

In *Te Mana Te Kāwanatanga* discussion about self-determination is shaped by a two-dimensional framework which incorporates the foundations of Māori control and authority, ngā pou mana, as well as factors relevant to Māori realisation of self-determination, te mana whakahaere. The framework is shown in table 1.4.

Ngā pou mana are the sources, the foundations, of authority and standing for Māori. Each chapter in this book will consider a particular pou mana with respect to Māori authority and control and will examine recent developments, the points of consensus between Māori and the Crown, the disagreements, and Māori aspirations. Because all domains cannot be examined seven key areas have been selected for closer attention on the basis of their widespread concern to Māori and their continuing relevance to Māori well-being, identity, security, and endurance, now and in the future. All seven areas have important lessons for Māori self-determination, though it will be shown that Māori control and authority are often threatened by unreasonable expectations of conformity or even assimilation.

Table 1.4 A Māori Self-Determination Framework

Te Mana Whakahaere	Ngā Pou Mana						
	Mana Atua	Mana Tūpuna	Mana Tāngata	Mana Whenua	Mana Moana	Mana Tiriti	Mana Motuhake
Goals							
Māori advancement							
Cultural affirmation							
Protection of the environment							
Key Participants							
Hapū							
Iwi							
Local, regional, and national leadership							
Strategic Relationships							
The state in NZ							
Pacific nations							
Indigenous peoples							

Chapter 2, Mana Atua: A Resourceful Environment, takes its Māori title from the authority and control vested in the children of Rangi and Papa, the sky father and the earth mother. In the struggle to separate their parents, the children assumed god-like qualities and became champions for the environment. Tāne Mahuta is the deification of forests, Tangaroa the oceans, Tāwhirimātea the wind and the elements, Haumia-tiketike, ferns and crops. Māori participation in environmental protection, the application of traditional practices to contemporary environmental management, and tension between the interests of conservationists and Māori claims to ownership of natural resources and parts of the conservation estate will be discussed. The giant forests of New Zealand are part of this debate. Whether it be the struggle to develop new forests or the battle to cut down older ones, or more fundamental questions about who owns the forests, Māori have asserted certain rights based on their own understandings of a relationship with the world of Rangi and Papa. There is also a reminder in this chapter that Māori attitudes to the environment played no small part in shaping the national ethos and in refocusing the balance between development and sustainability.

In chapter 3, Mana Tūpuna: Identity and Heritage, the focus shifts to the cultural legacies of ancestors, tūpuna. Current expressions of culture, including the continuing relevance of tribes to Māori development and especially to self-determination, are discussed. Māori language usage, mātauranga Māori (indigenous knowledge), and Māori identity are also explored within the context of change, westernisation, intellectual property rights, and urbanisation. Cultural adaptation with the accompanying concerns about adulteration will form part of the debate; and the emergence of the print, broadcasting, and television media as forces for cultural affirmation are examined.

Mana Tāngata: The Power of Numbers, the fourth chapter, is about the well-being of Māori individuals. It examines Māori performance in several social policy areas and as well reports on recent research on Māori households, the whānau (extended family), and the delivery of a range of services by Māori. While gaps between Māori and non-Māori are highlighted, the chapter is not primarily about disparities; rather it embraces concepts relevant to social justice and considers the increasing diversification within Māori society. Importantly, changing demographic trends are analysed and there is particular attention to kaumātua, Māori elderly. By 2031 the numbers of older Māori will have grown eightfold, a sufficiently dramatic increase to warrant greater interest in planning for their future needs. Finally, this chapter analyses Māori participation in political processes and discusses current Māori standing in the first MMP (Mixed Member Proportional System) Parliament.

Chapter 5 is called Mana Whenua: The Lore of the Land. Even though alienation has seriously eroded tribal holdings, land remains a substantial economic base for Māori. It is an important reason why the Ture Whenua Māori Act 1993 is of such significance, since its purpose is to encourage the retention of Māori land in Māori ownership and to make better use of the little land that does remain in Māori hands. Nonetheless the Act itself does not increase Māori land holdings and has sometimes been criticised as coming too late, after tribal lands had been reduced to a mere four per cent of total land ownership. The extent of land loss is one thing; the mechanisms through which land was alienated is another. Both the Tainui and Taranaki claims are vivid illustrations of the unjust exercise of power—through sheer might as well as through the pen—to remove Māori from their land, and the long saga leading to restitution forms a significant part of this chapter. Then there is the equal travesty of the Crown leases of Māori land, in perpetuity, another injustice for which an even longer-term resolution is proposed.

While land-based economies are important, the potential of the sea to provide a further substantial economic base has become increasingly apparent, as Māori participation in commercial fishing ventures has escalated. Chapter 6, Mana Moana: The Business of Fishing, reviews events leading up to the Sealord agreement and then examines some of the complexities surrounding the distribution of assets, including quota. It traverses a range of largely unresolved issues—the interpretation of Māori custom law and its application to modern times; the relative rights of inland and coastal tribes; the position of urban Māori and the authorities that advocate on their behalf; distinctions between inshore and deep water fisheries; large tribes and small tribes. At the same time the significance of the fisheries settlement to both Māori and the Crown is recognised as a key event which continues to have repercussions for other settlements as well as for the ongoing relationships between tribes and for Māori society generally.

One of the themes emerging from the decade of Māori development was the Treaty of Waitangi, and in this book it is the subject of chapter 7, Mana Tiriti: Application of the Treaty of Waitangi. Attitudes to the Treaty and the varying interpretations of its significance, in the past but more particularly in modern times, are discussed alongside government policies for Māori and the emergence of a Crown Treaty settlement policy. But attention also comes to rest on the mechanisms in place to address Treaty issues, including the Waitangi Tribunal, the courts, the Crown Forest Rental Trust, Te Ohu Kaimoana (Treaty of Waitangi Fisheries Commission), the Office of Treaty Settlements, and the Cabinet Treaty Committee. Treaty policies are not the same as policies for Treaty settlements, a distinction which is important when settlement frameworks are under negotiation. More to the point, without a clear Treaty policy, it is difficult for Māori to negotiate settlements which take account of future needs as well as past injustices. In addition there is the added question of the utility of the Treaty and the sometimes overly optimistic expectation that it will provide solutions for all aspects of Māori self-determination.

Mana Motuhake: Autonomy, Governance, and Nationhood (chapter 8) continues the theme of Māori control and authority by discussing the relevance of terms such as sovereignty, tino rangatiratanga and self-determination. Existing tribal and community arrangements for governance are highlighted and compared. Marae, Māori trust boards, runanga, councils, wānanga (Māori institutes of learning), and committees perform varying roles in the promotion of Māori interests and together could be said to make up an extensive, though diffuse, system of governance. Māori governance at a national level is another matter. The MMP environment raises fresh hopes of a Māori caucus within the new Parliament, though such a caucus is also regarded by advocates of Māori sovereignty as a second-best alternative to a distinct and separate Māori body politic. Since 1995, a range of views have surfaced about the need for a confederated Māori organisation; and, if there is a need, the most appropriate structure. The New Zealand Māori Council and the Māori Women's Welfare League have both provided leadership at a national level, and the emergence of the National Māori Congress in 1990 further expanded the options for kotahitanga (Māori unity) and the exercise of rangatiratanga. Moreover, the Congress has fuelled the debate by considering not only the formal recognition of the Māori nation but also the development of a Māori nation state. Meanwhile there is every indication that the government is embarking on a journey of similar fundamental constitutional significance, the development of a Republic with greatly lessened ties to a colonial past. In this respect, Māori and the Crown may have more in common than is generally appreciated.

That, however, is not the final conclusion of the book. More predictably it is that the search for Māori self-determination and the realisation of its three broad aims will require much more debate among Māori and between Māori and the state. Not all Māori agree that a single Māori nation exists or even that it should exist; nor does the Crown accept the possibility of any semblance of divided sovereignty or a dual voice for the country. Neither, however, have the issues been subjected to a coherent and systematic debate. One conclusion advanced in chapter 8 is that current constitutional arrangements are inadequate for today's realities. Before further piecemeal solutions are cemented into place, New Zealanders should have the opportunity to build a broad framework upon which Māori aspirations for self-determination can take shape in a constructive and deliberate manner.

In each chapter, two broad themes will be evident. One is about the role of the state in either facilitating or blocking Māori interests; the other is about Māori capacities to take advantage of changing situations in order to realise aspirations for cultural, social and economic advancement. The state's role hinges largely on government policies and laws, arrangements for power-sharing, and the establishment of national priorities which accord with the realities of the ballot box. Māori prerequisites for advancement, on the other hand, depend on access to cultural and physical resources, the level and type of organisation, and leadership and expertise. These themes are summarised in table 1.5.

Table 1.5 Barriers to Self-Determination Framework

	Legislation and policy	Arrangements for power-sharing and decision making	National priorities
Access to Māori resources			
Level and type of Māori organisation			
Leadership and expertise			

Te Mana Te Kāwanatanga: The Politics of Māori Self-Determination does not prescribe a solution nor does it offer a quick-fix remedy for Māori economic ills or better relationships between Māori and the state. However, it does attempt to bring together many of the major concerns integral to Māori advancement, and in the process examines the interaction between Māori and the state. Sometimes agreement between the two can be detected. Regrettably, all too often there is disagreement, misinformation, and frank misunderstanding. The prime purpose of this book is to examine the issues so that, if differences cannot be always avoided, they might at least be better understood.

NOTES FOR CHAPTER 1

1 'The Kōtuku (bird) with its neck outstretched.' Quoted by Denese Henare at the Hui Taumata in 1984. 'I believe we are like the kōtuku with its neck outstretched, ready to take flight. We are determined to be uplifted from our present position; we are determined to make progress,' in Department of Māori Affairs, (1984), *Māori Economic Summit Conference, Conference Proceedings*, Wellington.

2 The English and Māori texts of the Declaration of Independence are contained in Appendix 1. The original Declaration is in the National Archives, Wellington.

3 Bruce Biggs, (1989), 'Humpty Dumpty and the Treaty of Waitangi' in I. H. Kawharu (ed.), *Waitangi*, Oxford University Press, Auckland, pp. 303–304.

4 Motuhake is often used to mean a capacity for independence, while arikitanga, derived from ariki, conveys a sense of jurisdiction over a certain territory.

5 The Declaration of Independence was translated into Māori by the missionary Henry Williams who also translated the Treaty of Waitangi. In the Treaty he translated the sovereignty of the Crown as 'te Kawanatanga', whereas when describing Māori sovereignty in the Declaration he used the phrase 'Ko te Kingitanga, ko te mana'.

6 The Māori and English texts of the Treaty of Waitangi are contained in Appendix 2.

7 Biggs, 'Humpty Dumpty and the Treaty of Waitangi'.

8 Douglas Sinclair, (1975), 'Land: Maori View and European Response', in Michael King (ed.), *Te Ao Hurihuri: The World Moves On*, Hicks Smith, Wellington, p. 136.

9 Peter Cleave, (1989), *The Sovereignty Game: Power Knowledge and Reading the Treaty*, Victoria University Press, Wellington, p. 41.

10 Lindsay Cox, (1993), *Kotahitanga: The Search for Māori Political Unity*, Oxford University Press, Auckland, pp. 42–43.

11 Peter Adams, (1977), *Fatal Necessity: British Intervention in New Zealand 1830–1847*, Auckland/Oxford University Press, Auckland, pp. 164–165.

12 Claudia Orange, (1987), *The Treaty of Waitangi*, Allen and Unwin/Port Nicholson Press, Wellington, pp. 159–184.

13 M. Pomare, (1908), 'The Māori' in *Transactions of the Eighth Session of the Australasian Medical Congress*, Government Printer, Melbourne.

14 Ngātata Love, (1994), 'The Hui Taumata and the Decade of Māori Development in Perspective', in *Kia Pūmau Tonu: Proceedings of the Hui Whakapūmau Māori Development Conference*, Department of Māori Studies, Massey University, pp. 21–27.

15 Conference Steering Committee, (1984), *A Briefing on Māori Economic Affairs*, Māori Economic Development Summit Conference, Dunmore Press, Palmerston North.

16 Hon. K. T. Wetere, Minister of Māori Affairs, (1984), in Department of Māori Affairs, *Māori Economic Summit Conference, Conference Proceedings*, Wellington.

17 Kōhanga Reo are early childhood education centres where the operating language is Māori. Now numbering over 400, the first had only opened in 1983.

18 Te Runanga o Waitangi Planning Committee (1984), *He Kōrero mo Waitangi*, Te Runanga o Waitangi.

19 Hon. K. T. Wetere, (1994), 'Opening Address Hui Taumata—Hui Whakapūmau Ten Years of Māori Development', in *Kia Pūmau Tonu*, pp. 11–13.

20 Hon. K. T. Wetere, (1988), *Tirohanga Rangapū: Partnership Perspectives*, Office of the Minister of Māori Affairs, Wellington.

21 Hon. K. T. Wetere, (1988), *Te Urupare Rangapū: Partnership Response*, Office of the Minister of Māori Affairs, Wellington.

22 M. H. Durie, (1995), 'Beyond 1852: Māori, the State and a New Zealand Constitution', *Sites*, no. 30, pp. 31–47.

23 Adapted from M. H. Durie, (1994), 'An Introduction to the Hui Whakapuumau', in *Kia Pūmau Tonu*, p. 5.

24 Ministerial Planning Group, (1991), *Ka Awatea: Report of the Ministerial Planning Group*, Office of the Minister of Māori Affairs, Wellington.

25 Denese Henare, (1995), 'The Ka Awatea Report: Reflections on its Process and Vision', in Margaret Wilson and Anna Yeatman (eds.), *Justice & Identity: Antipodean Practices*, Bridget Williams Books, Wellington, pp. 45–60.

26 Jane Kelsey, (1993), *Rolling Back the State: Privatisation of Power in Aotearoa/New Zealand*, Bridget Williams Books, Wellington, pp. 257.

27 Waitangi Tribunal, (1993), *Māori Development Corporation Claim (Wai 350)*, Waitangi Tribunal, Wellington.

28 Tainui Maaori Trust Board, (1996), *Annual Report 1996*, Ngaruawahia.

29 The influence of free market policies on policies for Māori development is well discussed in Jane Kelsey, (1990), *A Question of Honour*, Allen and Unwin, Wellington.

30 Working Group on Indigenous Populations, (1993), *Draft Declaration on the Rights of Indigenous Peoples: Report on the Eleventh Session of the United Nations Working Group on Indigenous Populations*, United Nations, Geneva.

31 Te Puni Kōkiri, (1994), *Mana Tangata: Draft Declaration on the Rights of Indigenous Peoples 1993: Background and Discussion on Key Issues*, Ministry of Māori Development, Wellington.

32 Lilikalā Kame'eleihiwa, (1992), *Native Land and Foreign Desires*, Bishop Museum Press, Honolulu, pp. 321–327.

2

MANA ATUA

A RESOURCEFUL ENVIRONMENT

. . . ko te whānau takato a Rangi;
Ko Tāne-tūturi, ko Tāne-pēpeke,
Ko Tāne-ua-tika, ko Tāne-ua-hā;
Ko Tāne-te-wai-ora, ko Tāne-nui-ā-rangi,
Nāna i toko te rangi i runga nei.
Tū kē ana Rangi; tū kē ana Papa;
Ka tangi te hau, mātao i raro, he ao mārama.[1]

A BEGINNING

When the sky was forced apart from the earth, light entered the world and the environment was able to take shape. Although life soon flourished in every imaginable situation, the infinite variety of forms was not without pattern, nor did germination occur in isolated spurts without reference to a wider level of accord. Instead, the separation of the primordial parents was accompanied by a new set of transactions in which consensus was forged between the wind and the rain, the forests, fisheries, rivers, birds, and human inhabitants. As the story of Rangi and Papa suggests, the saga had all the hallmarks of a family epic, the parents sacrificing intimacy for the growth and well-being of their offspring, and eventually the children finding balance between their own aspirations and vendettas, and the need for cooperation, at least while the parents were alive.

Māori views of the world are based on the proposition that the environment is an interacting network of related elements, each having a relationship to the others and to earlier common origins. The personification of the earth and the sky as the parents Rangi and Papa underlines that point. Not only is a distinctly human dilemma presented as an explanation for creation, but by comparing the features of the environment to a family, a model is proposed for examining the connections and interdependencies which occur between forests and oceans, fish and fowl, the rivers and the soil and between people and the elements. In this sense, and well before the enactment of the Resource Management Act 1991, Māori gave some priority to the principles which underlie sustainable management and the needs of future generations.

In contrast to their more humble parents, the children of Rangi and Papa took on elevated—even grandiose—identities and as atua, gods, they became critical determinants of human well-being. It is not clear exactly how many atua existed or continue to exist, perhaps six, perhaps dozens.[2] Neither is there consistency across the tribes as to who were first generation atua and who came later. Sometimes Tāne is referred to as the atua responsible for forests and birds but he is also described as one of several siblings, all with the prefix Tāne: Tāne-tūturi, Tāne-pēpeke, Tāne-ua-tika, Tāne-ua-hā, Tāne-te-wai-ora and Tāne-nui-ā-Rangi.[3] Te Rangihiroa describes six atua and associates their names with authority over certain environmental elements.[4] Some are well known and are still afforded deference by modern practitioners of environmental ethics. Others are all but forgotten though they are retained in the deeper memories of tribal endeavour and periodically surface to offer guidance as new threats to nature emerge.

Tūmatauenga, often referred to as a god of war, though more accurately having responsibilities which extended over various human pursuits, is usually represented as the victor during the battle to separate the earth from the sky; and indeed he achieved a degree of power over Tāwhirimātea, the god of winds, surpassing the efforts of the siblings.[5] But it did not guarantee him, or his successors, pre-eminence over others. Instead, people remain a part of nature rather than superior to it; they exist in a state of balance with other elements, without dominion over the natural environment.[6] Rivers, lakes, trees, rocks, like men and women, all have a mauri (life force) of their own and in that sense have equal claims to a place in the order of things.

Table 2.1 contains a list of atua and their domains.

Table 2.1 Ngā Atua Māori: Guardians of the Environment

Atua	Domain	Resource Interests
Tangaroa	the seas and waters	fisheries and fish
Rongomatāne	kumara	cultivated crops
Haumiatiketike	fern roots	bush undergrowth
Tāne Mahuta	the forests	trees and birds
Tāwhirimātea	the elements	wind, rain
Tūmatauenga	humankind	human exploitation

Arising from this conceptualisation of the environment, a four-part framework for understanding Māori values has been proposed by Hirini Matunga.[7] He recommends that culturally responsible environmental management decisions should take into account four fundamental Māori values: taonga, tikanga, mauri, and kaitiaki. Taonga is interpreted to mean, in its broadest sense, an object or resource which is highly valued. Taonga was used in Article 2 of the Treaty of Waitangi as a translation for 'other objects', though clearly its meaning in Māori is far broader than the implied English focus on physical objects. It has been said to cover cultural properties such as language, social properties including children, and environmental properties—rivers, birds, and special land sites.

The way in which a taonga is valued varies according to particular methods of recognition practised by different tribal groups—the tikanga. Tikanga are used as 'guides to moral behaviour'[8] and within an environmental context refer to the preferred way of protecting natural resources, exercising guardianship, determining responsibilities and obligations, and protecting the interests of future generations. Few tribes have committed tikanga to writing or reduced them to a simple set of rules. Instead the most appropriate tikanga for a group at a given time, and in response to a particular situation, is more likely to be determined by a process of consensus, reached over time and based both on tribal precedent and the exigencies of the moment. Tikanga is as much a comment on process as it is on fixed attitudes or knowledge.[9]

In Māori terms all living things, including natural and physical resources, possess a mauri, a life principle or life essence. Distinctions between inanimate and animate objects are therefore blurred, because each is afforded a spiritual existence which complements the physical state. Nothing is lifeless. Damage to a resource not only creates physical impairment but also causes spiritual damage and in the process impinges on the mauri of other objects, including people. Cultural pollution, a term introduced by the Waitangi Tribunal in the Motunui claim, incorporates that meaning.

The fourth part of the framework for understanding Māori environmental values is kaitiaki. It denotes the burden incumbent on tangata whenua (i.e. tribal members in a particular area) to be guardians of a resource or taonga for future generations. The act of guardianship, kaitiakitanga, requires clear lines of accountability to whānau, hapū or iwi and is more frequently associated with obligation than authority. Transfer of the ownership of a resource away from tribal ownership does not release tangata whenua from exercising a protective role to the environment, although it does make the task more difficult since others will also have an interest. In environmental terms the kaitiaki approach is holistic and provides for restoration of damaged ecological systems, restoration of ecological harmony, increased usefulness of resources, and reduced risk to present and future generations.[10]

Table 2.2 A Framework for Understanding Māori Environmental Values

Key Value	Applications	
Taonga	ancestral land	wāhi tapu
	water seas, rivers	estuaries, coasts
	air	atmospheric change
	minerals	energy (geothermal)
	native animals	native plants
	mahinga kai (traditional food sources)	
	taonga raranga (flax, weaving material)	
Tikanga	wairuatanga	respect
	manaakitanga	protection
	rangatiratanga	recognition
	manawhenua	authority
Mauri	status of resource	extent of pollution
	abundance	regenerative capacity
Kaitiaki	guardianship	future generations
	restoration of balance	
	reduced risk to present generations	

Source: adapted from Matunga, 1994

THE WAITANGI TRIBUNAL AND ENVIRONMENTAL PROTECTION

Differing beliefs and values in relationship to the environment have contributed to the mistrust and misunderstanding between Māori and the state about the wise management of natural resources and the environment. Māori have long been suspicious of the motives behind untrammelled land development and large-scale exploitation of the earth's wealth, especially when cultural values have been offended or local wisdom ignored. It was not surprising, therefore, that environmental concerns were prominent in the first major claims to the Waitangi Tribunal. Sewage disposal, especially water-based schemes, formed the basis of many, but there was equal anxiety about local authority planning which had failed to take account of Māori spiritual and cultural values, traditional resources, and usages.[11]

In the Te Ati Awa case (1983) the Waitangi Tribunal found that pollution of reefs by the discharge of sewage and industrial waste at Motunui not only threatened the survival of seafood but also diminished the standing of the people in terms of their customary obligations.[12] The claimants, Aila Taylor and Te Ati Awa, demonstrated a pattern of ownership of the coastal reefs that was not unlike hapū land rights. They also claimed that, as a result of the pollution, they were prejudiced spiritually and culturally since they were unable to fulfil the expectations of their visitors or demonstrate their customary manaakitanga (hospitality).

Crown negligence had contributed to the problem, and the Tribunal agreed that within the meaning of the Treaty of Waitangi Act Te Ati Awa had a legitimate claim. 'After a great deal of evidence on this subject from a number of people we were convinced that there is a need for a much greater awareness of the spiritual and mental concepts of the Māori in relation to seafood and water by non-Māori who share the seafood resource and by those who are charged with its protection. It would be particularly wrong if the administration of Māori fishing grounds were entrusted only to those whose judgements are founded upon cultural values that are entirely irrelevant to Māori people.'

Land-based disposal of industrial waste was recommended by the Tribunal and a proposed coastal outfall at Motunui for a synthetic fuel plant was opposed. At that time, in 1983, cultural pollution and Māori ownership of fisheries were far from the mind of the state. It was the time of 'think big', synthetic fuels, and urgent large-scale development. Māori cultural values and beliefs were an irritation to the National Government as it geared itself for the 1984 general election. Eventually the Crown did support the Tribunal's recommendations but not before conservationists and recreational fisherman had joined the Taranaki tribes in effective lobbying. In the Motunui case the Tribunal also took the opportunity to bring together concerns about pollution of the reefs and ownership. 'The reefs, in their view, are their reefs just as they were the reefs of their forefathers, but they have not the ownership of them nor the control. The control is in fact vested in others who may or may not be aware of their customs and preferences or who may be constrained by an empowering statute that does not enable them to give to the Māori interests any greater weight than which must be given to the general public interest.'

A case generated by similar concerns was brought by Ngāti Pikiao in 1984 in respect of the Kaituna River and a proposed pipeline to discharge effluent into the Kaituna (to reduce pollution of Lake Rotorua).[13] As in the Motunui dispute, the claimants emphasised that the river had spiritual and economic associations; sewage discharge into the river would create both biological and cultural pollution, thereby reducing the material circumstances of the iwi and insulting their mana. To them, the Kaituna river had its own wairua (soul) which should be kept apart from other waters. To mix the polluted waters of Lake Rotorua, contaminated by human waste, with the waters of the Kaituna, used for fishing, would be highly offensive. The Tribunal agreed and suggested alternative ways of disposing of sewage, principally on land. Again, the Crown endorsed the recommendation. Land-based disposal of waste was eventually to become the norm but it was over a decade before it was accepted by local authorities elsewhere in the country. In 1996, for example, the City Wastewater Community Liaison Group consulted widely about options for a future sewerage system for Palmerston North and brought back recommendations for a land-based option. Despite the greater cost, the option was supported by more than two-thirds of those who had responded.[14]

A third case was heard in 1985, regarding the sorry state of the Manukau Harbour.[15] Failure by the authorities to keep the harbour free of pollutants had led to the destruction of customary Māori fisheries and a consequent demeaning of the people who traditionally lived on the harbour shores. 'Although there is some opinion that the Māori did not come to a full environmental awareness until several generations after his arrival in Aotearoa, it also seems clear that the Māori brought with him a magico-religious world-view of the environment that readily lent itself to the conservation of the earth's resources. The natural world of the Māori was not divided into seen and unseen parts, but the physical and spiritual dimensions formed an integral and indivisible entity.' The Tribunal's view was that the Crown had indeed been negligent, and a massive clean-up program was recommended along with a restoration of Māori cultural values and the appointment of harbour guardians. Some of these guardians were to be kaitiaki appointed by the Minister of Māori Affairs 'to seek the well-being and preservation of the traditional status of the tribes of the harbour and its hinterland.'

As part of the Manukau Harbour claim, submissions about New Zealand Steel's mining operations at Maioro were considered. Two main concerns had created anger and distress for the claimants, Ngāti Te Ata. First, in order to convey ironsand concentrate from the mine site to the mill at Glenbrook, water from the Waikato River was used in an underground slurry pipe. After separation of the ironsands the water would then be discharged into the Manukau Harbour. To the Māori claimants the proposal was culturally offensive since the mauri of two bodies of water are incompatible and should not be mixed. A second concern related to the area used for mining. At least four of the blocks contained wāhi tapu—sacred sites—where burials had taken place in distant times. The Tribunal was sympathetic to both concerns but did not recommend against the pipeline. Rather, a strong case was made for the inclusion of Māori values in the law, and the more careful identification of wāhi tapu to limit (but not prevent) mining operations.

Finally, the 1987 Mangonui sewage claim also protested against a proposed sewage disposal scheme which would distribute effluent (human waste) over land of particular spiritual significance to Ngāti Kahu.[16] The Tribunal acknowledged the cultural and spiritual affront which would be imposed on the iwi, and noted the importance of early consultation, but did not recommend a new system. Instead, they considered that the impact of the scheme would be slight and that the land-based disposal scheme would, in the long run, provide little, if any, pollution. 'Ngati Kahu as a tribe were prejudiced in the planning proceedings, for consultation came too late, but the prejudice is not in itself such as to warrant the relief that was mainly sought . . .'

Mangonui was important for other reasons as well. In its Report the Tribunal introduced the principle of compromise and the need for practical solutions. 'This is a case in our view, where the Treaty requires a balancing of Māori concerns with those of the wider community of which Māori form part. . . . The Māori spiritual ethic was singularly suppressed or overlooked in the past but recent Planning Tribunal and High Court decisions show that need no longer be so. A balance must be maintained, however, not an over-redress. . . . Construction of any sewage works necessarily imposes certain costs, both financial and cultural, on the local community. Ngati Kahu had good cause to bring their claim and reason to feel aggrieved, and yet the cost to the community, of which Ngati Kahu forms part, would be too great in this instance if their claim was allowed.'

These four cases, summarised in table 2.3, have several features in common. All emphasise the link between water and land, the separateness of bodies of water (each with its own mauri or wairua), the spiritual associations between the environment and the people, the link between the mana of a tribe and the surrounding environment, and the significance of Article 2 to environmental management.

Table 2.3 Claims to the Waitangi Tribunal: Environmental Protection

	Motunui (1983)	Kaituna (1984)	Manukau (1985)	Mangonui (1987)
Tribal claimants	Te Ati Awa	Ngāti Pikiao	Ngāti Te Ata	Ngāti Kahu
Claim	Pollution of reefs	Pollution of river	Pollution of harbour	Pollution of wāhi tapu
Offending Crown policies	Petrochemical industry; Motunui outfall	Diversion of sewage from Rotorua	NZ Steel & harbour management	Mangonui County Sewerage scheme
Main objections	Loss of food sources; cultural offence	Loss of food sources; cultural offence	Loss of food sources; cultural offence	Cultural offence
Remedies	Motunui outfall abandoned	Land-based sewerage disposal	Harbour management plan; appointment of kaitiaki	Need for compromise

In the respective reports the Tribunal took on the role of protector of the environment. At a time when pollution of natural resources threatened lakes, rivers, and coastlines, the Tribunal stood out as a powerful voice for the growing conservation movement. The Resource Management Act (1991) owed much of its spirit to those early claims and the views expressed by Māori claimants.

THE RESOURCE MANAGEMENT ACT 1991

The Resource Management Act was eventually enacted by Parliament in July 1991. Conceived by a Labour Government in 1988, but passed in modified form by the National Government, it replaced more than 20 major statutes, including the Town and Country Planning Act 1977, water and soil legislation, and legislation concerning geothermal resources, air and noise pollution, and coastal reserves. By bringing together laws governing land, air, and water resources, the Resource Management Act (RMA) introduced a totally new approach to environmental management. The purpose of the Act was to promote the sustainable management of natural and physical resources, i.e. 'managing the use, development, and protection of natural and physical resources in a way, or at a rate, which enables people and communities to provide for their social, economic and cultural well-being and for their health and safety.' In meeting those goals the needs of future generations must be considered, life-supporting ecosystems (in air, water, and soil) safeguarded, and adverse effects of activities on the environment minimised.

Māori Interests and the Resource Management Act 1991

In response to increasing Māori concern, expressed during Waitangi Tribunal hearings and during the extensive consultation process between 1989 and 1991, the Act incorporated a number of Māori values and beliefs, as well as provisions for special Māori interests. To assist local authorities, tribes, and planners, the Ministry for the Environment outlined the range of Māori interests in its publication *Resource Management Consultation with Tangata Whenua* and pointed to at least 30 relevant provisions.[17] The Act is long, but it is possible to identify four broad categories of provisions in the Act that are of particular relevance to Māori: the Treaty of Waitangi, cultural interests, iwi interests, and Māori language usage.

Recognition of the Treaty of Waitangi is contained in section 8 of the RMA: 'In achieving the purpose of this Act, all persons exercising functions and powers under it in relation to managing the use, development and protection of natural and physical resources shall take into account the principles of the Treaty of Waitangi (Te Tiriti o Waitangi).' Though a significant restraint on the way in which the Act is administered, section 8 is less powerful than section 9 of the State-Owned Enterprises Act 1986: 'Nothing in this Act shall permit the Crown to act in a manner that is inconsistent with the principles of the Treaty of Waitangi.' In its earlier draft form the RMA provision had used similar wording, and reference to Treaty 'provisions' rather than Treaty principles had been considered. In the event, and after a change of government, wording was adopted which was less likely to lead to litigation, even though Māori preference was clearly for the type of provision found in the SOE Act.[18]

The decision to refer to the principles of the Treaty of Waitangi was ration-alised on the basis that the Treaty provisions, even though they had been referred to in the 1877 Fish Protection Act, were not sufficiently explicit in either the English or the Māori text, and there was the added complication that because the two texts differed, the provisions could not be determined with any precision. As well, at least some principles had already been defined by the Waitangi Tribunal,[19] the High Court, and the Court of Appeal.[20] There is reasonably wide agreement that the principles of tribal self-regulation, partnership, consultation, and active protection, within the wider understanding of a bargain between Māori and the Crown ('the essential bargain'), are important in considering the interpretation of the RMA.[21]

Recognition that cultural attitudes and values are significant for resource management is first raised in section 6(e) of the RMA, a section which empha-sises the need to consider matters of national importance. All functionaries and decision makers under section 6 of the Act, when managing the use, develop-ment, and protection of national and physical resources, must recognise and provide for a number of matters of national importance. One of the matters is 'the relationship of Maori and their culture and traditions with their ancestral lands, water, sites, wāhi tapu and other taonga.' While section 6(e) does not override the main purpose of the Act it clearly indicates that Māori views and practices are to be part of the national interest and in that respect the Act has similarities with the Māori Language Act 1987, which recognised the Māori language as an official language of New Zealand.

Of the various cultural values, kaitiakitanga and wāhi tapu warrant further attention. Kaitiakitanga is included in section 7 and is defined as 'the exercise of guardianship; and in relation to a resource, includes the ethic of stewardship based on the nature of the resource itself.' In the joint submission from the three major national Māori organisations, there was criticism of the definition because it introduced new concepts largely unknown to Māori, and certainly not adequately debated. [22] A broader explanation was proposed: 'Kaitiakitanga refers to Māori perspectives in the use, management and control of Māori resources.' Further criticism of the use of kaitiakitanga was linked to a more general concern about the distortion of meaning when a Māori term is incorporated into a document which has its own contextual constraints. 'Herein lies the failure of the RMA. It attempts, by statutory definition, to recognise certain choice elements of kaitiakitanga while failing to account for any of the remaining elements. . . . Māori concepts when treated in isolation are incapable of proper function and development. In fact any concept when divorced from its cultural base is subject to dysfunction and cultural reinterpretation or hi-jack.'[23]

Wāhi tapu, Māori cultural sites, had been included in legislation prior to 1991. The Treaty of Waitangi (State Enterprises) Act 1988 recognised the importance of revesting alienated wāhi tapu to the appropriate iwi rather than transferring title to the state-owned enterprise.[24] Section 27D refers to wāhi tapu as '. . . being land of special spiritual, cultural, or historical tribal significance.' However, although the RMA makes provisions for wāhi tapu, it does not define the term in any detail and leaves it up to local authorities to consult with Māori to determine the meaning in a particular situation. Nor does the RMA require the location of a wāhi tapu to be precisely identified if the preservation of privacy is regarded as important. Yet while something of the significance of wāhi tapu to Māori has been captured in the Act, there is some concern that the mechanism available through the RMA, a heritage order, is a potentially long, litigious, and costly process, daunting to many applicants.[25] Thus while some iwi authorities have used the provisions of the Act, others have been critical, not only of the provisions but also of the latitude given to Crown agencies where purchase of the site is necessary for its protection.

Although the RMA recognises a number of Māori cultural beliefs, the omission of reference to mauri, a key Māori concept which links resources with both the environment and with people, caused some concern, especially as it had been included in the original bill. Moreover, its replacement with the phrase 'intrinsic values of ecosystems' fails to convey the same sense of interconnectedness or an appreciation of the environment as a network of living entities. It was also seen as undervaluing the Māori language and a missed opportunity for the government to support Māori as an official language of New Zealand.[26]

Iwi (tribal) interests feature in several parts of the Act. Most significant is the opportunity for iwi to develop their own management plans, statements about the environment which forms part of their own territory, and which indicate how the iwi wishes to manage the natural resources in order to ensure that future generations may benefit. Sections 61(2)(a)(ii), 66(2)(c)(ii), and 74(2)(b)(ii) all refer to iwi management plans and require that in preparing or amending regional policy statements and district plans, local authorities must have regard to any relevant planning document recognised by an iwi authority which might be affected by the plans.

Some iwi have prepared and published iwi management plans which deal with such matters as wāhi tapu (how to identify and protect them), mahinga kai, and iwi proposals for management or development of Māori land and other resources. Assistance to tribes in the preparation of plans was contained in a useful booklet, *Mauriora ki te Ao*, prepared by Te Puni Kōkiri.[27] Its intention was to detail a process to develop an environmental inventory to assist iwi, hapū, and marae planning. What was less certain, however, was how these documents would be received by local authorities. While they provide a basis for consultation and discussion, iwi sometimes feel that their plans have to be more or less consistent with the wider district plan to be recognised at all. Nonetheless, some iwi have prepared plans which leave no doubt about their role in environmental management. Ngāti Hauiti for example, a relatively small tribe in the Rangitīkei, published an environmental policy statement in 1996.[28] It gives a clear indication of the tribe's uniqueness as well as an intention to develop alliances with neighbouring hapū and iwi, regional and national Crown agencies, and the general public in the kaitiakitanga (guardianship) of waterways, freshwater fisheries, marine fisheries, land, indigenous flora and fauna, and heritage sites. Like other tribes, and despite a modest population base, Ngāti Hauiti has asserted rangatiratanga over its own mana whenua.

An underlying theme of the RMA is the need for local authorities to consult, and when consulting with Māori the Act refers to consultation with tangata whenua. In distinguishing between Māori people generally, and Māori who belong to a particular tribal grouping which has traditional rights in an area, the Act emphasises the special place of tribes. The purpose is to acknowledge section 6 of the Act and the special relationship of Māori and their environment. A key component of that relationship is the concept of mana whenua, the authority of tribes (as iwi or hapū) by virtue of traditional occupations. Although it sometimes puzzles local authorities as to which particular tangata whenua group should be consulted, the important point is the law has finally recognised that tribes have rights which stem from being indigenous without necessarily demonstrating continuing ownership or a direct commercial interest.

The Resource Management Act contains many Māori words and phrases: wāhi tapu, kaitiakitanga, tangata whenua, mana whenua, tikanga Māori, iwi. Several inferences arise from this practice. First, it supports the contention that, however slowly, a bicultural jurisprudence is emerging in New Zealand. Māori custom law is now part of several statutes, especially the RMA. Second, it places additional responsibilities on those who interpret the law to have some understanding of Māori custom, a difficult task since few, including Māori members of the judiciary, have had any formal educational exposure to Māori custom law. The law is, it appears, ahead of the teachers. A third implication, and it follows from the second, is that because the Māori terms are largely unfamiliar to the legal profession and local authorities, they are translated into English, at least for the purposes of the Act. The translations, however, may or may not accord with Māori understandings of a particular concept. Reference has already been made to kaitiakitanga and the differing shades of meaning which may be attached to it. It is not surprising; each tribe has its own wealth of traditions which explain and give substance to fundamental concepts such as those used in the RMA.[29] Further, very often the meaning behind a term such as mana whenua cannot be fully appreciated without recourse to a wider spiritual context; a two-word or three-word English translation runs the risk of diminishing the deeper meaning.

Categories of Māori interest in the RMA and the implications arising from them are summarised in table 2.4.

Table 2.4 Māori Interests in the RMA

Type of Interest	Implication
The Treaty of Waitangi	Requirement on those who administer the Act to take into account the Treaty
Cultural interests	Environmental planning must be responsive to Māori values and beliefs
Iwi interests	Iwi, as opposed to other groups (Māori or non-Māori), have expectations of special recognition under the Act
Māori language usage in the Act	Interpretation of Māori phrases or words requires an understanding of Māori custom law

Limitations of the Resource Management Act

A comprehensive critique of the RMA with particular reference to Māori interests has been completed by the James Ritchie and P. Nuttall.[30] Among their findings was the conclusion that the needs of councils to meet legal requirements had compromised the recognition of the very concepts which had been incorporated to protect Māori interests. By using English equivalents of Māori words, there had been a tendency to assume that Māori and Pākehā were saying the same thing, when often they were not. Central to the increasing Māori discontent with the administration of the Act is the distinction between consultation and participation. Because the Act requires councils to consult, and does not further define consultation, Māori are often left as passive respondents in the process of resource management. The Māori preference is for involvement as participants, equals in the planning process or not at all. Further, even apart from the fact that few council plans were produced with benefit of reference to iwi plans, relatively few iwi have actually prepared plans. Nor have resources been allocated to them for that purpose. In this respect, local authorities have adopted a minimal interpretation of their responsibilities to 'take into account' the Treaty of Waitangi, when the reality is that Māori 'wish to see a full and effective role for themselves in resource management in a way which reflects the partnership to which they signed in 1840.'[31] It would be relatively straightforward were it not for the political costs for councils if a genuine partnership with tangata whenua was actually implemented. Nonetheless, there are ways in which the generally unsatisfactory situation can be addressed. Ritchie and Nuttall have recommended a four-pronged approach: clarity of intent (including a statement about what is not attainable—to avoid misleading Māori), demonstration of willingness, understanding of values, and education and resourcing.[32]

The Waitangi Tribunal has also expressed concerns about some aspects of the RMA. In the *Ngawha Geothermal Resource Report* the Tribunal concluded that the RMA was deficient because it did not require those who administer the Act to ensure that the claimants' Treaty rights are fully protected. They may do so but are not required to do so.[33] Further, in the *Te Arawa Representative Geothermal Claims*, the Tribunal considered that the Act did not provide sufficient scope for iwi to exercise authority in relation to the management of the resource. While section 33 allows for the transfer of certain powers to iwi, this is at the discretion of the local authority, who in any event continues to be responsible for the exercise of any such powers.[34]

The Tribunal has recommended that an amendment be made to the RMA so that those who administer the Act will move beyond 'taking into account' the Treaty of Waitangi but 'shall act in a manner which is consistent with the principles of the Treaty of Waitangi.'

Fundamental differences in philosophy, as well as quite different frameworks for describing environmental issues and policies, are discussed in detail by Hemi in an analysis of the RMA according to Māori understandings of tino rangatira-tanga. He proposes nine growth stages as expressions of tino rangatiratanga: te pū (origin or source), te more (cause or purpose), te weu (beginning), te aka (establishment), te rea (growth), te ao nui (a suitable environment), te kune (the development), te whē (potential for change), and te kore (chaos). Because the RMA uses Māori terms to suit its own ends, though without giving sufficient weight to the underlying Māori values, he concludes that it would be less misleading if all Māori terminology were withdrawn from the Act.[35]

Māori are not on their own in having concerns about the RMA and its capacity to provide for sustainability, let alone resource development. The Commissioner for the Environment, in one of a series of reports dealing with Māori interests in environmental matters and the implications of the Treaty of Waitangi for environmental and resource management, was critical of the mechanisms available for the protection of cultural and historic heritage. Omission of heritage values from matters of national importance under section 6 of the RMA has contributed to local authorities being able to exercise the discretion to do little; and she considered there was insufficient linkage between the RMA and the Historic Places Act 1993 (HPA). This is particularly so in relation to a potential gap between the archaeological provisions of the HPA and the RMA when local authorities fail to provide for the protection of sites in their policies and plans. More attention to tangata whenua was recommended.[36]

Communities may be also disadvantaged by the costs of obtaining expert evidence and the seeming abdication of the government in favour of local authorities. A planning academic, Peter Horsley, sees the dream of direct community participation in environmental management being increasingly compromised by the outrageous costs of resource consent hearings where the 'largest budget buys the best brains'. Usually it is the developers who have the necessary resources to recruit the type of expertise that is likely to persuade authorities. He doubts that a community-focused balance between development and sustainability can be maintained.[37]

Under the RMA there has been a major transfer of responsibility from central government to local authorities. In New Zealand's history local authorities have never been comfortable with Māori issues, nor has the Crown always had confidence that they could respond in a fair way to Māori. Disagreement between Parliament and provincial governments as far back as 1855 was often related to responsibility for Māori policy, and Governor Browne feared that if the settlers had control their policies would lead to war against Māori.[38] He argued that central government should retain responsibility. Concern about central government withdrawal was also raised in 1996 by the OECD in a report, *Environmental Performance*. Local authorities were described as slow to carry out planning tasks required of them under the Act, and planning was said to be hampered by insufficient understanding of the links between the environment and the economy—a reference to the gap between local and central government.[39]

However, by 1996 there were also several instances of productive relationships between Māori and local authorities. The Horowhenua District Council, for example, working closely with iwi, has provided a clear statement of how it will recognise Māori environmental values, the Treaty of Waitangi, and, within its District, the distinctiveness of the three iwi, Muaupoko, Ngāti Raukawa, and Rangitane. Among other things the district plan will permit the occupation, use, subdivision, and development of Māori-owned land, subject to constraints relating to sustainable management, and will enable the development of particular Māori resources such as marae and kainga. The plan will also include standards and/or processes to protect Māori taonga and values against inappropriate use and development. Commitment is made to observing the Treaty principles of mutual benefits, active protection, iwi self-regulation, shared decision-making, and iwi and hapū resource development and consultation.[40]

THE CONSERVATION ESTATE

Access to and ownership of natural resources remain unresolved issues in New Zealand, at least for Māori. Rivers, lakes, harbours, minerals, native flora and fauna, and forests comprise much of the disputed resources and often form part of the conservation estate, the lands and properties administered by the Department of Conservation on behalf of all New Zealanders. Increasingly tribes are sensing that the creation of a national heritage has been at their expense and that the separation of resource management (through the RMA) and conservation management (by the Department of Conservation) has led to an incoherent series of policies in which they have had little influence.

Late in 1993 Māori alienation from their traditional lands and forests became more than an academic issue. A small group of protesters, impatient with the lack of progress in settling a Treaty of Waitangi claim, decided to occupy a Department of Conservation hut at Tieke, along the Wanganui River. Their intention was to remain until the government agreed to return the land the hut stood on, and the surrounding block. Trampers visiting the area were not turned away, nor made to feel unwelcome, but they were exposed to the history of the complaint from a Māori perspective. The occupiers felt that other avenues for negotiation had failed, especially with the Department of Conservation, and that there was no alternative but to take the law into their own hands. Government response was predictably terse, and a serious confrontation was only avoided by the intervention of tribal elders who eventually persuaded the Department of Conservation to enter into an arrangement with the protesters that would enable them to occupy the hut, lawfully, though without preventing the access of others. It was not of course an arrangement that could endure, but it provided a moratorium until the wider Waimarino claim could be settled.

Tieke was not the only conservation property subject to Māori occupation, and although it was a protest against the slowness of processing a claim, it was also symptomatic of a more general discontent between Māori, the Department of Conservation, and the government in response to perceived alienation from traditional lands, rivers, and forests. In a submission to the Royal Commission on Social Policy Tuhoe had already expressed concern about lack of reasonable access to the Urewera National Park and the irony that an acute housing shortage was occurring within kilometres of the park and its rich supply of timber.[41] Later, in 1996, criticism was again expressed by the tribe because of the Department of Conservation's restrictive and narrow policies for a joint approach to management. In responding to *Conservation Management Strategy for the East Coast Conservancy*, Tuhoe met with Crown representatives at the Ohotu marae, Ruatoki, in September 1995. There was disagreement about the assumptions made by the Department of Conservation (DOC) in regard to which areas of land should come under Crown guardianship, and within the Urewera National Park, and even greater concern that the language used in the documents had alienated the Tuhoe readers as much as they had been alienated for the park. 'Tuhoe are surrounded by Te Urewera National Park and yet we do not have any one individual in a management role or with appropriate formal qualifications in environmental planning, to safeguard our tikanga.'[42]

The Department of Conservation was not unmindful of Māori opinion and had in fact gone to considerable lengths to seek Māori advice and to recognise Māori values in respect of conservation issues. Māori members had been appointed to all conservation boards, a Māori deputy director-general, Piri Siascia, had been appointed, and a Māori unit, Kaupapa Atawhai, provided policy advice in respect of Māori issues. Over time the department had established extensive consultation processes with Māori as well as an active role in Treaty of Waitangi settlement negotiations. However, there was also recognition that DOC would be in an unenviable position as settlements proceeded. The director of the Kaupapa Atawhai unit, Eru Manuera, was hopeful that the department would be able to 'maintain a positive relationship with iwi, particularly at regional level, and one of the ways of doing this is through tikanga atawhai projects. The aim is to support and inform iwi in order to maintain conservation values and achieve mutual benefits.'[43]

An extensive critique of the Department of Conservation's Māori policy and practices has been compiled by Dr Margaret Mutu, one of the original appointees to the New Zealand Conservancy Authority. She has drawn attention to the department's apparent 'lack of clear understanding' about section 4 of the Conservation Act (to 'give effect to the principles of the Treaty of Waitangi') and the inadequacies of the consultation process with Māori. Likewise the non-availability of conservation lands to settle Treaty of Waitangi claims was seen as 'dishonest and dishonourable.' But her most severe criticism relates to customary Māori use of native flora and fauna and the department's 'nil use, preservationist policy' to the exclusion of cultural practices and contemporary realities.[44]

While the Department of Conservation has been the focus of much Māori discontent, in fact government policy regarding natural resources and environmental heritage has been the more fundamental issue. Thus, despite unilateral declarations by the government, automatic Crown ownership of minerals, river beds, lakes, and harbours has never been accepted by Māori, nor has it been unconditionally confirmed by the judiciary. In the courts and before the Waitangi Tribunal, claims for the return of natural resources have been frequently heard. The Manukau Harbour claim, for example, was (among other things) for the return of the harbour to Ngāti Te Ata on the grounds that it formed part of the traditional tribal estate and that, unlike British law, Māori custom law did not differentiate between ownership of land and ownership of rivers or harbours. In the event, the Tribunal declined to make a recommendation about harbour ownership but did recognise a tribal interest in the harbour and, as mentioned earlier, recommended the appointment of kaitiaki.

Nor did the debate settle there. When the government introduced its proposals for the settlement of Treaty of Waitangi claims, 'the fiscal envelope', the conservation estate and natural resources were excluded from the settlement formula. Tainui were able to accommodate the policy in the landmark settlement concluded in 1995, and, with some reluctance, so did Whakatohea in 1996. But it remains a sore point for tribes who have never willingly abandoned rights to those resources. During the Whakatohea negotiations other options, short of outright return to Māori, were canvassed. They included the creation of topuni reserves which would acknowledge the cultural, spiritual, and traditional values of particular sites and take them into account in future management. The Department of Conservation would generally retain administrative responsibility, but agreement would be needed from Whakatohea about management practices to fully recognise those values. It was a different approach from the Tainui settlement, which had simply provided for a tribal appointment to the Conservation Board.

In the South Island, Ngai Tahu adopted a much more determined approach to the conservation estate. Insisting that Whenua Hou (Codfish Island), other outlying islands, and parts of national parks be returned to the tribe, loud outcries from conservationists and recreational interests led to public reaction and protest. But Ngai Tahu were adamant that conservation was not 'the prerogative of the conservation lobby'[45] and reiterated that not only would public access be retained but resource development would be entirely consistent with the Ngai Tahu philosophy towards the environment.[46]

Pounamu and Coal

In respect of minerals, Ngai Tahu were more successful than most tribes in claiming back a natural resource, pounamu (jade or greenstone). They had argued before the Waitangi Tribunal that tribal ownership of pounamu had never been extinguished. When the Crown purchased the Arahura Block, the title to the Arahura River was promised to Ngai Tahu, largely to enable them to retain pounamu. However, since pounamu boulders are found on the land adjacent to the river, rather than only on the riverbed itself, the claim by Ngai Tahu alleged that the Crown had breached its Treaty obligations in failing to meet the wishes of Ngai Tahu to retain ownership of the pounamu in the area adjacent to the Arahura and its tributaries.

The Waitangi Tribunal agreed. 'The Tribunal considered that the unique nature of pounamu and its deep spiritual significance in Māori life and culture is such that every effort should now be made to secure as much as possible to Ngai Tahu ownership and control. . . . We believe all such pounamu [on Crown land] and any other owned by the Crown should be returned by the Crown to Ngai Tahu.' For pounamu on private land the Tribunal recommended that an amendment be made to section 7 of the Mining Act 1971 to ensure that mining privileges were granted only to Ngai Tahu.[47] Ngai Tahu have now been able to resume ownership of greenstone with exclusive mining rights.

In 1989, Tainui also sought legal determination of their right to the Huntly coal mines. When the Crown sought to transfer the mines to Coalcorp, a state-owned enterprise, Tainui objected and the matter was referred to the Court of Appeal.[48] Tainui were concerned that an agreement between the Crown and

Coalcorp would mean that valuable coal rights and lands would be sold off into private hands with no mechanism to ensure that the Crown could, if necessary, take them back to satisfy Tainui's claim concerning confiscations (or raupatu) before the Waitangi Tribunal. Tainui argued that the provisions of the Treaty of Waitangi (State Enterprises) Act 1988 and the decision of the Court of Appeal preceding this legislation (in *NZ Maori Council v Attorney-General*) should cover mining rights and land so that the raupatu claims could be satisfied.

The essence of the Court of Appeal decision was that coal mining rights and properties held or managed by Coalcorp should not be passed to private ownership until the mechanism provided in the Treaty of Waitangi (State Enterprises) Act 1988 was in place. Then it would be possible for the return of those lands or rights to Waikato/Tainui to take place in the event that a claim before the Tribunal was successful. The court agreed that Tainui had an interest in coal mining, an interest which had a strong bearing on the raupatu lands, already the subject of a claim before the Waitangi Tribunal. But the court did not say that Tainui owned the coal. To some extent the matter was left in abeyance and, as it happened, Tainui withdrew any claim over minerals, especially coal, during negotiations for their wider settlement.

Following the Coalition agreement between National and New Zealand First in 1996, the government indicated a possible review of the policy on natural resources, and Taranaki tribes were quick to assert that they would be placing oil and gas on the agenda when it came time to negotiate their settlement. To a large extent, however, any agreement to include natural resources such as oil in a settlement package would depend on how important the resource was to the Crown. Pounamu was less valuable than gas. Nonetheless Ngāti Tama negotiator Greg White expected that royalties from oil and gas, if not the resource itself, could well form part of a settlement.[49]

Water Rights

Māori ownership of waterways has long been a source of contention. When the Water Power Act 1903 was being debated, the Hon. Hone Heke, who was then the Member for Northern Māori, objected to the Crown's presumption of ownership of the rivers which would be used for the generation of electricity. 'It would not be proper for a Bill like this to take the right from Māori owners of the use of water power on their land. There is no telling to what use even the Māori may desire to put such water-power for themselves. It would be entirely different if the Crown desires to acquire water-power on Māori land; it remains for them to acquire it from natives. . . . The Bill is an attempt to take it away from native rights.' In reply the Minister for Public Works, Mr Hall-Jones, gave an assurance that the sole rights to use water would be vested in the Crown but would also be subject to any (other) rights lawfully held.[50]

Subsequently, however, the Crown assumed rights with scarcely any recognition of Māori interests. In 1992 the issue was again debated between Māori and the Crown. First, it was the subject of the Waitangi Tribunal *Mohaka River Report.*[51] When the Hawke's Bay Acclimatisation Society and the Council of North Island Acclimatisation Societies applied to the Minister of Works for a water conservation order over the Mohaka River, Ngāti Pāhauwera protested. They insisted that the prior issue was a determination of rangatiratanga over the river, i.e. possession and control of the river and its waters. However, the Planning Tribunal did not consider that it had the authority (under the Water and Soil Conservation Act 1967) to recognise rangatiratanga and proceeded to confirm the conservation order, though with some amendments. Subsequently the tribe's claim to the Waitangi Tribunal challenged the Crown's view on possession and contended that the Treaty of Waitangi had guaranteed full exclusive and undisturbed possession to Ngāti Pāhauwera.

Although land on the south side of the river had been purchased by Donald McLean in 1851, there was insufficient evidence that the sale had included any part of the river bed, nor could there be an automatic assumption of a riparian right. The Tribunal concluded that when the Treaty was signed the Mohaka River was a taonga of Ngāti Pāhauwera, who had never relinquished te tino rangatiratanga over it. In recommending against a water conservation order over the river, the Tribunal also advised the Crown to enter into discussions with the tribe on vesting the river bed in Ngāti Pāhauwera and reaching agreement on a regime for the future control and management of the river.[52]

Also in 1992 a separation of Trans Power from the Electricity Corporation (ECNZ) was proposed. At a meeting between Māori representatives and the Crown at Parliament, the Māori delegation emphasised the indivisibility of resources such as land and water, and the people, and expressed difficulty in accepting the separation without taking a more holistic perspective. In effect, Māori wanted to discuss issues relating not only to the transmission of power but also to the generation of power and Māori claims to water rights. On that basis the Māori Congress proposed that twenty per cent of the shares in Trans Power be retained by the Crown in a separate trust for Māori pending the settlement of the Treaty issues.[53] But the Crown had other views on water rights, and Māori claims to ownership were dismissed.

When the Crown announced its intention to split ECNZ and establish two SOEs to act as competitors, it consulted with Māori about aspects of the proposal. Any land transferred to the new SOEs would retain the protections afforded by the amended section 27 of the State-Owned Enterprises Act, and would also be subject to a Crown undertaking to be consistent with the principles of the Treaty of Waitangi, as required under section 9 of the SOE Act. There was, however, to be no special recognition of Māori water rights. Instead, the sale of small hydro stations would consider local Māori interests. The relevant stations were Cobb, Coleridge, Highbank, Matahina, Mangahao, and the Waikaremoana group (Tuai, Paripaua, Kaitawa).[54] In 1996, among others, the tribes of Manawatu and Horowhenua had exercised the right and successfully bid for the purchase of Mangahao.

Meanwhile two other hui had been convened, in 1993, to consider iwi water rights. For many years, the Whanganui tribes had sought a return of the Whanganui River, maintaining that ownership had been wrongfully assumed by the Crown. Although Judge Brown at a Native Court hearing in 1939 concluded that the Whanganui tribes were the owners of the river, the Crown appealed first to the Māori Appellate Court and then to the Supreme Court.[55] Concerned that other tribes might take similar action, Judge Hay ruled that the Coal Mine Amendment Act 1903 had vested ownership of the river bed in the Crown. Whanganui interests were overlooked in a series of actions, including the diversion of the river headwaters into Lake Taupo in 1960. A lengthy hearing before the Planning Tribunal regarding water flows in the river again raised the issues of ownership, and in 1991 negotiations with the Crown commenced regarding river ownership. They were, however, soon suspended pending a wider river policy.

After the 1993 hui, and concerned that their views were seldom given adequate consideration, the Whanganui River Māori Trust Board published a charter setting out principles which should determine the ownership, use, and management of the river. The text of the charter appears below:

The Whanganui River Charter hereby affirms the following principles of Tino Rangatiratanga and calls upon all concerned to actively redress the political and ecological imbalance which has occurred.

1   THE PRINCIPLE OF TINO RANGATIRATANGA AND KAITIAKI
    TANGA (INTERGENERATIONAL RESPONSIBILITY)
    Hapū and Iwi have inherited an intergenerational responsibility to ensure that
    they pass on to their descendants an environment which has been enhanced
    by their presence and efforts.

2   THE PRINCIPLE OF HAPŪ/IWI DETERMINATION
    Hapū and Iwi continue to apply their own tikanga in respect of the
    Tiakitanga of their waters. Any negotiations with Hapū and Iwi must therefore recognise the uniqueness of their interests and aspirations.

3   THE PRINCIPLE OF INTERDEPENDENCY
    Waters are taonga and are interdependent with all other taonga of the
    environment, physical, social and cultural. Any activity involving waters will
    therefore directly impact on the rest of the environment.

4   THE PRINCIPLE OF COLLECTIVITY

Hapū and Iwi are collective identities whose responsibilities and aspirations extend beyond any individual, organisation and generation.

5   THE MAURI PRINCIPLE

Waters come from Papatuanuku and Ranginui, they are part of the Mauri of the peoples. If the Mauri of waters is damaged so too will be the Mauri of the peoples.

6   THE PRINCIPLE OF DEVELOPMENT

Hapū and Iwi have the right to development of their resources.

7   THE PRINCIPLE OF USE MANAGEMENT

In the exercising of Tino Rangatiratanga, Hapū and Iwi maintain the right to grant or withhold permission for the use or development of their environment.

The charter reiterated Māori views of the environment as a network of inter-related components and stressed not only tribal control and authority but also the right to develop the resource. Quite apart from its impact on the Crown, which had anyway decided that Māori claims on waterways were untenable, the significance of the charter was its clear signal that Māori had not abandoned a claim to ownership of natural resources such as rivers and that every opportunity to have the claim recognised would be taken. Tuhoe had already made the point during their attempt to prevent a powerboat rally from proceeding up Ohinemataroa (Whakatane River) in 1991 and as a consequence were made to face legal proceedings at the Whakatane court. A submission to the court from Taiarahia Black emphasised not only the spiritual significance of the river to tangata whenua but the blatant disregard for Māori environmental values shown by the rally organisers. [56] The case was eventually dismissed, and since then the rallies have not gone beyond the Pekatahi bridge.

However, nearly two years after the Pakaitore (Moutoa Gardens) occupation,[57] and with the Whanganui claim not yet heard by the Waitangi Tribunal, one Whanganui hapū, Tamahaki, followed a similar course of action, thereby demon-strating the seriousness with which they were taking the Whanganui River Charter. When Winston Oliver, a tourist operator, tried to take his new house-boat, the MV *Georgina*, up the river, he was met by a flotilla of canoes and a hail of stones from hapū members led by Ken Mair and Niko Tangaroa, both of whom had played prominent roles at Pakaitore. A spokesman for the hapū, John Maihi, delivered a letter setting out the basis for their actions: inadequate consultation, environmental impact on the river wilderness, pollution, effects on the river's ecology. '[T]his river is our spiritual, cultural and historical ancestor. It has aspects that must always be protected.' Unfortunately Oliver had forgotten to read the letter before setting out.[58]

Ownership of Lake Rotorua prompted further open protest in 1996. The Te Arawa tribes, unhappy about the failure of the Crown to increase the annual annuity paid to the Te Arawa Māori Trust Board to compensate the tribe for loss of title to the lakes, threatened a campaign of civil disobedience. In October they marched through the streets and down to Lake Rotorua demanding either the return of the lake or a more realistic annuity. Set in 1922, attempts to have the annual amount increased had been unsuccessful, and the Board was now seeking an immediate payment of $2 177 000. Te Arawa were adamant that they had never voluntarily ceded the lakes.[59]

Native flora and fauna

As much as anyone, Māori became worried that many native plants, animals, and birds faced extinction or, perhaps worse, transformation through genetic engineering and deliberate hybridisation. Former member of Parliament for Northern Māori, Bruce Gregory, had long been advocating the rearing of native birds on a large commercial scale, to avoid extinction but also to provide a sustainable basis for harvest. There was also the question of patents and the rights of indigenous peoples to ownership over indigenous resources, such as flora and fauna. Del Wihongi successfully fought for the return of an original kumara plant from Japan, one of the few which had not been hybridised. She also played a key role in the establishment of an ethnobotanical garden in Auckland, where native flora could be both protected and propagated in a safe manner. Seeking to have those rights recognised, Te Rarawa and others lodged a claim to the Waitangi Tribunal. The claim objects to the exploitation of plant genotypes, the sale and export of native species, the extinction of rare and endangered species, the extraction and sale of plant extracts and products, and patenting of plant varieties. It is also concerned about the management and control of native animals, traditional harvesting, the collection and export of native fauna, and the ethics of scientific research.[60] Hearings for the claim, Wai 262, commenced in September 1997.

Forests

By 1994 it was evident that while Māori had pioneered a conservation ethic in New Zealand, both in the distant past but also in modern times, species protection was not their only interest. Equally, tribes were adamant that the principle of tino rangatiratanga should not be overlooked. In effect, they sought to exercise the right to utilise resources, not just care for them. Concerned that there might be wholesale destruction of native trees or birds, and unable to comprehend what seemed to be an about-turn by Māori, conservationists expressed outrage. In fact the Māori position was consistent with a philosophy of balance and interdependence, and tribes were equally incensed that conservationists, having been virtually silent while New Zealand was systematically cleared of acre after acre of native bush by settlers and their descendants, had only become vocal when the majority of remaining indigenous forests were on Māori land or under claim by Māori.

At Taumarunui, the National Māori Congress highlighted that point in a submission to Ngā Whenua Rāhui, a body established to advise on indigenous forest policy. 'Morally, the policy [of forbidding commercial harvesting of indigenous forests] should not be applied to Māori land especially where Māori don't want it. Indigenous forests are the product of generations of Māori management prior to European arrival. Substantial areas of high quality stands of indigenous forests have been acquired by the Crown for protective purposes and some of these have been commercially harvested. It is difficult to accept that a forest conservation regime should be imposed on Māori land to the detriment of other uses and to the exclusion of financial gains in a climate where Māori land grievances remain unresolved . . .'[61]

The aims of Ngā Whenua Rāhui, however, were gradually accepted. In the first month of the 1996/97 financial year a total of 75 280 hectares had been approved for protection, and additional proposals were being processed for a further 19 000 hectares of indigenous forests in the Whanganui and East Coast regions. Māori appeared to have warmed to Ngā Whenua Rāhui agreements, which emphasise cultural use of Māori-owned forests and iwi ownership, control, and management.[62]

But aware of the growing tension between DOC and iwi, the Conservation Authority sought to ease the situation by promoting informed discussion on Māori customary use of native flora and fauna.[63] The department recommended setting up iwi committees with the power to make decisions over customary uses in their own areas, recognising the principles of sustainable harvest and restoration of resources. Delegations could be made under the Conservation Act to iwi representatives or to a regional Kaupapa Atawhai manager (DOC). Though not exactly what Māori had in mind, the recommendation was an attempt to reintroduce a concept of partnership into the management of flora and fauna and to recognise the sometimes conflicting views of Māori and conservationists.

At the same time, Ngāti Porou, an East Coast tribe, were having their own disagreements with the Department of Conservation and the large-scale development of forestry on their own tribal lands. After many years of campaigning to reclaim Mount Hikurangi, a landmark with particular significance to the tribe and as much part of the tribal identity as the people themselves, the Crown agreed to its return. In an arrangement negotiated initially with the Minister of Māori Affairs Koro Wetere, Mount Hikurangi became part of the tribal estate in 1991. However, the terms of the agreement gave the Department of Conservation a continuing role in its management and control, a sore point with Ngāti Porou who argued that they were perfectly capable of doing the job themselves.

But the greatest sense of injustice came just as Ngāti Porou were completing arrangements for the establishment of a large exotic forest on tribal lands. A bilateral development scheme between Ngāti Porou landowners and Tasman Forestry Limited involved clearing mature mānuka and kānuka in order to establish a forest estate of at least 50 000 hectares. It was to be part of an economic package which would reverse the downward economic spiral that had affected the East Coast and would at the same time provide much-needed employment. Although conservationist groups had been involved in the discussions, the Forest and Bird Protection Society, Maruia, and Greenpeace objected to the clearing and withdrew. Because Tasman had been a signatory to a Forest Accord, they were also pressured by the conservation activists to withdraw, and did.[64]

Ngāti Porou had been left without a partner. To them mānuka and kānuka, though native trees, did not hold the same attractions that they did for others; for generations they had battled to control the 'scrub' and were unimpressed by claims that the clearing process would threaten the species. What was under greater threat was the tribe's economic survival. Unable to convince the government that the signing of the Forest Accord (to which there had been no Māori signatories) was inconsistent with the Treaty of Waitangi, they sought offshore partners and eventually negotiated an arrangement with a Korean development company, Hansol Forem. But the experience left them disappointed with the state's commitment to Māori forest rights and the aggressive tactics of the conservation lobby.

When the Crown decided to exit from the business of forestry and to establish Forestcorp, a state-owned enterprise, to manage its exotic forests, Māori objected on the grounds that Treaty interests in the land and perhaps the forests would be jeopardised. As a result the Crown Forestry Rental Trust (CFRT) was established in 1990 under section 34 of the Crown Forest Assets Act 1989. Both the Crown and Māori (through the New Zealand Māori Council and Federation of Māori Authorities) make up the trustees. The purpose of the CFRT is to receive the licence fees paid by forest owners for the rental of Crown Forest land and to use the interest earned from investment of those fees to assist claimants in negotiations for claims involving those lands. Licence fees have made the CFRT wealthy. In 1991 alone income from licence fees was $16.8 million, and by 1995 the fees received totalled $93.5 million. Accumulated interest from 1991 until 1995 was $22.5 million.[65] Māori criticism of the CFRT emerged at several meetings of the Māori Congress in 1990 and 1991 and continued into 1996, when calls were made for the Trust to be disestablished. New member of Parliament, Donna Awatere, aware that not a single claim had been settled six years after its establishment, argued for the funds to be given over to the claimants. Tama Nikora, from the Federation of Māori Authorities and a former Trustee, was similarly disillusioned, and called for greater levels of transparency and accountability so that the performance of the trust could be assessed and a more equitable system introduced.[66] Some tribes had received no assistance while others, for claims which were essentially the same, had. And the narrow base for Māori representation among the trustees was increasingly regarded as a flaw in the Act. Neither the New Zealand Māori Council nor the Federation of Māori Authorities could be seen as having a sufficiently broad mandate to warrant their exclusive appointments and, to aggravate the situation, the Māori trustees and their Crown counterparts were not in accord, at least according to the trust chairman, Sir Graham Latimer.[67]

In 1996 the sale of cutting rights to Crown forests attracted a great deal of debate. It was a three-way argument. The Crown had long since concluded that commercial activities should not be a function of the state and Cabinet made a decision that Forestcorp, a state-owned enterprise with cutting rights on state forests, should be sold. Many New Zealanders, including the Alliance Party, which subsequently organised a petition to Parliament, considered that because the forests had been developed with taxpayers' money they should remain the property of the Crown for all New Zealanders. Additionally there was further anxiety that the Waipa Mill could well close, with the loss of Māori employment; a fear not dispelled by assurances that Fletchers intended to invest $16 million at Waipa and create a further 700 jobs through the processing of logs in New Zealand. Forestcorp had exported logs for processing. Meanwhile Māori groups, mainly from Te Arawa, were opposed to any sale before tribal interests in both the land and the cutting rights had been determined by the Waitangi Tribunal.

After lengthy negotiations, Forestcorp was sold to a Fletcher Challenge-led consortium for $2.026 billion on 20 August 1996. Fletcher Challenge had a 37.5 per cent interest (and will manage the corporation), 37.5 per cent had been purchased by Citic (a Chinese Government investment firm), and Brierley Holdings had a 25 per cent interest. Bids had also been considered from Carter Holt Harvey and Weyerhaeuser (USA) as well as from a consortium of Te Arawa, Tuwharetoa, and Mātaatua tribes, Te AMA.[68]

The principal forests were at Kaingaroa, Rotoehu, and Whakarewarewa and covered some 188 000 hectares of land owned by the Crown. The land did not form part of the deal and left the way clear for the 37 claims for Forestcorp lands to proceed. If the lands are returned to Māori, then the cutting rights purchased by Fletcher Challenge would not necessarily be in perpetuity, at least for those lands, a point emphasised by Te AMA after losing the bid. Obviously, by express-ing an interest in purchasing cutting rights, the collective tribes were also positioning themselves well for conducting business with the successful bidders in the future. Should the tribes represented by Te AMA be successful in their claim for the land, then it will be good economic sense for the Fletcher Challenge consortium to come to some understanding with the Māori parties.

The New Zealand Māori Council, seeking to secure cutting rights as a Māori investment (not only a tribal right) and worried about the possible loss of jobs, threatened to take court action to prevent the sale. But by 19 August, because there was insufficient support from Council members, no action was taken. However, Māori interest in exotic forests continued, and discussions were held at Taupo to consider establishing a Māori Forest Industry Association.[69] To prevent a repeat of the tribal divisions which emerged during the Sealord's negotiations, some tribes in the central North Island were interested in a cooperative approach to claims involving forest lands, including the formulation of clear rules for determining ownership after grievances with the Crown were resolved. Taking advantage of the Forest Accord which had come together during the sale of the Forestry Corporation, the Te Arawa and Mātaatua tribes sought to continue the alliance.[70]

Following the release in 1997 of the Waitangi Tribunal's *Muriwhenua Land Report*, the status of Crown forests was again called into question. The 20 000 hectare Te Aupouri forest, now leased to the Japanese firm Juken Nissho for two rotations of tree growth, was part of the wider land claim, and there was considerable evidence that, far from being purchased in a fair manner, it had more of the hallmarks of a lease than an outright sale. A warning was sounded in the Report's recommendations that the forest might be required to help settle the claim and that if necessary the Tribunal could make a binding order to that effect.[71] Under the Treaty of Waitangi (State Enterprises) Act 1987 the Tribunal has the power to force the return of land from a state-owned enterprise if it were required to settle a claim. The option was clearly within the law, though the possibility was perceived by the Crown as a 'gauntlet to the Government'.[72] Rent on the land is over $300 000 and is paid to the Crown Forestry Rental Trust.

Understanding the Māori Position

So far this chapter has outlined many of the concerns voiced by Māori about the management of natural resources, the environment, and the widely differing perspectives of Māori and the Crown, not so much in regard to the ethics of conservation or the importance of environmental values, but in relationship to the context within which decisions about resources are made. While Māori prefer to place resources and the environment within a Māori development framework, and in that respect share common ground with the authors of the Resource Management Act, conservationists, including the state's own advisers, appear to view the environment in a much less integrated manner. The close relationship between tangata whenua and their environs, the central message contained in the story of Rangi and Papa, has been weakened by legislation, the practices of the state, and the vociferousness of the conservation lobby. Moreover, iwi have been offended by assumptions of Crown ownership to rivers, minerals, harbours, lakes, and forests, without clear extinguishment of title.

In an otherwise polemical arena, however, some signs of reconciliation are evident. The RMA now provides a legal basis for Māori values to be recognised; the Treaty of Waitangi has been shown to have practical significance for environmental management; and, although there is much yet to be done, there are some encouraging examples of partnership between Māori and the state so that the environment and its abundant resources may be protected for future generations. The many unresolved issues should not prevent the creation of new strategies to address particular situations. Sometimes, in the end, ownership may be a less critical issue than the capacity for active participation in decision-making. Sometimes, public access may be a lower priority than the recognition of tribal property rights; and sometimes Māori may be more effective conservators than the state.

NOTES FOR CHAPTER 2

1 This excerpt from an ancient oriori (traditional tribal recital) relates the well-known story of the separation by Tāne Mahuta of his parents, Rangi and Papa (the sky father and the earth mother). The postures adopted by Tāne as he forced the two apart are reflected in the verse. The complete version, attributed to Te Wi of the Rangitane tribe, is recorded in J. McEwen (1986), *Rangitane: A Tribal History*, Reed Methuen, Auckland, p. 197.

2 John White, (1887), *The Ancient History of the Māori*, Vol. 1, George Didsbury, Government Printer, Wellington, pp. 17–35.

3 In contrast to the verse at the beginning of this chapter, Hoani Meihana Te Rangiotu described Tane-tuturi, Tane-pepeke, Tane-ua-tika, Tane-uaha, Tane-te-wai-ora and Tane-nui-a-Rangi as one family in John White, (1890), *The Ancient History of the Māori*, Vol. VI, George Didsbury, Government Printer, Wellington, p. 172.

4 Te Rangihiroa (Peter Buck), (1949), *The Coming of the Māori*, Māori Purposes Fund Board, Whitcombe and Tombs, Wellington, pp. 438–441.

5 Ranginui Walker, (1978), *Ngā Tau Tohetohe: Years of Anger*, Penguin Books, Auckland, p. 21.

6 John Patterson, (1992), *Exploring Māori Values*, Dunmore Press, Palmerston North, p. 23.

7 Hirini P. Matunga, (1994), *The Resource Management Act 1991 and Māori Perspectives*, Centre for Māori Studies and Research, Lincoln University.

8 *ibid.*

9 Margaret Mutu, (1994), *The Use and Meaning of Māori Words Borrowed into English for Discussing Resource Management and Conservation in Aotearoa/New Zealand: A Discussion Paper Prepared for the Conservation Board Chairpersons Conference*, New Zealand Conservation Authority, Wellington.

10 Matunga, (1994), *The Resource Management Act 1991 and Māori Perpectives.*

11 W. H. Oliver, (1991), *Claims to the Waitangi Tribunal*, Waitangi Tribunal Division, Department of Justice, Wellington, pp. 18–37.

12 Waitangi Tribunal, (1983), *Report Findings and Recommendations of the Waitangi Tribunal on an Application by Aila Taylor for and on Behalf of Te Atiawa Tribe in Relation to Fishing Grounds in the Waitara District (Wai 6)*, Waitangi Tribunal, Department of Justice, Wellington.

13 Waitangi Tribunal, (1984), *Kaituna River (Wai 4)*, Waitangi Tribunal, Department of Justice, Wellington.

14 'Land-based option best', Editorial, *Evening Standard*, Thursday 14 November 1996.

15 Waitangi Tribunal, (1985), *Finding of the Waitangi Tribunal on the Manukau Claim (Wai 8)*, Waitangi Tribunal, Department of Justice, Wellington.

16 Waitangi Tribunal, (1988), *Report of the Waitangi Tribunal on the Mangonui Sewerage Claim (Wai 17)*, Waitangi Tribunal, Department of Justice, Wellington.

17 Ministry for the Environment (1994), *Resource Management Consultation with Tangata Whenua*, Ministry for the Environment, Wellington.

18 National Māori Congress, NZ Māori Council, Māori Women's Welfare League, (1991), *A Collective Submission on Supplementary Order Paper No. 22 Resource Management Bill*, National Māori Congress, Wellington.

19 Waitangi Tribunal principles relating to the environment and resource management are summarised in a report from the Commissioner for the Environment (1988), *Environmental Management and the Principles of the Treaty of Waitangi*, Parliamentary Commissioner for the Environment, Wellington.

20 *The New Zealand Māori Council v Attorney General* [1987] 1 NZLR 641 (Court of Appeal).

21 Diane Crengle, (1993), *Taking Into Account the Principles of the Treaty of Waitangi: Ideas for the Implementation of Section 8 Resource Management Act 1991*, Ministry for the Environment, Wellington.

22 National Māori Congress, NZ Māori Council, Māori Women's Welfare League, (1991), *A Collective Submission on . . . Resource Management Bill*.

23 M. A. Hemi, (1995), 'Tino Rangatiratanga: Assessing the Resource Management Act', Masterate thesis, Lincoln University.

24 Manatu Māori, (1991), *Wāhi Tapu: Protection of Māori Sacred Sites*, Ministry of Māori Affairs, Wellington.

25 Tony Sole, (1991), *Protection of Indigenous Sacred Sites: The New Zealand Experience*, Manatu Māori Ministry of Māori Affairs, Wellington.

26 Taiarahia Black, (1991), *Submission to the Planning and Development Select Committee on the Supplementary Order Paper Resource Management Bill*, Department of Māori Studies, Massey University.

27 Te Puni Kōkiri, (1993), *Mauriora ki te Ao: An Introduction to Environmental and Resource Management Planning*, Ministry of Māori Development, Wellington.

28 Ngāti Hauiti, (1996), *Kaupapa Taiao: Environmental Policy Statement*, Te Rūnanga o Ngāti Hauiti, Hunterville.

29 Margaret Mutu, (1994), *The Use and Meaning of Māori Words Borrowed into English for Discussing Resource Management and Conservation in Aotearoa/New Zealand*.

30 P. Nuttall, J. Ritchie, (1995), *Maaori Participation in the Resource Management Act: An Analysis of Provision Made for Maaori Participation in Regional Policy Statements and District Plans Produced under the Resource Management Act 1991*, Tainui Maaori Trust Board and Centre for Maaori Studies and Research, University of Waikato, Hamilton.

31 *ibid.*

32 *ibid.*

33 Waitangi Tribunal, (1993), *Ngawha Geothermal Resource Report (Wai 304)*, Waitangi Tribunal, Wellington.

34 Waitangi Tribunal, (1993), *Te Arawa Representative Geothermal Claims (Wai 32)*, Waitangi Tribunal, Wellington.

35 Hemi, 'Tino Rangatiratanga'.

36 Parliamentary Commissioner for the Environment, (1996), *Historic and Cultural Heritage Management in New Zealand*, Parliamentary Commissioner for the Environment, Te Kaitiaki Taiao a Te Whare Pāremata, Wellington.

37 John Saunders, (1996), 'View Point: Only high-paid experts benefiting', *Evening Standard*, Friday 25 October 1996.

38 Raewyn Dalziel, (1981), 'The Politics of Settlement', in W. H. Oliver (ed.), *The Oxford History of New Zealand*, Oxford University Press, Wellington, p. 87.

39 'OECD report critical of management', *Evening Standard*, Wednesday 20 November 1996.

40 Working Party, (1996), *Matters of Importance to Tangata Whenua*, Horowhenua District Council.

41 Royal Commission on Social Policy, (1988), *The April Report*, vol. 1, Royal Commission on Social Policy, Wellington, p. 264.

42 T. E. Black, (1996), *Tuhoe and the Conservation Estate*, paper presented at Environmental Conference, University of Otago, (unpublished), Department of Māori Studies, Massey University.

43 Department of Conservation, (1994), *Conservation Action: Department of Conservation Achievements and Plans*, Department of Conservation, Wellington, p. 16.

44 Margaret Mutu, (1995), *Report to the Minister of Māori Affairs on the New Zealand Conservation Authority*, Department of Māori Studies, University of Auckland, Auckland.

45 Tipene O'Regan, *Mana News*, Radio New Zealand, 19 September 1996.

46 See also chapter 7 for further discussion of the Ngai Tahu settlement.

47 Waitangi Tribunal, (1991), *Ngai Tahu Report 1991, (Wai 27)*, vol. 1, Brooker and Friend, Wellington, pp. 128–131.

48 Waitangi Tribunal, (1990), *Te Manutukutuku*, Newsletter of the Waitangi Tribunal, Wellington.

49 'Tribes add oil, gas and rivers to claim', *The Dominion*, Saturday 15 February 1997.

50 In National Māori Congress, (1992), *Submission on the Energy Sector Reform Bill to the Planning and Development Select Committee*, National Māori Congress, Wellington.

51 Waitangi Tribunal, (1992), *The Mohaka River Report 1992 (Wai 119)*, GP Publications, Wellington.

52 *ibid.*, pp. 78–79.

53 Justice Committee, (1992), *Electricity Sector Reforms Trans Power, a Report to the Congress Executive*, National Māori Congress, Wellington.

54 Minister of Finance, (1995), *Proposed Restructuring of ECNZ into Two SOES*, Circular letter, Office of the Minister of Finance, Wellington.

55 The Māori Appellate Court upheld the Brown decision.

56 Taiarahia Black, (1991), *Our River! To Matau Awa*, Submission to the Whakatane District Court, March 1991.

57 See chapter 5.

58 Lin Fergusson, (1997), 'Law of the River', *The Dominion*, Saturday 1 February 1997.

59 'Heat on in Te Arawa Lakes Dispute', *Te Māori Magazine*, 1996, vol. 5, no. 13, p. 8.

60 Congress Executive, (1991), *Waitangi Tribunal Claim: The Native Flora and Fauna of Aotearoa, A Resume of the Issues*, National Māori Congress, Wellington.

61 National Māori Congress, (1991), *Submission to Ngā Whenua Rahui from the National Māori Congress*, NMC 91/2/12, National Māori Congress, Wellington.

62 Department of Conservation Te Papa Atawhai, (1996), *Conservation Action Department of Conservation Achievements and Plans 1995/1996 – 1996/1997*, Wellington, p. 52.

63 Conservation Authority, (1994), *Māori Customary Use of Native Birds, Plants and Other Traditional Materials: A Discussion Paper*, New Zealand Conservation Authority, te Whakahaere Matua o Aotearoa, Wellington.

64 Nguha Patuwai, (1994), 'Kia Tu Kia Ora: A Māori Perspective on Ethnodevelopment', M. Phil. thesis, Department of Māori Studies, Massey University, pp. 40–51.

65 Controller and Auditor-General, (1995), *The Settlement of Claims Under the Treaty of Waitangi*, Second Report for 1995, Controller and Auditor-General, Wellington, p. 47–48.

66 Television New Zealand Channel One, *Marae*, 10 November 1996.

67 *ibid.*

68 *The Dominion*, 21 August 1996.

69 'Proposed Māori forest industry group hailed as vital step', *Newsletter*, Te Puni Kōkiri, Ministry of Māori Development, 37, December 1996.

70 'Forestry claimants stress Maori unity', *The Dominion*, Thursday 23 January 1996.

71 Waitangi Tribunal, (1997), *Muriwhenua Land Report (Wai 45)*, GP Publication, Wellington, p. 404.

72 Anthony Hubbard, Ruth Berry, (1997), 'Backing for Maori claims to forests', *Sunday Star Times*, 23 March 1997.

3

MANA TŪPUNA

IDENTITY AND HERITAGE

Ehara au nā tēnei ao,
Engari nā te aroha i wae aku mātua.
Ko aku kahu, ko te mauri me te wehi o oku tīpuna.
Ko aku kupu whakaaro, ā rātau tikanga . . .[1]

BEING MĀORI

Ten years after the 1984 Hui Taumata, the Hui Whakapūmau looked back on a decade of Māori development and tried to anticipate developmental strategies and priorities for the next ten years. At the 1994 hui the Hon. Koro Wetere emphasised the importance of Māori people being able to remain Māori. Reflecting on his own accomplishments as Minister of Māori Affairs from 1984 until 1990, he considered that the passage of the Māori Language Act 1987 ranked high and he hoped that the message of kōhanga reo[2] and kura kaupapa Māori[3] would be felt across other educational levels.[4] At the same conference, the keynote speaker, Chief Judge Eddie Durie, also acknowledged the progress towards positive Māori development, as well as the areas requiring greater effort. He noted the very considerable gains in economic development but had some reservations about the processes used: 'It would therefore appear important . . . that the leadership and direction should remain with those who have developed from out of the people, and who share a commitment to the cultural values that have sustained past generations. There is not much point in an efficient Māori organisation if it lacks a Māori heart.'[5]

Both Wetere and Durie were sounding the same cautionary note. Māori self-determination and positive Māori development amounted to little if, in the establishment of a strong economic base, no room were left for the strengthening of a Māori identity and the continuing expression of Māori culture—the advancement of Māori peoples as Māori. The history of New Zealand, at least since 1840, suggests that Pākehā New Zealanders have had some difficulty tolerating a strong Māori cultural presence alongside Eurocentric values and beliefs. Assimilation, rather than the retention and development of Māori language and culture, was the usual goal, and in that process presumptions were made about a common New Zealand identity that overrode claims to being Māori. In 1896 there were even doubts about Māori physical survival; the population had declined to a mere 42 000, and during the previous two decades it had been periodically predicted that the race would become extinct.[6]

Before European contact, the word māori simply meant normal or usual. There was no concept of a Māori identity in the sense of cultural or even national similarities. Instead, the distinguishing features which demarcated groups were mainly attributable to tribal affiliations and the natural environment. Thus members of Rangitane, a tribe in the lower half of the North Island, took their identity from Rangitane ancestors as well as the Manawatu River and the Ruahine mountain range,[7] whereas their neighbours, Ngāti Apa, identified with other ancestors and another river, the Rangitikei. In that sense, identity reflected historical, social, and geographic characteristics. The original inhabitants of New Zealand did not refer to themselves as Māori; rather they were Rangitane or Ngāti Apa or Tuhoe or any of forty or more tribes.

The Creation of a Māori Identity

The evolution of a collective national Māori identity was heralded at a meeting in 1835 when the Declaration of Independence was signed.[8] A Māori body politic was prescribed, as well as a 'Congress' to pass laws and make regulations for all Māori. Though the Māori legislature never eventuated, the declaration was recognised in Britain as evidence of a Māori nation and served to support a unified front by Māori as settlers from other countries arrived. Early missionaries had also encouraged a new Māori identity based on both conversion to Christianity and new alliances between tribes, even an abandonment of tribal differences. However, it was only after the signing of the Treaty of Waitangi in 1840 and the subsequent rapid colonisation of New Zealand that a more widely accepted Māori identity emerged. By 1857 māori had lost some of its meaning as normal; by then Māori accounted for fifty per cent of the population, and by 1874 they had become only fourteen per cent, a minority in their own country.[9]

Often the culture of the newcomers, because of its stark contrasts, provided Māori with a reason for emphasising their common features, rather than their tribal differences, if only when interacting with the settlers. Even then it was an identity more obvious to the newcomers, and in truth largely determined by them, rather than a true reflection of any sense of homogeneity on the part of Māori people. Anthropologists (e.g. Best, Cowan, White), missionaries (e.g.

Taylor, Cervantes) and even a Governor (Grey) created their own versions of Māori identity, using terms that reflected Eurocentric views of the world rather than Māori perceptions of tribe and the Māori world. The new constructions of a Māori identity were accompanied by the promotion of a range of stories, 'legends', and traditions, based on various tribal accounts but amalgamated to form new pan-Māori versions which frequently also drew heavily on both European tradition and the Old Testament. It was part of a colonising process which not only led to alienation of land and other resources but also brought Māori history and culture into a regimented framework so that it could readily be understood and controlled by the colonisers. In the process new myths were created and a new type of Māori identity was forged. Māori, however, were not entirely convinced that they were the different ones; they were perplexed enough trying to understand the peculiarities of western ways and did not think it necessary to try to decipher their own 'normal' culture.

The emergence of a nineteenth century Māori identity was, then, a product of several forces: colonisation, Christian conversion, an emerging sense of Māori nationalism, and immigration with a rapid reversal of population dominance. For the most part the story was told by the newcomers and in their language, so that Māori themselves, through a monocultural education system, were exposed to the new perspectives of their own culture. Often the new views became the accepted wisdom. Māori initiative gave way to imperial domination and, following the nineteenth century land wars, the 'passing of the Māori' was confidently predicted. The widely held government view was that the Māori population would become extinct and that the government's obligation was to 'smooth the pillow of a dying race.'[10]

By 1900, however, and against all odds, it became clear that Māori would not become extinct although they had come perilously close to it. Had it not been for the efforts of Māori leaders themselves, the outcome might have been entirely different. But with new vigour and the capacity to embrace rather than reject new knowledge and technologies, tribes regrouped and set about to recapture some-thing of their own past and their own sense of direction, albeit within the imposed constraints of successive regimes that had little sympathy for Māori aspirations, let alone autonomy. Of course, there was no going back to the past, nor did the tribes necessarily want to restore the past. Rather, they were interested in playing more decisive roles in determining their own futures and in creating their own structures and processes to meet changing times.[11]

The new challenge came after World War II. Whereas, a century earlier, Māori identity had been moulded as much by the forces of colonisation as by Māori themselves, from 1945 urbanisation became the unmarshalled force which called for fresh understandings of what it meant to be Māori. In the space of 25 years 80 per cent of the population moved away from tribal areas to live in cities and towns. Moreover, high fertility rates coupled with reduced mortality had resulted in a population explosion. By the time of the 1991 census Māori accounted for some 13 per cent of the total population, and over one-third were under the age of 25 years; 85 per cent were urban dwellers and one in four lived in the greater Auckland area.[12] The speed of urbanisation, rather than its inevitability, brought new problems. Retention of tribal links was difficult enough for economic reasons but government policies also actively discouraged tribal organisation.[13] 'Pepper-potting', the housing policy of sprinkling Māori families among Pākehā ones, was to ensure that Māori were dispersed throughout urban centres—a necessary step for full integration, though in Māori eyes a stepping stone to assimilation. Under the Māori Community Development Act 1962, an earlier reference to tribal committees was changed to Māori committees to underline the significance of a new cultural identity based less on tribe than on simply being Māori.

Tribal Identity

As the realities of urbanisation dawned, Māori began to question the validity of a universal Māori identity. Tuhoe leader John Rangihau even wondered whether the notion of Māoritanga had been created 'by the Pakeha to bring the tribes together. Because if you cannot divide and rule, then for tribal people all you can do is unite them and rule.' A Māori identity did not make a lot of sense to him. More relevant was a cultural identity based on tribal origin: 'Although these feelings are Māori, for me they are my Tuhoetanga rather than my Māoritanga.'[14] By 1984 his sentiments were echoed in many quarters. Encouraged by government policies of iwi (tribal) management, which rather than continuing to dismiss the relevance of tribe supported tribal development, Māori reaffirmed a tribal identity in preference to the more bland Māori identity. A decade of iwi development followed, and in that time there was a resurgence of tribal pride accompanied by new opportunities for the second and third generations of urban migrants to learn tribal history, language, and song. Statistics New Zealand, acting on a Māori request, decided to include tribal questions in the 1991 census. After an initial trial in 1991, the Schedule of Iwi was refined for the 1996 census and is shown in table 3.1.[15] The schedule recognises that some iwi have different identities in more than one region. Ngāti Raukawa, for example, migrated to the Horowhenua and Manawatu areas where they re-established themselves, setting up a number of marae based on hapū. At the same time, their relatives who did not travel south continued to occupy traditional lands in the Waikato area. Now each grouping has distinctive characteristics and operates independently, regardless of a shared early history.

The 1996 census was the second attempt in recent years to record tribal affiliation in a systematic manner. Although the nine largest iwi were unchanged from 1991, the numbers who indicated an affiliation with each had grown substantially. Ngāpuhi remained the largest iwi with 95451 members, while Ngāti Porou with 54219 and Ngāti Kahungunu with 45261 were again larger than most others. Ngai Tahu reported the greatest inter-census increase, 43.5 per cent, from 20304 in 1991 to a total of 29133 in 1996.[16] Nineteen per cent of the 1996 respondents, however, did not know the name of their iwi.

Table 3.1 Schedule of Iwi for Statistical Purposes

Northland Auckland	Hauraki	Waikato King Country	Te Arawa Taupo
Te Aupouri	Ngāti Hako	Ngāti Haua	Ngāti Pikiao
Ngāti Kahu	Ngāti Hei	Ngāti Maniapoto	Ngāti Rangiteaorere
Ngāti Kuri	Ngāti Maru	Ngāti Raukawa	Ngati Rangitihi
Ngāpuhi	Ngāti Paoa	Waikato	Ngāti Rangwewehi
Te Rarawa	Patukirikiri		Tapuika
Ngai Takoto	Ngāti Rahiri-		Tarawhai
Ngāti Wai	Tumutumu		Tuhourangi
Ngāti Whātua	Ngāti Tai		Uenuku-Kopako
Te Kawerau	Ngāti Tamatera		Ngāti Whakaue
Te Uru-o-Hau	Ngāti Tara Tokanui		Tuwharetoa
	Ngāti Whanaunga		

Bay of Plenty	East Coast	Hawke's Bay Wairarapa	Taranaki
Ngāti Pukenga	Ngāti Porou	Rongomaiwahine	Te Atiawa
Ngaiterangi	Te Aitangi-a-Mataki	Ngāti Kahungunu	Ngāti Maru
Ngatiranginui	Rongowhakaata	ki te Wairoa	Ngāti Mutunga
Ngāti Awa	Ngai Tamanuhiri	ki Heretaunga	Ngāti Rauru
Ngāti Manawa		ki Wairarapa	Ngā Ruahine
Ngāti Whare		Rangitane	Ngāti Ruanui
Ngai Tai			Ngāti Tama
Tuhoe			Taranaki
Whakatohea			Tangahoe
Whanau-a-Apanui			Pakakohe

Whanganui	Manawatu Horowhenua Wellington	South Island Chatham Islands	
Ngati Apa	Te Atiawa	Te Ati Awa	Ngāti Rarua
Te Ati Hau Nui-a-	Muaupoko	Ngāti Koata	Ngai Tahu
Paparangi	Rangitane	Ngāti Kuia	Ngāti Tama
Ngāti Haua	Ngāti Raukawa	Kati Mamoe	Ngāti Toa
	Ngāti Toa	Moriori	Waitaha
		Ngāti Mutunga	Ngāti Apa
		Rangitane	

Source: Statistics New Zealand

While a tribal identity was lauded by Māori, and from 1984 actively promoted by the state, the 1991 census also showed that as many as 29 per cent of all Māori did not identify with any particular tribe and, predictably, many of those who did actually had very little contact with tribe or tribal life.[17] In 1994 some reappraisal of an exclusively tribal focus was called for by urban Māori. The situation came to a head after the signing of a fisheries settlement between Māori and the Crown in 1992. A distribution of fishing quota and associated resources along tribal lines was proposed, even though the settlement was for 'all Māori'.[18] By now many urban dwellers were no longer prepared to accept that tribal approaches were sufficient to accommodate all Māori interests and were concerned that Māori who were not included in tribal activities, or language programs, were being afforded lesser status as Māori.[19] They called on the government to recognise the diverse realities of Māori without presuming that all Māori could be stereotyped and they instigated court action against the Treaty of Waitangi Fisheries Commission.

In 1996 the Court of Appeal ruled that urban Māori had rights akin to tribal rights (at least in respect of the allocation of fishing rights). By then, however, it was also apparent that there was a lack of empirical evidence to describe the several realities of Māori or to appreciate the links between socio-economic circumstances and cultural identity. Māori had, it seemed, acquired a range of cultural meanings and associations, which went beyond notions of tribe, but did not negate a tribal identity.

BEING MĀORI IN THE 21ST CENTURY

In order to better understand contemporary Māori values and identities, the Department of Māori Studies at Massey University is undertaking an extensive survey of 700 Māori households in four regions of New Zealand: Auckland, Tairawhiti, Manawatu–Whanganui, and Wellington. Te Hoe Nuku Roa is a longitudinal study which tracks the progress, problems, aspirations, and circumstances of Māori people from all walks of life and over a ten- or fifteen-year period. It explores the realities of Māori lives using social, economic and cultural indicators which can then be analysed and synthesised to obtain an integrated view. The study is based on a multi-axial framework made up of four interacting dimensions—paihere tangata (human relationships), te ao Māori (Māori culture and identity), ngā āhuatanga noho-a-tangata (socio-economic circumstances), ngā whakanekeneketanga (change over time).[20]

An important component of Te Hoe Nuku Roa is cultural identity, and using responses to a detailed questionnaire a number of cultural identity profiles have been developed. Cultural identity is conceived as an amalgam of personal attitudes, cultural knowledge, and participation in Māori society. Particular attention is focused on self-identification, knowledge of whakapapa (ancestry), participation in marae activities (customary social and cultural centres), involvement with whānau (extended family), access to whenua tipu (ancestral land), contacts with other Māori people, and use of Māori language. These key markers are summarised in table 3.2.

Table 3.2 Māori Cultural Identity: Key Markers

	Markers	Indicators
Identification	Ethnic identity	identification as Māori
Knowledge and understanding	Cultural knowledge	tribal history, whakapapa (genealogy), tikanga (custom), social arrangements
Access and participation	Access to, and participation in, Māori institutions and society	marae whānau, hapū, social links land, forests the environment, fisheries
Communication	Māori language	level and place of usage print and broadcasting media fluency

Underlying this approach to cultural identity is the assumption that despite personal values and beliefs, the development of a cultural identity also depends on access to key cultural institutions and resources such as land, whānau, language, and marae. Preliminary analysis has enabled the construction of four cultural identity profiles: a secure identity, a positive identity, a notional identity, and a compromised identity. [21]

The concept of a secure identity rests on definite self-identification as Māori together with quantifiable involvement in, and/or knowledge of, whakapapa (ancestry), marae participation, whānau (extended family), whenua tipu (ancestral land), contacts with Māori people, and Māori language. The positive identity profile has lower levels of involvement in Māori society, te ao Māori, and the notional identity profile has no access—notwithstanding self-identification as Māori. A compromised identity, on the other hand, reflects non-identification as Māori, often despite quite considerable access to te ao Māori.

Of the 200 responses so far analysed, 35 per cent fit the criteria for a secure identity, 53 per cent a positive identity, 6 per cent a notional identity, and a further 6 per cent a compromised identity. Although the study is insufficiently complete to draw definite conclusions, it does appear that many Māori people do not have secure access to the Māori world and as a consequence are unable to enjoy full participation in Māori society. Nor does it always matter where a person is living; dispossession (of land, language, or marae) is not confined to urban Māori, nor does a rural residence guarantee access to either cultural or physical resources. What is suggestive, however, is that a secure identity may have advantages beyond cultural affirmation. It may, for example, afford some protection against poor health; it is more likely to be associated with active educational participation and with positive employment profiles. The corollary is that reduced access to the Māori resources, and the wider Māori world, may be associated with cultural, social, and economic disadvantage.[22]

At the same time, it is now evident that there is no single Māori cultural stereotype, and being Māori may have quite different connotations for various groups.[23] Māori are as diverse as any other people—not only in socio-economic terms but also in fundamental attitudes to identity. Nor can a Māori identity any longer be entirely dismissed in favour of a tribal identity. The reality is that some Māori also choose to identify with a particular tribe, others might wish to but have lost access, and others still might be content simply as Māori, with no desire to add a tribal identity.

MĀORI LANGUAGE AND CULTURE

The late Sir James Henare was in no doubt when he gave evidence to the Waitangi Tribunal that language is fundamental to culture and a key marker of cultural identity. 'The language is the core of our Māori culture and mana. Ko te reo te mauri o te mana Māori. If the language dies, as some predict, what do we have left to us? Then I ask our own people who are we?'[24] The fight to retain, revitalise, and extend Māori language typifies Māori determination to assert a positive cultural identity in a contemporary world.

It was not surprising therefore that quite early in the life of the Waitangi Tribunal a claim was made against the Crown for failing to protect Māori language. Brought by Huirangi Waikerepuru and Ngā Kaiwhakapūmau i te Reo (the Wellington Māori Language Board), the claim alleged that government policies had contributed to the decline of te reo Māori, not only through neglect but also by way of active prohibition of Māori in schools and a refusal to allow the use of Māori in court or in dealings with the government. Several features made this particular case distinctive: the claim was for loss of cultural properties (not land or fisheries); though having the support of all tribes, it was brought by a Māori interest group (rather than a particular tribe); and it was a claim made for and on behalf of all Māori.[25]

The claimants' case was that te reo Māori should be recognised as an official language throughout New Zealand and for all purposes. The Māori Affairs Act 1953 (s 77A), the Broadcasting Act 1976, the Education Act 1964, the Health Act 1956, the Hospitals Act 1957, and broadcasting and educational policies were said to be inconsistent with the principles of the Treaty and as a result the claimants were prejudiced in that they and other Māori were not able to have the Māori language spoken, heard, taught, learnt, broadcast or otherwise used for all purposes and in particular in Parliament, the courts, government departments, and local bodies, and in all other spheres of New Zealand society including hospitals.

Two proverbs recurred during the hearing: 'Ko te reo te mauri o te mana Māori' and 'Ka ngaro te reo, ka ngaro tāua, pera i te ngaro o te moa'. Both illustrated the close link between language and well-being and the likely fate of Māori language which, without restorative measures, could become as extinct as the moa.[26] Ample evidence was produced to show how Māori language use had declined. In 1913, for example, 90 per cent of Māori school children could speak Māori. By 1953 the percentage had reduced to 26 per cent, and in 1975 fewer than 5 per cent of Māori schoolchildren could speak Māori.

As much as anything, general policies of assimilation and the promotion of English as the only language of progress and advancement were blamed for the decline. As well, policies of urbanisation and 'pepperpotting', along with largely monolingual and monocultural media, reduced social opportunities for speaking and hearing Māori, while the exclusive use of English in official documents and in the courts diminished the standing of Māori not only in the eyes of the public but also in the bureaucracy.

The Tribunal was told that no Māori was able to use te reo Māori in the courts of New Zealand if there was a capacity to speak English. As recently as 1979 a High Court decision, confirmed the following year by the Court of Appeal (*Mihaka v Police*), ruled that Māori could not be used. In that case the appellant, Dun Mihaka, claimed the right to address the court in Māori. He was refused. He then appealed, using the Treaty of Waitangi as the basis for his claim. The Appeal Court found that the Treaty did not cover the right to use Māori in the courts according to present law. That was correct. A person who could speak and understand English could not use Māori in court, a decision based on an English statute, the Pleadings in English Act 1362, which became part of New Zealand law by virtue of the English Laws Act 1858 when the settler government adopted all the laws of England that were in force on 14 January 1840.

Ironically, the Pleadings in English Act was passed at a time when there was concern that the language of the government, Norman French, was making too many incursions and the native English-speaking litigants were consequently disadvantaged. In 1980 the same law was being used to protect the language of government (English) at the expense of native speakers of Māori.

But the most severe criticism in the Māori language claim was reserved for policies which had forbidden the use of Māori in school grounds from the beginning of the century. Witnesses, including Sir James Henare, described incidents of punishment for speaking Māori and contested the Department of Education view that it was never a practice to forbid Māori. Policy or not, 'there was an extremely effective gentlemen's agreement!' Sir James went on to recount his own experiences while at school. An inspector made it very clear that 'English is the bread-and-butter language, and if you want to earn your bread and butter you must speak English.' Then he recalled being sent into the bushes to cut a piece of supplejack with which he was caned for failing to leave 'te reo Māori at the school gates.'[27]

Although there were signs that Māori language was being encouraged through government policies and practices, the claimants maintained Department of Education policies still actively discriminated against Māori language learners. The national School Certificate examination was a particularly disturbing point. In 1983 candidates sitting School Certificate Māori had a pass rate of 37 per cent, while candidates sitting Latin, French, and German had pass rates of 80 per cent. A scaling system operated so that 80 out of every 100 candidates sitting the foreign examination passed, but only 38 out of every 100 Māori language candidates were allowed to pass; i.e. 62 per cent had to fail.

There was also concern that the organisation and structure of schools was generally monocultural and that the teaching of Māori was very much an optional extra. Many children had to take it by correspondence because their own (often large) school was not able to offer it as a regular subject. The method of teaching Māori similarly caused criticism. Literacy in Māori was being favoured over fluency in speaking Māori (80 per cent of the School Certificate exam was written, 20 per cent oral) and the kōhanga reo system for children under five years old had shown up the inadequacies of secondary school teaching of Māori.

During the claim hearings the Waitangi Tribunal received many complaints about broadcasting policy but, because there was already an inquiry under way, did not make any further recommendations about the Māori language in radio or television. However, in the *Te Reo Māori Report*, the Tribunal was strong in its criticism of government policy and made recommendations which would lead to the enhancement of the status of Māori language. Little difficulty was encountered in concluding that the Māori language had not been accorded the status it warranted as an indigenous language or as promised in the Treaty, a finding which was consistent with the notion of language as a taonga, a resource protected in Article 2 of the Treaty: 'Language is an essential part of culture and must be regarded as "a valued possession".'[28]

Five recommendations were made by the Tribunal. First, Māori should be a lawful language in all courts of law and in any dealings with government departments, local authorities, and other public bodies. Second, a supervising body should be established by statute to supervise and foster the use of the Māori language. Third, there should be an inquiry into way Māori children are educated, including the opportunity to learn te reo. Fourth, broadcasting policy should recognise that the Treaty obliges the Crown to recognise and protect the Māori language. Finally, bilingualism should be a prerequisite for some appointments to state service.

The recommendations did not go as far as the claimants wished, but they were instrumental in securing major change at governmental and policy levels. The Māori Language Act 1987, introduced as a bill shortly before the Waitangi Tribunal's *Te Reo Māori Report* was released, declared the Māori language to be an official language of New Zealand and conferred the right to speak Māori in any legal proceedings, regardless of ability to understand or communicate in English or any other language. In the preamble to the Act the Tribunal's findings were accepted: 'Whereas in the Treaty of Waitangi the Crown confirmed and guaranteed to the Māori people, among other things, all their taonga; And whereas the Māori language is one such taonga: . . . ' When enacted in 1987 the Act also established Te Taura Whiri i te Reo Māori (Māori Language Commission) to actively promote Māori as a living language and to advise and assist the Crown on the implementation of Māori as an official language. Subsequently, changes to broadcasting policy were introduced and the State Sector Act 1988 required chief executives of government departments to recognise the aims, aspirations, and employment requirements of the Māori people.

Some recommendations were not implemented, and others were accepted but within narrower frameworks than sought. For example, the Māori Language Act did not make provision for Māori language to be spoken in dealings with public authorities, and some felt that the Māori Language Commissioner would be constrained by a lack of regulatory power.[29] An inquiry into Māori education was announced in September 1989 but not under terms suggested by the Tribunal; instead, it focused on the Māori Education Foundation with scant regard for school policies, workforce development, or the place of Māori in the curriculum. Suggested amendments to the State Services Act 1962 and the State Services Conditions of Employment Act 1977 to make provision for bilingualism were not accepted. Yet, despite incomplete acceptance, for the first time in New Zealand's modern history, the Māori language had been afforded recognition, and the way was clearer than it had been to develop other strategies for revitalisation.

Māori Language Revitalisation

Recognition of Māori language as an official language will not by itself guarantee its survival and continuing use. More important is the actual use of te reo Māori by Māori and across all domains. The state has a role to create favourable circumstances (in schools and work places) for Māori language development and to allocate funds, but the initiative must come from Māori. Wiremu Kaa made a similar suggestion when discussing the relative roles of the state and Māori: 'The Department's willingness to share the decision-making and to give Māori people power to determine future policy for the development and maintenance of Māori as a living language in Aotearoa, will surely pave the way for a brighter future.'[30] His point was a relevant one insofar as language is cradled not in the statutes of the land, or the policies of state, but in the hearts and mouths of families and whānau, in their homes and marae. Revitalisation strategies therefore needed to be centred on Māori aspirations and initiative. While school programs were regarded as very important, and Māori programs on television and radio essential, Māori communities themselves were the critical determinants for the successful maintenance of Māori language.

After the 1986 *Te Reo Māori Report*, several revitalisation strategies evolved more or less in parallel. Table 3.3 summarises the eight main thrusts.

Table 3.3 Strategies for the Revitalisation of Te Reo Māori

Focus	Programs
Early childhood education	Kōhanga reo
Primary school	Kura kaupapa Māori Bilingual classes and units
Secondary, tertiary education	High schools, polytechnics, universities, wānanga
Policy and promotion	Te Taura Whiri i te Reo Māori (Māori Language Commission) Ministry of Education Te Puni Kōkiri
Community	Whānau, marae, wānanga
Workforce development	Teachers of Māori
Māori language resources	Toi te Kupu, Ministry of Education
Media content	Radio, TV, print media

No single approach can claim to be totally successful, nor can the usefulness of different approaches be easily compared with each other. The inclusion of Māori language teaching in regular state schools at primary and secondary levels probably impacts on a greater number of pupils than the immersion methods allow, and even though the potential for fluency may be less, the significance and success of such classes should not be discounted. Turoa Royal, who pioneered a bilingual program in a large Wellington secondary school, concluded that the inclusion of Māori language and culture across the curriculum had positive spin-offs for Māori language development as well as for examination success and the personal confidence of Māori students.[31] Monty Ohia, also working in Wellington, found that children in bilingual units in a primary and a secondary school were achieving well in both English and Māori, including in School Certificate subjects.[32]

Kōhanga Reo and Kura Kaupapa Māori

While the progressive inclusion of Māori language and culture allowed Māori children and others to receive formal language teaching, and often a sound introduction to Māori culture, international attention also focused on the immersion approaches of kōhanga reo and kura kaupapa Māori. Kōhanga reo programs combined three objectives. First, they aimed to provide a vehicle for the promotion of Māori language; second, they wished to stimulate whānau centres which offered quality child care within tikanga Māori; and third, they sought to maintain a totally Māori environment by using immersion modes of learning. The first program started at the Pukeatua Kōkiri Centre, Wainuiomata, in 1981, and others followed in rapid succession, so that even by 1983 there were 94 centres catering for 1 377 children.[33] By 1993 that number had swelled to 819 centres and 14 027 children, though there was a decline in 1995 to 13 839 children.[34] Several studies have shown the success of kōhanga reo in imparting Māori language to new generations — and to their parents.[35] But benefits beyond language acquisition have also been described. Margie Hohepa found that kōhanga reo play a significant role as an enculturating environment in which, apart from language learning, Māori cultural beliefs, values, and practices are transmitted.[36]

Objections to the establishment of kōhanga reo, however, were not infrequent. Two were based on the assumptions that an all-Māori environment would be detrimental to children when they moved on to English-speaking schools and that a type of separatism was being developed. Neither objection stood up to close scrutiny. Examples from elsewhere in the world suggest that bilingualism is not only possible but in many countries it is the rule and has led to advantage rather than disadvantage. Moreover, far from encouraging separatism, kōhanga reo were going some way towards compensating for the large numbers of Māori children who had no early childhood education at all. If anything, they created the potential for less division in a society which was (and still is) characterised by unacceptable disparities between Māori and non-Māori. It was difficult not to conclude that early objections to kōhanga were based on a prejudice against Māori and a fundamental belief in assimilation.

However, with the growth of kōhanga additional concerns have arisen, often voiced by Māori. Whereas early critics feared that children exposed to Māori language would never learn to speak English, some Māori linguists are concerned that the standard of Māori within kōhanga is so variable that children will emerge speaking a type of second-language Māori, which is based on English language structures and lacks any sense of the vernacular. The point was made by Timoti Karetu, the Māori Language Commissioner, in a Ngāhuru lecture delivered at Massey University in 1995. He also took the opportunity to advocate a more focused approach to the training of teachers of Māori so that they might deliver an authentic high-quality product, not devoid of the nuances and idiom which enrich language.[37] Other concerns have surfaced from time to time—about having all kōhanga reo under the Te Kōhanga Reo National Trust, rather than directly under iwi control, and high weekly fees which act as barrier to needy families. Related to the latter is an awareness that fewer than half of all Māori children involved in early childhood education are attending kōhanga. For some parents the exercise of choice is important (kindergarten, play centre, 'parents as first teachers' may be preferred), but for others, reasons for not sending children to a kōhanga include costs, location, a parent who is not Māori, and lack of parental involvement and support.[38] A different concern is the limited opportunity for kōhanga reo pupils to continue their education in Māori at primary and secondary levels.[39]

Combined objectives of Māori language promotion and quality primary school education contributed to the formation of kura kaupapa Māori schools. Like kōhanga reo, immersion Māori was the norm, though the curriculum conformed to state expectations. The first kura was established on the Hoani Waititi marae in Auckland, outside the state system, but by 1995, 34 had been approved by the Ministry of Education, with a total of 2475 enrolments.[40] The largest, Te Arawhanui in Petone, had a roll of 350 by 1997 and, according to Chairman Ritchie Luke, was planning to build a college for secondary pupils.[41] Between 1995 and 1998 fifteen new kura have been forecast, all now within the state system. Although more time is needed to draw definitive conclusions, the early indications are that kura kaupapa are successfully meeting their objectives.[42] In a study of children in six kura kaupapa for example, Reedy found good development in oral Māori, literacy in Māori, and numeracy skills;[43] and Aspin reported higher than average mathematics achievement in a group of students who were being taught mathematics in Māori.[44]

While language immersion is a key ingredient of these schools, the notion of whānau is a core feature of both kura kaupapa theory and practice. The success of kura kaupapa has been largely attributed to the whānau method, and Graham Smith has identified four key whānau elements: knowledge, pedagogy, discipline, curriculum.[45] In a whānau approach, knowledge is regarded as belonging to the whole group or whānau, individuals being repositories only for the benefit of the wider group. The cultural obligation is to share. Whānau-derived pedagogies incorporate those cultural values and beliefs which facilitate learning such as manaakitanga (sharing and caring), aroha (respect), whakaiti (humility). Older children help younger ones and advantage is taken of group activities within which culturally preferred learning styles can flourish. Discipline in kura kaupapa depends on the whānau models of authority and respect, teachers being known as pāpā (father), whāea (aunty), matua (uncle), while pupils adopt sibling roles towards each other. In kura kaupapa the curriculum reflects the realities of the children, and the values and practices of whānau are reinforced through the curriculum content. Far from providing a lesser standard of education, as some sceptics predicted, and even allowing for the high motivation of parents, kura kaupapa pupils have generally excelled both at primary and later at secondary schools. Not surprisingly, their standard of Māori language has also surpassed expectation, many form two pupils being able to cope with School Certificate Māori, some three years before their peers. In turn this language capacity, advanced in comparison with late-entry second-language learners, has led to difficulties providing courses beyond the level of form seven for students who were in lower forms and not yet eligible to enter university.

Māori Language Teachers and Resources

At all levels of education, both formal and informal, the shortage of well-trained Māori language teachers has been rivalled only by the non-availability of suitable Māori language resource material. Both have been major obstacles to teaching and learning Māori. Several strategies have been tried, including the recruitment of native speakers into short teacher-training programs. The Te Atakura program, for example, encouraged Māori speakers who were mandated by their tribe or community to enrol in a one-year training program, after which they were eligible for teacher positions in secondary schools. Not all found the transition easy, nor was the duration of training always sufficient to provide both theoretical and practical skills. But their deployment throughout the country at least enabled schools to introduce Māori language programs. Bridging programs such as the one-year Raukura program at the Palmerston North College of Education gave some potential teachers the chance to upskill before embarking on regular teacher training, while at the Whanganui Community Polytechnic a condensed teacher-training program for kura kaupapa teachers attracted Māori-language speakers from various parts of the North Island. Meanwhile, the mainstream colleges of education had also introduced programs to cater for students who wished to teach in the Māori immersion mode, as well as for those who would teach in bilingual units.

However, the relative dearth of resources created problems for students and for young teachers, many of whom were forced to spend as many hours writing their own booklets as actually teaching. Often they have had little option but to use any resource, regardless of the quality of the Māori or the cost. In addressing the situation, a number of publications have appeared, and Te Taura Whiri o te Reo Māori has played a facilitating and expert role, developing valuable lexicons and dictionaries, and introducing a wide range of words to describe modern ideas and objects.[46] Avoiding where possible transliterations, the approach has been to convey a new concept by using old words in new senses. Sometimes the resulting phrase has been unclear, even to native speakers, but sufficient progress has been made to demonstrate that the extended Māori vocabulary is capable of representing a range of technical, commercial, scientific, and philosophical ideas. At the same time, there is a dearth of suitable texts in subjects such as science, technology, geography, and mathematics, an area where Christensen considers that there is an urgent need for quality resource materials. In meeting this goal, and allowing for the possibility that classroom teachers might become overloaded, there is also the potential for good materials to be catalytic for teacher, as well as student, development.[47]

At the more academic end of the learning spectrum the situation may be less pressing. Several English texts have been also published in Māori,[48] and an increasing number of quality Māori language books have appeared, sometimes (but not always) translated into English.[49] Generally, however, there is a crucial gap in the provision of very advanced Māori language courses.[50] For less advanced learners, iwi newspapers have filled part of the resource void, providing information of interest to local iwi and hapū, written from a Māori perspective and seldom available in the mainstream print media. Generally, however, they have devoted more space to commentaries in English than to articles in Māori.

A particular problem confronting teachers of Māori has been to ensure that the quality of language is high and that it provides good models of language use for second language learners. In response, Te Tau o te Reo Māori, Māori Language Year 1995, provided an opportunity for a renewed focus on quality resources suitable for teachers and learners. The Ministry of Education, through Learning Media Limited, published a series of readers, charts, and audio tapes, and distributed a Māori education bibliography, *Whaia te Matauranga II*.[51] In the same year the Department of Māori Studies at Massey University embarked on another research program, Toi te Kupu, aimed at developing a mechanism for cataloguing and describing Māori-language resources so that teachers of Māori could make better assessments of the quality and suitability of a resource for a particular purpose.[52] The Toi te Kupu framework incorporates a number of resource characteristics such as accessibility, purpose, dialect, reading level, language level, content, the type of language employed, and the suggested uses of the resource.

For many years the media were slow to include Māori language in regular productions. However, Derek Tini Fox played a major role in promoting Māori participation in both the print and broadcasting media. Despite considerable opposition from colleagues in the field, and with extremely limited resources, he consistently argued for a stronger Māori presence. Not only did he establish the Mana News radio broadcasts, but he also launched *Mana, A Māori News Magazine for all New Zealanders* in 1993. Though written mainly in English, the magazine contains regular articles in Māori and includes a wide range of material relating to contemporary Māori, including a heavy emphasis on education, health, sport, and politics. Fifteen issues had been published by the beginning of 1997.

Broadcasting

Although in 1986 the Waitangi Tribunal was unable to make significant recommendations in respect of broadcasting because a Royal Commission and a Broadcasting Tribunal were meeting at the same time as te reo Māori claim hearings, the Tribunal did recognise the tremendous potential which radio and television had for promoting Māori language: 'It is consistent with the principles of the Treaty that the language and matters of Māori interest should have a secure place in broadcasting.' Veteran Māori broadcaster Haare Williams agreed: 'Radio and television are the main instruments of mass communication and have the capacity to reach every living room, common room, classroom, factory floor and motor car, . . . There is a moral obligation on New Zealanders to make certain that te reo Māori remains a part of the communication process . . .'[53] According to the late Sir Kingi Ihaka, a former Chairman of the Māori Language Commission, television and radio broadcasting were 'an essential component of institutional support for the maintenance and revival of the language.'[54]

Māori dissatisfaction with broadcasting policies continued after the *Te Reo Māori Report* was released, and grievances increased from 1988 when the restructuring of broadcasting commenced. Two sets of court action followed. First, there were concerns about the tendering process for AM and FM radio frequencies, and, second, objections were lodged over the proposed transfer of state assets to two new state-owned enterprises, Radio New Zealand and Television New Zealand. In both instances High Court and Court of Appeal suits followed and in the asset transfer case the matter was eventually taken to the Privy Council.

The Radiocommunications Act 1989 established government's policy regarding the disposal of radio frequencies. The New Zealand Māori Council and Ngā Kaiwhakapūmau i te Reo contended that the Act did not adequately meet the need to promote the Māori language and culture and that the government had called for tenders for radio frequencies without taking Māori broadcasting claims sufficiently into account. Again they took a case to the Waitangi Tribunal, this time claiming that radio frequencies were a 'taonga', guaranteed within tino rangatiratanga. The Tribunal heard the claim in 1990 and found that broadcasting was a vehicle for the protection of Māori language and that Māori should have access to airwave spectrums. They recommended a six-month suspension of the government tendering process and the allocation of FM frequencies to Māori.[55]

But the government was impatient and did not wish to delay the tendering process; further, they did not consider that Māori-language broadcasting would be adversely affected by the AM/FM tenders. As it stood, however, none of the FM frequencies reserved for Māori were in either Auckland or Wellington. In 1990, therefore, the New Zealand Māori Council challenged the Crown in the High Court seeking assurances that Māori access to FM frequencies would form part of government policy. Justice Heron ruled that Article 2 of the Treaty did cover Māori language and that the Crown had an obligation to devise safeguards, not only to avoid present damage but also to facilitate future revival and development of the language. He made an order that the Crown ought to delay the sale by tender of frequencies for a period of six weeks. That would give the Waitangi Tribunal time to complete its investigations. The Crown appealed but on a split vote, three to two, the appeal was dismissed.[56]

At a national hui in 1990, Māori debated the significance of broadcasting for Māori language development against the background of the restructuring of the Broadcasting Corporation, the allocation of radio frequencies, and the possibility of additional television channels. The hui concluded that Māori broadcasting required sufficient and independent funding to maintain a television channel, a Māori radio network, a full Māori news service, and a strong Māori presence in mainstream media. It was also agreed that bilingual and bicultural policies should be vigorously pursued in the programming and management of Māori broadcasting bodies and that a Māori Broadcasting Commission should be established.

Although proceedings were commenced towards the end of 1988, it was not until 1991 that the High Court heard the case brought by Ngā Kaiwhakapumau i te Reo Māori and the New Zealand Māori Council to block the transfer of state broadcasting assets to the newly corporatised Radio New Zealand and Television New Zealand. The court did not find that there had been a breach of the Treaty, and in the first of two judgements did not obstruct the transfer of assets to Radio New Zealand. But the release of television assets was blocked at least until a protective scheme was in place. Nonetheless, it was only a temporary injunction. Once the Crown had produced a protective scheme, Justice McGechan made a declaration that the transfer of assets could proceed.

The Māori claimants took the matter to the Court of Appeal in 1992.[57] Their essential question was whether the proposed transfer of broadcasting assets by the Crown would go beyond the powers conferred by the State-Owned Enterprises Act 1986. That Act prohibited the Crown from acting in a manner inconsistent with the principles of the Treaty of Waitangi. The President of the Court, Sir Robin Cooke, considered that the protection suggested by the Crown, and sanctioned by Justice McGechan, would not be very substantial and that the devolution of assets left the Māori language relatively unprotected. Justice Hardie-Boys, on the other hand, was concerned that language protection would fare badly against market forces, though he did not consider that issue relevant to the case. On a majority decision, the appeal was dismissed.

In the wake of defeat, the plaintiffs took the case to the Privy Council in 1993. Although the Council did not support the appeal, the judgment went some way to supporting Māori views and endorsed the opinion of the Waitangi Tribunal that language was indeed a taonga. The Privy Council also accepted Justice McGechan's assessment that Māori language was in a perilous state, that there had been default by the Crown in the past, and that there was an obligation on the Crown to ensure that Māori language had a proper place in broadcasting. However, in meeting an obligation to protect taonga, the Council considered that the Crown was not required to go beyond what was 'reasonable in the prevailing circumstances.' They were satisfied that the protective mechanisms arranged in response to the High Court ruling were adequate.

Part of the protection offered by the Crown was the establishment of Te Māngai Pāho, originally described as Te Reo Whakapuaki Irirangi in the Broadcasting Amendment Act (No. 2) 1993. The function of the new agency was to 'promote Māori language and Māori culture by making funds available, on such terms and conditions as Te Reo Whakapuaki Irirangi thinks fit, for broadcasting and the production of programs to be broadcast.'[58] A Board was appointed in 1993: James Brown (Chairman), Timoti Karetu, John Dyall, Annette Sykes, Hone Harawira, and Katerina Mataira, and Ripeka Evans as Executive Officer. A proportion of the Public Broadcasting Fee was allocated to Te Māngai Pāho, and funding directly from the government was promised for new projects.[59]

There was criticism about the relative absence of Māori broadcasters on the board and later about the policies adopted. Te Māngai Pāho was a funding agency, a purchaser of broadcasting, not itself a provider of services. Iwi radio often felt marginalised by funding priorities, although in fact a large number of iwi radio stations were established in a relatively short time. Prior to the broadcasting reforms there was only one iwi-based radio station (Te Upoko o te Ika), but by 1996 the number had increased to 24, 23 of which operated on frequencies reserved by the Crown for the promotion of Māori language and culture. In addition Radio Aotearoa (which had appeared on occasions to compete with iwi for limited funds) established broadcasts to Auckland, Wellington, and Christchurch. Concern about the extent to which Te Māngai Pāho could adopt a pure purchasing role without also actively promoting Māori broadcasting was to become a major issue by 1997. The hands-off approach, in the absence of any other responsible agency, was seen to be inconsistent with government obligations to actively protect Māori language.

Not all iwi stations have sufficiently high levels of Māori language, and there have been occasional concerns about managerial capacity, but the objective of Te Māngai Pāho is nonetheless that at least 50 per cent of all programs funded will be in te reo Māori. There are expectations that providers will progressively move to that goal, and language incentive payments have been made to assist stations increase Māori language content above the minimum 20 per cent required. A national Māori radio service was launched in 1996 and the tender was awarded to Ruia Mai, a division of the Ngāti Whātua Mai FM in Auckland. Ruia Mai broadcasts quality language programs for five hours a day on the national distribution system.

Māori Television

In addition to radio, Māori have actively promoted the establishment of a Māori television channel. When a third and independent channel was proposed in 1984, the New Zealand Māori Council decided to step up its longstanding protest against the broadcasting authorities by applying for the new channel warrant. Led by Professor Whatarangi Winiata, who played a major role in many aspects of Māori broadcasting, the Aotearoa Broadcasting System (ABS) was created for that purpose. Early discussions with the Broadcasting Corporation of New Zealand (which then controlled television) led to an agreement that BCNZ would provide funding and make its transmitting equipment available to ABS if they successfully obtained the warrant.[60] It was not an entirely selfless gesture but an attempt to keep other competitors, with programs similar to their own, at bay. However, in May 1986 BCNZ reneged on their 1985 commitment, greatly weakening the Māori case.[61]

The ABS case was further undermined when independent Māori advisers were engaged by other bidders to demonstrate how Māori language and culture could be promoted in the proposed new channel. Most Māori were sceptical about the capacity of a mainstream channel to make any serious effort to promote Māori language, but insufficient funds and a lack of responsiveness from Crown-related broadcasting bodies resulted in Tele-Vid 3 (TV 3) being awarded the warrant. An appeal was lodged but without effect. A similar proposal (for a national Māori television channel) was later developed by the Iwi Television Trust but did not eventuate.

Regardless, Māori determination to use television to promote te reo Māori was strong, and litigation was aggressively pursued. After the High Court ruling in 1991, the Ministry of Commerce produced a booklet outlining the perceived advantages and disadvantages for various options and sought Māori views at a series of hui in the main centres.[62] Based largely on submissions made at those meetings, a report was prepared by officials for Justice McGechan. While it did not recommend a Māori television channel, it did recommend a time-frame for the development of special purpose Māori television and for the extension of Māori-language programming on commercial television (mainstreaming).[63] In any event it was sufficiently convincing for the court to remove restrictions on the transfer of assets to Television New Zealand, as already noted, a decision upheld by the Court of Appeal and the Privy Council.

In a separate series of consultations, the Wellington Māori Language Board and the New Zealand Māori Council, considered several other options. All would have led to Māori television as a nationwide service with provision for independent iwi-based developments to use 'break-outs'.[64] But the autonomy sought by the Māori interests was poles apart from the government's proposals for Māori television and came to little. Though mainstream television appeared to be the government's preference as a vehicle for Māori language programs, doubts about its capacity to provide anything other than a token Māori presence were reinforced when *Te Karere*, a Māori news program was shifted from primetime viewing in favour of a 4.40 p.m. burial, and the popular *Marae* program was relegated to an early Sunday morning slot.[65]

Te Māngai Pāho subsequently became the focus for Māori television and arranged a hui in September 1994. The second chairman of the agency, Hiwi Tauroa was instrumental in moving the final resolution to 'endorse the establishment of a steering group comprising Māori broadcasters and Te Māngai Pāho to progress matters and to report back to Māori interests by February 1995.'[66] As a result, in May 1996, a Māori Television channel, Aotearoa TV Network, commenced broadcasting. Establishment funding of $2.6 million had come from Te Māngai Pāho and a broad mix of news, documentaries, cultural performances, and comedy reflecting the indigenous population of NZ was screened. The channel sought to celebrate Māori life in Aotearoa in the 1990s and quickly attracted a large audience, Māori and non-Māori.[67] Program scheduler Robert Pouwhare announced a program line-up which included E Tipu e Rea (Māori pre-schoolers) and Tai Oho (teenagers), with a commentary from Tukuroirangi Morgan each night. The network employed more than ninety people and could be picked up on UHF channel 35 from five to 10.30 p.m. daily. Initially the new channel would screen in the Auckland region but there were plans to extend coverage later.[68] However, after two pilot roll-overs, the funding levels were insufficient to maintain the scale of the operation and major staff cuts were necessary less than twelve months after commencement. Te Māngai Pāho was unable to offer additional funds, and some concerns about long term viability re-emerged. Chief Executive Puhi Rangiaho vowed to keep the channel going, and a deal with a private business was raised as a possible solution. The new Minister of Māori Affairs, Tau Henare, meanwhile planned to fight for the survival of Aotearoa Television,[69] and within a month the government announced that an additional $4 million ($2 million from New Zealand on Air and $2 million from tax revenue) was being granted to keep the network going, at least until June 1997.

Opposition members in Parliament were critical, maintaining that the network was overly sympathetic to a political party, New Zealand First, and that public funds were being used to support what was a private company, with exorbitant salaries and questionable commercial practices.[70] But Henare supported the government decision, maintaining that Māori television contributed to the whole of society in a distinctive way. Moreover, the court had required a commitment from the government to support Māori broadcasting, including television, and the Aotearoa network was the only serious provider with any significant capacity.

However, a flurry of questions asked about the management of the company were an embarrassment to New Zealand First. Further, a new member of Parliament, Tukuroirangi Morgan, had been a director up until August 1996, and there was some doubt about his continuing influence and about a trip to Europe after his election that had been paid for by the television company. The Serious Fraud Office as well as the government needed to satisfy themselves that all was above board before the bail-out $4 million could be transferred. In the process the new coalition government was seriously tested, as was New Zealand First itself.[71] With new information about the organisational structures of the network, the government withdrew its promise of additional funding. Parliament debated the issues for the first two days of the 1997 session, not in terms of government strategies to advance the Māori language, but whether Morgan's extravagances constituted legitimate spending. Calls for his resignation had less to do with Māori broadcasting than with the delicate balance of power between the coalition government and the collective opposition. And there were claims that the accusations were simply Māori bashing, a backlash against emerging Māori strength in Parliament and in the wider community.[72] In the event, the Serious Fraud Office was unable to conclude that there had been any wrongdoing, though it acknowledged that accountability mechanisms were lax.

Given the continuing concerns about standards, funding, and the level of Māori content in broadcast programs, and then early in 1996 the proposals to sell the commercial operations of Radio New Zealand, Māori and the Crown had agreed to establish a joint working party to assist in the development of Māori broadcasting policy. The joint Māori–Crown working party included representatives from the Treasury, the Office of the Prime Minister, the Ministry of Commerce, Te Puni Kōkiri, Te Māngai Pāho, Māori broadcasters, the Māori Congress, the Māori Women's Welfare League, the New Zealand Māori Council, and Bishop Whakahuihui Vercoe, who chaired many of the meetings. In its first report, the group expressed some concerns about Māori television, especially about the level of Māori language use, the reflection of iwi and regional issues, and sources of funding which would give a greater sense of security. It was also agreed that the pilot Auckland project should not necessarily have implications for the development of long-term Māori television services. Māori members of the group were unhappy that the legislative framework did not contain more specific provisions for Māori broadcasting and were especially concerned about the lack of a statement of Crown commitment and a detailed implementation schedule.[73]

However, a government decision to disestablish the joint working party fuelled growing Māori impatience with the politicians and the state. There was also mounting criticism of Te Māngai Pāho, especially its lack of broadcasting experience and commercial acumen, manifest in the inadequacies of its tendering and vetting processes.[74] Not surprisingly, though to the dismay of the relevant ministers, the Māori Congress, the Wellington Māori Language Board, and the Māori Women's Welfare League lodged a further claim with the Waitangi Tribunal in May 1997. They asked the Tribunal to oversee policy development— a clear indication that they considered the government to be reneging on its obligation to protect the Māori language, especially in television. It was the fourteenth legal action relating to broadcasting and underlined Māori exasperation with the formulation of Māori policies by the Crown and inconsistent consultation or opportunity for Māori participation. Despite the fifteen Māori members in Parliament, confidence in the political process was not at a high point.

Māori Language Status

A decade or more of innovative Māori language development has almost certainly saved te reo Māori from extinction. Though not on an absolutely secure footing, the level of awareness, and the enthusiasm for learning and, perhaps more importantly, for speaking Māori escalated well beyond the popular forecasts of 1984. Success in one sphere has generated enthusiasm in another, a snowballing effect which has given confidence to both young and old speakers of Māori. But concerns still remain about the quality of spoken Māori and the number of fluent speakers. Although it is extremely difficult to determine the number of competent Māori speakers, estimates in the 1970s ranged from 50 000 to 70 000.[75] In 1995 Te Taura Whiri i te Reo Māori attempted to assess the use of Māori language throughout New Zealand. From a random sample of 20 297 households, 1 904 Māori households were identified and a total of 2 241 Māori individuals were interviewed. The provisional findings of the survey showed that more than half of the Māori population over the age of sixteen years spoke some Māori, but the number of fluent Māori speakers was less than it was in 1970. Of those who spoke some Māori, only 6 per cent could be regarded as fluent. And less than one-third of all Māori speakers (fluent and not so fluent) could carry out a daily conversation with ease. Greater fluency was evident in the Waikato, Bay of Plenty, and East Coast regions.

The Māori language also featured in the 1996 census. Not only was the whole census questionnaire available in both English and Māori, but a question about the ability to speak Māori was also asked. There were 153 666 people who said they could speak Māori, a figure not too far from the 163 000 who had indicated some degree of expertise in the 1995 Taura Whiri survey. But, although suggesting that 'the language was reinvigorating itself', neither survey gave an accurate measure of fluency.[76]

Findings from the households surveyed in the Manawatu–Whanganui region during the Hoe Nuku Roa study revealed similar levels of competence. Of the respondents over the age of fifteen years, 50 per cent identified themselves as having a limited or zero level of proficiency, 39 per cent a basis ability, and 11 per cent an advanced or native speaker ability. As with the national profile, the vast majority of proficient speakers of Māori were in the 55 years plus age groups.[77]

The International Social Survey Programme also conducted a nationwide mail survey of 1 810 people (Māori and non-Māori) over the age of eighteen years, with 1 043 valid responses.[78] The sample was considered to be representative of Māori: 10 per cent of the total sample spoke some Māori at home, but only 5 per cent claimed to speak it well. Most believed that the language was worth preserving for the sake of all New Zealanders though as many as 45 per cent thought that its use could lead to divisions within society. A similar attitudinal study had been carried out in 1990 among 225 respondents, Māori and non-Māori. While two-thirds considered Māori language had a place in New Zealand society, only one-quarter indicated that the language should be used to a greater extent than it already was.[79] It was consistent with the later more general finding that there were relatively low levels of support for practices which would increase the use of Māori in everyday life.[80]

In a survey of the health and well-being of older Māori, the Oranga Kaumātua study, 400 kaumātua, men and women, were selected from rural, urban, and metropolitan areas using a networking sampling method.[81] While it could not be seen as a representative sample, the numbers recruited amounted to around 3 per cent of the total population over 60 years and are therefore not insignificant. People who regarded themselves as native speakers, i.e. with Māori as their first language, made up 23 per cent of the total; a further 40 per cent claimed equal fluency in English and Māori, and 38 per cent spoke only English; 90 per cent reported that members of their whānau were learning Māori and 97 per cent thought it important that young people continue to use Māori.[82]

The combined results of these surveys give cause for concern as well as some measure of hope. What is not yet clear is the impact of kōhanga reo on Māori language fluency in the years to come. But beyond doubt the enthusiasm of Māori to promote te reo Māori is high. More than any other single factor it is that enthusiasm which is probably the most essential prerequisite for language revitalisation.

TRADITIONAL KNOWLEDGE

The retention and affirmation of Māori culture presents some ironies. Until the 1950s, and even beyond, there was little encouragement for Māori to retain their own language, traditions, or culture. As already noted, Māori language use was actively discouraged, urbanisation presumed there would be an adaptation to western lifestyles, and knowledge was organised around western constructs with little recognition of mātauranga Māori, Māori systems of knowledge. It was a common pattern the world over. In New Zealand the Tohunga Suppression Act 1907, although purportedly about positive health promotion, outlawed the guardians of Māori knowledge, tohunga, and their distinctive methodologies.[83] Moreover there was a lack of government tolerance of Māori culture for any other than ceremonial purposes. From a Māori perspective it became extremely difficult to have Māori culture recognised outside an academic context, and even in that situation it was regarded with either suspicion or anthropological curiosity.

By 1990, however, another dimension to the debate was emerging. Māori culture had been, so to speak, discovered, and Māori energies were now being increasingly channelled into protecting traditional knowledge and preventing its uninhibited use in commercial, educational, scientific, and political spheres. To some extent the situation could be attributed to Māori advocacy for the recognition of Māori knowledge and culture within the New Zealand mainstream. So major institutions in both the public and private sectors, seeking to give practical effect to biculturalism, have incorporated Māori culture into the institutional culture, sometimes for their own advantage but more often to provide a platform for seriously addressing the realities of a bicultural society and the growing Māori demands for greater visibility within the machinery of state. Too often, however, the emphasis appeared to Māori to be on cultural capture rather than on the more effective delivery of the organisation's core business to Māori, and in the process there was a fear that Māori culture itself would be lost to well-meaning Pākehā students. Particular concern centred on the relationship between Māori and the state, and at a conference for senior public servants in 1993 the audience was warned about the state's assumptions to ownership of cultural properties: 'There is increasing concern from Māori and from other indigenous peoples that without safeguards, Māori intellectual and cultural property could be claimed by the State. That is not to say the public service has set about to acquire Māori knowledge or traditional skills in an unethical way, or that the material they have accumulated is inaccurate. But there is a sufficient volume of publications from Government departments covering a variety of Māori scientific, technological and cultural matters, to warrant serious debate on the State's assumptions of property rights.'[84]

The same had been true in universities and schools. Arohia Durie recommended a cautious approach to the inclusion of traditional knowledge in academic frameworks and institutions. At the national Matawhānui Hui for Māori university staff in 1995, she raised the question of the 'proper place for Māori knowledge, how it should be passed on, to whom and in what context. . . . The wider question is related to the relative roles of a university, an iwi, a wānanga, and a whare wānanga. . . . A university can never be a wānanga nor should it attempt to emulate one.'[85] In a similar vein, Monty Soutar has posed questions about the nature of tribal histories and emphasises the inherent difficulties in separating history itself from the people whose story is being told. Though not concluding that only tribal members are qualified to write about a particular tribe, he doubted that a single academic historian, Māori or Pakeha for that matter, could capture an authentic record of a tribe unless tribal members were active participants, not merely informants.[86]

Cultural and intellectual property rights assumed greater importance as indigenous peoples in several conferences around the world expressed concerns about the unilateral appropriation of culture and knowledge by non-indigenous decision makers. Article 12 in the Draft Declaration on the Rights of Indigenous Peoples specifically recognises that: 'Indigenous peoples have the right to practise and revitalise their cultural traditions and customs. This includes the right to maintain, protect and develop the past, present and future manifestations of their culture, such as archaeological and historical sites, artefacts, designs, ceremonies, technologies and visual and performing arts and literature, as well as the right to the restitution of cultural, intellectual, religious and spiritual property taken without their free and informed consent or in violation of their laws, traditions and customs.'[87] A Waitangi Tribunal claim, Wai 262, included that matter.

Largely at the instigation of the Māori Congress in June 1993, the foreign policy convenor, Aroha Mead, arranged the first international conference on the cultural and intellectual property rights of indigenous peoples, at Whakatane. During the final plenary session a declaration was passed reaffirming indigenous ownership of cultural properties. Known as the Mātaatua Declaration, because the Conference had been convened by the nine tribes of Mātaatua, states were urged to repatriate indigenous knowledge and devise a comprehensive intellectual property rights regime which included indigenous rights to native flora and fauna.[88] Particularly worrisome was the GATT agreement which the New Zealand government signed. Within it there was a lack of authority to define what is Māori intellectual property, a failure to recognise Māori rights to the development of Māori knowledge, and an inadequacy of legislation and the proposed reforms to protect Māori interests.[89] During a select committee hearing Te Puni Kōkiri presented a range of Māori objections to the GATT Agreement and identified three threats to Māori traditional knowledge: expropriation (e.g. through the use of a registered trademark registration over a modification of a traditional Māori symbol); inappropriate use of traditional knowledge (which might give cause for offence); and overprotection (leading to underutilisation and possible loss of developmental potential).[90]

Traditional healers, now that they were no longer outlawed, also faced the questions of ownership and protection of their knowledge. Widespread interest in alternative healing among both Māori and non-Māori was one factor which prompted Māori healers to form a national association, Ngā Ringa Whakahaere o te Iwi Māori. As well as seeking entry into the public health sector as providers of traditional healing services, they were equally keen to ensure that their proprietary rights were maintained. So were their counterparts overseas. Following a World Health Organisation (Western Pacific Region) conference in Hong Kong in 1995, a paper was prepared for the Ministry of Health setting out a framework within which traditional healing could be developed in New Zealand.[91] Three principles were proposed as a basis for the framework: cultural integrity, medical pluralism, and self-determination. The latter was seen as an important principle for accreditation and formalisation of traditional healing. A bureaucratic response to demands for the inclusion of traditional healing in the public health system that does not recognise the significance of autonomy and decision-making by traditional healers or their advocates was seen as contrary to the rights of indigenous peoples.

Similarly at the Health Research Council conference on human genetic information in 1995, Māori participants reiterated concerns about Māori knowledge and Māori property rights. They were unanimous that tissue and other body materials taken from Māori belonged to Māori and that a Māori world-view ought to be acknowledged in all scientific research. Criticism of the human genome diversity project prompted a call for the 'absolute and immediate halt of the project as well as an endorsement of the Mātaatua Declaration', section 3.5 of which protested about the project '. . . until its moral, ethical, socio-economic, physical and political implications have been thoroughly discussed and understood and approved by indigenous peoples.'[92]

What had been missing was an appropriate forum where Māori might debate the issues themselves and reach agreement about a policy for mātauranga Māori. NAMMSAT[93] went some way to addressing that situation. Although its primary objective was to accelerate Māori entry into science, at the inaugural conference there was debate about traditional knowledge and its relationship to science. Shane Munn from Manaaki Whenua (Landcare, a Crown Research Institute) argued that science was a process and that the elaboration of Māori knowledge observed similar processes to scientific methods.[94] He was of course making a case for funding to be available for research into Māori knowledge.

A different approach was taken by a taskforce convened by Eru Potaka-Dewes in 1996 to consider a framework for Māori knowledge and its appropriate place alongside other forms of knowledge. There was agreement on the following points: mātauranga Māori belongs to iwi and should remain under Māori control; mātauranga Māori is different to science and should not be confused with it; Māori participation in science and technology should be encouraged but not as a goal that is directly linked to mātauranga Māori; the government bears some responsibility for the protection of mātauranga Māori and should make funding available for its transmission and development, without confusing the issue with

Māori participation in science. A working party with a national mandate was recommended to promote Māori control over mātauranga Māori and its retention, transmission, and development.[95] The taskforce was mindful of increasing Māori discontent with the Public Good Science Fund's (PGSF) criteria for funding projects. The difficulty, though, was not necessarily with the criteria used by the PGSF so much as the lack of an alternate fund for research into mātauranga Māori as a body of knowledge which was distinct from science. Applicants to the PGSF often found it demeaning that, in order to access funding, traditional knowledge needed to be rationalised in scientific terms.

DETERMINING MĀORI CULTURE AND IDENTITY

This chapter has explored the concept of identity as it applies to contemporary Māori and has highlighted some of the issues that need further discussion, including the distinction between a tribal identity and a Māori identity. Both are seen as valid but in some contexts one may be more significant than the other. Access to cultural institutions and the resources which nurture culture has also been identified as a key determinant of identity, and in that regard language, te reo Māori, has received special consideration. For its survival much will depend on continued Māori enthusiasm for revitalising te reo Māori as well as on the state's performance of its obligations to ensure that the legal and funding frameworks are properly supportive. In radio and television, especially, because of their critical importance to the promotion of Māori language, purchasing and funding policies must be appropriate for Māori and should involve Māori in more than a token way. And while language is central to culture and identity, there is a range of traditional knowledge bases that are also important; their retention, transmission, and development demand Māori ownership and control. This does not relegate a Māori cultural identity to an absolute alignment with the past. Cultures change and develop but 'in shaping a vision for the future the configuration of the past often provides a framework for reconfiguring that future.'[96]

Māori self-determination is a shallow goal if a Māori identity is not part of the equation. Two factors stand out in the struggle to retain and develop a positive identity and a strong cultural base. First, despite overwhelming odds and state opposition, Māori language, tribal identity, and Māori values and beliefs have survived. Second, survival alone has become less important than the sense of authenticity that comes through ownership and control. In other words, efforts by the state to assimilate Māori into a pale mainstream and attempts by the state to define Māori cultural realities have been rejected. While there is a role for the state, it is essentially a facilitatory one. In contrast, Māori leaders have insisted that Māori knowledge, and Māori heritage generally, belong to Māori and must form the seed from which positive Māori development can grow.

NOTES FOR CHAPTER 3

1 'I am not solely from this world. Instead I am the embodiment of the love of my parents. My clothes are fashioned from the vitality and greatness of my ancestors and my thoughts are shaped by their manners . . .' An excerpt from 'He Whakaaro Huri Roto', by Hirini Melbourne (1982) in Witi Ihimaera and D. S. Long (eds), *Into the World of Light: An Anthology of Māori Writing*, Heinemann, Auckland, p. 211.

2 Early childhood education centres where Māori is the operative language.

3 Māori-speaking primary schools.

4 Hon. K. T. Wetere, (1994), 'Opening Address: Hui Taumata–Hui Whakapūmau— Ten Years of Māori Development', in Department of Māori Studies, *Kia Pūmau Tonu, Proceedings of the Hui Whakapūmau Māori Development Conference*, Department of Māori Studies, Massey University.

5 E. T. Durie, 'Keynote Address', in Department of Māori Studies, Kia Pūmau Tonu.

6 M. H. Durie, (1994), *Whaiora: Māori Health Development*, Oxford University Press, Auckland, pp. 30–32.

7 J. M. McEwen, (1986), *Rangitane: A Tribal History*, Reed Methuen, Auckland.

8 H. Ross, (1980), 'Busby and the Declaration of Independence', *New Zealand Journal of History*, vol. 14, no. 1, pp. 83–89.

9 Ian Poole, (1991), *Te Iwi Māori: A New Zealand Population Past, Present and Projected*, Auckland University Press, Auckland, p. 245.

10 J. Miller, (1958), *Early Victorian New Zealand*, Oxford University Press, London, p. 104.

11 Ranginui Walker, (1990), *Ka Whawhai Tonu Matou: Struggle Without End*, Penguin, Auckland, pp. 177–178.

12 Statistics New Zealand, (1994), *New Zealand Now Māori*, Department of Statistics, Wellington.

13 J. K. Hunn, (1961), *Report on the Department of Maori Affairs, Appendix to the Journals of the House of Representatives, 1960*, Wellington.

14 John Rangihau, (1975), 'Being Māori', in M. King (ed.), *Te Ao Hurihuri: The World Moves On*, Hicks Smith and Sons, Wellington, pp. 221–233.

15 Statistics New Zealand, (1994), *Statistical Standards for Iwi*, Department of Statistics, Wellington.

16 Statistics New Zealand, (1997), *1996 Population Census Iwi Affiliation*, Statistics New Zealand Te Tai Tatau, Wellington.

17 In the 1996 census, the number of Māori who did not report being affiliated to any tribe dropped to 26 per cent. Similarly, the number of people of Māori descent who did not know the name of their iwi reduced from 22 per cent in 1991 to nineteen per cent in 1996.

18 The Treaty of Waitangi (Fisheries Claim) Settlement Act 1992 will be discussed in chapter 6.

19 Te Whānau o Waipareira (1995), *Claim to the Waitangi Tribunal,* Waitangi Tribunal, Department of Justice, Wellington.

20 M. H. Durie, (1995), 'Te Hoe Nuku Roa Framework A Māori Identity Measure', *Journal of the Polynesian Society,* vol. 104, no. 4, pp. 461–470.

21 Te Hoe Nuku Roa, (1996), *Māori Profiles: An Integrated Approach to Policy and Planning:A Report Prepared for the Ministry of Māori Development,* Department of Māori Studies, Massey University, Palmerston North.

22 Te Hoe Nuku Roa (1996), *Report on the Baseline Manawatu–Whanagnui Survey,* Department of Māori Studies, Massey University, Palmerston North.

23 M. H. Durie, (1995), *Ngā Matatini Māori Diverse Māori Realities,* Paper Prepared for the Ministry of Health, Wellington.

24 Waitangi Tribunal, (1986), *Report of the Waitangi Tribunal on the te Reo Māori Claim (Wai 11),* Department of Justice, Wellington, p. 34.

25 *ibid.*

26 The moa was a giant New Zealand bird which became extinct before the nineteenth century.

27 Waitangi Tribunal, (1986), *Report . . . on the te Reo Māori Claim,* p. 9.

28 *ibid.,* p. 20.

29 Richard Benton, (1987), 'From the Treaty of Waitangi to the Waitangi Tribunal', in Walter Hirsh (ed.), *Living Languages: Bilingualism and Community Languages in New Zealand,* Heinemann, Auckland, pp. 69–70.

30 Wiremu Kaa, (1987), 'Policy and Planning: Strategies of the Department of Education in Providing for Māori Language Revival', in Walter Hirsh (ed.), *Living Languages,* p. 59.

31 Turoa Royal, (1987), 'A Bi-lingual Model for Secondary Schools', in Walter Hirsh (ed.), *Living Languages,* pp. 89–93.

32 Monty Ohia, (1993), *Bilingualism and Bilingual Education: Their Scope, Advantages, Disadvantages, and the Implications for Māori Learners,* MEdAdmin thesis, Massey University, Palmerston North.

33 Beatrice Kerr, (1987), 'Te Kōhanga Reo He Kakano i Ruia Mai i Rangiatea', in Walter Hirsh (ed.), *Living Languages,* pp. 95–97.

34 Ministry of Education, (1997), *Ngā Haeta Mātauranga: Annual Report on Māori Education 1995/96 and Strategic Directions for 1997,* Te Tāhuhu o te Mātauranga, Ministry of Education, Wellington, p. 14.

35 See Peter Keegan, (1996), *The Benefits of Immersion Education: A Review of the New Zealand and Overseas Literature,* NZCER, Wellington.

36 Margie Hohepa, (1990), *Te Kōhanga Reo Hei Tikanga Ako i te Reo Māori: Te Kōhanga Reo as a Context for Language Learning,* MA thesis, University of Auckland, Auckland.

37 Timoti Karetu, (1995), 'Te Tau o te Reo Māori', *He Pukenga Kōrero,* vol. 1, no. 1, pp. i–ii.

38 Dorothy Urlich Cloher, Margie Hohepa, (1996), 'Te Tū a te Kōhanga Reo i Waenga i te Whānau me te Tikanga Poipoi Tamariki: Māori Families, Child Socialisation and the Role of the Kohanga Reo', *He Pukenga Kōrero*, vol. 1, no. 2, pp. 33–41.

39 Peter J. Keegan, (1997), *1996 Survey of the Provision of Te Reo Māori*, New Zealand Council for Educational Research and Te Puni Kōkiri, Wellington, pp. 5–6.

40 Ministry of Education, (1997), *Ngā Haeta Mātauranga*, p. 40.

41 *The Dominion*, Tuesday 28 January, 1997.

42 Keegan, (1996), *1996 Survey of the Provision of Te Reo Māori*.

43 T. Reedy, (1992), *Kura Kaupapa Māori Research and Development Project Final Report*, Ministry of Education, Wellington.

44 C. Aspin, (1994), *A Study of the Mathematics Achievement in a Kura Kaupapa Māori*, MA thesis, Victoria University, Wellington.

45 Graham Smith, (1995), 'Whakaoho Whanau: New Formations of Whanau as Innovative Intervention into Māori Cultural and Educational Crises', *He Pukenga Kōrero*, vol. 1, no. 1, pp. 18–36.

46 Taura Whiri i te Reo Māori, (1995), *Te Matatiki: Contemporary Māori Words*, Oxford University Press, Auckland.

47 Ian Christensen, (1996), 'Māori Mathematics', *He Pukenga Kōrero*, vol. 1, no. 2, pp. 42–47.

48 The Dictionary of New Zealand Biography is a good example. Māori-language versions are available of the articles on Māori subjects.

49 *Ngā Uri o Tainui* (Pei Te Hurunui and Bruce Biggs) provides a further quality book in both English and Māori and Wiremu Kaa has edited Māori language books from the writings of Reweti Kohere and also Apirana Ngata

50 Keegan, (1997), *1996 Survey of the Provision of Te Reo Māori*, pp. 8–9.

51 Ministry of Education, (1995), *Ngā Haeta Mātauranga Annual Report on Māori Education 1994/95 and Strategic Directions for 1995/96*, Te Tāhuhu o te Mātauranga, Ministry of Education, Wellington.

52 S. McKinley, T. Black, I. Christensen, P. Richardson, (1996), 'Toi te Kupu: A Framework for Māori Language Resource Materials', *He Pukenga Kōrero*, vol. 2, no. 1, pp. 26–33.

53 Haare Williams, (1987), 'Broadcasting and the Māori Language', in Walter Hirsh (ed.), *Living Languages*, pp. 100–101.

54 Evidence given in the High Court bid to prevent the transfer of assets to Radio New Zealand and Television New Zealand.

55 Waitangi Tribunal, (1990), *Report of the Waitangi Tribunal on Claims Concerning the Allocation of Radio Frequencies (Wai 26 and Wai 150)*, Brooker and Friend, Wellington, p. 2.

56 *Attorney-General v New Zealand Māori Council* [1991] 2 NZLR 129 (Court of Appeal).

57 *New Zealand Māori Council v Attorney-General* [1992] 2 NZLR 576 (Court of Appeal).

58 Section 53B, Broadcasting Amendment Act (No. 2) 1993.

59 Te Puni Kōkiri, (1994), *Newsletter*, 23, June/July 1994, p. 6.

60 Derek Fox, (1988), 'The Mass Media: A Māori Perspective', in Royal Commission on Social Policy, *The April Report, Vol. IV*, Royal Commission on Social Policy, Wellington, pp. 487–494.

61 Aotearoa Broadcasting Systems Inc, (1988), *Report to Members*, ABS, Wellington.

62 Ministry of Commerce, (1991), *Māori Television: Options for Development Te Pouaka Whakaata Māori: me pehea—he aha ngā tikanga*, Ministry of Commerce, Wellington.

63 Officials Committee, (1991), *Report on the Officials Committee on Māori Television*, Ministry of Commerce, Wellington.

64 D. R. Hay, (1991), *Ko te Whakaata Irirangi Tikanga Māori—Nga whakaritenga: Tikanga Māori Television—the requirements*, Wellington Māori Language Board and the New Zealand Māori Council, Wellington.

65 Buddy Mikaere, (1997), 'What's Wrong with Maori Broadcasting?' *The Dominion*, Saturday 8 February 1997.

66 Te Māngai Pāho, (1994), *Māori Television Hui 29–30 September Proceedings*, Te Managi Pāho Māori Broadcasting Funding Agency, Wellington.

67 Te Māngai Pāho, (1996), *Annual Report 1995/96*, Māori Broadcasting Funding Agency, Wellington.

68 *Sunday Star-Times*, 28 April 1996.

69 'Aotearoa TV gets top-level support', *The Dominion*, Tuesday 14 January 1997.

70 'Charges of cronyism over Māori TV funds', *The Dominion*, Tuesday 28 January 1997.

71 Ian Templeton, (1997), 'Aotearoa affair wobbles coalition', *Sunday Star-Times*, 2 February 1997.

72 Paul Little, (1997), 'Tuku's trial', Editorial, *New Zealand Listener*, May 24–30 1997, p. 7.

73 Joint Māori/Crown Working Group, (1996), *Report of the Joint Māori/Crown Working Group on Māori Broadcasting Policy*, Wellington.

74 Mikaere, (1997), 'What's Wrong with Maori Broadcasting?'

75 R. A. Benton, (1991), *The Māori Language: Dying or Reviving*, New Zealand Council for Educational Research, Wellington.

76 'Maori language growth pleases commissioner', *The Dominion*, Saturday 10 May 1997.

77 Te Hoe Nuku Roa, (1996), *A Report and Analysis on the Initial Findings Regarding Māori Language in the Manawatu Whanaganui Region*, Department of Māori Studies, Massey University.

78 Department of Marketing, (1996), *National Identity International Social Survey Programme*, Massey University.

79 Rangi Nicholson, Ron Garland, (1991), 'New Zealanders' Attitudes to the Revitalisation of the Māori Language', *Journal of Multilingual and Multicultural Development*, vol. 12, no. 5, pp. 393–410.

80 Department of Marketing, (1996), *National Identity International Social Survey Programme,* Massey University.

81 Te Pūmanawa Hauora, (1996), *Oranga Kaumātua: The Health and Wellbeing of Older Māori, A Report Prepared for the Ministry of Health and Te Puni Kōkiri,* Department of Māori Studies, Massey University.

82 The study was carried out with the assistance of Māori community workers in the Bay of Plenty, Manawatu, Southland, and Auckland regions.

83 Mason Durie, (1994), *Whaiora: Māori Health Development,* pp. 45–46.

84 M. H. Durie, (1993), 'Māori and the State: Professional and Ethical Implications for the Public Service', in *Proceedings of the Public Service Senior Management Conference,* Wellington, pp. 23–35.

85 Arohia Durie, (1995), 'Kia Hiwa Ra: Challenges for Māori Academics in Changing Times', *He Pukenga Kōrero,* vol. 1, no. 1, pp. 1–9.

86 Monty Soutar, (1996), 'A Framework for Analysing Written Iwi Histories', *He Pukenga Kōrero,* vol. 2, no. 1, pp. 43–57.

87 Te Puni Kōkiri, (1994), *Mana Tangata: Draft Declaration on the Rights of Indigenous Peoples 1993: Background and Discussion on Key Issues,* Ministry of Māori Development, Wellington.

88 Mātaatua Tribes, (1993), *The Mātaatua Declaration on Cultural Property Rights of Indigenous Peoples,* presented at the First International Conference on the Cultural and Intellectual Property Rights of Indigenous Peoples, Whakatane.

89 Ngā Kaiwhakamarama i Ngā Ture, (1994), *Detailed Scoping Paper on the Protection of Māori Intellectual Property in the Reform of the Industrial Statutes and Plant Varieties Act: A Submission to Te Puni Kōkiri,* Wellington.

90 Te Puni Kōkiri, (1994), *Ngā Taonga Tuku Iho Nō Ngā Tūpuna: Māori Genetic, Cultural and Intellectual Property Rights,* Submission to Commerce Select Committee, Wellington.

91 M. H. Durie, (1996), *A Framework For Purchasing Traditional Healing Services,* a paper prepared for the Ministry of Health, Wellington.

92 Deborah Baird, Lloyd Geering, Kay Saville-Smith, Linda Thompson, Tose Tuhipa, (1995), *Whose Genes Are They Anyway? Report from the HRC Conference on Human Genetic Information,* Health Research Council, Auckland.

93 The National Association of Māori Mathmaticians, Scientists and Technologists was founded in 1994.

94 Shane Munn, (1995), 'Exploring Relationships Between Knowledge, Science and Technology', *Proceedings of the Inaugural NAMMSAT Conference,* Te Puni Kōkiri, Ministry of Māori Development, Wellington, pp. 64–69.

95 M. H. Durie, (1996), *Mātauranga Māori: Iwi and the Crown: A Discussion Paper,* Department of Māori Studies, Massey University.

96 Robert Jahnke, (1996), 'Voices Beyond the Pale', *He Pukenga Kōrero,* vol. 2, no. 1, pp. 12–19.

4

MANA TĀNGATA

THE POWER OF NUMBERS

Ko tini whetu ki te rangi
Ko te tini a Toi ki te whenua.[1]

A CHANGING DEMOGRAPHY

The Māori population has never been more numerous. Though comparisons
with earlier years are difficult because of incomplete enumeration and different
ways of defining who is a Māori, even conservative estimates acknowledge that
the population has increased by more than ten times over the past century. Table
4.1 highlights the growth between 1896 and 1996. A slow rise until the early
1930s gave way to an increasingly rapid growth rate, especially from 1960.[2]

Table 4.1 Māori Population Growth, 1896–1996

Year	Reported Māori Population
1896	42 650
1906	45 549
1936	82 326
1951	115 676
1966	255 000
1986	404 778
1991	511 278
1996	579 714

Source: Pool (1991), Te Iwi Māori, Statistics New Zealand
Note: The 1991 and 1996 figures include people of Māori descent as distinct from Māori who identify as Māori.

In the 1996 census, 579714 people indicated they were descended from a
Māori, an increase of some 68000 since the 1991 census.[3] Using Māori descent
criteria, approximately 14 per cent of the total New Zealand population are

Māori. Māori are a youthful population, the number of people under 15 years accounting for some 40 per cent of the total Māori population. Although the younger age groups will continue to increase in size, the population will quite rapidly begin to age, the proportion of men and women over the age of 65 years increasing from 3 per cent in 1991 to 13 per cent in 2031. With demographic change will also come social and cultural change. It is highly likely, for example, that many of the elderly in the next century will be neither fluent in Māori nor familiar with the customs and culture of the marae; moreover, they may not be able to count on consistent whānau support. Though Māori by choice as well as descent, their role within Māori society may be substantially different from the roles currently ascribed to kaumātua.[4] Further, value shifts will be necessary as societal demands for greater self-sufficiency impact on the elderly, creating particular stresses on Māori females.[5]

Internal and external migratory patterns will produce other changes that will affect social well-being. Following World War II more than 80 per cent of Māori migrated to urban areas, 25 per cent in the greater Auckland area, and there was a net Māori migration to the South Island. Emigration overseas has also become a significant trend, some 26 000 Māori now being recorded as resident in Australia. More recently still, there has been a shift in internal migratory patterns away from urban areas where unemployment is high and back to tribal areas such as Northland, from where grandparents had moved some thirty or forty years earlier.[6] Individuals moving back to rural Māori life will be challenged by new lifestyles and established social networks which may or may not conform with their own sense of community.

Māori are not uniformly distributed throughout all regions of the country. As already noted, nearly one-quarter live in the greater Auckland area, and a further quarter live in the Waikato and the Bay of Plenty. However, between 1986 and 1991 Auckland also experienced the greatest outflow, mainly to Northland.[7] An increasing emphasis on tribal development may be one factor contributing to recent Māori urban-to-rural and interregional migration. The proportion of the population who are Māori is higher than the national average in Gisborne, Northland, the Bay of Plenty, Waikato, Hawke's Bay and Manawatu/Wanganui. In the South Island only 6 per cent of the population is Māori.

Although it is not possible to determine the degree of Māori biological inheritance from ethnic data based on self-identification, it is highly probable that greater numbers of Māori will identify with more than one ethnic group and will correspondingly seek involvement with multiple sections of the community. Those activities will impact significantly on an evolving Māori culture and provide several points of interaction between Māori systems and other ethnic or even mainstream systems. That trend will be more obvious in regions where the Māori population is low compared to the national average.

DISPARITIES BETWEEN MĀORI AND NON-MĀORI

Statistics have drawn attention to the relatively low living standards of Māori and have been used as a rationale for a range of social policies and programs to improve health, education, housing, and levels of employment. In briefing papers to the incoming government in 1996, Te Puni Kōkiri warned that unless disparities in education, health, employment, and justice were eliminated, serious racial problems could arise.[8] On almost all socio-economic indices there are significant disparities between Māori and non-Māori. Examples are shown in the tables below.

Table 4.2 compares Māori and non-Māori participation in secondary schools and in tertiary education.[9] Although during the decade the number of Māori who left school without any qualifications fell, from over one-half to less than one-third, rates were still well short of the non-Māori rates, and Māori students gained lower grades in all senior school examinations. In the tertiary sector, there was also an increase in the numbers of Māori students, especially at polytechnics, where Māori enrolments have doubled, but Māori rates are still less than population ratios, particularly when the youthfulness of the Māori population is taken into account.

Table 4.2 Māori and the Education System

	Māori	Non-Māori
% school leavers with no qualifications in 1994	34.6	12.1
% enrolments in tertiary sector 1994		
university	9	91
polytechnic	12	88
college of education	12	88
wānanga	94	6

Source: Ministry of Education

Standards of health between Māori and non-Māori show similar patterns: improvement (in most areas) over a decade or more but Māori still significantly behind non-Māori. The extent of the disparities is well documented in *Hauora III* which examines patterns of mortality and morbidity over the period 1970–1991.[10] Of particular concern are the high Māori rates of cancer of the lung, stomach, and cervix, the increasing admission rates to psychiatric hospitals (as well as the differential treatment received),[11] and the relatively high rates of respiratory disease and diabetes. Table 4.3 shows the disparity rates for cancer of the lung, admissions to hospital for mental health problems, and hospitalisation for diabetes.

Table 4.3 Māori and Non-Māori Standards of Health
(Age-standardised rates per 10 000 population)

	Māori	Non-Māori
Lung cancer incidence 1989–1991	8.2	3.1
First admissions to psychiatric hospitals 1992		
females	18.0	10.1
males	23.2	12.0
Hospitalisation for diabetes 1992, ages 45–64	112.0	14.0

Source: Hauora Māori Standards of Health III

Relatively higher rates of unemployment have been a particular concern since the introduction of free market principles and the radical restructuring of the economy from 1984. Prior to the Hui Taumata there was concern that Māori unemployment could reach as much as 7.3 per cent by 1987.[12] Few had any idea, however, that it would reach three times that rate and three times the non-Māori rate. By 1990 Māori male unemployment had reached 20.5 per cent while non-Māori male unemployment had more than doubled to 7 per cent. Female unemployment increased at the much slower pace, the unemployment rate for Māori women reaching 19 per cent while the commensurate figure for non-Māori women was 6 per cent.[13] Māori bore the brunt of economic reform, and even when economic recovery was evident in 1996, the Māori unemployment rate of nearly 16 per cent was more than twice as high as the non-Māori rate and much higher than it had been in 1986.[14] Moreover, Māori were still disproportionately overrepresented in the poorly paid and insecure jobs.

Table 4.4 Māori and Non-Māori Unemployment Rates

	Māori	Non-Māori
1986	10.8	3.3
1990	19.8	6.7
1996	15.9	6.3

Sources: Māori and Work; Statistics New Zealand (Labour Household Survey)

Both Māori and the state have developed programs to address socio-economic disparities, though there have been differences in the approaches used and disagreements about levels of autonomy. Typically, Māori have pioneered a range of initiatives to encourage more active Māori participation in social policy areas and to provide services which are culturally appropriate. The state has then often incorporated the initiatives, or the foundations upon which the initiatives have been built, into mainstream services. In the education sector, for example, kōhanga reo and kura kaupapa Māori were launched by Māori before similar innovations occurred at secondary and tertiary levels. Even the Ministry of Education's ten-point plan for Māori education reflects Māori initiatives, though it relates them to the particular tasks of the ministry. The ten points are these: increasing the opportunities for Māori language learning; increasing the participation of Māori children in early childhood education; supporting and strengthening kōhanga reo; removing barriers to Māori achievement in schools; supporting and strengthening kura kaupapa Māori; increasing the number of Māori students in training and further education; developing indicators of Māori education outcomes; increasing understanding of Māori educational needs through research; developing the Ministry of Education's bicultural perspective; exploring options for Māori education in the future.[15]

The health sector has also recognised the valuable input of Māori into the delivery of health services and, consistent with government guidelines, regional health authorities have entered into a wide range of contracts with Māori providers to supply a range of health services, including traditional healing.[16] But, in addition, regional health authorities have required mainstream providers to address Māori health needs and to consult with Māori in order to develop services that are culturally acceptable. In a similar manner both Māori providers and Māori values have been recognised in broadcasting, penal services, and social service delivery, as well as in employment services and to a lesser extent in transport, consumer services, and cultural affairs.

For many reasons, however, Māori have been critical of the state's approach to social problems, not only because there has been a wide gap between policy and Māori realities but also because the devolution of control and delivery has been inconsistent and insufficiently resourced. The Māori Congress, for example, was unhappy with government employment policies and argued for two changes. First, employment services should be transferred to iwi and linked to wider aspects of Māori development.[17] 'What Congress is suggesting is to support projects that will encourage economic growth and create sustainable employment. If one were to consider utilising unoccupied Māori land and bringing that back into production through forestry for example, the down-stream benefits also create further employment opportunities.' The second change was for iwi programs to focus on outcomes which were connected to real markets. 'We need to break away from the training for training sake mode and look at the labour market needs and opportunities. We need to refocus our energies, our resources and our expertise into making something real happen.'

The significance of state programs for Māori should not be underestimated, nor should the now quite high levels of Māori participation be dismissed as too little too late. On the contrary, efforts to address disparities between Māori and non-Māori through more direct involvement of Māori in the delivery of social policy programs has been a major accomplishment in a state which, until a decade or more ago, refused to accept that culture was important or to recognise any good reason why Pākehā providers could not adequately meet Māori needs. However, not all Māori are satisfied with the amount of progress or the direction it is taking. Three issues (summarised in table 4.5) continue to cause particular concern: the fragmented approach to development inherent in the government's sectoral efforts; the use of inappropriate outcome measures; and the imbalance between Māori-centred services and mainstream services.

Table 4.5 Māori and Government Strategies for Reducing Disparities

	Māori Strategies	Government Strategies
Integrated development	Holistic approaches which incorporate economic, social, and cultural elements	Sectoral approaches with limited intersectoral planning
Outcome measures	Socio-economic advancement not divorced from cultural development and autonomy	Output focused with non-Māori benchmarks
Māori dimension	Māori-centred, i.e. based on tikanga Māori and Māori models for development	Māori perspectives added to core sectoral goals

Typically, Māori approaches to development are holistic insofar as they do not recognise clear sectoral demarcations between social, cultural, and economic areas. Attempting to modify iwi policies to fit in with government sectors has challenged many Māori authorities, to the point that they have often walked away from the discussion table in sheer frustration. Amazingly, there is often little coherence between departments in terms of policies, funding criteria, and joint activities, so that Māori policies for integrated development at tribal or community levels must be advanced in a piecemeal manner to fit in with government sectoral policies. Sectoral development also tends to mask the fact that social well-being may depend less on the delivery of services such as health or social welfare than on macro-policies which relate to employment, access to education, and immigration. Good health, for example, owes as much to good housing, a decent job, and education as to health services.[18]

The situation has not been alleviated by a move towards mainstreaming and a reduced role for the Ministry of Māori Development. Though not always efficient, the former Department of Māori Affairs was able to retain a generic approach and to offer an integrated model for social and economic growth. Mainstreaming will not necessarily mean that departments and ministries will be less responsive to Māori. They should in fact be increasingly required to quantify gains for Māori and Treaty of Waitangi outputs and to demonstrate that their workforce is representative of the communities they serve. But the focus for each will be sectoral, and the notion of integrated development—a key factor in Māori development—will defy bureaucratic frameworks.

Māori development will be difficult to justify if it is simply a pale imitation of state structures and roles. Integrated development is not simply a bringing together of separate sectors; rather, because it is based on concepts of whanau-ngatanga and hapūtanga[19] it has an inherent holism and is philosophically different from the strongly sectoral emphasis that pervades national development and policy formulation.[20]

The government makes relatively little use of outcome measures in social policy. Instead, progress is monitored according to outputs which are provider-focused more than client-centred. It is easier to gain information about teacher activities, or clinical interventions, or the number of case conferences, than it is to measure the outcomes for people who use services. Māori interest, however, is increasingly focused on the development of outcome measures so that progress can be charted in a meaningful way that makes sense to the users of services, rather than the providers. In this respect, there is some convergence between Māori and the advocates of the New Right who argue for the free market and the centrality of the individual client. But the outcome measures preferred by Māori are those which recognise the importance of being able to remain Māori in a cultural and lifestyle sense. It is not sufficient to obtain a high grade at school at the expense of cultural priorities. Nor does treatment for renal failure make sense if it requires alienation from whānau. Māori are interested in outcome measures which link well-being with cultural identity rather than simply with the attainment of a colourless score designed for a theoretical norm.

It therefore follows that comparisons between Māori and non-Māori, while they are useful in gaining a perspective and measuring overall progress, are of limited value in developmental programs which aspire towards the advancement of Māori as Māori. The 'universal' approach to social policy, at least as it had been practised in New Zealand, relied on excessive reference to the norms of the majority, and fell well short of being able to locate Māori at the centre of the exercise or even to seriously incorporate Māori needs. Nor did it significantly contribute to the development of a professional Māori workforce or the promotion of methodologies appropriate to Māori. Moreover, in practice, and despite the claim of cultural sensitivity, the formulation of social policies, if not the delivery of social services, is still heavily biased towards Eurocentric views and philosophies. Where other cultural views are admitted, they tend to be grafted on as perspectives but within conventional disciplinary frameworks that themselves may obscure key linkages and causal relationships. The Māori-centred approach does not ignore the importance of other approaches, and the contributions which have derived from a variety of policies and disciplines, but it deliberately places Māori people and Māori experience at the centre of the activity. In contrast to the state, which adds on the Māori dimension to the core sectoral business, a Māori-centred approach requires that Māori themselves are involved in the design, delivery, management, and monitoring of services.

MĀORI DIVERSITY

A further difficulty with the comparative approach is the assumption that Māori can be regarded as a homogeneous group at least in terms of socio-economic disadvantage. It has become increasingly apparent, however, that far from being homogeneous, Māori are as diverse and complex as other sections of the population, even though they may have certain characteristics and features in common. There is no one Māori reality nor is there any longer a single description that will encompass the range of Māori lifestyles.[21]

Differing socio-economic levels within Māori society were examined at the 1994 Hui Whakapūmau. 'A trend which has emerged during this decade has been one of increasing social stratification of Māori. Some Māori are improving their social and economic status but the vast majority, under the current system, are destined to be at the very bottom of the economic scale in the foreseeable future.'[22]

Thus, although Māori collectively are overrepresented in lower socio-economic groupings, there is nonetheless considerable variation between individuals. The gap between Māori and non-Māori is wide, but there is also an emerging gap between Māori who are employed and well qualified and those who are unemployed with poor prospects of employment. Health status and housing standards are likely to be reflected in that differential. On the other hand, and in contrast to the blacks in the United States, it is unusual for middle-class Māori to live entirely apart from their families. Each Māori whānau is inevitably represented across the social strata.[23] In this respect it is often difficult to separate socio-economic conditions from cultural and historical factors, even though some individuals may be relatively well off.

Educational achievement is probably the most significant determinant of socio-economic advancement, and there are signs that Māori are making substantial gains. The establishment of Māori alternatives such as kōhanga reo provided an incentive, but higher Māori participation rates have also occurred within the mainstream. Over the past ten years, the proportion of Māori students who remain at school through to the seventh form has increased dramatically. In 1983 only 4 per cent of Māori students stayed on to a seventh form year, compared to 31 per cent in 1993.[24] While those same proportions have not yet been observed at tertiary educational institutions, there has nonetheless been a fivefold increase in tertiary enrolments between 1986 and 1992, and between 1993 and 1994 the number of university graduates more than doubled, especially at the postgraduate level.[25] Yet, as already discussed, Māori are heavily over-represented among school leavers who have no qualification. In 1992 four out of ten Māori left school without any qualification, compared to one in ten non-Māori; and the gap may be increasing.[26]

Just as the range of educational achievement is expanding, so over time Māori have moved into a wider range of jobs and more have become self-employed.[27] But, as already noted, Māori unemployment remains at an unacceptably high level. Nor is it evenly distributed across the country. For young Māori, unemployment rates are highest in Northland (46 per cent) while in Taranaki, the Bay of Plenty, Waikato, and Hawke's Bay at least two out of every five in the labour force are unemployed.

Not surprisingly, income levels for Māori households are significantly lower than for non-Māori—the result of low-paying jobs, high unemployment, disability, and an excess of sole-parent households.[28] Māori are overrepresented in all categories, have uptake rates of more than three times the non-Māori rate for the domestic purposes benefit and are twice as likely to receive an unemployment benefit. Though Māori men receive, on average, a higher income than Māori women, the income position of Māori women, when compared with non-Māori women, has improved, while the position for Māori men has deteriorated. Both, however, are underrepresented in occupations with the highest median incomes.

A trend towards sole-parent households is now well established among Māori, with more than 43 per cent of Māori infants living in single-parent families. Whānau support is variable. One-parent families are likely to form part of an extended family (whānau) household, but not always. Little more than a third of Māori sole-parent families are closely linked to whānau.[29] Nor do most Māori children share their living arrangements with grandparents or other relatives for day-to-day practical purposes. In 1991 over three-quarters of Māori children lived in households with their parent or parents only.

At the other end of the life cycle, a higher proportion of Māori elderly (over 75 years) live alone rather than with other family members. Between 1981 and 1991 there was a relative reduction in the number of extended family households, at least for the over 75 years age group, so that they are now second to single-person households. For the not so elderly (60–74 years), the same trend is evident though there is a more even spread over the household types.[30]

Differences between Māori women and Māori men are reflected in income levels, educational achievement, the burden of caring (for children, elderly, and the disabled) and health risks. At the Hui Ara Ahu Whakamua, a lack of role complementarity was discussed as well as the many disadvantages facing women, often because of the attitudes of Māori men. Māori women as leaders was a theme which recurred at the Hui Whakapūmau. 'It is a tragic waste of much needed skill, energy and commitment to continue to deny Māori women their rightful place in Iwi/Māori decision-making.'[31] A prediction was made that Māori women would play greater roles in the development of Māori society as politicians, bureaucrats, consultants, lawyers and bankers and that Māori men might be best advised to encourage rather than resist the movement.[32]

Changes in the roles of rangatahi, Māori youth, were also debated at the Hui Whakapūmau and at the three Hirangi hui called by Sir Hepi Te Heuheu to discuss the position of Māori in society generally.[33] Forecasts were made that leadership for the future would emerge from the young and urban and that youthful leaders would not necessarily defer to their elders. Again elders were advised to welcome the new skills and the energy, to guide, not obstruct.[34]

Not only is there increasing diversity in terms of socio-economic indicators, but cultural diversity and a diversity of social affiliations are also apparent among Māori people. The theme was debated at the Hui Ara Ahu Whakamua in 1994. 'In considering policies for Māori, the diverse realities of Māori people must be taken into account. It can no longer be assumed that most Māori are linked to the conservative structures of hapū and iwi or that kōhanga reo will be accessed by all Māori children or that the marae will continue to be the favoured meeting place for all Māori.'[35] Even before then, however, and with a focus on culture rather than health or economic indicators, it will be recalled that John Rangihau pointed out the distinctions between members of different tribes, rejecting the concept of Māoritanga and favouring instead the term Tuhoetanga.[36] Before the end of the Decade of Māori Development, the aliena- tion of Māori individuals from tribal structures was to become another major issue for Māori. In addressing the orientation of many urban Māori, as well as those adopted by non-Māori parents, Karetu concluded that contemporary Māori were often without a base, iho ngaro; 'many of these children look Māori and are identified as such by their peers, but that is where their Māoriness ends.'[37] However, in contrast to the conclusions of Māori leaders with strong tribal identities, urban Māori did not necessarily regard themselves as any less Māori than their tribal relatives. In 1995 urban Māori authorities challenged both government departments and other Māori organisations for presuming that the rights (including the rights to Māori resources) of town and city Māori were somehow subordinate to Māori who were part of tribal networks.

During the 1984–1994 Decade of Māori Development an emphasis had been placed on iwi policies and iwi delivery mechanisms. Iwi development became the preferred vehicle for Māori development on the assumption that, no matter where they lived, Māori individuals would be able to relate to at least one iwi and therefore have more reliable access to social services such as Matua Whāngai or economic development packages such as Mana Enterprises. Two quite distinct parameters of iwi development were identified, though more often than not they were confused. The first was the unique position iwi occupied as tangata whenua in particular locations, a Treaty-derived political status of particular relevance to partnership (with the Crown) in respect of physical resources. The second parameter was rationalised because of the potential capacity of iwi organisations to provide social services for their members. Associated with the first parameter was Article 2 of the Treaty of Waitangi, while both Articles 2 and 3 anchored the second.

Of the two, the position in relationship to physical resources such as land, forests, water, and the environment is more clearly established, even though there is continuing uncertainty about the relationship between hapū and iwi and the consequent resource implications. The delivery of social services by iwi, however, had not been practised to any extent since World War II when 75 per cent of Māori still lived in their own tribal areas, often around marae. Urbanisation changed that. The Hunn Report did not favour tribal structures in urban contexts and implicitly encouraged the creation of new organisations geared to meet the needs of whānau within the towns and cities.[38] After the 1984 Hui Taumata, and partly because other structures seemed unable to satisfactorily address Māori needs, tribes were encouraged to establish representative authorities to which certain government services could be devolved and through which channels of communication could be opened with the Crown.

Social policies and programs were included as appropriate areas of focus for tribes on the assumption that iwi knew their own people better than other providers and were able to utilise networks which were not accessible by mainstream agencies.[39] The trend was compatible with the approach being taken by the Department of Social Welfare and other sectors. Creative responses occurred and new health programs emerged which incorporated Māori perspectives and philosophy, while at the same time including appropriate elements of modern health care. By the end of the Decade of Maori Development, however, three concerns raised doubts about the appropriateness of iwi authorities as the exclusive preferred providers of health care, education, and welfare programs. Of particular significance, there was mounting concern that urban Māori did not necessarily associate or affiliate with hapū or iwi structures. At the 1993 hui to discuss the appointment of Treaty of Waitangi Fisheries Commissioners, June Jackson estimated that fewer than one half of Māori living in the greater Auckland area had any meaningful contact with an iwi, nor did they wish to. The Hon. Peter Tapsell arrived at a similar conclusion and saw a need for Māori people to move away from 'outdated tribal structures.'[40] Treaty of Waitangi Fisheries Commissioner Shane Jones doubted that tribal sovereignty would make the slightest difference to 'most Māori people who face daily disadvantage and struggle to educate their children adequately and care suitably for their health and shelter.'[41]

At the Hui Ara Ahu Whakamua, John Tamihere, chief executive of a large urban authority in Auckland, Te Whānau o Waipareira Trust, discussed a need for new regional Māori organisations to meet the requirements of the 'new environment'.[42] Then at the Hui Whakapūmau, Irihāpeti Ramsden urged a wider range of strategies for Māori in order to negotiate for change and for the reallocation of resources. 'Iwi, hapū and whanau remain fundamental to traditional Māori social structure but they are no longer accessible to all Māori.'[43]

While there is an obvious and enduring place for iwi and hapū structures, especially in relationship to Treaty-based political negotiations and possibly the ownership and management of physical resources, social policies and programs must relate primarily to Māori whānau and individuals across the range of social and cultural conditions. An exclusive focus on tribal structures will bypass many Māori who, for reasons of their own, are not active participants in tribal society. The Court of Appeal went further, ruling in 1996 that urban Māori, through non-tribal urban Māori authorities, had a right to receive benefits from Māori fisheries and required Te Ohu Kaimoana (the Treaty of Waitangi Fisheries Commission) to make appropriate allocations.[44] (Subsequently, however, the Court of Appeal decision was quashed by the Privy Council.)[45]

THE MĀORI VOTE

Māori diversity is not only evident in demographic and socio-economic terms. It has also become a characteristic of political affiliation and voting patterns. In addition, the rapid growth in the Māori population over the past fifty years has been accompanied by a new political might activated through the ballot box and in the democratic show of hands. By the time Māori representation in Parliament was assured, Māori were a minority in the country as well as in the corridors of power, and all too often were forced to depend on the goodwill and sympathies of their Pākehā colleagues for support. As a result, over the years a mistrust of Parliament as an effective means of advancing Māori interests developed—at least up until the 1996 general election.

The inclusion of Māori in government had its beginnings in the Legislative Council, one of the constitutional bodies established by the New Zealand Constitution Act 1852 (UK). A type of Upper House with 'no fewer than ten' members being appointed by the Crown, it met for the first time in 1854. In 1872, two Māori members, Wiremu Ngatata and Mokena Kohere, were appointed to the Council, and from then on there were usually two Māori members. The Council was abolished altogether in 1950, leaving New Zealand with a unicameral system, a single house of Parliament.

Like the Legislative Council, the House of Representatives had no specific provision for Māori representation when it was established under the 1852 Act.

Pressure both from Māori communities and from Parliament itself was mounting, however, for direct Māori representation in the House. After the rejection of a resolution in 1862 that Māori people should be brought into government with fair representation in both Houses, provincial councils, juries, and the courts, a select committee on representation recommended in 1863 that thirteen new seats should be established, ten for the South Island (where the population had suddenly increased because of the gold rush), three for the North Island, and two for Europeans elected by Māori voters. The proposals were never passed into law.

Surprisingly, in view of his reputation for alienating Māori land and openly siding with settlers in land disputes, Donald McLean introduced the Māori Representation Bill, which was enacted in 1867 and provided for three Māori representatives for the North Island and one for the South. His motives were complex. Some saw it as an equalising measure which retained the balance between North and South after two extra South Island seats were created in Westland. McLean, however, described it as a peace measure, which would divert Māori discontent away from warfare and into Parliament. There was some opposition to the philosophy of special representation but that was not large, possibly because most saw the measure as temporary until assimilation had become a reality.[46]

The decision to limit the number of seats to four was based neither on the Treaty of Waitangi nor on the principles of fair representation. Some 50000 Māori constituents were given four seats (a ratio of 1:12500) whereas 250000 Europeans had 72 seats (ratio 1:3500). On a population basis there should have been fourteen or fifteen Māori seats. The situation did not improve over the years although, when Māori had the option to vote in general electorates and to come off the Māori roll, the comparisons, shown in table 4.6, became less dramatic.

Table 4.6 Māori Representation in Parliament, 1868–1984

Election year	Māori population	No. of Māori	Average population per seat	Non-Māori population	No. of non-Māori seats	Average population per seat
1868	50 000	4	12 500	250 000	72	3 500
1890	41 873	4	10 500	626 500	70	9 000
1908	48 500	4	12 100	960 000	76	12 600
1949	110 032	4	27 500	1 780 000	76	23 500
1969	217 000	4	54 000	2 583 000	80	32 000
1984	300 000	4	72 500	3 000 000	91	32 500

Source: Sorrenson, (1986), in Report of the Royal Commission on the Electoral System

Over the years there has been considerable debate about the four Māori seats, their effectiveness and retention. From 1935 until 1996 they had given a political advantage to the Labour party, but that party had never acted on the advice of its Māori caucus to increase the number to ten or more. Neither had any party actually recommended the abolition of the seats, even though National not infrequently hinted at the option. In truth, according to Sorrenson there was 'little political advantage in abolishing the seats in the face of what was bound to be considerable Māori opposition.'[47] At the same time Māori often became impatient with the four Māori seats, and by 1993 more than half of enrolled Māori voters had opted to transfer to the general roll. There were several reasons. The capture of the four seats by Labour after the historic 1935 agreement between T. W. Ratana and the Rt. Hon. Michael Joseph Savage[48] meant that the seats were guaranteed for Labour, and the Māori vote might be better employed in marginal general seats where Māori voters could make a difference. There was also frequent dissatisfaction with the performance of the four Māori members and their low levels of accountability back to the electorates. For one thing the size of the electorates made it difficult if not impossible to maintain the same links with constituents that other members of Parliament enjoyed. For another, even when cabinet ranking had been achieved, Parliament rarely gave full effect to Māori concerns voiced by the Māori members. The Māori members were often seen to be sidelined, especially when in opposition. National underlined that point when it established the New Zealand Māori Council as an alternative source of advice on Māori policy (in preference to the four Labour Māori members). Finally, Māori have often concluded that, in the search for tino rangatiratanga, there is an irony in Māori becoming part of an institution which has used its powers, at least in the past, to exploit Māori rather than empower them.[49]

Though not based on an explicit commitment to the Treaty of Waitangi, the retention of the Māori seats, however, may suggest an underlying recognition in New Zealand that Māori claims to political power do in fact stem from a legitimate cause. Certainly the Royal Commission on the Electoral System recommended that there be no change to the system of Māori representation prior to a decision on whether or not the Mixed Member Proportional System (MMP) was to be introduced.[50] The Commission further recommended, however, that should MMP be introduced then the separate Māori seats, the Māori roll and the Māori option could be abolished.[51] In any event, in view of the Commission's inability to comment on fundamental constitutional matters, it was recommended that Parliament and government should enter into consultation and discussion with a wide range of representatives of the Māori people about the definition and protection of the rights of the Māori people and the recognition of their constitutional position under the Treaty of Waitangi.

Politicians were generally reluctant to move away from the comfortable First-Past-the-Post system but eventually agreed to let the country decide about future arrangements for parliamentary representation. The 1992 electoral reform referendum presented several options, including MMP and First-Past-the-Post. It also offered an opportunity for the introduction of a senate. Many Māori saw the MMP option as offering potential advantages because it could favour a party such as Mana Motuhake. Others were sceptical: a new system could mean the abolition of Māori seats without firm guarantees of Māori participation in Parliament. Nonetheless a large majority voted in favour of MMP, and it was also the preferred option in the second referendum the following year. (There was, however, no substantial support for a senate.)

Prior to the second referendum conducted during the 1993 general election, the Electoral Reform Bill was introduced. In line with the Royal Commission's report, though without genuine consultation with Māori, the bill made no provision for any Māori seats. Widespread Māori indignation was expressed at several hui, the abolition of the seats being seen as an erosion of an established constitutional convention.[52] During the committee stage the bill was therefore amended to retain Māori seats according to the strength of the Māori roll. Henceforth the number of Māori seats would not be tied to the fixed formula which had prevailed since 1867, but would be based on the size of the electorate; it could be more than four—or less.

When legislation enabling MMP was passed in 1993, the government also moved to provide electoral choice for Māori. Although the option to register on either the Māori or the general roll was available every five years, a provision confirmed for all Māori (not only 'half-castes') in the Electoral Amendment Act 1975, a special Māori option was to be held, largely because of a change in the number of Māori electorates but also because of a consequential change to the number of single-member electoral districts. Between February and April 1994 the option was open. It was an unnecessarily short time with minimal resources to conduct an effective campaign. At stake was the number of Māori seats. If all Māori had enrolled on the Māori roll, some twelve or so Māori seats would have been possible and the Māori presence in Parliament considerably augmented.

After a national hui organised by the Māori Congress at Ngaruawahia in January 1994, the Māori Congress, the New Zealand Māori Council, and the Māori Women's Welfare League supported a claim by Hare Puke to the Waitangi Tribunal that resources to inform Māori of their options under the Electoral Act 1993 were grossly inadequate. The Tribunal agreed.[53] They found that the Crown is under a Treaty obligation to actively protect Māori citizenship rights and in particular existing Māori rights to political representation conferred under the Electoral Act 1993. This duty of protection arises from the Treaty generally and in particular from the provisions of Article 3.

According to the Tribunal the level of funding and services provided by the Crown through the agency of New Zealand Post and Te Puni Kōkiri was substantially less than could be reasonably required to meet the Crown's Treaty obligation to protect Māori citizenship rights and in particular the effective exercise of the Māori Electoral Option. The Crown was in breach of Treaty principles which require the Crown actively to protect Māori rights to political representation conferred under the Electoral Act 1993. As a consequence the effective exercise of the electoral option by Māori would be seriously prejudicially affected by such a breach.

The Tribunal recommended that the Crown funding to Māori be increased as a matter of urgency to a level sufficient to achieve the maximum possible enrolment of Māori electors and to achieve adequate promotion and information on the exercise of the Māori option. Cabinet declined on the grounds that, in the view of the ministers, sufficient funds had been allocated. Despite concern from the Minister of Justice that a successful challenge could delay the implementation of MMP,[54] the Māori plaintiffs contested the government's actions in the High Court. Justice McGechan, presiding, concluded that 'While the Minister . . . acted in good faith and reasonably on information available at the time, there was an important underlying misconception as to the actual degree of Māori understanding of option implications. . . . That misconception carried through into Cabinet's decision on 21 February 1994. . . . In the result Māori have been disadvantaged to an extent not precisely measurable, but of some significance. The Crown, as a Treaty partner acting in good faith, should recognise past error when it comes to light, and consider the possibility of remedy under present conditions.'[55] After the ruling the government chose not to modify its position, and the Māori claimants[56] took action through the Court of Appeal, where a bench of seven judges dismissed the appeal, placing some importance on the provisions in the legislation for further Māori options—the 1994 result would not last forever, a further option being available in 1997. The court concluded that 'What was done [to advertise the option] was far from perfect, but it passes the test of reasonableness.'[57] Further action followed at the Privy Council but the result was unchanged.

Although the exact number of eligible Māori voters who were not enrolled was not known, it was estimated that the number was not less than 50 000 and could be between 50 000 and 60 000.[58] Table 4.7 provides a summary of Māori enrolments and non-enrolments. The latter had become a target for the Māori roll and there was a positive response to a trial project, using a team of Māori with strong community knowledge. Successfully enrolled were 1 323 Māori, of whom 459 lived in the targeted Elsdon/Titahi Bay area.[59] But for many would-be voters, there was both a sense of resignation and a certain cynicism, a lack of confidence in the parliamentary system to deliver to Māori, and, if for reasons which were unclear, a decided lack of enthusiasm to be seen joining a system which had 'failed' Māori. In the event, although large numbers of Māori voters transferred from the general roll, and many more enrolled directly on to the Māori roll, only one extra seat was confirmed, bringing the total number of Māori seats from four to five: Te Tai Tokerau (based on the old Northern Māori electorate), Te Tai Hauāuru (Western), Te Tai Rāwhiti (Eastern), Te Puku o te Whenua (a new electorate) and Te Tai Tonga (Southern). These five seats were contested in the 1996 general election. For the first time the Māori electoral populations were similar in size to the general electorates. Electoral quotas for the South Island were around 51 747, for the North Island 51 866, and for each Māori electorate close to 52 844. Shortly after the 1996 general election the caretaker National government wanted to set in place arrangements for another Māori electoral option, early in 1997, so that new electoral boundaries could be set in time for the next election. But Māori Labour MPs objected, claiming that the matter was of constitutional importance and should not be pursued by a caretaker government, nor rushed while coalition talks were in progress.[60]

Experience from the 1994 option was valuable in 1997 when the option was again eventually opened. This time it was extended for a slightly longer period, from 28 April to 27 August and was more generously funded. Moreover, the issues were clearer and the prospect of more seats in the next Parliament spurred would-be Māori voters to at least enrol and give consideration to moving to the Māori roll. When the option opened, there were 291 850 voters identified as Māori with 146 138 (50 per cent) of those on the Māori roll. A shift of even half from the general roll would guarantee an extra two seats. Not all Māori, however, wanted to increase the number of Māori seats. Disappointed by the public and private lives of some New Zealand First members, and the 'negative cloud hanging over Māori politics', Māori organisations and opposition MPs claimed that Māori were being turned off signing the Māori roll.[61]

Table 4.7 The Māori Roll

	Māori Roll	General Roll	Māori on no roll
Prior to April 1993	93 131	136 890	est. 59 000
Post-1994 option	136 708	127 826	est. 50 000
Prior to 1997 option	146 138	145 712	est. 30 000

MMP More Māori in Parliament

The 1996 general election was exceptional for many reasons. It was, of course, the first election under MMP and would lead to a larger Parliament than New Zealand had ever known. There were also more political parties contesting seats than ever before, and although only a minority would be represented in

Parliament, it was clear that New Zealanders were ready to cast aside old loyalties in favour of new policies and fresh faces. It was also to become evident that the election was less about electing a government than electing members of Parliament. On election night there was no outright winner. National gained 44 seats, Labour 37, New Zealand First 17, Alliance 13, ACT New Zealand 8, and United 1 seat. Short of forming a minority government, a coalition would be necessary, and for two months after the election secret talks continued until eventually a National–New Zealand First combination was formed. In the meantime the outgoing National government had maintained a caretaker government.

For Māori, however, the 1996 general election will be remembered as the dawning of Māori political might. Five features deserve particular mention. First, there were more Māori candidates in a wider range of parties than ever before. Second, whereas in 1993 a Māori boycott of the election was planned, and the so-called tino rangatiratanga vote was advocated as a deliberate decision not to vote,[62] by 1996 Māori interest in mainstream political participation resulted in the largest ever turnout of voters and no mention of a boycott. This time activists were themselves candidates. Third, interest in the Māori seats was high, not only because there was a new seat, Te Puku o te Whenua, but also because voters in the Māori electorates were instrumental in establishing New Zealand First as the vital third party that would determine the next government. The fourth feature was the record number of Māori candidates—apart from those in the Māori electorates—who were successful in gaining seats in Parliament. But, most significantly, and somewhat to the surprise of commentators, Māori members of Parliament were crucial in determining the composition of the new government. In the period leading up to the final agreement between National and New Zealand First to form a coalition government, it became increasingly apparent that Māori parliamentarians, and behind them Māori voters, held the balance of power.

Early in 1996, it was evident that there would be no single Māori party, even though the possibility was raised in the report of the Royal Commission on the Electoral System and in 1994 and 1995 the New Zealand Māori Council had considered establishing the Aotearoa Party. The more obvious fact was that Māori were affiliated to a wide range of mainstream parties. 'Māori hold diverse opinions, and the complex nature of tribalism pervades tribal politics. They cannot be classified as a pan-group of people who are going to vote for one particular party, nor should it be assumed that the majority of Māori would want a Māori party.'[63] As it happened, an estimated 88 Māori candidates presented themselves for election to Parliament either through electorates or party list seats. In a effort to test the level of agreement on Māori issues, the Māori Congress invited all Māori candidates to a Congress Executive meeting at Hopuhopu, near Ngaruawahia, and some 33 attended representing the Alliance, Independent

Morehu, Labour, Mana Māori, National, Natural Law, New Zealand First, Progressive Green, Republican, and United parties. While many delegates at the hui expressed disillusionment with the parliamentary system, by far the greatest interest was in the possibility of forming a Māori caucus within Parliament. Candidates were asked to indicate how committed they would be to such a body and how it might work. There were few detailed replies but a sufficiently high level of enthusiasm was apparent that the Congress arranged further meetings and began actively promoting the idea, offering at the same time to provide opportunities for Māori parliamentarians to meet Māori people outside the confines of electorates or political parties.

Immediately following the election, a Māori caucus was debated by some of the successful candidates.[64] Donna Awatere, a list candidate for ACT, was emphatic about the need for Māori MPs to work together and pledged to do so. Others were a little more cautious, Tau Henare of New Zealand First doubting that a formal caucus could be established but agreeing about the need to cooperate, and Rana Waitai (New Zealand First) confessing to a prior party loyalty. John Delamere, also New Zealand First, hoped that Māori would be able to lift the spirit of Parliament by introducing tikanga Māori and demonstrating models for collective decision-making.

By October 1996, Māori interest in the general election had gathered momentum and the Māori turnout at voting booths was higher than ever before. Of the 140 004 on the Māori roll, about 63 per cent (88 400) voted, including those casting special votes. Though not as high as the turnouts in general seats, participation in the Māori seats was higher than in the past. A former member of the Royal Commission on the Electoral System, which had recommended a change to MMP in 1986, was impressed by the high levels of Māori voting. 'From a Māori point of view the willingness to get on the roll and take part in the process is especially pleasing.'[65] Reasons for the higher participation levels could be attributed to the large number of Māori candidates but also to a new sense of vigour, partly linked to MMP and also to the perception of New Zealand First as a pro-Māori party. Professor Ranginui Walker interpreted the trend as a demonstration that Māori wanted to play a part in mainstream politics rather than in ethnic minority politics. He may well have been right. The Alliance Party, incorporating the Mana Motuhake Party founded by Matiu Rata, did not become the major opposition force it had expected though two Māori candidates gained list seats. Votes for Māori parties, including the Mana Māori Party which had promoted candidates such as activists Eva Rickard, Tame Iti and Ken Mair, were relatively low, neither Mana Māori nor the Ringatu-linked Te Tawharau party obtaining the necessary 4 per cent of the vote to qualify for a seat (Mana Māori 0.14 per cent, Te Tawharau 0.01 per cent). Even so, in the four Māori electorates where candidates were fielded, Mana Māori scored slightly more votes than the National party.

Without doubt, however, Māori had spread themselves across almost all parties. The extent of the participation is shown in table 4.8, which details the party list candidates, their rankings and their success.

Table 4.8 Māori Party and List Candidates 1996

	Candidate	Ranking	Result (L = List Seat) (E = Electorate)
ACT	Donna Awatere-Huata	4	L
	Mereania Karuaria	18	
	Peggy Luke-Ngaheke	35	
Alliance	Sandra Lee	2	L
	Alamein Kopu	12	L
	Hone Kaiwai	15	
	Willie Jackson	20	
	Bill Hamilton	26	
	Te Pare Joseph	58	
	Huia Mitchell	64	
Christian Coalition	Maahi Tukapua	34	
Labour Party	Dover Samuels	3	L
	Nanaia Mahuta	8	L
	Joe Hawke	15	L
	Tariana Turia	20	L
	Matiu Dickson	26	
	Norah Walker	45	
	Tamati Kruger	49	
	Hori Awa	59	
Mana Māori	Angeline Greensill	1	
	Tame Iti	2	
	Moana Sinclair	3	
	Hone Harawira	4	
	Mereana Pitman	5	
	David Gilgen	6	
	Jackie Amohanga	7	
	Ken Mair	8	
	Joyce Maipi	9	
	Oneroa Pihema	10	
	Te Anau Tuiono	11	
	Waiariki Grace	12	
	Jim Perry	13	
	Dianne Prince	14	
	Kelly Pene	15	
	Rachael Raimona	16	
	Mere Grant	17	
	Jack Smith	18	

continued

	Candidate	Ranking	Result (L = List Seat) (E = Electorate)
New Zealand First	Winston Peters	1	E
	Tau Henare	2	E
	Tuku Morgan	10	E
	Ron Mark	11	L
	Ian Peters	16	
	John Delamere	18	E
	Rana Waitai	27	E
	Tu Wyllie	26	E
	Keri Kingi	41	
	Jack Tamihana	56	
	Clem Huriwaka	59	
	Thomas Moana	60	
National	Georgina Te Heuheu	7	L
	Wayne Taitoko	37	
	Dick Dargaville	55	
	Peta Butt	56	
	George Mathews	62	
	Cliff Bedwell	63	
Te Tawharau	William Coates	1	
	Koro Wikeepa	2	
	Hawea Vercoe	3	
	John Maihi	4	
	Steven Te Kani	5	
	Rangitukehu Paora	6	

One of the more dramatic results of the election was the capture of all five Māori seats by New Zealand First. Labour suffered a 22 per cent drop in Māori support, while New Zealand First were given 43 per cent of the vote. At an end was the 61-year-old alliance between Tahupotiki Wiremu Ratana and Michael Joseph Savage, and even two long-standing and respected Labour members were defeated. Peter Tapsell, the first Māori Speaker of Parliament, lost to John Delamere, and Whetu Tirikatene was narrowly beaten by Tutekawa Wyllie. (After special votes were counted, Wyllie's majority increased to 285.) Koro Wetere, sensing perhaps a new mood, had decided not to stand for a further term, but his Labour successor, Nanaia Mahuta, was also beaten by the New Zealand First candidate, Tukuroirangi Morgan. (Mahuta, however, was successful as a list candidate.) Public interest in the fate of the Māori seats was high throughout election night and later.[66] Without them New Zealand First would have been less significant than Alliance, and with them Labour could have increased its potential to form a government. Table 4.9 shows the final results for the five Māori seats.[67]

Table 4.9 The Māori Electorates 1996—Final Results
(Numbers of votes cast)

	Te Tai Tokerau	Te Tai Hauauru	Te Tai Rāwhiti	Te Puku o te Whenua	Te Tai Tonga
ACT	No candidate	Mereania Karauria 167	Hinemoa Awatere 352	Donna Awatere-Huata 923	No candidate
Alliance	Peter Campbell 1 468	Te Pare Joseph 1 370	Alamein Kopu 1 210	David James 1 571	Hone Kaiwai 1 916
Christian Coalition	Larry Sutherland 299	Rawiri Whare 369	No candidate	Maahi Tukapua 319	No candidate
Labour Party	Joe Hawke 4 408	Nanaia Mahuta 5 645	Peter Tapsell 6 432	Rino Tirikatene 5 388	Whetu Tirikatene-Sullivan 7 372
Mana Māori	No candidate	Angiline Greensill 952	Tame Iti 1 372	Ken Mair 1 066	Tuaiwa Rickard 1 220
National	Dick Dargaville 931	Tahuna Minhinnick 1 090	Peta Butt 506	Timoti Te Heuheu 877	Cliff Bedwell 1 115
New Zealand First	Tau **Henare** 12 826	Tukoroirangi **Morgan** 10 606	John **Delamere** 10 647	Rana **Waitai** 7 774	Tutekawa **Wyllie** 7 657
Te Tawharau	No candidate	No candidate	Wharekaihua Coates 389	Niko Maihi 128	No candidate
Independent	Mary-anne Baker 740	No candidate	No candidate	No candidate	No candidate
Aotearoa Legalise Cannabis	No candidate	No candidate	No candidate	No candidate	H Whaanga-Morris 873
Others	553	282	70	485	

Source: Mana

The departure of Whetu Tirikatene-Sullivan from the political scene marked the end of an era. Ratana's delivery of Māori votes to Labour had predetermined the outcome of the Māori seats since 1943, and even though New Zealand First had taken the Northern Māori seat in 1993, Tirikatene seemed safe enough even within a week or so of the ballot. Elected to replace her father, Sir Eruera Tirikatene, after his death in 1967, she had held the Southern Māori seat with such a large majority that her failure appeared to come as a surprise. She refused to concede defeat until after special votes were counted, and then attributed New Zealand First's showing to Winston Peter's 'messianic aura'. 'Māori were wanting to see the first Māori prime minister and Winston was the closest we've had in this generation.'[68] She also heaped blame on the Ngai Tahu leadership for using tribal resources in a subversive campaign against her.[69] It was no secret that she had opposed the new Ngai Tahu Runanga and Sir Tipene O'Regan's leadership, while for his part O'Regan had supported Wyllie because of a mistrust of Tirikatene, at least as an instrument to advance the Ngai Tahu settlement within Parliament. As well, Wyllie's views on the tribal ownership of fishing resources accorded with his own. Gone too was the chance to extend a family dynasty within the House; Rino Tirikatene, a nephew of Whetu, was defeated by Rana Waitai in the new Puku o te Whenua electorate.

Apart from those in the Māori seats, ten other Māori candidates were successful in the 1996 general election, nine being high enough on party list seats to gain a place. Winston Peters, leader of New Zealand First, successfully defended the Tauranga electorate seat and went to Parliament with a 7 481 majority. Donna Awatere-Huata was no match for Rana Waitai in Te Puku o te Whenua but entered Parliament as number four on the ACT list, while Sandra Lee unsuccessfully defended the Auckland Central seat but was successful as number two on the Alliance list. Joe Hawke was beaten by Tau Henare for Te Tai Tokerau but was number fifteen on the Labour party list, and Nanaia Mahuta, though failing to gain the seat vacated by Koro Wetere, was eight on the labour list. Alamein Kopu (Alliance), Georgina Te Heuheu (National), Dover Samuels (Labour), Ron Mark (New Zealand First), and Tariana Turia (Labour) did not contest electorate seats but entered Parliament as list members.

Table 4.10 Māori in Parliament 1996

Electorate Seats	Party List Seats
John Delamere (NZF)	Donna Awatere-Huata (ACT)
Tau Henare (NZF)	Alamein Kopu (Alliance)
Tukuroirangi Morgan (NZF)	Sandra Lee (Alliance)
Winston Peters (NZF)	Joe Hawke (Labour)
Rana Waitai (NZF)	Nanaia Mahuta (Labour)
Tutekawe Wyllie (NZF)	Dover Samuels (Labour)
	Tariana Turia (Labour)
	Georgina Te Heuheu (National)
	Ron Mark (NZF)

Among the Māori members there were some ironies. Tainui, and in particular the Kingitanga movement, was well represented but by members in different parties—Mahuta in Labour and Morgan in New Zealand First. Whakatohea, about to settle its Treaty of Waitangi claim, also had two members in the new Parliament, Kopu and Delamere. Alamein Kopu attracted some media attention in that she went from the unemployment benefit directly onto an MP's salary of $74 500.[70] But, by July 1997, the demands of both Parliament and party had proved too much. She opted to withdraw from the Alliance and continue as an independent member. Again media attention was high, and the Alliance and Mana Motuhake were critical of the perceived disloyalty. Meanwhile Tutekawa Wyllie of Ngai Tāmanuhiri and Rongowhakaata (Gisborne) had displaced a Ngai Tahu candidate in her own area; and Tariana Turia maintained that her fight for Māori independence, even a Māori Parliament, could continue within the parliamentary system. She was hopeful that Māori across all parties could work together for tino rangatiratanga.[71] There was though a sense of betrayal from some of those who followed her at Pakaitore; and a hint perhaps of an underestimation of the power of the party political system and the difference between working within a system and operating on the outside. Nor was it easy to reconcile her stated views on rangatiratanga with her decision to accept a list seat in the Labour party. Not convinced that Māori aspirations for greater autonomy could be realised within Parliament, some also considered that the strong position taken by Sir Hepi Te Heuheu about the fiscal envelope was weakened when his son Timi and daughter-in-law Georgina both stood for National.

However, the presence of fifteen Māori members in Parliament and their commitment to Māori advancement brought home to political leaders and to media commentators the importance of the Māori vote.[72] Māori members promised action, and posed something of a culture shock for Parliament.[73] During the eight weeks of coalition talks, all parties were mindful of the need to appear sympathetic to Māori positions. Labour doubted that Māori voters could be accommodated with National policies, while National showed a willingness to adapt and even to bend on the previously non-negotiable billion dollar cap on the fiscal envelope. Somewhat surprisingly, Māori MPs, at least those in New Zealand First, were more than a little embarrassed by their own high profiles and found it necessary to reiterate the importance of the wider party, not only the Māori electorates. John Delamere (now, at the request of tribal elders, known as Tuariki Delamere) was at pains to point out that Māori electorate MPs should be careful not to dominate New Zealand First and make it 'too Māori' in character. 'Because of our numbers and the personalities we have, there is a danger we could become overbearing. The last thing we want is to be part of a Māori party. There is no future in that, we are part of New Zealand.' Tukuroirangi Morgan agreed, endorsing the view of a united party caucus, and not a 'them and us situation.'[74]

In fact, the Māori MPs were highly influential in cementing the coalition between New Zealand First and National, eventually announced by Peters on 10 December in time for the opening of Parliament. They were even reported as influencing the course of law by persuading National not to support a contro-versial Court of Appeal decision ruling that urban Māori were a tribe entitled to benefit directly from Māori fisheries assets. According to the reports, unless the caretaker government used its powers to pull back the Crown Law Office to a neutral position when the matter went to the Privy Council, they would refuse to endorse a coalition deal with National. And even though the argument used in the Privy Council was that it was inappropriate for a caretaker government to take a stand on the issue, National did instruct the Crown Law Office to withdraw its support for the Court of Appeal decision.[75]

When New Zealand First opted to form a coalition with National, many Māori felt betrayed. After all, the Māori vote for National was much lower than for Labour (see table 4.11). However, a few days prior to the announcement of the coalition decision, Peters released a letter from the Māori Queen, Te Atairangikaahu, written on her own behalf, but urging him to consider the national interests rather than either the party position or the level of popular party support. It was the sanction he needed to put aside Māori voting prefer-ences in order to negotiate a new position with a government that he had earlier sworn to remove from power. At the same time, Māori now had a stronger presence in Cabinet than ever before. As Deputy Prime Minister and Treasurer Peters had control of the budget; Henare was sworn in as Minister of Māori Affairs, Minister of Racing, and Associate Minister for Sport, Fitness and Leisure, while the youthful Tuariki Delamere had become Associate Treasurer, Minister in Charge of the Valuation Department, and Minister in Charge of the Public Trust Office.

Table 4.11 Party Vote in Māori Electorates, 1996
(Main parties by percentage of total vote)

	Te Tai Tokerau	Te Tai Rāwhiti	Te Puku o te Whenua	Te Tai Hauauru	Te Tai Tonga
National	4	2	5	5	6
Labour	21	31	29	28	37
NZ First	60	51	42	52	38
Alliance	7	6	8	7	10
Mana Maori	n/a	7	6	5	6

Source: Mana

In the first few months of the new government, Māori politicians were subjected to close scrutiny and a seemingly orchestrated series of media attacks and revelations, often without sound supporting evidence. Depicted (largely by themselves) as 'warriors', critics seized on a sense of arrogance, especially in relationship to the Aotearoa Television Network scandal and Morgan's unrepent-ant attitude. As well, Wyllie was accused of not declaring an amount of four or five hundred dollars spent on his election campaign. Then Peters's refusal to apologise for what the parliamentary privileges committee found to be an assault on MP John Banks added to the image of bullies rather than warriors.[76] Disappointment with the performance of the New Zealand First Māori members was also said to be one reason why fewer than expected transferred from the general roll to the Māori roll during the 1997 Māori option and why some opted to leave the Māori roll in favour of the general roll. At the same time, however, the influx of fifteen Māori into Parliament brought a change to the House itself. It was evident in the maiden speeches, in the galleries, and in the media misrepresentation of the many subtleties that characterised Māori oratory. The significance of Māori voting power had also been recognised, and the Māori vote would be actively courted in the next election. The Hon. Jenny Shipley advised National party delegates that a further two or so extra Māori seats could be expected as a result of the 1997 Māori option and a separate Māori party might emerge. In any event, she warned that Māori voters could hold the balance of power between National and Labour.[77]

Some maintained that it was Tau Henare, not Winston Peters, who appealed to Māori voters in the 1996 election, while others blamed the poor performance of previous incumbents and growing dissatisfaction with Labour's lukewarm Māori policies. But it may not have been party policies, or past inadequacies which captured Māori imagination so much as a sense of new direction, youthful political leaders, and a desire to make the best of the new system. Most Māori, it seemed, were not swayed by the loyalties of the past, or the concept of Māori sovereignty, or the power of boycott. At least for now they had opted for a strong Māori presence within the system, and the prospect of a new generation of Māori politicians to negotiate arrangements for power, resources, and policy. Not the same as autonomy or tino rangatiratanga, nor even a step in the direction of a separate order, but a serious bid to capture the mainstream and to locate Māori at the political centre.

NOTES FOR CHAPTER 4

1 There are several versions to this proverb. All compare the size of a population to the myriad of stars in the sky.

2 Ian Pool, (1991), *Te Iwi Māori: A New Zealand Population Past, Present and Projected*, Auckland University Press, Auckland.

3 Statistics New Zealand, (1997), *1996 Census of Populations and Dwellings: Iwi Populations and Dwellings*, Department of Statistics, Wellington.

4 M. H. Durie, (1994), 'Kaupapa Hauora Māori: Policies for Māori Health', in *Te Ara Ahu Whakamua Proceedings of the Māori Health Decade Hui*, Te Puni Kōkiri, Wellington, p. 133.

5 Edward Te Kohu Douglas, (1994), 'Demographic Changes and their Social Consequences for Māori', in Department of Māori Studies (ed.), *Kia Pūmau Tonu: Proceedings of the Hui Whakapūmau*, Department of Māori Studies, Massey University, p. 87.

6 Statistics New Zealand, (1994), *Population Issues for New Zealand: New Zealand National Report on Population*, Department of Statistics, Wellington.

7 W. Wereta (1994), 'Māori Demographic Trends', in *Kia Pūmau Tonu*, pp. 75–84.

8 Te Puni Kōkiri, (1996), *Briefing Papers to the Incoming Government*, Ministry of Māori Development, Wellington.

9 Ministry of Education, (1995), *Ngā Haeata Mātauranga: Annual Report on Māori Education 1994/95 and Strategic Direction for 1995/96*, Ministry of Education, Wellington.

10 Eru Pomare, Vera Keefe-Ormsby, Clint Ormsby, Neil Pearce, Paparangi Reid, Bridget Robson, Naina Wātene-Haydon, (1995), *Hauora Māori Standards of Health III: A Study of the Years 1970–1991*, Te Roopu Rangahau Hauora a Eru Pomare, Wellington.

11 Lorna Dyall, Geoff Bridgman, (1996), *Ngā Ia o te Oranga Hinengaro Māori 1984–1993: Māori Mental Health Trends*, Mental Health Foundation, Auckland.

12 Conference Steering Committee, (1984), *A Briefing on Māori Economic Affairs*, Māori Economic Development Conference 1984, Dunmore, Palmerston North.

13 Manatu Māori, (1991), *Māori and Work: The Position of Māori in the New Zealand Labour Market*, Manatu Māori Ministry of Māori Affairs, Wellington.

14 Statistics New Zealand, (1996), *Household Labour Force Survey September 1996*, Department of Statistics, New Zealand.

15 Ministry of Education, (1995), *Ngā Haeata Mātauranga*.

16 Hon. Jenny Shipley, (1995*), Policy Guidelines for Māori Health: Ngā Aratohu Kaupapahere Hauora Māori*, Parliament, Wellington.

17 Full Employment Committee, (1994), *Employment: an Iwi Perspective*, Māori Congress, Wellington.

18 Core Services Committee, (1994), *Core Services for 1995/96*, National Advisory Committee on Core Health and Disability Support Services, Wellington, p. 24.

19 Networks and social interaction based on the models of the extended family (whanaungatanga) and tribal obligations and cohesion (hapūtanga).

20 M. H. Durie, (1995), *Principles for the Development of Māori Policy*, paper presented at the Māori Policy Development AIC Conference, Wellington.

21 M. H. Durie, (1994), *Whaiora: Māori Health Development*, Oxford University Press, Auckland, p. 214.

22 Love, Ngātata, (1994), 'The Hui Taumata and the Decade of Māori Development in Perspective', in *Kia Pūmau Tonu*, p. 25.

23 D. Henare, (1994), 'Social Policy Outcomes Since the Hui Taumati', in *Kia Pūmau Tonu*, p. 40.

24 Ministry of Education, (1994), 'Maori in Education', *Education Trends Reports*, vol. 6, no. 1.

25 *ibid.*

26 Statistics New Zealand, (1994), *New Zealand Now Māori*, Department of Statistics, Wellington, pp. 25–32.

27 *ibid.*, pp. 35–44.

28 New Zealand Government, (1994), *Report Submitted by the New Zealand Government to the United Nations World Summit for Social Development*, Wellington.

29 J. Davey, (1993), *From Birth to Death iii*, Institute of Policy Studies, Victoria University of Wellington, p. 13.

30 *ibid.*, pp. 141, 164–167.

31 Aroha Mead, (1994), 'Māori Leadership: The Waka Tradition: The Crews Were the Real Heroes', in *Kia Pūmau Tonu*, pp. 109–115.

32 W. Gardiner, (1994), 'Marae to Global Village: 1000 Years of Māori Development', in *Kia Pūmau Tonu*, pp. 67–73.

33 John Roberts, (1996), *Alternative Vision He Moemoea Ano: The Significance of the Hirangi Hui*, Joint Public Questions Committee of the Methodist Church of New Zealand and the Presbyterian Church of Aotearoa New Zealand, Wellington.

34 B. Puketapu, (1994), 'Hokia ki te Kopae a ngā Pāheke: The Classical Māori Journey', in *Kia Pūmau Tonu*, pp. 161–171.

35 M. H. Durie, (1994) 'Kaupapa Hauora Māori: Policies for Māori Health', in *Te Ara Ahu Whakamua: Proceedings of the Māori Health Decade Hui*, Te Puni Kōkiri, Wellington, p. 131.

36 John Rangihau, (1975), 'Being Māori', in M. King (ed.), *Te Ao Hurihuri: The World Moves On*, Hicks Smith, Wellington, pp. 232–233.

37 T. Karetu, (1990), 'The Clue to Identity', *New Zealand Geographic*, no. 5, pp. 112–117.

38 J. K. Hunn, (1961), *Report on the Department of Maori Affairs, Appendix to the Journals of the House of Representatives 1960*, Wellington.

39 Māori Health Committee, (1987), *Tribal Authorities as Advocates for Māori Health*, New Zealand Board of Health, Wellington.

40 'Move with the times, says Tapsell', *The Dominion,* Wednesday 8 December 1993.

41 S. Jones, (1993), 'Beyond the boundary of tribalism', *The Dominion,* Friday 19 November 1993.

42 J. Tamihere, (1994), 'Management of Māori Health Programmes', in *Te Ara Ahu Whakamua.*

43 I. Ramsden, (1994), 'Māori Policy', in *Kia Pūmau Tonu,* pp. 117–123.

44 This case is discussed in greater detail in Chapter 6.

45 See chapter 6.

46 Danny Keenan, (1996), 'A Permanent Expedient?', *He Pukenga Kōrero,* vol. 2, no. 1, pp. 58–61.

47 M. P. K. Sorrenson, (1986), 'A History of Māori Representation in Parliament', in *Towards a Better Democracy: Report of the Royal Commission on the Electoral System,* Wellington, p. B–58.

48 J. Henderson, (1963), *Ratana: The Man, the Church, the Political Movement,* The Polynesian Society, Wellington, pp. 90–91.

49 Tina Dahlberg, (1996), 'Māori Representation in Parliament and Tino Rangatiratanga', *He Pukenga Kōrero,* vol. 2, no. 1, pp. 62–72.

50 Royal Commission on the Electoral System, (1986), *Towards a Better Democracy: Report of the Royal Commission on the Electoral System,* Wellington, p. 108.

51 *ibid.,* pp. 43–44.

52 Justice Committee, (1993), *The Treaty of Waitangi and Constitutional Implications of the Electoral Reform Bill, A Discussion Paper,* National Māori Congress, Wellington.

53 Waitangi Tribunal, (1994), *Report of the Waitangi Tribunal on the Maori Electoral Option Claim (Wai 413),* Waitangi Tribunal, Wellington.

54 'Māori roll case could delay MMP', *The Dominion,* Monday 27 June 1994.

55 *Atawhai Taiaroa and others v Minister of Justice,* Wellington, High Court, CP No 99/94, 4 October 1994, McGechan J.

56 Atawhai Taiaroa, Hare Puke, Henare Ngata, Charles Bennett, Ralph Love, Mira Szaszy, Areta Koopu, Graham Latimer.

57 *Taiaroa v Minister of Justice* [1995] 1 NZLR 411 (Court of Appeal).

58 Waitangi Tribunal (1994), *Report . . . on the Maori Electoral Option Claim,* p. 25.

59 *ibid.,* p. 21.

60 'Call to delay Maori option', *The Dominion,* Friday 22 November 1996.

61 'Bad publicity turns people off Māori roll', *Sunday Star-Times,* 18 May 1997.

62 Jane Kelsey, (1993), *Rolling Back the State: Privatisation of Power in Aotearoa/New Zealand,* Bridget Williams Books, Wellington, pp. 239–240.

63 Ann Sullivan, (1997), 'Māori Politics and Government Policies', in R. Miller (ed.), *New Zealand Politics in Transition,* Oxford University Press, Auckland, pp. 368–369.

64 Television New Zealand, *Marae,* 13 October 1996, Channel One.

65 'MMP architects review handiwork', *The Dominion,* Thursday 14 November 1996.

66 'The Māori Switch', Editorial, *The Otago Daily Times,* Thursday 17 October 1966.

67 'Māori political muscle—at last', *Mana: The Maori News Magazine for All New Zealanders*, (Summer 1996/97), no. 14, pp. 38–39.

68 'Political dynasty ends after 64 years', *The Dominion*, Friday 25 October 1966.

69 'Tirikatene-Sullivan lashes out at Ngai Tahu leaders', *Evening Standard*, Tuesday 29 October 1966.

70 'Dole queue leads to Parliament', *The Dominion*, Thursday 7 November 1966.

71 Tariana Turia, *Mana News*, Radio New Zealand, 31 October 1996.

72 'Māori chance to lead way', Editorial, *The Dominion*, Wednesday 16 October 1966.

73 'Culture shock of new Māori MPs', *The Dominion*, Friday 25 October 1996.

74 'Māori MPs warned not to dominate NZ First', *The Dominion*, Thursday 14 November 1996.

75 'National yields to NZ First's Maori MPs', *The Dominion*, Wednesday 20 November 1966.

76 'The warriors turned bullies', Editorial, *The Dominion*, Monday 19 May 1997.

77 'Maori party key to power says Shipley', *The Dominion*, Monday 19 May 1997.

5

MANA WHENUA

THE LORE OF THE LAND

Ka ngaro ra aku whenua
Ka ngaro ra aku tika;
Mataotao ana te aroha
Mōmona ana ngā iwi whai rawa
Tūpuhi ana ngā iwi rawakore.[1]

WHENUA TŪPUNA

Land is necessary for spiritual growth and economic survival. It contributes to sustenance, wealth, resource development, tradition; land strengthens whānau and hapū solidarity, and adds value to personal and tribal identity as well as the well-being of future generations. Though its ownership may change, land itself cannot be made to disappear nor can it be separated from the lives and deaths of the people for whom it has been home, or for whom it should have been home. In this sense it has abiding qualities which go well beyond utilitarian considerations to encompass existential dimensions and to give solidarity to the often abstract state of belonging. A Māori identity is secured by land; land binds human relationships, and in turn people learn to bond with the land. Loss of land is loss of life, or at least loss of that part of life which depends on the connections between the past and the present and present with the future. 'Whatu ngarongaro te tangata, toitū te whenua. People perish but the land is permanent.'[2]

It is no source of amazement that people will willingly die to defend their land or that generations after the event, they will return to take up where their ancestors left off. Nor is it remarkable that for 160 or more years Māori energies have been consistently focused on land retention and the return of land alienated by force or unjust laws. What has not been forgotten are the explicit policies of the last century, which encouraged settlers to occupy the land while

115

systematically removing the Māori landowners. A key task for central government in the nineteenth century was creating and operating devices for separating Māori from their land.[3] In the North Island, war and the law were the twin instruments through which a major part of the usable land was transferred to Pākehā hands. In the South Island no war was needed; Crown purchases achieved a similar effect.

Two consequences of land alienation remain problematic for contemporary Māori advancement. First, the major erosion of land as an economic base has had 'a crippling impact on the welfare, economy and development' of the Māori.[4] Second, social cohesion between whānau and within tribes has been seriously undermined by the individualisation of land titles and the forced abandonment of collective ownership. Caught somewhere between a group philosophy of shared histories and aspirations, and an increasing emphasis on individual rights, many Māori find themselves in a situation in which land, or its absence, is the main cause of their discontent. Nor is it simply land loss which has created the problem; arrangements for tenure of the little land that remains in Māori hands are often equal causes of conflict.

Many of the difficulties in reconciling customary land tenure with modern times, and in understanding the transfer of substantial tracts of land from Māori to settlers, can be traced to the differing cultural values placed on land by tribes and colonists.[5] According to the Chief Judge of the Māori Land Court, E. T. Durie, Māori tenure could be characterised as an ancestral trust estate of indefinite magnitude vested in hapū but with internal use rights distributed among such ancestral descendants and incorporated outsiders who used them. Use rights were transferable within families but not outside the group unless through general group sanction.[6] Customary Māori title included take tipu (ancestral land passed down according to Māori custom), take raupatu (land acquired by conquest and followed by occupation), take ōhākī (land allocated through the wish of a dying chief), and take tuku (gifted land).[7] Use rights were also held on sufferance, being known as 'noho tikanga kore' or 'noho noa iho'.[8] Take taunaha described land claims based on discovery, and for all land an entitlement was conditioned by occupation, the maintenance of a continual presence—ahi kā.[9]

In the European tradition ownership of land was established by deed of sale, not by use. There was a distinction between landowners and tenants—a social hierarchy based on individual wealth and land ownership. A written deed of sale led to possession of title regardless of intent to occupy or the interests of long-standing occupiers. Moreover, the value of land was determined by its market potential with little recognition of spiritual or cultural values. Table 5.1 compares Māori and colonial attitudes to land and highlights the essential sources of conflict and misunderstanding which were to lead to tension, war, and then large-scale alienation.

Table 5.1 Māori and Colonial Attitudes to Land

	Māori	Colonial
Ownership	Collective (tribal)	Individual title
Proof of Ownership	Occupation, use	Deed of sale
Significance	Economic, spiritual	Economic status
Transfer	By conquest or abandonment or succession	By sale or lease or Crown directive
Occupants	Part-owners, trustees	Owners or tenants
Classes of Land	Ancestral (take tupuna) Gifted (take tuku) Conquered (take raupatu)	Freehold Leasehold Waste land/arable land
Utilisation	Agriculture Hunting Resource management	Agriculture Horticulture Mining Settlements
Value	Tribal identity and security for next generations	Market potential Employment

The differing attitudes are nowhere better illustrated than in the Waitangi Tribunal's *Muriwhenua Land Report*. Whereas other tribes lost land through confiscation or aggressive Crown purchasing strategies, land transactions in Northland were often poorly understood and reflected fundamental differences in values and philosophies concerning land. From 1834 the Muriwhenua tribes parted with some 204 785 hectares. As transactions concerning 60 705 hectares were made even before 1840, though they were subsequently confirmed by the Crown, the clash of custom and differing understandings of land tenure was not surprising. According to the Tribunal, Māori contracts were not about transferring property but about defining relationships between people. Thus the pre-Treaty transactions (and even transactions up until 1865) could not be regarded as binding since the parties 'were not of sufficient common mind for valid contracts to be formed'. Rather than selling the land, Māori were observing tuku whenua, a form of leasing without any intention to alienate interests for ever. To Māori the transaction was a social contract, to settlers a property conveyance.[10]

These understandings of land transfers were not only held by Muriwhenua but were common to all tribes and were similarly evident in the wider Pacific.

ALIENATION AND DISPOSSESSION

The alienation of land from Māori was sanctioned in laws passed by the settler government and was effected through three mechanisms: confiscation, Crown land purchases, and Māori Land Court decisions. Together, they resulted in the loss of most of the land held by Māori.

Despite Lord Normanby's instruction to Hobson that tribes should retain sufficient land as an economic base for the future, after the Treaty of Waitangi and the establishment of a settler parliament in 1854 alienation occurred at great pace and with little regard for Māori welfare. Supposedly to prevent exploitation of Māori and unfair land acquisitions, the Treaty of Waitangi contained (in Article 2) a clause (the pre-emption clause) which gave the Crown the exclusive right to purchase Māori land. It was a contentious clause and was first violated by Governor FitzRoy in 1844. Almost immediately after the Treaty was signed, there were complaints about land transactions and confusion about the role of the Crown. The pre-emption clause was not well explained either in the Treaty or at gatherings to sign the Treaty. It could have meant that the government had the first option on land that tribes wished to sell. In fact, it meant that the Crown had the only option; i.e. tribes could only sell to the Crown.

There were two reasons for the clause: to validate titles, thereby protecting Māori from unscrupulous dealers, but also to fund emigration by creating a price differential and providing a mechanism for colonisation. In 1844, however, Governor FitzRoy waived the pre-emptive clause. He was swayed by the government's lack of funds to purchase land as well as by increasing settler demand for land which far exceeded the government's rate of land purchase. Māori were also dissatisfied with a situation in which land could be bought for sixpence an acre but sold for one pound and wondered why they could not sell to the highest bidder. FitzRoy's actions meant that direct sales were permitted but were subject to approval. At first a levy of 10 shillings an acre was charged (Crown revenue) but land sales were so slow that the levy was dropped to one penny an acre.

After FitzRoy's recall, the new Governor, George Grey, resumed the Crown's right of pre-emption. He overcame the problem of inadequate funds by obtaining off-shore finances from the British government and proceeded with an active land purchase policy, a deliberate move to stop the practice of long-term leases which impeded the process of alienation.

However, the sale of land was still too slow for settlers, and there was pressure to smooth the way for direct purchasing by enabling deals to be made with Māori individuals. The Native Lands Act 1862 was the answer. Its purpose was to do away with tribal ownership, the greatest barrier to land purchasing, and it also suspended once again the Crown's right to pre-emption. For a brief period the right was restored in the 1893 Native Land Purchase and Acquisition Act, which among other things enabled the Crown to declare any Māori land suitable for settlement. But the government finally abandoned its right to pre-emption under the 1900 Maori Lands Administration Act. Far from protecting Māori land and discouraging purchases by unscrupulous settlers, the clause had been used by the Crown to further its own ends and to launch a range of land policies formulated to destroy Māori opposition to sale and hasten occupation by settlers.

Table 5.2 Patterns of Māori Land Ownership

Year	Acres	Hectares
1840	66 400 000	29 880 000
1852	34 000 000	15 300 000
1860	21 400 000	9 630 000
1891	11 079 486	4 985 000
1911	7 137 205	3 211 000
1920	4 787 686	2 154 000
1939	4 028 903	1 813 000
1975	3 000 000	1 350 000
1986	2 626 091	1 181 740
1996	3 743 689	1 515 071

Confiscation

Although by far the greater losses occurred through the government's aggressive purchasing policies and the decisions taken by the Native Land Court, war was the most visible conflagration and in the short term the most injurious. Māori opposition to land sales was countered by armed troops and the punishment was confiscation of tribal lands, legalised through two Acts of Parliament, the New Zealand Settlements Act and the Suppression of Rebellion Act, both passed in 1863. Under them the government gave itself wide-ranging powers to confiscate tribal lands. Tribes who actively or passively resisted surveyors or sales were regarded as rebels and their lands were confiscated. Even if there were little more than a suspicion of 'rebellion', land could be taken—and in that way over three million acres were appropriated by the Crown.

Of the 3.25 million acres confiscated in the North Island, 1 199 622 acres were in Taranaki, 1 217 437 in Waikato, and the remainder in the Bay of Plenty. Although approximately half was returned later, often it was inferior land, and not always given to rightful owners. Proportionately less land was given back to Waikato.

Table 5.3 Disposal of Confiscated Land
(Acres)

	Opotiki	Tauranga	Taranaki	Waikato
Total land confiscated	448 000	290 000	1 199 622	1 217 437
Area returned to tribes	230 600	240 250		50 000

Sources: Sorrenson (1981), Waitangi Tribunal (1996)

Apart from legislation which gave a veneer of justification to the confiscation process, other laws were passed with the express purpose of speeding up sales and transferring ownership from tribal collectives to individuals. The Native Land Act 1862 and the Native Land Act 1865 largely did away with customary land titles, freeing up land for sale and in the process undermining the social links between families and within tribes. Māori society had depended on common interests in traditional lands for cohesion and purpose. As land was transferred, through one means or another, so Māori identity and well-being were rendered vulnerable, until eventually even survival appeared unlikely. Out of nearly 66.5 million acres, by 1896 only eleven million acres remained in Māori ownership. By then, in parallel fashion, the Māori population had declined to less than 43 000.[11]

Government Land Purchases

Under the 1852 New Zealand Constitution Act, New Zealand was to have a general assembly and provincial councils in each of six provinces. When the general assembly first met in Auckland in 1854, the main business was the transfer of the powers of the Governor to the Cabinet, and at the second meeting in 1856 the focus was on the relationship of the provincial councils to the new central government.[12] Both issues were concerned with the acquisition of land, the procurement of power, and the neutralisation of Māori opposition. Governor Gore Browne was not convinced that the new assembly would be fair to Māori and insisted on retaining direct control over Māori affairs. Ministers were ambivalent; on the one hand they wanted to be able to embark on a sweeping land purchasing strategy but, aware of Māori opposition in Taranaki and elsewhere, they did not want full responsibility and were mindful of the Governor's control of the Imperial forces. The Governor won, but increasingly his powers were transferred to the Cabinet, until in 1863 the House of Representatives passed resolutions accepting full responsibility for Māori affairs, rather than a system of dual control.[13] Any prospect of a Treaty-inspired role for the Governor as a protector of Māori interests had by then run its course.

Not that governors distinguished themselves as defenders of Māori rights. More often than not they demonstrated the reverse, and if up until 1858 policies for land purchasing were in conformity with Māori systems,[14] the aggressive land purchasing policies developed in Governor Grey's time were evidence of an intention to conveniently leave aside notions of mutual benefit or the future economic security of tribes. McLean was the best-known government purchasing agent. First appointed by FitzRoy as a Sub-protector of Aborigines, he later entered a long career as a land purchasing agent under Grey and, like his master, used his associations with Māori leaders 'for the purpose of manipulating them and securing their land.'[15] Deals with chiefs known to be in favour of selling land were made in secret, and many more transactions were made with supposed chiefs who, in fact, had no authority to commit others. In essence it was a divide and rule approach and tuku whenua (land selling) factions fought with pupuri whenua (land holding) groups. Government sympathies were very much with the tuku whenua groups. In 1853 alone, 32 million acres were bought for £50 000.

It is hard to say exactly how much land was alienated through government land purchasing policies, and how many of those purchases could be said to breach Treaty of Waitangi principles. In the South Island the three million acre Wairau block, the 20 million acre Canterbury–Otago block, and the Murihiku and Waipounamu blocks were sold for less than £15000.[16] Over a century later they were the subject of a formal Waitangi Tribunal hearing followed in 1996 by a proposal for a settlement with the Crown. Similarly, the Taranaki claim to the Waitangi Tribunal included not only claims relating to the unjust confiscation of tribal lands but also to the government's earlier and later purchasing policies.[17] The blunder of the Waitara purchase in 1860 for £600 stemmed from a failure to ascertain who the actual owners were and to side with one owner who wished to sell. But even when the mistake was recognised, Māori opposition to sales had been reconfigured as a cause for armed intervention, and war followed.[18] One way or another, settlers were determined to move on to Māori land.

The sale of the Rangitikei Manawatu block in 1866 for a mere £25000 was a good example of a pressured purchase which was concluded despite extensive opposition and uncertainty about ownership. Ngāti Raukawa, Rangitane, Muaupoko, Ngāti Apa and Ngāti Toa could all claim some interest in the block, but there was a lack of agreement about the relativity of those claims and conflicting views on verbal agreements made some years before. In addition, within each tribe there was division about the proposed sale. As government agent, Dr Featherston played one party against the other, seeking out allies and electing to deal with them at the expense of the greater majority who remembered only too well the unfair terms of earlier purchases. And when an agreement was finally signed the government reneged on its promises about reserves; sellers were as dissatisfied as the non-sellers. McLean intervened, setting aside additional reserves though without the support of central government. The irregularities surrounding the purchase caused enduring discontent for tribes in the area, and between 1988 and 1991 eight claims relating to Featherston's purchase were registered with the Waitangi Tribunal.[19]

Māori Land Court Purchases

The third way of moving Māori off their lands was through the Native Land Court. Although procedures to establish a Native Land Court were contained in the Native Land Act of 1862, it was not until 1865 that the court was actually in operation. Modelled on the conventions of British courts of law, there was little room for incorporating Māori forms of justice, evidence, and debate, and earlier promises to give local chiefs roles in determination were never realised. Between 1865 and 1900 the main judicial tasks were to determine ownership and then to facilitate individualisation of title, with greater likelihood of transferring title to settlers.[20] Though increasingly it came to adopt a protective role towards

Māori owners in the alienation of their lands, the clear purpose of the court when it was established was to bring Māori land on to the market.[21]

Individualisation of title was a key method, despite Māori objection. In the Poverty Bay areas, after defined shares had been awarded by the court, Māori leaders moved to create a massive trust for all their lands to give a united front against sales and to develop the land themselves. They formed the East Coast Native Trust, which had a chequered career but still survives in part as the Mangatu Incorporation. The Tuhoe people, as well, were opposed to the individualisation of titles and successfully promoted legislation resulting in the Urewera District Native Reserve Act 1896, to provide a system of tribal management for all Tuhoe lands. Eventually, however, individualisation arrived, even there.[22]

Despite Māori opposition the Maori Land Court was unable to award land to tribes as distinct entities. Instead the law required that tribal estates should be carved up and awarded to individuals. Those in actual occupancy were given priority, and earlier tribal arrangements and sanctions, which had imposed terms on the right to occupy, were ignored. Further, anyone who had fought against the Crown forfeited any share—to the Crown. In this way Ngāti Paoa of Waiheke Island were dispossessed. The ten blocks remaining in tribal ownership in 1865, and amounting to some 5700 acres, were awarded to the few at the expense of the majority, and nine of the ten were sold before the turn of the century.[23] In Hawke's Bay alone nearly four million acres of Māori land had been purchased by fewer than fifty Pākehā farmers. Chiefs who were reluctant to sell were trapped into accepting enormous sums of credit—which sometimes included credit against alcohol—and were subjected to unreasonable pressure by missionaries and provincial and central government politicians and to the promises of unscrupulous entrepreneurs.[24]

The role of the Native Land Court in failing to protect Ngāti Whātua interests at Orakei forms a considerable part of the Waitangi Tribunal Orakei Report. Had Chief Judge Fenton recorded the names of all tribal beneficiaries, as well as the thirteen entered on the title, the tribe as a whole might not have suffered alienation to the extent that they did. But he justified his decision not to use section 17 of the Native Land Act 1867[25] because he felt that it could negate the 'great object' of the Act which was 'the abolition of communal ownership of land.'[26] In considering the case some 120 years later, the Tribunal attributed blame to the Crown rather than the court; the court had acted within the terms of the 1867 Act but the Crown should have ensured that the provisions of section 17 were not overstepped by the Native Land Court.

It was the same throughout the country. In the Waikaremoana district, the Native Land Court was the final phase in the alienation of the Tuhoe tribal estate. Investigations were rushed and tribes were played off against each other to the detriment of Tuhoe and the benefit of Ngāti Kahungunu.[27]

There is some debate as to whether the actions of the court can be taken into account by politicians when it comes to settling Treaty claims. The Tuhoe claim is yet to be heard, but following the 1996 Deed of Settlement between Whakatohea and the Crown, John Delamere considered that land alienation, from whatever cause, demanded action and constituted just cause for Crown recompense. He concluded that the Crown could not avoid a measure of responsibility for unjust decisions made by a court that was sympathetic to government objectives for land purchases from Māori. Neither did he agree with the Minister in Charge of Treaty Negotiations, who had argued that the Crown had no place overturning the decisions made by a court last century, and pointed out that appointments to the Māori Land Court were very often linked to political favours. In Delamere's opinion alienation through raupatu was not necessarily any more unjust than alienation from pressured government land purchases or purchases sanctioned by the Native Land Court.[28]

MĀORI STRATEGIES FOR LAND REVITALISATION

In an effort to retain what little land remains in Māori hands or to extend Māori land holdings, and to make best use of land in economic terms, five strategies adopted by Māori over the past two decades can be identified. They are summarised in table 5.4.

Table 5.4 Māori Land Revitalisation Strategies

Strategy	Case Studies	Action
Land occupation	Bastion Point	Land returned (Orakei Act 1991)
	Moutoa: Pakaitore	High Court claim dismissed
Waitangi Tribunal claims	Orakei claim	Orakei Act 1991
	Te Roroa claim	Negotiations with Crown
	Ngai Tahu claim	Deed of settlement
	Taranaki claim	Negotiations with Crown
Claims over Crown land	SOE Appeal Court challenge	Treaty of Waitangi (State Enterprises) Act 1988
	Surplus railways land	Congress-Crown joint working party
	Surplus Crown lands	Consultative Clearance Process
Land retention	Māori freehold land	Te Ture Whenua Māori Act 1993
	Māori lease lands	Māori Reserved Land Amendment Bill 1996
Land development	Greater economic returns from Māori land	Incorporations
		Aotearoa Financial Services
		Federation of Māori Authorities
		Māori Land Investment Group

Bastion Point

In 1975 Whina Cooper, who had been the first president of the Māori Women's Welfare League, led a march from Te Hapua in the far north to Parliament. Joined by 5000 marchers, she presented a Memorial of Rights to the Prime Minister, petitioning the government to cease unjust alienation of Māori land.[29] The memorial, signed by over 60000 people, and the land march itself demonstrated the extent of Māori dissatisfaction and the desire to take the initiative in a variety of social and economic endeavours. There had been promises but little action, and Māori were no longer willing to sanction further land losses or efforts to assimilate Māori land into general land.

In 1977 more direct action followed. The Orakei Māori Committee Action Group, worried that the government was unsympathetic to Ngāti Whātua concerns for their lands at Orakei, and impatient with the minimal gains made by tribal elders, took the matter into their own hands. Gathering support from other (but not all) tribal members, trade unionists, the Matakite movement, the Citizens' Association for Racial Equality, and leaders such as Whina Cooper, the committee established a camp at Bastion Point.[30] The immediate focus of concern was the government's proposal to subdivide 24 hectares of Crown land for residential purposes, largely to satisfy a growing demand by wealthy Aucklanders for undisturbed harbour views and escape from the crowded suburbs. But behind the flash point was a history of oppression and dispossession dating back at least to the Orakei Native Reserve Act 1882, which disregarded previous undertakings to protect the land for the tribe and instead allowed for long-term leasing as a first step towards alienation. By 1898 the 'inalienable' reserve of 280 hectares had been reduced to 15.6 hectares. Protest followed, and there was some support for Ngāti Whātua from the Stout–Ngata Commission of 1907 and the Kennedy Commission of 1939, but one way or another the city and the government were bent on driving Ngāti Whātua out, regardless of legal or moral niceties. The 1951 eviction of the residents from the papa kāinga and their reinstatement into state houses in Kitemoana Street was further evidence of disregard for Māori opinion. But following the 1975 land march and under the leadership of Joe Hawke, a new generation was not prepared to accept the government's latest proposal for subdivision.

During the occupation Māori opinion became divided on the use of protest as the most effective means to make change. There was little disagreement about the wrongs of the land alienation but some, including Whina Cooper, and the Ngāti Whātua establishment, thought more progress could be made outside the threat of protest.[31] The government meanwhile sought to make an agreement with the more moderate elders, and a deal was struck for the return of around thirteen hectares and some $200000 in cash.[32] The protesters were scornful of the offer and considered that the moderates were selling out. Effectively the government had again divided the tribe, so that any solid basis for negotiation was distorted by internal disagreement and a 'take it or leave it' approach to settling the dispute. It was also true, however, that the Bastion Point case was being used as a focus for other tribal dissatisfactions, and the protesters included people who had no direct interest but a deep sympathy for the principles at stake.

Finally, on a court ruling, an eviction notice was served. The occupation had lasted for 506 days and the numbers of protesters had swelled from 150 to many more; on the final day, 222 were arrested by the 600 policemen and army personnel. Bulldozers and television cameras added a sense of drama. But the cause was far from over, and in 1987 the Waitangi Tribunal recommended a much more realistic settlement. Eventually in 1991 the recommendations had been accepted and implemented by the Crown. The protest leader, Joe Hawke, was also to follow new directions. Not only did he join the ranks of the Ngāti Whātua establishment and continue to work on behalf of his people, albeit in a different manner, but in 1996 he became a member of Parliament, having obtained a list seat in the Labour party.

Moutoa: Pakaitore

Though lasting for only 80 days, from 28 February until 18 May 1995, the occupation of the Moutoa Gardens in Whanganui shared many features of the Bastion Point occupation: land alienation was the main concern of the protesters; there was division over the handling of the matter between tribal elders and the protesters as well as between central and local government; other groups took the opportunity to protest about separate issues; and one of the protest leaders from each occupation was to become a member of Parliament after the 1996 general election. In addition at both there was loss of life, with the accidental deaths of two children, Joanna Hawke at Bastion Point and Judge Darcy Hayes at Pakaitore.

From December 1994 into February 1995 there was a mood of both anger and rejection in relationship to the government's proposals for the settlement of Treaty of Waitangi claims, the so-called 'fiscal envelope'.[33] Signs that Whanganui might become the focus for protest were evident by 20 December when the statue of Sir John Ballance in the Moutoa Gardens had a head and foot knocked off. The Māori rights action group, Te Ahi Kaa, claimed responsibility, saying Ballance was anti-Māori. Then in January 1995 Sir Hepi Te Heuheu called a hui at Hirangi which condemned the government proposals and may have acted as a signal for more radical groups to express their outrage in other ways. On 3 February the motorway north of Whanganui was barricaded with old refrigerators and whitewear by members of Te Ahi Kaa, to draw attention to long-standing grievances over Whanganui river lands and as a challenge to weekend holidaymakers to consider what Waitangi Day stood for. Celebrations at Waitangi on 6 February became a further opportunity for protest and defiance. The Crown representatives, including the Governor-General, were the recipients of verbal and gesticulated insults, generated by the government's Treaty settlement proposals, and prompting Court action and a decision to transfer official celebrations to Wellington in the future. At the same time Māori were coming to the conclusion that talk about partnership, consultation, and mutual regard were fine words but amounted to little if economic and political imperatives demanded otherwise. They too felt insulted.

At Whanganui meanwhile the repaired statue of John Ballance was again decapitated on 13 February and the mayor, Chas Poynter, expressed outrage on behalf of the city. On February 27, however, he was invited by telephone to attend a function at the Moutoa Gardens to celebrate 'Whanganuitanga', though at least as far as the timing was concerned it was more likely to have been a deliberate distraction from, or boycott of, the Crown's fiscal envelope hui being held further up the Whanganui River on 28 February. Certainly on the 27th some 150 Whanganui Māori established the Pakaitore marae at the gardens. Kaumatua Niko Tangaroa maintained then that they were there to celebrate Whanganuitanga, but when the mayor visited the marae later, he was advised that Māori wanted the return of the land and that the occupiers were simply exercising rights to use land which they already owned. Confusion between Poynter and the police about the terms of the occupation did not help. A poll of district councillors had shown strong support for settling the dispute by dialogue. However, there was also pressure from the community to take more decisive action and to prevent the incident from becoming another Bastion Point.

Regardless, by mid-March the situation had come to resemble Bastion Point in more ways than one. Construction of a substantial meeting house had begun and the occupiers showed signs of settling in for a long winter. Niko Tangaroa was adamant that the Māori occupiers were 'at the gardens to stay'. The mayor took a negotiating role himself and tried to convince the Māori protesters that the gardens belonged to the people of the district, not to Māori. He also made it clear that the council would not negotiate while the gardens were being occupied. Spokesman Ken Mair replied by saying iwi would not be bound by Pākehā law. In turn, Poynter, on behalf of the council, presented a five-point plan which proposed a trust, research into ownership by iwi and council, identification of other disputed sites, the resiting of offensive monuments, and a solution to be reached within the Whanganui community. Tangaroa reacted by shifting attention from Pakaitore and announcing that the plan would be discussed on marae throughout the area. The occupiers themselves, however, now demanded sovereignty over 33 590 hectares bordering the Wanganui River, from the mountains to the sea.

Mayor Poynter's five-point plan received considerable publicity. It also led barrister Christopher Harder to publish his own five-point plan to settle the Moutoa protest. In his version further fiscal envelope hui should be renamed Māori equality hui; the term Māori sovereignty should be replaced by the less provocative joint consensus; government should call a halt to all Crown land transfers for two years until an elected Māori Congress was sworn in; a longer Treaty claim repayment period, perhaps fifty years, should replace the emphasis on current affordability over ten years. Economic vision was needed and the development of an industry with billion dollar potential—fresh water fisheries—was recommended.[34]

The protest at Moutoa was about a village known as Pakaitore, used by Māori from up the river during the fishing season. After the establishment of the township Whanganui by settlers, Pakaitore remained a market-place and was still used by the tribes to sell produce when they visited the town even after 1900. It had been the site of the 1848 Whanganui sale agreement and from then was known as Moutoa Gardens. Later a monument was erected to commemorate Māori opposition to the Hauhau at a battle on the upriver island of Moutoa in 1864. Doubts about the ownership of the gardens had been expressed over the years, some Māori maintaining that it had never been included in the sale of Whanganui.[35]

When it was clear that the protesters at Pakaitore did not have the full backing of tribal elders, both the police and the district council entered into discussions with kaumātua from neighbouring marae. Of major concern to the Whanganui tribes was the resolution of long-standing grievances which had already been filed with the Waitangi Tribunal; they were keen to make progress with their claims and, as at Orakei, did not see the occupation as an advantage. Nor did they seriously entertain the thought that a show of force or defiance of the law would bring speedier results. Yet notwithstanding whatever reservations they had, and despite the Prime Minister's call for Māori leaders to speak out against the occupation, there was no outward rebuke of the occupiers from the elders. Pākehā sometimes saw the lack of condemnation by Māori leadership as a failure to take a responsible stand, though more likely it was an attempt not to inflame the situation or to give the council an opportunity to promote a divide-and-rule strategy. In fact, there were several meetings between Whanganui iwi and the protesters, but the issues they debated were more complex than simply law and order or the maintenance of good public relations. Instead, the focus was on relationships between hapū, iwi strategies, observance of tikanga, and the relative merits of various iwi claims. The occupiers always denied any iwi opposition to the occupation and in the long run the maintenance of reasonably clear lines of communication and goodwill between the occupiers and the kaumātua outside Pakaitore enabled the occupation to be concluded without force or loss of dignity—for anyone—including the council and the government. By resisting the Crown's invitation to condemn the occupation, the iwi had shown that it was possible to resolve disputes between Māori in a positive way.

Differences between the district council and central government also surfaced during the occupation but were not handled with as much diplomacy as Māori had shown. Early in April, Poynter made a request to the Prime Minister for the government to intervene, only to be told that it was a local government matter and should be dealt with at a local level. Meetings with the ministers of Māori Affairs and Justice had similar results. Central government sympathies had not been helped when it was revealed that Poynter had written to the police on Friday 28 April, saying that Māori could stay at the gardens for an indefinite period. Swayed by the apparent impotence of local government and the interest of the protesters in talking to government, New Zealand First MP Tau Henare suggested that Māori members of Parliament act as mediators in the dispute. His colleagues, however, were less enthusiastic. Representatives from Pakaitore were also now beginning to shift the focus of the protest from local to central government and met with the Speaker of the House, Peter Tapsell, to arrange a meeting with the Prime Minister. No meeting occurred but Minister in Charge of Treaty Settlements, Doug Graham, invited the protesters to write to him setting out the details of their claim.

Throughout the occupation, the police tried, with some success, to avoid provocation or intimidation. Even when the council served notice on March 22 that the gardens should be evacuated within seven days, Superintendent Waugh argued that all other methods should be tried before forced eviction. Nor did the March 25 bomb scare, which led to temporary evacuation, or supposed threats against the mayor precipitate police action. An equal problem for the police, however, was the control of community groups who were not satisfied with a wait-and-see policy. A memorial to Māori leader Major Kemp was cut down, apparently in retaliation for the decapitation of the John Ballance memorial. Then a protest outside Moutoa by the One New Zealand Foundation was intentionally provocative, and an Anzac Day procession of some 500 people marched past Moutoa to demonstrate against the Māori occupation. Organiser Brian Turner maintained it was not a race issue but a vote for law and order, though the march itself gave some impetus to the formation of a group known as 'One Wanganui', which was opposed to any action based on the Treaty of Waitangi. 'The Treaty is hardly relevant today because of our mixed blood.'[36] Christian groups took a more reconciliatory position, calling for calm and rational discussion. Methodist, Anglican, and Catholic clergy wrote to the occupiers begging forgiveness 'for our years of silence and ignorance concerning your hurts.'

By the end of March the number of Māori at the gardens increased to more than 400 and included Titiwhai Harawira, Mike Smith, and other veteran protesters. It also included disaffected Māori from various persuasions, and their presence posed some problems for the core protesters, who not only had to retain credibility with the tangata whenua, the Whanganui tribes, but now also with supporters who had quite different agendas. Led by Niko Tangaroa, Ken Mair, and Tariana Turia, a strong sense of purpose was maintained and even if at times the rationale for the occupation appeared to shift—from the fiscal envelope, to a celebration of Whanganuitanga, to the reclamation of Pakaitore, to wider sovereign rights—the clear message was one of self-determination and an impatience with the due process of the law.

When no response to the council plan had been received, High Court action was taken by the council, seeking clarification of ownership to the gardens. Tangaroa refused to recognise the authority of the court and, since the protesters did not want to be represented, Wanganui barrister John Rowan refused to take their case. 'They see this as a political matter rather than a legal matter.'[37] Wellington barrister Hugh Rennie was then appointed to act in the High Court case as an *amicus curiae* (friend of the court), an independent agent to communicate between the court and the occupiers. In the event the court found in favour of the Whanganui District Council, and after being served an eviction notice, the protesters marched off Pakaitore to stay at a local marae before disbanding. As required of them by the court, they also dismantled the makeshift buildings.

Whanganui iwi are still waiting for the the outcome of their claim to the Waitangi Tribunal, and it is unlikely that the Moutoa Gardens occupation will add credence to their case. But, as at Orakei, the occupation was proof that Māori who are not themselves involved in decision-making either with their own people or with the Crown will not be inclined to show infinite patience, or even respect for the law. The message is equally pertinent to the Crown and to tribes; unless all people are valued regardless of education, whakapapa (ancestry), wealth, or influence, they will be unlikely to show confidence in tribal or civic structures and will prescribe their own solutions even in the face of opposition from their own people.

Te Roroa

Once the jurisdiction of the Waitangi Tribunal had been extended back to 1840, by the 1985 amendment to the Treaty of Waitangi Act, claims against the Crown for land which had been unfairly alienated rapidly increased. Some claimed unfair pressure by Crown purchasing agents; others blamed the Māori Land Court; and a few contested the government's right to confiscate lands. The *Waiheke Island Report (Wai 10)*, the *Orakei Report (Wai 9)*, the report on

Ngāti Rangiteaorere (Wai 32), and the *Ngai Tahu Report (Wai 27)* were among the early cases and in each instance the Tribunal recommended the return of the land.

A particularly contentious claim concerned Te Roroa, a northern tribe who maintained that they had been unfairly deprived of several large blocks of land, some of which were now in private ownership. The Tribunal's *Te Roroa Report (Wai 32)*[38] caused considerable discussion and comment because it recommended that land owned by a private farmer be purchased by the Crown and returned to Te Roroa. Some politicians and Federated Farmers wanted the Tribunal's powers reduced so that it could not (again) recommend about land currently owned by private individuals.

In fact, the recommendation was based on sound argument. There was little doubt that Te Roroa had a valid claim and that only the land in question would right an injustice. The problem for the government was that it could not force the farmer, Alan Titford, who had bought the land in good faith and legally, to sell to the Crown. However, reducing the powers of the Tribunal, Māori argued, would not remove the injustice. And, in any event, the recommendation was just that: a recommendation for the Crown to consider. If the Crown were disinclined to implement it, for whatever reason, then the problem rested with the Crown, to be solved when circumstances permitted. In that process the Crown could take an active or a passive approach. Māori views were that the Tribunal should not be put in a position where it could not comment on injustices in relationship to the Crown and the Treaty. There was some sympathy for the farmer; but the disagreement was with the Crown and the issue was that land had been taken in breach of the Treaty.

The recommendation in the Te Roroa Report was: 'we recommend the return to tangata whenua of all the land which should have been set aside from Crown purchases of Maunganui, Waipoua, Waimamaku and Wairau lands.' In respect of Kahurau and Te Taraire lands, the recommendation was 'that the Crown take all steps to acquire these lands . . . which should not have been included in its purchases, and to return the same to tangata whenua as hapū estates.'

The Crown was left in a difficult position. It could not ignore the strength of the Tribunal recommendations, but neither could it forcibly reclaim the land from the private owner. To avoid similar circumstances in the future, it took steps to block the Tribunal from recommending on privately owned land by amending the Treaty of Waitangi Act. As well, the farmer who owned the land, and who was by then living in Tasmania, was paid $3.5 million for the 672-hectare property, which he had purchased for a fraction of the cost. Now in Crown ownership, part of the farm (of which 38 hectares are under Māori claim) will be returned to the Te Roroa people. Ironically, though maintaining that he had been run off the property by local Māori, Titford wanted to purchase back the farm from the Crown for the original cost, $800 000, less than a year after the Crown had purchased it from him.[39]

The Taranaki Claim

The claim of the Taranaki tribes to the Waitangi Tribunal was based on all three mechanisms to alienate Māori from their land: confiscation, aggressive government land purchasing strategies, and dubious decisions from the Native Land Court. The *Taranaki Report*, released in June 1996, covers 21 claims: five for Taranaki generally (the Taranaki Māori Trust Board, the Taranaki Iwi Katoa Trust, Ngā Iwi o Taranaki, the Paraninihi-ki-Waitotara Incorporation, and Taranaki Tribes); and the remainder for various kin groupings (Ngāti Tama, Ngāti Maru, Ngāti Mutunga, Te Ati Awa, Taranaki, Ngā Ruahine, Ngāti Ruanui, Tangahoe, Pakakohi, and Ngā Rauru).[40] Although described as an interim report (the Crown had yet to be heard on all matters), the Tribunal appeared confident that the report was sufficiently indicative to be used to expedite negotiations for a settlement.

When the war with the British troops began in 1860, there had already been 19 years of turmoil, with attempts to constrain settlers and fighting among Māori groups in response to the pressure to sell land. At the heart of the matter, though, was the confiscation of land following the 1860s wars. The Tribunal emphasised the long-standing nature of the Taranaki land conflicts. Although history suggests that the war continued for over nine years, military action on the government's part did not end till 1881 with the invasion of Parihaka. As a result of these conflicts, alienation and confiscation were extensive and severe: 1 199 622 acres were confiscated as punishment for the 1860s wars, with a further 296 578 acres illegally purchased, and 426 000 acres expropriated by land reform and the government's Native Land Court process, making 1 922 200 acres in all. Five categories of unjust alienation were described by the Tribunal: lands confiscated after 1860s war; early purchases in North Taranaki and Waitotara; land purchased in a hostile climate (1872–81); Ngāti Tama land wrongly awarded by the Native Land Court; land expropriated through court awards.

But the absolute amount of land taken was not seen as important as the impact of loss by reference to the proportion of land taken and the amount retained. Some hapū lost everything, others virtually everything, and no hapū had sufficient lands returned to provide even minimum relief. Using these measures, the Tribunal assessed the Taranaki land losses as the most severe in the country. Even after the wars, when hapū were promised lands for survival, none were returned and, when the government was pushed, some reserves were eventually defined but given over to administrators rather than to the owners.

Leases in perpetuity were then sold to settlers. Expropriation of land continued after the confiscations. Māori living away from Taranaki were excluded from an interest in land, and land was bought under such conditions that in terms of the Treaty it should be set aside. Imposed tenure reform was probably the most destructive and demoralising in that all land was put in individual titles, even reserves. The Tribunal concluded, 'This land reform, so clearly contrary to the Treaty, made alienations more likely, undermined or destroyed the social order, jeopardised Māori authority and leadership and expropriated the endowments to which hapū, as distinct from individuals, were entitled.'

The *Taranaki Report* was released before final conclusions could be made, and as a consequence recommendations are not made either, though the report itself will be a valuable starting point for both sides when negotiations with the Crown commence. Like the *Ngai Tahu Report*, the expectation of the Tribunal is that specific remedies will be determined jointly by the claimants and the Crown. Compensation for the impact of land loss, for social and economic destabil-isation, for personal injuries, and for current social and economic performance are regarded as important for a satisfactory resolution.

However, a warning is sounded by the Tribunal. Aware of the political deter-mination to negotiate settlements which are full and final, the report doubts that the present political frameworks for Treaty settlements will be able to do justice to the extent of tribal suffering, and cautions against requiring the tribes to sign for a full and final settlement when legal principles do not apply or must (perhaps of necessity) take second place to political expediencies. The Taranaki claim may be assessed in billions of dollars, yet it is highly likely that negotia-tions will be for a fraction of one billion dollars. The Tribunal urged the Crown to make a generous reparation and to seek a solution which will restore the people, remove prejudice, and prevent similar prejudice from arising again. 'If a full pay-off for the past on legal lines is impractical, and a massive sum would be needed in this instance, it is more honest to say so and to reconsider the juris-prudential basis for historical claims settlements. . . . Any requirement for tribal leaders to sign a full and final settlement which does not adequately recognise the extent of suffering would only serve to destabilise their authority.'

Direct negotiation with the Crown had not commenced before the 1996 general election, and there was some concern that the MMP parliamentary environment would complicate settlement negotiations. There were other com-plications as well. Unlike the Tainui and Ngai Tahu settlements, which in each case were negotiated by a single body (the Tainui Māori Trust Board and the Ngai Tahu Māori Trust Board, respectively) the Taranaki claim will be led by five or six groups, each with a mandate for certain hapū within Taranaki but without claiming to represent others. It will make for a more complex negotiating process and will challenge the Crown as much as Māori to maintain an overall sense of justice while avoiding a modern version of divide and rule. That had been a further consequence of the Taranaki land conflicts, and it would be ironic and of little comfort if a fragmenting process were repeated under the guise of a settlement. By 1997 three northern Taranaki tribes, Ngāti Tama, Ngāti Maru and Ngāti Mutunga, had their mandates to negotiate recognised by the Office of Treaty Settlements, but Te Ati Awa were unable to agree on a broadly based team which represented all hapū. Ngāti Ruahine and Ngā Rauru, on the other hand, were said to be close to seeking recognition of tribal mandates.[41]

Claims over Crown Land

Māori opposition to the State-Owned Enterprises Act 1986 stemmed from a fear that the Crown would divest itself of land and then not be in a position to honour Treaty claims, especially when land (rather than compensation) was required as a remedy. In the landmark Court of Appeal case in 1987, the court ordered the government to make provisions to safeguard Māori interests in Crown land for future Treaty settlements.[42] After discussions between the New Zealand Māori Council and the government, the Treaty of Waitangi (State Enterprises) Act 1988 was introduced, providing a mechanism whereby land sold by the Crown to a state-owned enterprise would carry a memorial, warning a purchaser that reversion to Crown ownership might be necessary in order to meet a Waitangi Tribunal order. Although the provision has never been implemented, it is important for three reasons. First, it represents a joint effort by Māori and the Crown at drafting legislation; second, the Act gave the Tribunal power to make a binding ruling in respect of land transferred to a state-owned enterprise; and third, it was the first of a series of protective mechanisms introduced between 1987 and 1994.

Because the restructuring of New Zealand Railways had commenced before the SOE Act was passed, surplus railways lands were not subject to the Treaty of Waitangi (State Enterprises) Act. Māori interest in the lands was high as many tribes had been required by law to give over their land to the Crown for railways development and, now they were no longer needed, there was good reason to expect that they would be returned. Railcorp had not foreseen the interest and feared that the sale process would suddenly be subject to litigation and lengthy delays. During 1991, however, the National Māori Congress and the Crown agreed on a clearance procedure for land no longer required by Railcorp. All surplus properties were scrutinised by a joint Congress–Crown research team, and tribes were invited to indicate a possible claim. If research showed there were no Māori interests in a particular site, the land was cleared for sale. If a claim were contemplated, disposal of the land was not to proceed until the claim had been settled.[43]

Considerable advantages to both Māori and the Crown were evident in this model: land was not sold into the private sector until iwi had the opportunity to systematically review each property, and for the Crown there was an avoidance of expensive litigation, enabling land to be cleared much more speedily and without expensive legal costs. In this way the surplus Auckland railway lands were cleared, Ngāti Whātua acquiring the Railway station.[44]

Despite the success of the Congress–Crown joint working party, the Minister of Justice was unhappy about the model and closed it down once the major railway properties had been cleared. He considered that too many properties had been the subject of a general claim, when the intention had been to identify specific claims, and he thought that Māori had misinterpreted their role.[45] In its place, and without wide consultation, he introduced another scheme to accommodate surplus Crown properties from almost all government departments, including health, education, social welfare, and defence. Known as the Consultative Clearance Process (CCP), the scheme was to be administered by the Department of Survey and Land Information (DOSLI) and applied to Crown land which was neither required for another public work nor constrained by any offerback provisions. The CCP did not apply to land owned by territorial authorities, land under the Crown Forest Assets Act, state-owned enterprises land, land transferred under section 206 of the Education Act, or land transferred under section 6 of the New Zealand Railways Corporation Restructuring Act 1990.

Under the CCP, DOSLI is obliged to notify iwi of Crown land intended for disposal so that they have a chance to give their views on any reasons for withholding sale. The time allowed for response is one month from public notification and assumes that a claim has already been lodged with the Waitangi Tribunal. Iwi views need to be based on the classification of land according to A, B, or C categories. Category A sites are essential to the settlement of a claim and recognise the importance of the land as having particular historical, cultural, or spiritual significance, such as burial sites. Category B sites are not essential to a claim but include lands which have special importance to a tribe such as lake beds, mountains, and river beds. Category C sites are not essential to a claim, nor of special tribal significance, but are lands particularly sought by claimants.

Māori have not been impressed by either the model or its outcomes. Even though there is provision for kaumātua participation, too much power is thought to be given to officials, who are able to decide on the merits of claims and the basis for iwi not clearing a particular site. A report from the Auditor-General confirms the small number of successful claims to prevent surplus Crown assets from being sold, at a time when additional Crown properties are needed for Treaty settlements. Up until July 1995, of the 1 194 properties advertised for sale, only 43 (four per cent) with an estimated value of $4.126 million, had been granted protection by Cabinet.[46] To that extent, Māori concern that the Crown will be unable to meet a 'land for land' policy when considering settlements appears warranted.

In anticipation of settlements, however, the Crown has used the CCP to hold strategic lands. The Crown Settlement Portfolio holds all surplus properties within confiscation (raupatu) boundaries; claim-specific landbanks hold land for a specific claimant; while regional land banks hold land where a claim-specific land bank has not been established, and the land falls outside a Crown Settlement Portfolio. As at 31 May 1996, the estimated values of land in the three groupings were thought to be in the order of $2 million (Crown Settlement Portfolio), $51 million (claim-specific landbanks) and $6 million (regional landbanks).

Māori Land Retention

Less than six per cent of New Zealand's land mass is Māori land. Table 5.5 shows the current extent and location of Māori land. It is not evenly distributed, and very little is in Te Wai Pounamu (where the Māori population is small), or for that matter in the Takitimu district (Hawke's Bay, where the Māori population is large). Because so little land remains, retention of existing holdings is of critical importance, and this was to become one of the prime objectives of Te Ture Whenua Māori, the Māori Land Act of 1993.

Table 5.5 Māori Land per District
(Hectares)

Māori Land District	Total Land Area (ha)	Total Māori Land (ha)	% of Māori Land
Tai Tokerau	1 592 842	139 873	8
Maniapoto	2 019 874	143 388	7
Waiariki	1 780 502	426 595	23.5
Tairawhiti	1 075 041	310 631	28
Takitimu	1 780 706	88 608	5
Aotea	1 180 967	334 207	28
Te Wai Pounamu	15 370 489	71 769	0.5

Source: Ministry of Māori Development 1996

Te Ture Whenua Māori Act 1993

Māori and government have had quite different views on the retention of Māori land, even in recent times. Contrary to the Treaty of Waitangi, for example, the Maori Affairs Amendment Act 1967, sponsored by the Hon. Ralph Hanan, made provision for Māori land to be converted to general land if held by not more than four joint owners. The jurisdiction of the Māori Land Court would be consequently reduced and land could be alienated with greater ease. Moreover, the Māori Trustee would be able to sell Māori lease lands to owners even if not all owners agreed. There was a predictable outcry from Māori and disillusionment that the government was still determined on assimilating Māori into a Pākehā-dominated mainstream.[47] The Hon. Matiu Rata had the Act repealed through the Māori Affairs Amendment Act 1974 but not before 96 000 hectares had been compulsorily converted to general land.

Following the 1975 Māori Land March, the establishment of the Waitangi Tribunal, and a clear Māori view that whatever land remained in Māori hands should be retained, Parliament began to rethink its Māori land policy. Minister of Māori Affairs, Duncan McIntyre, generally sympathetic to Māori aspirations, introduced a new Māori Affairs Bill in 1978, but in view of the continuing wide opposition by Māori it was subsequently withdrawn. The New Zealand Māori Council then asked for the chance to rewrite the bill and, somewhat to their surprise, McIntyre agreed. In 1983 the council published its proposals for a new bill and they were more or less accepted.[48] Ben Couch, now Minister of Māori Affairs, introduced the new Māori Affairs Bill, based on the New Zealand Māori Council proposals in 1983, but a change of government in 1984 led to the bill being withdrawn and additional parts added. However, they were never introduced. Instead Koro Wetere, the new minister, tabled an amended version of the bill in 1987 and it was referred to a Māori Affairs select committee for further submissions and marae hearings.

But another change of government in 1990 caused further delay, and it was not until 1992, when Doug Kidd was Minister of Māori Affairs, that it was returned to the House for a second reading. Known now as Te Ture Whenua Māori, a brief consultation round was conducted between December 1992 and February 1993 before it was enacted in 1993, some fifteen years after Macintyre's original bill and ten years after the New Zealand Māori Council had submitted proposals for new legislation.

The new Act represents a departure from the agenda of dispossession, alienation and fragmentation that had characterised the trend of Māori land law in the past. According to the Minister of Maori Affairs the Act was the first piece of major legislation framed according to what Māori have said they need. It was based on the Treaty of Waitangi and recognised that Māori land is a taonga tuku iho, an asset inherited from earlier generations. The purpose of the Act is to make sure that the owners of Māori land keep the land so it is passed on to future generations. In short, it has made Māori land more difficult to alienate. At the same time provision has been made for owners to make maximum commercial use of their land.

Among other provisions, five types of trust are available under Te Ture Whenua Māori Act 1993. Putea trusts are small, uneconomic interests pooled for the common benefit without individual dividends. They can be created to prevent further fragmentation and to assist cultural and social development, while at the same time retaining ownership of ancestral land. Whānau trusts are not dissimilar, preserving family links to particular land, tūrangawaewae, but without expectation of individual interests or dividends. Consent from all owners is required.

Ahu Whenua trusts are similar to section 438 trusts in the old Māori Affairs Act. They are intended to promote and facilitate the use and administration of the land in the interests of the owners. Whenua tōpu trusts are tribal trusts for the interests of an iwi or hapū, while kaitiaki trusts are available for persons under disability who are unable to manage their own land. As well as trusts, Te Ture Whenua Māori encourages the formation of incorporations, shareholders being the owners while day-to-day activities remain in the hands of an elected committee of management. Table 5.6 shows the number of land blocks subject to trusts, incorporations, or trust boards, under Te Ture Whenua Māori.

Table 5.6 Māori Land Structures

Structure	Number of Land Blocks	% of Total Area
438/Ahu whenua trusts	6 303	50
Whānau trusts	108	6
Kaitiaki trusts	8	0.01
Whenua topu trusts	10	2
Putea trusts	1	0
Incorporations	259	13
Trust boards	106	4
No clear structure	16 405	13
Other	1 129	2
Not described	1 307	4
Total	25 636	100

Source: Ministry of Māori Development 1996

The Act reaffirms Māori concepts of land ownership and represents a legal interpretation of whānau and hapū relationships and their joint interest in a particular piece of land. Its slow progress through Parliament suggested a reluctance to introduce legislation that would make it more difficult to alienate Māori land. In contrast the 1862 and 1865 Native Land Acts, which speeded up the process of land alienation, were passed with little delay, even though they were clearly contrary to the Treaty of Waitangi.

Under the 1993 Act, unlike the 1967 Act, it has now became easier for owners to change general land back to Māori freehold land, but some provision to convert Māori land to general land, under special circumstances, has also been retained. The Act recognises the important role of the Māori Land Court and allows for people other than judges to hear cases relating to tikanga Māori. There is also provision for lay members to be appointed to the Māori Appellate Court when a question of tikanga Māori has been referred to it by the High Court.

Under Te Ture Whenua Māori, owners of Māori land are not free to dispose of their interests as they might wish. If they intend to sell or if they die intestate, the first claim on their interests lies with 'preferred classes of alienees', usually other owners who have a traditional interest in a particular block of land by virtue of a common ancestor. Unless spouses are from the same hapū, they are only entitled to a life interest. Individual liberties to dispose of land interests have been traded off against the objective of retaining land for future generations.

Criticism of the Act is twofold. First, not all Māori individuals agree that their interest in Māori land should be confined to being a trustee for future generations. They argue that they have been denied the right to use land as an investment, or to sell it to the highest bidder, or to leave it to a spouse. In this sense the New Zealand Māori Council's ideological position (that Māori land does not belong to any individual, but to the whānau or hapū), may no longer find commonality with Māori who have become estranged from Māori values and beliefs or who have decided to act quite independently of their relatives or who place commercial objectives ahead of others. The Act, however, is explicit on the overriding purpose: '... to promote the retention of that land in the hands of its owners, their whānau and their hapū... .'

Second, there is some concern that the Act is not conducive to land development and that it falls short of meeting its second objective: '... to facilitate the occupation, development, and utilisation of that land... .' Despite assurances that the Act would allow wider management options for land,[49] there are concerns about the disincentives for commercial initiative, and the Māori Land Court has been accused of paternalism and over-caution. Judge Norman Smith, Deputy Chief Judge of the court, agrees that the judges are cautious but maintains that it is the Act, not the court, which is paternalistic. 'The Act is far more paternalistic than the 1953 Act and the Court must conform to the purpose of the Act which is to retain land.'[50] That indeed is what the New Zealand Māori Council intended although other national Māori bodies, including the Federation of Māori Authorities and the government-appointed Māori Land Investment Group are unhappy about the restrictions.

On some matters the Act is not always clear and there are some minor inconsistencies. Section 228 requires that no trustee can sell Māori land without consent from 75 per cent of the owners, while section 135 allows for Māori land to be converted to general land (and then to be sold) without 75 per cent agreement. And while section 276(7) states that all incorporations must file accounts with the Māori Land Court, it is uncertain whether the court has particular responsibilities thereby in terms of a management audit.

Māori Reserved Land Amendment Bill 1996

Perhaps the most glaring and ongoing injustice in the administration of Māori land can be found in the Crown's handling of Māori reserved lands. Following the large-scale land purchases of the nineteenth century by the government and the New Zealand Company, reserves were set aside for the original Māori owners. Others were established after confiscation, and when townships such as Rotorua and Te Kuiti were built on Māori land. Vested lands resulted from government investigations at the end of the nineteenth century and, like reserved lands, if government considered they were excessive to the needs of a tribe or that a tribe could not themselves manage the land, they were administered by the Crown in trust for Māori owners. Some were sold or used for Crown purposes but others were leased in perpetuity. By 1996 lands leased in perpetuity totalled 26 000 hectares with an estimated value of $200 million. The 2 236 leases included farmlands, commercial sites, and urban residential properties.[51]

In effect, Māori were denied access to their own lands and were seldom consulted about the terms of lease or the distribution of the benefits. It was another form of alienation. Rents were reviewed every 21 years, and the lease arrangements meant that lessees could expect to retain the land for ever, for themselves and their descendants. The 1955 Māori Reserved Land Act brought together some 43 statutes and set the rules for reserved lands on a national basis. Farm rents were fixed at 5 per cent of government valuation, and rent for residential land in towns was set at 4 per cent. Rents could be changed every 21 years (depending on up-to-date valuation) but tenants were given the automatic right of renewal. Lessees were favoured over owners, and the Māori Trustee was given powers to purchase lands for ongoing sale to lessees.

A 1975 Commission found that the Māori owners had been treated unfairly and recommended that rents be reviewed more often and according to a fairer formula. It also recommended that the administration of the lands (but not the powers to alter the terms of the leases) should be vested in incorporations established for the purpose. Reserved lands were brought a step closer to Māori control, but there was recognition that the nature of Māori land ownership had changed. Although original purchases were made from hapū, reserved lands were administered by regional organisations remote from hapū. In Taranaki the Paraninihi-ki-Waitotara Incorporation, established for that purpose, spelled an end to a direct interest in the land by hapū. Owners received rent but little else, and hapū interests were subsumed by the commercially driven policies of the incorporation, which included selling the land but not buying back leases. 'The reserve administration was an overt exercise in cultural displacement and racial subjugation.'[52]

In the face of increasing Māori exasperation, the government established a review team in 1991 to re-examine the 1975 recommendations and to hear submissions from owners and tenants. Their report was to become the basis for extensive discussions over the next five years.[53] Three main approaches were suggested by the review team. First they proposed a plan, extending over a possible 63 years, to bring the system to an end by enabling owners to resume ownership of the land and to buy back the improvements. The long lead time was considered necessary so as not to disadvantage the lessees. Second, they did not favour compensation for anyone, owners or lessees, and, third, they wanted to bring rents up to market rates and make them subject to seven-year reviews.

Between August and October 1993 a government-appointed panel led by Waitangi Tribunal member Judge Peter Trapski and including Georgina Kirby, a former President of the Māori Women's Welfare League, and Rob Cooper, an independent valuer from Ngāti Whātua, consulted with owners and lessees in seventeen areas which would be most affected by the proposed changes.[54] Neither owners or lessees were satisfied, though for different reasons. Māori owners were appalled by the 42–63 year delay before they could resume the rights of ownership and were unhappy that compensation, which could amount to millions of dollars, was not to be entertained. Overlooking the benefits of years of low rents and sometimes now speaking as if they were owners of the land, lessees were furious about proposed changes in rent (from 5 per cent to market rates) and also demanded compensation. And both parties were keen to know how rents would be fixed.

When the government released a report based on the recommendations of the panel, there were significant differences from the 1993 report.[55] Compensation of between 1.85 per cent and 2.9 per cent of the unimproved value of the land was to be paid to lessees for the loss of the perpetual right of renewal, but not to Māori owners, who could try and claim compensation through the Treaty claims process. On the other hand, a move to fairer rents would be introduced earlier; after a three-year delay market rents would be phased in over a four-year period and would then be reviewed every seven years. Farmers were vocal in their opposition to the proposed level of compensation and, having had the privilege of minimal rents, remained unhappy about having to pay the owners rents that reflected the true value of the land. Many cried disadvantage, although the purchase of a neighbouring lease for $800 000 by the chairperson of an association of lessees battling with the government over compensation did little to sway public sympathy in the lessees' favour.[56]

In 1996 the government tabled the Māori Reserved Land Amendment Act in Parliament. At pains to point out that the bill was not about a Treaty grievance but rather a relaxing of inappropriate government controls over a commercial relationship between Māori owners and lessees, the Minister of Māori Affairs, John Luxton, welcomed the bill as a 'landmark step towards resolving a long-standing inequitable relationship.'[57] The bill expanded the arrangements for compensation. It promised owners payments for the delay in moving rents to market levels, and lessees payments for the introduction of market rentals and more frequent rent reviews. Concerns by owners and lessees about compensation and the formula for setting the level led government to appoint an independent review panel, Dr T. Boyd, Mr R. W. Davison, and Mr R. G. Calvert, to provide an opinion to the Minister of Māori Affairs, who would refer it to the select committee. Compensation totalling $62 million was recommended, $20 million more than originally forecast in order to recognise 'justifiable but unquantifiable loss' in relation to the costs of more frequent rent reviews. Resolution of the legitimate complaint of lessors was seen to be as necessary as the provision of 'certainty' for lessees. But there was to be no compensation to lessors, other than through recourse to the Waitangi Tribunal. Deputy chairman of the Federation of Māori Authorities, Paul Morgan, was disappointed. The focus in terms of compensation had been on payments to lessees for the move to market rents and the phasing out of perpetual leases, and 'the Committee had not had the courage to recognise the owners' right to compensation.'[58]

From the outset, the Māori reserved lands policies reflected close collaboration between settlers and the government and their mutual determination that Māori land should be used by Pākehā in a productive manner. The government's bias, towards one group at the expense of the other, contributed as much as anything to the wider Māori perception of a system that was flawed to the point of being incapable of addressing Māori interests, let alone Māori values and beliefs. The eventual introduction of Te Ture Whenua Māori and the Māori Reserved Land Amendment Bill went some way to addressing that perception, even though they appeared when Māori land holdings had been reduced to less than six per cent of the total land mass.

Māori Land Development

Māori land development schemes were a hallmark of Sir Apirana Ngata's time as Native Minister from 1928 until 1934. Unlike his predecessor, Gordon Coates, Ngata's aims were not only to assist individual Māori farmers but also to use land development to create a sound economic base for tribes. It was a distinctive Māori viewpoint which went against the popular Pākehā perception of tribalism as a barrier to efficient agricultural productivity, and it was costly to Ngata in terms of parliamentary support.[59] But, by enlisting the support of tribal leaders, including Te Puea, he was able to demonstrate that Māori energies were stronger when a collective strategy was employed and when tribal aspirations were celebrated rather than contested. Unfortunately the Department of Māori Affairs lost some of Ngata's philosophy and, especially from 1945, played an increasingly paternal role with respect to Māori. That was nowhere more obvious than in the management of land and the conviction that departmental officers could bring about greater efficiencies than the owners. As it happened, the departmental advice received was often second-rate, and the farm management policies adopted by the department were costly without necessarily leading to improved productivity.

During the wind-down of the Department of Māori Affairs in the 1980s, many of the large land blocks which had been administered by the department for thirty or more years were returned to the owners. As Minister of Māori Affairs when devolution was introduced, Koro Wetere recognised the importance of whānau and hapū working and managing their land themselves and hastened the hand-back process. By then, however, urbanisation and a move away from agricultural vocations had depleted the level of Māori expertise as far as land development was concerned. It was apparent that a sustained focus on the many aspects of modern development would be necessary, especially with the prospect of additional lands being returned through Treaty of Waitangi claims, without developmental funding attached. Larger tribes with extensive land holdings had less difficulty, but all experienced a similar range of problems: coping with a large number of owners, obtaining developmental financing, gaining accurate information about the land, acquiring the necessary expertise, and working within an imperfect law.

Table 5.7   Obstacles to Māori Land Development

Problem	Implication
Large numbers of owners	Need for better communication systems and strategies to involve dormant owners
Difficulty obtaining developmental funding	Need for new arrangements with finance lending bodies
Inadequate land information	Information systems that will link land profiles with iwi, hapū, and whānau development
Low levels of expertise	Education relevant to the sector
Legal restraints	Amendments to Te Ture Whenua Māori Act

Fragmentation of title has been an obstacle for land development for decades, and various remedies have been attempted including amalgamation of title, incorporations, trusts, compulsory purchase of uneconomic shares, individualisation of title, and conversion to general land. But the large number of owners in single blocks, many of whom are unaware they are owners, makes it extremely difficult to reach decisions about land development. It would be easier if land titles were accompanied by up-to-date records of owners or if dormant owners were advised of their interests, but in the meantime the effort of trying to reach distant or even non-existent owners is out of proportion to the wider task. Computerised Māori Land Court records may help.

Limited access to developmental funding is a further problem. As government funding has declined, including Rural Bank loans, Māori land-owners have turned to the private sector for assistance. In 1994 the Māori Congress and a commercial bank, Westpac, established Aotearoa Financial Services to address the needs of Māori incorporations and large-scale ventures who wanted to borrow money for economic development. Other banks have made similar moves, though not without reservations about lending against Māori land. Because Te Ture Whenua Māori prohibits alienation of land, banks will not be able to seize the asset if it is land, nor can they count on hapū and whānau to find funds from other sources. On the other hand, the developmental prospects for many lands are sound and there are opportunities as well as risks. Links with overseas financial institutions are another option. When the so-called Hawaiian loans affair was publicised by Winston Peters in 1987, government warned against international money markets and many Māori backed away. But a number of financiers in other countries appear less frightened of indigenous development than the cautious New Zealand lenders, and some innovative arrangements have been made with Māori. However, of particular concern is the limited availability of funds to smaller land holders, either within New Zealand or overseas.

Māori landowners, meanwhile, are becoming dissatisfied with a lack of representation on agriculture producer boards, especially the Meat and Wool Boards, despite paying levies. Most boards are made up of non-Māori. In a submission to the primary production select committee Paul Morgan of the Federation of Māori Authorities warned that, unless there were provision for Māori representation, the already established Māori Exporters Council might be a better option. In any case the one-farm one-vote system disadvantaged the very large Māori runholding incorporations and did little to convince Māori farmers that they were getting value for their levies.[60]

Developmental finance and higher returns from exports are not the only concerns relevant to the better utilisation of Māori land. Information has become an equally significant issue. In order to provide improved information systems, Te Puni Kōkiri has been developing a national Māori land data base.[61] Using a geographic information system and Māori Land Court records, regional offices of the ministry have been able to complete summary forms for each current block of Māori freehold land, including information on how the land is administered.[62] Widespread Māori interest in better information systems was evident at the Conference on Geographic Information Systems (GIS) for Māori in 1996. The new computerised technology enables tribes to gain a comprehensive picture of land in relationship to other social and economic priorities and to focus more imaginatively on land use patterns. Links between land, demography, loans, markets, legislation, and policies can be brought together as a sound basis for developmental planning. GIS would have made important differences to Tainui during Treaty negotiations with the Crown; still, it now holds promise as an aid to more efficient utilisation of the tribal land base in a context which is consistent with iwi and hapū plans.[63]

As with other sectors, low levels of Māori expertise in agriculture and horticulture, as well as financial planning and management, are an impediment to speedy development. Some progress since 1984 has been made, and developments at Tuhono near Rotorua and Whakatu near Nelson demonstrate the effectiveness of collective Māori action. But a highly developed professional Māori workforce has yet to emerge in sufficient strength to convert hopes and aspirations across the tribes into economically viable schemes. One implication is that, for some time yet, iwi will have to rely on non-Māori to provide the necessary expert advice and planning. At the most, that should be seen as a temporary measure and should not be a signal for Māori to limit their direct involvement in land development to manual roles, no matter how expert they might be as shearers, fencers, or stockmen. Most tribes are now keen to train their own people as leaders in agricultural, forestry, and horticultural development, and expect greater numbers to enter tertiary education at polytechnics, wānanga, and universities. Partnership with educational institutions has accelerated the process. Te Arawa, for example, have signed an agreement with the Waiariki Polytechnic and Massey University to provide courses in agriculture and horticulture for their own people. Under the agreement, students will be able to complete the first year of a Bachelor of Applied Science degree at Rotorua (in the polytechnic) and will then be guaranteed a position in the second-year university courses. Opportunities for postgraduate work and research are also part of the agreement.[64]

Inadequacies in the legislation have been noted by several Māori groups, including the Māori Land Investment Group (MLIG), established by the Ministry of Māori Affairs in 1995. They consider that Te Ture Whenua Māori Act limits the effective utilisation and development of multiple-owned Māori land because of the current provisions for organisational governance, management structures, decision-making frameworks, financing options, and the discretionary powers awarded the Māori Land Court.[65] In the group's opinion, the court is too involved in the economic utilisation decision-making and an investigation into its role and discretion has been recommended.[66] They have also concluded that Māori land should be available to owners to use as mortgage security, if they so wish—a step that would require legislative amendment. But the exclusive focus on financial arrangements has been at the expense of addressing the other main aim of the Act which is to make Māori land inalienable. Instead the MLIG implies that the two goals are incompatible.

Working with the MLIG is another national Māori organisation established in 1985 as a forum for Māori incorporations and other organisations. The Federation of Māori Authorities (FOMA) is a business network of over one hundred Māori resource-based businesses whose main objectives are to encourage active and economic business development and to provide professional and commercial services to members. The federation has had a strong influence on land policy and has also contributed to shaping legislation, including the Māori Reserved Land Amendment Bill and Te Ture Whenua Māori Act. FOMA accepts that its commercial imperatives sometimes clash with social objectives and takes pride in having eliminated the 'socialist dangers' in the bill before Te Ture Whenua Māori was enacted.[67]

Although iwi control and private sector funding are important features of contemporary Māori land development, the Treaty of Waitangi does not excuse government from an ongoing role; clearly not the paternalistic role which strangled Māori initiative in the past, but one which at least commits some Crown resources to future development in a cooperative way. Te Puni Kōkiri has identified pre-commercial facilitation as an appropriate area for Crown involvement: the provision of guidance, assistance and resources, and the coordination of services, by both the public and private sectors, in support of the sustainable development of Māori land. Business development boards, community employment groups, Trade NZ, and the Māori Land Court all have some responsibilities in the area, but there is a lack of coordination and there are gaps in service provision such as trustee training, business planning, and an adequate monitoring framework for analysing Māori land development.

Māori land is important for economic development but, more than that, remains a cornerstone for Māori identity and a sense of continuity with the past. Although there are thousands of Māori who can claim ownership (in part) over blocks of Māori land, there is also evidence than many Māori have been totally alienated from a customary land base. The longitudinal study of Māori households, Te Hoe Nuku Roa, reveals that in the Manawatu–Whanganui, Wellington, and Tairawhiti regions more than one-third of Māori adults have no access to Māori land, nor do they receive any financial benefits from it. Almost half as many again do not know whether they have land entitlements at all.[68] A challenge for the future will be to repatriate all Māori people so that being Māori makes real sense, not only in cultural terms but also in having a place to call home, tūrangawaewae. There is otherwise the risk that Māori will be divided into land-owning and landless categories, a short step from status and non-status. Nor is it helpful to heap blame on the landless themselves for not being more vigilant in keeping the fires burning or to accept that Treaty land settlements are just if they simply confirm the position of those who already have title to land. Although the policies, legislation, and practices of successive governments have conspired to separate Māori from their land, Māori land still remains. The task now is to extend the holdings, develop them, and make connections between people and the land, so that future generations may come to experience first hand the nurturance of Papatuanuku.

NOTES FOR CHAPTER 5

1 'My lands have gone; My rights have disappeared; Love has become cold, The rich become fatter; While the poor have become leaner.' Excerpt from a haka composed by Kingi Ihaka, in Witi Ihimaera and D. S. Long (eds), *Into the World of Light: An Anthology of Maori Writing*, Heinemann, Auckland, pp. 24–26.

2 Quoted by George Asher, David Naulls, (1987), *Māori Land*, Planning Paper No. 29, New Zealand Planning Council, Wellington.

3 W. H. Oliver, (1988), 'Social Policy in New Zealand: An Historical Overview', in *The April Report*, Vol. 1, Royal Commission on Social Policy, Wellington, pp. 6–8.

4 Waikato Raupatu Claims Settlement Act 1995.

5 Asher and Naulls, *Māori Land*, pp. 10–11.

6 E. T. Durie, (1994), *Custom Law, A Discussion Paper*, Waitangi Tribunal, Wellington.

7 Douglas Sinclair, (1975), 'Land: Māori View and European Response', in Michael King (ed.), *Te Ao Hurihuri: The World Moves On*, Hicks Smith, Wellington, pp. 118–121.

8 E. T. Durie, (1994), *Custom Law*.

9 Ranginui Walker, (1987), 'Maori Myth Tradition and Philosophic Beliefs', in Jock Phillips (ed.), *Te Whenua te Iwi: The Land and the People*, Allen and Unwin, Wellington, p. 43.

10 Waitangi Tribunal, (1997), *Muriwhenua Land Report (Wai 45)*, GP Publications, Wellington, p. 108.

11 Asher and David Naulls, *Māori Land*, Appendix 1.

12 Harold Miller, (1966), *Race Conflict in New Zealand 1814–1865*, Blackwood & Janet Paul, Auckland, pp. 5–6.

13 G. V. Butterworth, (1990), *Maori Affairs*, GP Books, Wellington, pp. 123–124.

14 Miller, *Race Conflict in New Zealand*, p. 15.

15 Alan Ward, (1973), *A Show of Justice: Racial Amalgamation in Nineteenth Century New Zealand*, Auckland University Press & Oxford University Press, Auckland, pp. 92–95.

16 M. P. K. Sorrenson, (1981), 'Maori and Pakeha', in W. H. Oliver (ed.), *The Oxford History of New Zealand*, Oxford University Press, Wellington, pp. 174–175.

17 Waitangi Tribunal, (1996), *The Taranaki Report Kaupapa Tuatahi (Wai 143)*, GP Publications, Wellington.

18 Sorrenson, (1981), 'Maori and Pakeha', pp. 180–182.

19 Jane Luiten, (1992), *An Exploratory Report Commissioned by the Waitangi Tribunal on Early Crown Purchases Whanganui ki Porirua, Wai 52, 88, 108, 113, 182, 207, 265, 287*, Waitangi Tribunal, Wellington.

20 E. T. J. Durie, (1979), *Submission to the Royal Commission on the Māori Land Courts*, No. 11, Wellington.

21 Asher and Naulls, *Māori Land*, p. 29.

22 E. T. J. Durie (1979), *Submission . . . on the Māori Land Courts*.

23 Waitangi Tribunal, (1987), *The Waiheke Claim (Wai 10)*, Waitangi Tribunal, Wellington.

24 M. P. K. Sorrenson, (1965), 'The Politics of Land', in J. G. A. Pocock (ed.), *The Māori and New Zealand Politics*, Blackwood and Janet Paul, Auckland, pp. 40–41.

25 Section 17 required the compilation of a list of each and every member of the tribe to be recorded separately on a memorial entered in the records of the Court.

26 Waitangi Tribunal, (1987), *Orakei Report (Wai 9)*, Department of Justice, Wellington, p. 153.

27 Rapata Wiri, (1966), 'Land Alienation at Waikaremoana', *He Pukenga Kōrero*, 1, 2, 48–60.

28 John Delamere, *Mana News*, Radio New Zealand, 31 October 1996.

29 Michael King, (1983), *Whina: A Biography of Whina Cooper*, Penguin Books, Auckland, pp. 212–222.

30 Ranginui Walker, (1990), *Ka Whawhai Tonu Matou: Struggle Without End*, Penguin, Auckland, pp. 215–219.

31 King, (1983), *Whina*, pp. 229–231.

32 Waitangi Tribunal, (1987), *Orakei Report (Wai 9)*, Department of Justice, Wellington, pp. 106–118.

33 The Government's proposals are discussed in detail in chapter 7.

34 *Sunday Star Times*, 26 March 1995.

35 *The Dominion*, Saturday 15 April 1995.

36 *Evening Standard*, Thursday 27 April 1995.

37 *The Dominion*, Tuesday 25 April 1995.

38 Waitangi Tribunal, (1992), *Te Roroa Report (Wai 38)*, Waitangi Tribunal, Wellington.

39 'Graham says Titford can't buy back farm', *The Dominion*, Tuesday 21 January 1997.

40 Waitangi Tribunal, (1996), *The Taranaki Report*.

41 'Taranaki tribes recognised', *The Dominion*, Friday 22 November 1996.

42 The SOE case is discussed in chapter 7.

43 Crown Congress Joint Working Party, (1991), *Information Brief for Iwi Arrangements in Respect of Surplus Crown Railway Properties and Treaty of Waitangi Claims*, Crown Congress Joint Working Party, Wellington.

44 Though plans to convert the Auckland Railway Station into a casino were blocked when the licence was awarded to the Brierleys-backed Sky City, the property remains a substantial tribal asset.

45 Carol Archie, (1995), 'Doug Graham', in *Māori Sovereignty: The Pakeha Perspective*, Hodder Moa Beckett, Auckland, pp. 118–120.

46 D. J. D. Macdonald, (1995), *The Settlement of Claims Under the Treaty of Waitangi*, Second report for 1995, Controller and Auditor-General, Wellington, p. 40.

47 Butterworth, *Māori Affairs*, pp. 105–106.

48 New Zealand Māori Council, (1983), *Te Wahanga Tuatahi – Kaupapa*, NZMC, Wellington.

49 Te Puni Kōkiri, (1993), *Newsletter Special*, March 1993, Ministry of Māori Development, Wellington.

50 *Marae*, Television New Zealand, Channel One, Sunday 16 November, 1966.

51 Hugh Barlow and Alison Tocker, (1996), 'Government moves to right Māori land injustice', *The Dominion*, Tuesday 6 August 1996.

52 Waitangi Tribunal, (1996), *The Taranaki Report*, pp. 269–271.

53 Review Team, (1993), *A Framework for Negotiation Toitū te Whenua*, Te Puni Kōkiri, Wellington.

54 'Reserved Lands Hearings Underway', *Newsletter*, Te Puni Kōkiri Ministry of Māori Development, (1993), no. 14, p. 7.

55 Hon. John Luxton, Hon. Dennis Marshall, (1994), *Toitū te Mana Toitū te Whenua Māori Reserved Lands: Government Policy Decisions 1994*, Te Puni Kōkiri, Wellington.

56 Hugh Barlow, (1996), 'Campaigner buys another lease', *The Dominion*, Monday 19 August 1996.

57 'Maori reserved land Bill introduced', *Te Maori News*, Hepetema 1996, pp. 1, 10.

58 'Report lists $62m tag on Maori land', *The Dominion*, Saturday 15 February 1997.

59 Butterworth, *Māori Affairs*, pp. 74–75.

60 Alison Tocker, (1997), 'Maori exporters want more say', *The Dominion*, Tuesday 27 May 1997.

61 'Ministry sees exciting potential in national Māori land database', *Newsletter*, Te Puni Kōkiri Ministry of Māori Development, Wellington, 1996.

62 Te Taru White, Glenn Webber, (1996), *A National Māori Land Data Base*, paper presented at the Maaori Geographic Information Systems Conference, Wellington.

63 Wayne Taitoko, (1996), *Preparation is Everything Information is Power: A Tainui Perspective*, Maaori Geographic Information Systems Conference, Wellington.

64 'One man's vision opens door to educational opportunities for iwi', *Newsletter*, Te Puni Kōkiri, Ministry of Māori Development, (1994), no. 25, p. 7.

65 Māori Land Investment Group, (1996), *Securing Finance on Multiple-owned Māori Land*, Te Puni Kōkiri, Wellington.

66 *ibid.*

67 Federation of Māori Authorities, (1996), *Report of the Executive to the 9th Annual General Meeting of the Federation, Whanganui*, Federation of Māori Authorities, Wellington.

68 Te Hoe Nuku Roa, (1996), *Reports on the Manawatu–Whanganui, Tairawhiti, Wellington Regional Baseline Surveys*, Department of Māori Studies, Massey University.

6

MANA MOANA

THE BUSINESS OF FISHING

Kia timata ra ano te hiku o te ika i te akiaki,
i te upoko o te ika katahi ano ka tika te haere.[1]

Until the passage of the Fisheries Amendment Act in 1986 and the introduction of a quota management system for fishing stock, there had been little public discussion on the ownership of fisheries. However, the Act created a property right that had been appropriated by the Crown without consultation and without consideration that others might have prior claims. In a series of court cases and Waitangi Tribunal hearings Māori successfully challenged the government and eventually dispelled the widely held views that customary Māori usage was confined to subsistence fishing interests and that the Treaty of Waitangi was about freezing Māori in an 1840 time warp.

Even though the Treaty of Waitangi, especially the English version, guaranteed Māori the 'full exclusive and undisturbed possession of their Lands and Estates Forests Fisheries and other properties,'[2] by 1866 there were already signs that a much narrower view of Māori fishing rights was being adopted. The Oyster Fisheries Act 1866 was the first fish law in New Zealand. It provided for the leasing of oyster beds for commercial purposes but made no specific provisions for Māori apart from not allowing them to sell oysters from their own reserves until 1874, by which time it was anticipated that they would have 'acquired other tastes.'[3]

It was surprising, therefore, that the Fish Protection Act of 1877, the first comprehensive fisheries control measure, recognised the Treaty. Apart from purporting to recognise Māori rights, section 8 is interesting because it refers to the provisions of the Treaty rather than the principles: 'Nothing in this Act shall be deemed to repeal, alter or affect any of the provisions of the Treaty of Waitangi. . . .' However, in all other respects the Act was a gross negation of the guarantees in the Treaty and assumed that Māori fishing rights (though not explicitly defined) were limited in some way. The purpose of the Act was to regulate the general fish resource, and in so doing it assumed that the public was entitled to exploit it, and Māori interests would not encroach upon it.

By the time of the Sea Fisheries Act 1884, reference to the Treaty had been omitted altogether and the limitation of Māori rights was explicit. In forbidding the sale of oysters from beds reserved for Māori, there was token acknowledgment of Māori interests, but in a way which reduced them to subsistence levels: 'Provided that when shellfish in the Middle Island are required as an article of food by the aboriginal native population they shall be exempt from the operations of this Act.' In 1903, Māori fishing rights were provided for in the Sea Fisheries Amendment Act but never defined: 'Nothing in this Act shall affect any existing Maori fishing rights.' By then the association of Māori fishing interests with small-scale subsistence rights was complete, at least in the mind of the Crown, and remained that way until 1986.

Various subsequent Acts such as the Native Purposes Act 1937 and the Maori Social and Economic Advancement Act 1945 provided for fishing reserves, but within the context of limited, non-commercial interests, and mostly in respect of shellfish. Major changes to fishing laws, however, were introduced in the sweeping Fisheries Act 1983. Serious overfishing of the inshore fisheries could be traced back to 1963, when restrictions on licensing had been removed, and the government had introduced new policies to provide for major fishing expansion. Large operators were rapidly depleting the supplies and within two decades it was apparent that new conservation measures were needed, quite urgently. The 1983 Act was the result. It was a consolidation and reform of the law relating to the management and conservation of fisheries and fishery resources and included, though without any clear definition, section 88(2): 'Nothing in this Act shall affect any Maori fishing rights.' It appears that the legislators were simply assuming, as their predecessors had done, that Māori rights were synonymous with personal needs, gathering shellfish for the family, or small-scale catches of fin fish for customary purposes. Section 28 of the Fisheries Amendment Act 1986 was more specific: 'The Minister may, after allowing for the Maori, traditional, recreational and other non-commercial interests in the fishery, specify the total allowable catch to be available for commercial fishing for each quota management area in respect of each species or class of fish subject to the quota management system.' Clearly Māori interests had been categorised as non-commercial, and the Crown would now be able to lease fishing quota without considering Māori further.

MĀORI FISHING PRACTICES

In contrast to later generations, early European settlers were amazed at Māori fishing exploits, and the *Muriwhenua Fishing Report* contains evidence of the scale of customary fishing practices as well as the sophisticated technology and commercial motivation.[4] For example, Joseph Banks, a botanist on board the *Endeavour*, described a net measuring 700–900 metres, while L. J. Nicholas in a record dating back to 1814 concluded that 'Their nets are much larger than any that are made use of in Europe.'[5] The scale of fishing was also noted by early explorers and settlers, and R. H. Mathews has left a graphic description of a massive operation in 1855 during which over 7000 sharks were caught, 265 on one canoe alone.[6] Fish trading followed with other tribes and with early settlers, evidence that Māori fishing interests were commercial in nature, even before the Treaty of Waitangi.

Fishing sites were well known to local fishermen. Several hundred fishing grounds in the Taitokerau alone were named and identified in detail, up to 25 miles out to sea. Each fishing ground was located by cross bearings from the land and was associated with particular species of fish and the times of the year when fishing was best.[7] Muriwhenua fishermen worked the whole of the inshore seas (twelve miles from shore) and even beyond.

Emerging from the detailed *Muriwhenua Fishing Report* was a redefinition of customary Māori fishing activities, away from the depiction of a subsistence interest in fishing, widely promulgated by the state, to a representation of fishing as a mainstay of the economy, at least in the far north, and having much in common with commercial and business practices. Evidence reviewed by the Tribunal confirmed that the Māori economy depended to a large extent on fishing, and fishing activities covered most of the continental shelf, utilising the most advanced technology available at the time. One fishing ground was located 48 miles from shore. Ownership of fisheries was determined along tribal lines, fishing grounds being apportioned to at least one Muriwhenua hapū or tribe. Fishing was a commercial venture; tribes depended on the products of an aquatic economy that was essential to survival and well-being, and when early settlers arrived, trading was extended to their villages. The Tribunal findings were to become crucial in the negotiations that soon took place between Māori and the Crown, and they played a major role in reversing the Crown's appreciation of the extent of Māori fishing rights. Moreover, in moving from a subsistence to a commercial framework, it became abundantly clear that the quota management system, when it was first introduced, was the very antithesis of the guarantees of the Treaty of Waitangi.

THE QUOTA MANAGEMENT SYSTEM

By 1980 overfishing of inshore fish stocks threatened the industry, and new measures were needed to manage the fisheries and protect the rapidly diminishing supplies. The quota management system introduced in 1986 was promoted as a conservation and management tool and gave fishermen who had purchased quota from the Crown the right to catch the total amount of any species that might be safely caught in any area at any time. Individual Transferable Quotas (ITQs) allowed for trading of quotas, which could be transferred by sale, lease, or licence. However, no regard for customary fisheries was made, and small and part-time fishermen were disadvantaged. Fishermen whose catch returns were under a specified amount or whose income was mainly from other sources had their licences removed, and between 1984 and 1985 nearly 300 fishermen in Northland lost their licences, an outcome that contributed to the escalating poverty in that region.

Because quotas were expensive and could be held in perpetuity, small businesses were disadvantaged. But, more significantly, the scheme had created a property interest in an exclusive right of commercial fishing. Tribunal concerns about quota management policy proposals had been raised in the Manukau Report (1985), but under the Act Māori interests were grouped along with other non-commercial users, including recreational users, though they were also still recognised in section 88(2) of the 1983 Act ('Nothing in this Act shall affect any Maori fishing rights'). Tom Te Weehi had discovered that the section was not inconsequential. In 1986 the High Court quashed a District Court conviction for taking 46 undersized paua, concluding that Te Weehi was exercising a customary right and that other provisions of the Act did not affect his right to take paua.[8]

But the *Te Weehi* decision did not hinge on the Treaty of Waitangi, nor did it offer any comfort to the Muriwhenua claimants who considered that their fisheries, including the right to fish commercially, should stand outside the quota management system on the grounds that the Treaty secured to them the fisheries of Muriwhenua. The Ministry of Agriculture and Fisheries was caught somewhat unprepared when, in December 1986, the Waitangi Tribunal first cautioned that the quota management system could be inconsistent with the Treaty of Waitangi and that no quotas should be issued until the Tribunal had had the chance to report. By way of response the Director-General of Fisheries advised that the request for delay (in implementing the quota management system) could not be acceded to.[9] In thus capitulating to the fishing industry, the ministry bought a lengthy legal battle with Māori and was acting against the Tribunal's conclusion that 'the [quota management] system we find is in fundamental conflict with the Treaty's principles, apportioning to non-Māori the full exclusive and undisturbed possession of the property in fishing that to Māori was guaranteed.' But the Tribunal added the QMS need not be in conflict if an agreement could be reached: 'It appears that Māori interests could be accommodated within it.'[10]

A further report which examined Māori fishing rights was prepared by the Law Commission in 1989.[11] Acknowledging that neither the law or past government policies gave adequate recognition to Māori interest in fisheries, particularly sea fisheries, the commission noted that governments have tended to decide Māori fishing claims on the basis of English rules, principles, and priorities, without giving Māori views full weight. The law regarding Māori fishing interests was uncertain enough that any solution should take the form of negotiated settlements ratified by legislation.

Just how unjust some laws were, however, was the subject of another Waitangi Tribunal report, in August 1992.[12] The second part of the Ngai Tahu claim was related to fisheries, and the Tribunal found that Ngai Tahu were prejudicially affected by the various acts and omissions, policies, and statutes of the Crown relating to their sea fisheries. These breaches were inconsistent with the principles of the Treaty of Waitangi. A further serious breach was the assumed right of the Crown to dispose of Māori fisheries without consent or consultation with the iwi, as if the fisheries were Crown property. The report was critical of the quota management scheme for its effect on Ngai Tahu Treaty rights.

At the time it attracted a great deal of attention, partly because the media had confused Tribunal findings with Tribunal recommendations. In the Ngai Tahu case, the Tribunal finding was that Ngai Tahu had an exclusive Treaty right to the sea fisheries surrounding the whole of their coastline to a distance of twelve miles or so but not 100 per cent of all sea fisheries off their boundaries. On the other hand, the Tribunal's recommendations proposed a solution to the Ngai Tahu sea fisheries grievance through a negotiated settlement, which should include an additional percentage of quota to Ngai Tahu under the quota management system delivered through the Māori Fisheries Act 1989. As far as noncommercial fisheries were concerned, the Tribunal recommended the return to Ngai Tahu of exclusive eel fishing rights in Waihera (Lake Ellesmere) and a change to the Fisheries Act 1983 to provide for certain mahinga kai reserves for iwi or hapū (as proposed in the Sustainable Fisheries Report of the Ministerial Task Force, April 1992). Importantly, though the point was misunderstood by the media, the Tribunal did not recommend that most of the South Island fisheries be handed over to Ngai Tahu or that all the fisheries within twelve miles of the coast be returned to Ngai Tahu.

Well before the Tribunal and Law Commission Reports, however, Māori had turned to the courts to seek justice and to protest against their exclusion from the QMS. By the time the *Muriwhenua Fishing Report* was released, a Māori challenge to the system was under way in the High Court.

NEGOTIATIONS BETWEEN MĀORI AND THE CROWN

Court action to block the quota management system was initiated by several tribes in 1987. Along with the New Zealand Māori Council, Te Rūnanga o Muriwhenua petitioned the High Court for a restraining order to prevent the Minister of Fisheries from issuing fishing quotas. Justice Grieg found in favour of the Māori plaintiffs and issued an order to 'stop any further action.'[13] Similarly the Ngai Tahu Māori Trust Board, Raukawa Marae Trustees, Taranaki Māori Trust Board, Taitokerau District Māori Council, and Tainui Māori Trust Board all sought a further injunction to prevent the minister from issuing quotas for squid, Jack mackerel, rock lobster, paua, and eel. Again Justice Grieg ordered the minister not to lease further quotas, in effect bringing the system to a halt.[14]

A stalemate had developed, and, in an attempt to solve the impasse, a Joint Working Group on Maori Fisheries was established. Tipene O'Regan, Matiu Rata, Robert Mahuta, and Sir Graham Latimer, representing claimants who had taken action in the High Court, were invited to join Crown representatives to seek solutions. The expectation was that the group would make definitive recommendations by September 1988. However, talks were hampered, partly because the Māori team was not confidently able to act on behalf of all tribes or all Māori. In order to speak with a greater authority, they needed a stronger indication of the level of Māori support. A national hui at the Takupuwahia marae, near Wellington, in June 1988, mandated the Māori fisheries negotiators with securing a just and honourable settlement of fisheries claims and instructed them to settle for not less than 50 per cent of the quota. The figure of 50 per cent was a consensus view not a unanimous one. At the hui, many tribes, giving a literal interpretation to 'the full exclusive and undisturbed possession of their . . . fisheries. . . .' maintained that the Treaty gave tribes a right to 100 per cent of the fishing quota; settling for only half was unnecessarily generous to the Crown. But the moderate view prevailed and 50 per cent became the accepted target. Predictably the fishing industry, far from being impressed by Māori generosity, was scathing in their disbelief that a Treaty right could still be used as the basis for contemporary commercial advantage. But the Māori negotiators were able to return to the bargaining table with a clearer mandate and a definite brief.

The government, however, though unimpressed by the Māori claims for 50 per cent of the quota, were less inclined to dismiss a Treaty argument as haughtily as the fishing industry had done, and of course were mindful of the court's concerns. The minister handling negotiations, Richard Prebble, introduced a bill which provided for a progressive transfer of 50 per cent of the quota to Māori in exchange for a suspension of Treaty-based fishing claims in court or in the Waitangi Tribunal. Its unpopularity with Māori, expressed at a specially convened national hui, led to a number of quite major amendments. Finally passed in December 1989, the Māori Fisheries Act provided for 10 per cent of the quota to be transferred to a new Māori Fisheries Commission, over a four-year period. In addition, an amount of $10 million was allocated to assist in the establishment of Aotearoa Fishing, a commercial company wholly owned by the commission. Proceeds were to be applied to Māori social and economic development. The other half of the 10 per cent of the quota was to be made available for lease to Māori fishermen.

The Māori Fisheries Act 1989 was not received enthusiastically by Māori, nor did the Māori negotiators accept it as the last word. For one thing, it offered a level of quota far short of the 50 per cent; for another, the establishment of an intermediary body (the new Māori Fisheries Commission) was seen as an unnecessary compromise of tribal rights. So Crown and Māori negotiators continued to talk and by early 1990 had agreed to discuss the development of the QMS in a manner that would meet both conservation requirements and the principles of the Treaty of Waitangi. Agreement was also reached that court proceedings would be suspended and no further species would be introduced to the QMS until a satisfactory resolution was reached. Uncertainty within the industry had been partially alleviated, but sufficient remained to give the negotiators continued leverage.

SEALORD PRODUCTS

Keen to advance Māori fishing, and aware that ownership of 50 per cent of the quota was still the Māori goal, the negotiators looked for opportunities that might be acceptable to Māori and to the Crown. As early as August 1991 the option for a large commercial purchase was discussed by the negotiators. For the Crown, a real problem was that additional quota was simply not available, having already been leased to other interests. It was with some relief therefore that it was learned in May 1992 that Sealord Products Limited was likely to be available for purchase. Sealord held 26 per cent of quota and the possibility of it being acquired for Māori was an opportunity not likely to be repeated. While the negotiators appealed to the Crown to purchase the company outright for Māori, the government opted instead to buy only half and to seek a partner to purchase the other half. Brierleys was interested.

Events then moved swiftly, too hastily to allow adequate debate on all the implications of either endorsing or rejecting the deal. Urgency was compounded by the knowledge that overseas interests were preparing to tender for the purchase of Sealord Products. A Memorandum of Understanding was prepared in August 1992 and the negotiators, who now included a representative from the Māori Congress, undertook a national round of consultation with iwi and other

Māori groups, seeking ratification. The Crown had always maintained that the Sealord deal was to be an 'all-in' settlement with no room for groups who wished to remain outside its provisions. In other words, it would be for all Māori, or none. This meant ascertaining the overall level of support for the deal and, before proceeding, being assured that Māori support was, if not total, then very considerable.

The proposal taken to the people by the negotiators was essentially a recommendation that the Crown pay $150 million to enable Māori to enter into a joint venture purchase of Sealord Products Ltd. As well, 20 per cent of new species quota would be reserved for Māori, and the Māori Fisheries Commission would be restructured into a more representative body to be known as the Treaty of Waitangi Fisheries Commission. In return, Māori would need to agree to discontinue current court action in respect of fishing claims and to accept that legislation recognising Māori fishing rights would be repealed. Furthermore, neither the courts or the Waitangi Tribunal would have any further jurisdiction over Treaty-based commercial fishing matters.

Meetings were held on 23 marae, in addition to two national hui, and almost every regional hui produced a statement of support for the proposal, qualified, however, by three concerns. First, because the proposal was to be accompanied by the repeal of section 88(2) of the Fisheries Act, iwi were adamant that traditional fishing rights, including traditional fisheries, must nonetheless be protected. There was acknowledgment that the enforceability of section 88(2), and its meaning, was uncertain but, regardless, Māori were unhappy about abandoning what was perceived as a Treaty-derived guarantee. Second, inland tribes in particular were opposed to the inclusion of traditional and freshwater fisheries. Third, because of its commercial sensitivity, no opportunity was given to iwi to make their own examinations of the deal in commercial terms.

However, not all iwi or all sections of each iwi supported the proposal. For many, the major objection was the extinguishment, for ever, of the right to seek redress in the courts or with the Waitangi Tribunal. In a report to the Executive of the National Māori Congress at the Ruamata marae, Rotorua, in October 1992, negotiator Whatarangi Winiata considered that the crunch question was 'whether this proposal could, and would be managed, at an acceptable level of risk, so as to ensure that all iwi would be in a better position with respect to enjoying the fruits of their fisheries, in three to five years (and beyond) than if they followed other approaches—such as the Waitangi Tribunal/High Court/Negotiation way.'[15]

In terms of acquiring a percentage of fish quota, the negotiators believed that the Sealord deal would move Māori close to the desired 50 per cent. Ten per cent was already in Māori ownership (Māori Fisheries Act 1989), an additional 1.5 per cent, leased by Moana Pacific was Māori-owned, and the Sealord Products agreement would bring in a further 26 per cent (half Māori-owned, half owned by Brierleys but subject to Māori scrutiny), giving a total of 37.5 per cent. In addition, as new species were included in the QMS, Māori would receive 20 per cent of each quota.

With outspoken confidence the negotiators maintained that the proposal would deliver in a more certain way than ongoing litigation or claims procedures. Ngai Tahu and the iwi of Muriwhenua had also reached the conclusion that even if their claims were successful (and there was no guarantee that they would be), the Crown would simply not have access to sufficient quota to make good the tribal entitlement. For them the deal seemed a practical and a realistic way of meeting their goals for fishing. And two of the negotiators, Rata and O'Regan, reached a tacit agreement that South Island interests would not prejudice the far north. The role played by most of the negotiators in the purchase of Sealord, especially Sir Graham Latimer and Sir Tipene O'Regan, attracted criticism from Māori, partly because their mandate was not always sure, and partly because sometimes it appeared that, in return for delivering Māori consent, they were being rewarded with lucrative chairmanships.[16]

Rightly or wrongly, the negotiators believed that enough Māori were in favour of the deal for them to make positive recommendations to the Crown. They did so in a 260-page report, and on that basis the Crown considered there was sufficient Māori support for the deal to proceed, a view also taken by the Waitangi Tribunal in its own report, *The Fisheries Settlement 1992*.[17] A formal deed was then drawn up, hastily, and signed on 23 September by the Crown, the Māori negotiators, 43 signatories from some 17 different iwi, and 32 of the Māori plaintiffs in various fish actions in the courts.

Later, even some of those who had signed the historic document admitted being confused about what they had actually signed. It was no wonder. Although many had heard about the deed, on the night of signing they had been given an hour to read a 26-page document, understand its legal and economic significance, and make a commitment on behalf of their people.[18] Few had a chance to grasp the significance of the document as a whole, let alone specific clauses such as clause 4.6, which forecast the fiscal envelope: 'Māori recognise that the Crown has fiscal constraints and that this settlement will necessarily restrict the Crown's ability to meet from any fund which the Crown establishes as part of the Crown's overall settlement framework, the settlement of other claims arising from the Treaty of Waitangi.'

The actual signing was wrought with ambiguity. At least three thought they were signing an attendance record, an understandable impression given that they were handed a blank sheet of paper. In fact two documents were completed that evening. One was the deed of settlement and the other was an agreement to withdraw court action in respect of fishing claims. The distinction was far from clear.

Concern was also expressed about the mandate which some of the signatories presumed to carry. Did the appendage of tribal affiliation after a signature carry with it mandated tribal authority? Several tribes were to protest that the signatures of one or two members who had not been given authority to sign on behalf of the tribe did not mean consent by the tribe. And, more to the point, what was to be the position of tribes who refused outright to sign the deed?

In the end their opposition amounted to little. Like the signing of the Treaty of Waitangi, scant notice was taken of the non-signatory tribes, nor was there serious debate on the standing of the various signatories. In Parliament, meanwhile, both sides of the House spoke of the night's work as an historic undertaking, and there was a rare outpouring of emotion from ministers of the Crown. Media reaction was also generally favourable. 'There will be relief all round that the vast majority of Maori tribes have shown themselves sufficiently trusting, pragmatic and far-sighted to sign the Beehive agreement confirming the Sealord deal.'[19]

Almost immediately, however, claims were lodged with the Waitangi Tribunal and the High Court by those opposed to the deal. The Moriori of the Chatham Islands, Tuhuru, Rangitane ki Wairau, Rongomaiwahine, Ngāti Kahungunu, Muaupoko, Ngāti Porou, Ngāti Ranginui, and Waitaha all had serious reservations about the process which had been adopted, and the legitimacy of the completed deed. In October 1992, they approached the High Court in a bid to block it. They claimed that 'only sixteen of 54 tribes approved the agreement.' But the court could find no legal impediment to the deal and did not support the disgruntled iwi. Undeterred, the iwi concerned took their case to the Court of Appeal. On Tuesday, 3 November 1992, the Court of Appeal reached its decision. In not overturning a High Court refusal to have the deal delayed, as the Māori objectors wished, the agreement was said by the Appeal Court President, Sir Robin Cooke, to be a responsible and important step forward. According to the court, Māori failure to agree to the Sealord deal might have been seen as a failure of duty by a partner in a position akin to partnership. While the court was not able to assess the level or range of Māori support for the deal, it was confident that the negotiators were responsible Māori leaders. The deed was in any case only binding on those who had signed it and was a political compact. In no way, said the court, did the deal repeal the Treaty of Waitangi and, in the end, it was over to Parliament to introduce new legislation—or repeal parts of the Fisheries Act relating to Māori fishing quota—if it wished. With the court on its side, the House of Representatives was now free to draft laws that would legalise the Sealord agreement.

Three days later, on November 6, the Waitangi Tribunal released its report. Though not dismissing the deal outright, the Tribunal considered that it was wrong that Treaty-based Māori fishing rights would be extinguished. More specifically, it recommended that legislation to enforce the deal should provide for Treaty fishing interests, rather than extinguishing them, and that the legislation should state the goals of the settlement. Then a Māori–government body should be appointed to review progress on achieving the goals. The Tribunal did not agree that the courts should have no further jurisdiction and recommended that they have the power to review fisheries regulations on policies and Treaty principles. Rather than a complete ban on fishing claims, the Tribunal considered it would be more reasonable to have a 25-year moratorium.

The Tribunal's practical approach was, however, ignored and the deal went a decisive step further on 18 November when Carter Holt Harvey announced that Sealord Products had been sold to the joint venture between Brierley Investments and the Māori Fisheries Commission for $350 million. The sale of shares and quota holdings to Te Ika Paewai (the Brierley–Māori partnership) removed any commercial obstacle to the settlement.

The government then proceeded to draw up legislation and introduced the Treaty of Waitangi (Fisheries Claim) Settlement Bill on 3 December. It was given urgency, bypassing the usual select committee hearings; Justice Minister Doug Graham argued that consultation had already been very extensive. When introducing the new bill, he outlined the advantages to Māori: a $150 million government grant towards the purchase of Sealord's; a quota value of $286 million; a $22 million value from 20 per cent of new quota; all on top of an estimated $174 million value from quota and cash transferred to the Māori Fisheries Commission under the 1989 interim settlement of fisheries claims— a total package, he claimed, worth around half a billion dollars. On the other hand, the Crown would have no further obligations to Māori regarding commercial fishing, and all fishing claims before the courts or the Waitangi Tribunal would be deemed to be discharged. Customary fishing rights would receive some protection provided they were not of a commercial nature. The agreement did not spell out how dividends would flow on to iwi or to Māori people generally. Nor did it make any comment about tribes who refused to sign except that the settlement was 'for all Māori'.

Opposition Māori Affairs spokesman, Koro Wetere, supported aspects of the deal but opposed the wiping of future commercial fishing claims. Wider Māori reaction remained mixed. The Māori negotiators had strongly supported the deal as the best Māori could expect now and in the future, and said so. But other leaders were vigorously opposed to the removal of Treaty rights as part of the settlement. Taking advantage of opening addresses at the launch of the 1993 International Year of the World's Indigenous People at the United Nations in New York on 10 December, Dr Tamati Reedy delivered a scathing attack on the government, accusing them of trampling Treaty and indigenous rights. He denounced the government's handling of the Sealord deal as being 'in utter violation of the rights of its own minority.' Though speaking as a National Māori Congress representative, Reedy did not add that some Congress members had supported the deal or that the Congress had been represented on the Māori negotiators' team. Offended, and concerned that it could be used as a platform for dissidents, Ngai Tahu withdrew from the Congress in February the following year. Nonetheless, Reedy's statement, designed to gain international attention, had irritated the government at a time when they were congratulating themselves on what was seen as a major achievement.[20]

Ironically, on the same day that Reedy was speaking in the United Nations, Parliament in Wellington enacted the Treaty of Waitangi (Fisheries Claim) Settlement Act. None of the six Māori members of Parliament were completely in favour, and they earned some rebuke from the Minister of Justice, who advised them to be more realistic. He also warned that 'the public's patience will soon be exhausted if what is seen as a fair deal is rejected and Māori want to reserve the right to come back again later for more.'

Plans to establish the Treaty of Waitangi Fisheries Commission proceeded with minimal consultation, and it appeared that the old Māori Fisheries Commission would, in effect, select the new commissioners. Hariata Gordon of Ngāti Paoa objected to the haste and the process. She lodged a claim with the Waitangi Tribunal to secure a more open selection method, and the Tribunal released its report in December 1992, its second concerning the Sealord deal within six weeks.[21] The Tribunal recommended that a national hui be held so that the selection process could be more transparent and would lead to a more representative body. Though opposed to a hui, the Crown changed its mind after the Tribunal's report, and a meeting was held on 16 February 1993. Sir Henare Ngata had eventually agreed to chair the meeting but became unwell, and the Minister of Māori Affairs himself acted as chairman, assisted by Wira Gardiner, general manager of the Ministry of Māori Development. The invitation to iwi to gather at the Beehive emphasised the limited nature of the exercise. Only sixteen speakers were to be given speaking rights, each of whom had around five to ten minutes to address the forum.

Not surprisingly, Māori were opposed to such constraints and voiced their opposition at the National Māori Congress Executive meeting on 13 February. Some leeway was allocated, but the process nonetheless fell considerably short of Māori expectations and Māori methods of deciding policy. At the hui, set times were allocated to 23 groups, mainly iwi representatives, to give their views on the desired qualities of commissioners and the way in which they should be selected. There was considerable agreement that iwi should make the selection of commissioners and that the Crown should confine itself to making the appointments. Further, iwi generally rejected the idea that all commissioners should be selected on the basis of commercial experience.

In presenting the final formal submission, the secretary of the National Māori Congress took the opportunity to support previous speakers and underline points of agreement. 'It is important to remember that although there is no single Māori voice—and nor should there be—and though there is no single Māori viewpoint, there is nonetheless substantial agreement among iwi, between iwi and between waka. That high level of agreement needs to be emphasised at a time when some sections of New Zealand society, including the media, would make much of disagreements and highlight differences between Māori. Minister, this hui, despite the shortcomings that have been referred to, does demonstrate one thing: if there are divisions between iwi, or even within iwi, those divisions pale into insignificance alongside the many points of agreement and the high level of consensus that has emerged in this preliminary discussion on the establishment of the Treaty of Waitangi Fisheries Commission.'[22] Congress had emphasised three principles for the allocation of pre-settlement assets and future benefits: make haste slowly; respect the interests and circumstances of all iwi; protect the asset.[23]

In the end, the appointment of commissioners was a government decision made behind closed doors. It is doubtful that hui recommendations were afforded serious consideration. The first commissioners appointed later in 1993 were Tipene O'Regan (Ngai Tahu), Ben Couch (Ngāti Kahungunu), Whaimutu Dewes (Ngāti Porou), Craig Ellison (Ngai Tahu), Shane Jones (Muriwhenua), Robert Mahuta (Tainui), John Mitchell (Ngāti Tama), Naida Pou (Ngāti Whātua), Phil Pryke (the only Pākehā member), Anaru Rangiheuea (Te Arawa), Archie Taiaroa (Atihaunui-a-Paparangi), Evelyn Tuuta (Wharekauri). Much had been learned from the first experience of selecting commissioners and in 1996, when new commissioners were being considered, Sir Paul Reeves chaired a more amiable and more focused meeting, though the selection process was again left with the Crown. After a delay of nearly twelve months, during which Matiu Rata, Sir Robert Mahuta, Sir Graham Latimer, Maanu Paul, and Whatarangi Winiata unsuccessfully tried to have the appointment process stopped because of insufficient consultation,[24] the new Minister of Māori Affairs began canvassing Māori opinion about suitable members for the commission.

To some Māori, the Sealord deal signalled a departure from legally based Treaty arguments for the settlement of Māori claims. What had to be balanced, however, were practical economic considerations against more lofty Treaty principles which might or might not bear fruit. Could iwi afford to put aside the harsh realities of the contemporary Māori economy in favour of some future prospect of tino rangatiratanga? The same question must have been asked in 1865 when land titles were individualised and tribal representatives were pressured to sell tribal lands. Land-holding (pupuri whenua) factions fought against the land sellers (tuku whenua). In the 1990s the acrimony was no less than it had been in the 1860s as the pro-Sealord lobby confronted those who opposed any abrogation of Treaty rights.

CUSTOMARY FISHING RIGHTS

Following the fisheries settlement and the repeal of section 88(2) of the Fisheries Act, regulations needed to be made on non-commercial customary fishing rights. It had proved to be a stumbling block during the earlier negotiations and was no less demanding over the next four years. Te Ohu Kaimoana facilitated the establishment of a joint Māori/Crown Customary Fisheries Working Party (CFWP) which eventually produced a set of regulations designed to give substance to Māori non-commercial customary fishing rights.

The three main features were exclusive control of mataitai reserves by adjacent hapū or marae; kaitiaki would control customary take; and honorary officers would be appointed to protect and enforce customary fishing rights.[25] Extensive consultation with iwi and hapū assisted the process of drafting regulations, but significant differences between Māori and Crown members of the CFWP also emerged. In relation to the extent of by-laws Māori wanted to move beyond mataitai reserves, while Crown members were opting for a more limited arena. The use of Māori terms in the regulations caused considerable debate, the Crown wanting more specific definitions which the Māori words did not appear to offer. And the authority for kaitiaki to make prosecutions drew a sharp protest from the Crown. In response to the disagreements, the minister appeared to favour the views of the Crown members, though he felt unable to comment on the question of prosecutions, which 'is a matter for the Justice system.' Meanwhile, six years after the passing of the Māori Fisheries Act the Minister of Fisheries announced the establishment of the country's first two taiapure (fishing grounds reserved for hapū and iwi), Te Kopi and Te Kumenga on the southern Wairarapa coast.[26]

But if the Minister of Fisheries and the CFWP had difficulty deciding on the nature and extent of Māori customary fishing, the courts were beginning to reach their own conclusions. The 1986 *Te Weehi* case has already been referred to. It was followed in 1994 by a decision from District Court Judge R. L. Watson, who dismissed an action against two Hawera men, Tere Whanairoto and Rangiroa Rongonui, both being prosecuted for alleged whitebaiting offences. The Department of Conservation prosecutor, Geoff Hulbert, asked that charges against the pair be dropped as the Crown Law Office had determined that the defendants were exercising their customary fishing rights, which were protected by the Conservation Act.[27]

A similar case came before the Wanganui District Court in 1997. Kirk McRitchie of the Ngāti Hine, Ngāti Ruawai, and Ngāti Waikarapu hapū was fishing for trout in the Mangawhero River without a relevant licence. An honorary fish and game ranger confronted him and issued an offence notice, which led to prosecution under sections 26R(6) and 26ZI(1(a)) of the Conservation Act 1987. In his evidence, kaumātua Niko Tangaroa of the Whanganui tribes described McRitchie as 'a main provider' of local marae and contended that McRitchie was observing the tikanga, the lore, of local Māori and did not need a licence. The Māori Congress convenor, Te Atawhai Tairoa, also emphasised to the court three justifications for Māori to fish for trout without a licence: as an unqualified exercise of tino rangatiratanga; as a food source because of the depletion of native species; and because non-Māori have damaged traditional fisheries.

Judge Andrew Becroft dismissed the case. In concluding that McRitchie was exercising a customary Māori fishing right he drew on section 4 of the Conservation Act ('This Act shall be so interpreted and administered as to give effect to the principles of the Treaty of Waitangi') as well as section 26ZH ('Nothing in this part of this Act shall affect any Māori fishing rights'). He maintained that even though trout were an introduced species, the focus was on fisheries rather than species and in any case a developmental right was within a Treaty interpretation. The effect of the decision was to allow Māori from hapū or iwi having traditional territorial authority over a river fishery to fish for trout without a licence. However, he warned that the provision only applied if they did so according to the terms and conditions of local kawa (protocol) and were able to prove they are properly authorised to do so. Further, the fishing was to be for personal or family consumption, or for hui, and the fishing was not to impinge upon the conservation and sustainability of the trout resource.[28]

A predictable outcry followed from anglers and from the Taranaki Fish and Game Council, who threatened appeal, though possibly without Crown backing. Cabinet ministers were divided over whether to support an appeal, Conservation Minister Nick Smith and Attorney-General Paul East wanting to back the Council, and Māori Affairs Minister Tau Henare urging the government not to interfere with the judicial process.[29] However, lawyer Maui Solomon pointed out that the Conservation Act gave any landowner the right to fish for trout without a licence provided the property owned bordered a river.[30]

MĀORI QUOTA ALLOCATIONS

Negotiating the Sealord deal was, in hindsight, the easy part. Still to be resolved, apart from the very vexed questions of protecting customary rights, was allocating quotas to Māori.

In terms of commercial fisheries, however, Sealord was to be for all Māori, including those who had not signed the agreement and those who had no claim on fisheries because they were inland tribes. While Sealord Products Limited would give Māori virtual control over one third of all quota, there was no clear mechanism for the benefits to flow beyond the new Treaty of Waitangi Fisheries Commission, Te Ohu Kaimoana. As early as October 1992, Whatarangi Winiata had urged the Māori Congress to debate an allocation philosophy derived from an examination of mana whenua mana moana (coastline ownership), tribal population, dependency on fishing, and the state of development (of each iwi).[31] It was a chance for Māori outside government to decide key issues themselves before decisions were forced on them by the Crown or a Crown agency. But no clear agreement emerged and Te Ohu Kaimoana carried the burden of constructing an allocation formula.

By 1995 three quite distinct issues relating to allocation were being debated: aggregation or disbursement; mana moana or population-based distribution; urban Māori rights versus the rights of iwi. Support for quotas to be retained in a central holding and not to be distributed at all, though not widespread, was rationalised as an opportunity to protect and consolidate the asset. The Hon. Peter Tapsell and Sir Graham Latimer favoured aggregation of the resource but the chairman of Te Ohu Kaimoana, Sir Tipene O'Regan, as well as most iwi, favoured distribution of actual fishing quota, not just the dividends from fishing.[32] For them, however, the more important question was how quotas should be allocated and to whom. At stake were the so-called pre-settlement assets, the 10 per cent of quota transferred by the Crown according to the terms of the Māori Fisheries Act 1989 and amounting to some 57 000 tonnes or (when totalled along with shares in Moana Pacific) a book value of $200 million. In response to a discussion document circulated in 1993, Te Ohu Kaimoana identified three possible models as representative of the range of views.[33] The mana moana model would allocate quota to iwi on the basis that the fish off a tribe's coastline belonged to that iwi. Iwi entitlement to quota would be determined by extending the tribe's coastal boundary out to 200 miles offshore. The population model, mana tōtoru o te tangata, aimed to divide up quota on the basis of population, the more numerous an iwi, the more quota it would receive, regardless of holding coastal rights. In the progressive allocation model, quota would be allocated by a similar formula to the mana moana model but in a staged manner.

A number of tribal and other Māori groups were increasingly concerned that the commission was about to recommend to the Crown that the distribution of pre-settlement assets would be strongly influenced by the mana whenua mana moana principle. Tribes such as Ngai Tahu with a lengthy coastline would be greatly advantaged while those with less shoreline, or an inland base, would be disadvantaged. The differences could have been substantial. Under the mana whenua mana moana principle, Ngai Tahu, with a population of 22 269, would receive $4 533 per per person while Muriwhenua, with a population of 18 492, would receive $204 per person.

To lobby for the mana moana model, a Treaty Tribes Coalition was formed by Ngai Tāmanuhiri, Ngāti Tama, Ngai Tahu, Hauraki, Ngāti Kahungunu, Ngāti Rarua, Te Ati Awa, Ngāti Kuia, Ngāti Apa, Ngāti Toa, and Moriori (from the Chatham Islands). Though not a member of the coalition, Ngāti Porou were supportive. Led by Tutekawa Wyllie, who became the member of Parliament for Te Tai Tonga in 1996, the Treaty Tribes were fiercely opposed to any solution other than one firmly based on Treaty of Waitangi guarantees and notions of property rights. Heated arguments ensued, both in and out of court, with the protagonists of the population-based formula, particularly those in the Area One Consortium (Northland, Bay of Plenty), headed by Dick Dargaville. But by July 1995, when there was no clear winner and Māori were beginning to despair that Te Ohu Kaimoana would ever deliver, an agreement was reached between the two sides. Both acknowledged that there was room for the incorporation of both mana moana (coastline) and mana tōtoru o te tangata (population) in any final method of allocation.[34]

They also agreed that urban Māori had no rights to quota. Urban Māori claims had become increasingly forceful during 1995, and Te Ohu Kaimoana could not ignore them, no matter how much the chair and other commissioners disagreed. When High Court action followed, three commissioners, Sir Graham Latimer, Robert Mahuta, and Shane Jones, made an alternative proposal which could have recognised urban Māori, though without transferring quota. Seven regional fishing companies could be established with provision for leasing quota long term, while the assets would stay with the commission. Within the scheme, benefits for urban Māori were anticipated. However, Te Ohu Kaimoana officials dismissed the proposal because it was based on 'unsound' principles and failed to recognise the property rights of tribes.[35] At that stage they were not suggesting any alternative and seemed convinced that the special needs of urban Māori, as a group (or series of groups), were not part of their brief.

But on 30 April 1996, the Court of Appeal, under its President Sir Robin Cooke, now Lord Cooke of Thorndon, ruled that urban Māori interests must be taken into account in allocating Māori fisheries settlement assets. The appeal related to a direction given by Justice Anderson in the Auckland High Court on 30 June 1995 and to a judgment by Justice Ellis in the Wellington High Court on 31 July 1995. Both issues were to be dealt with simultaneously in the complicated Court of Appeal case. One was linked to the jurisdiction of the Waitangi Tribunal to hear fishing matters and the other was the position of urban Māori who did not have iwi links. The case had its origins in the inability of Te Ohu Kaimoana to reach a satisfactory conclusion about the distribution of pre-settlement fishing quota. As a result of the Treaty of Waitangi (Fisheries Claims) Settlement Act 1992, the commission was charged with distributing both pre- and post-settlement benefits to Māori. The Act did not specify iwi or hapū but rather was conceived as a settlement for Māori. Rightly or wrongly, it appeared to have been drafted as a pan-Māori settlement.

In addition, urban Māori authorities claimed that many urban Māori dwellers, because they had lost connections with a tribal base, or simply did not know what tribe they could lay claim to, would also be disadvantaged, though for different reasons. In the 1991 census, 22 per cent of Māori did not know the name of their iwi and, although reduced, in the 1996 census 19 per cent were still unable to state an iwi affiliation. Various groups, including two large urban authorities in Auckland, Te Whānau o Waipareira and the Manukau Urban Māori Authority, lodged a claim with the Waitangi Tribunal, seeking an inquiry into the commission's intentions. Ngai Tahu and the Treaty Tribes opposed any such inquiry and challenged the Tribunal's right to hear the matter. The High Court (Justice Ellis) ruled that the Tribunal did not have the authority to hear the matter and in any case it was premature since the commission had not actually formulated a scheme. The decision was appealed and formed a substantial part of this Court of Appeal case. In its 30 April decision, the Court of Appeal found that the passage of the Treaty of Waitangi (Fisheries Claim) Settlement Act 1992 had carried with it an amendment to section 6 of the Treaty of Waitangi Act which expressly prevented the Waitangi Tribunal from inquiring into Māori commercial fishing interests under the Treaty of Waitangi.

As for the position of urban Māori, the earlier direction by Justice Anderson at the High Court in 1995 had been inconclusive, because statutory interpretation would have been necessary to answer the question as to whether pre-settlement assets should be distributed solely to iwi or bodies representing iwi. The Court of Appeal considered first of all the meaning of the word iwi, in the context of the Treaty of Waitangi, and concluded that while authorities had been established to represent tribes, iwi referred to the people of a tribe, not the representatives or the tribal leaders. It also noted a Waitangi Tribunal finding that in the Treaty the term hapū was used to denote ownership of various resources. After hearing evidence from the Treaty of Waitangi Fisheries Commission that urban Māori, or for that matter individual Māori, were not to be excluded from settlement benefits, the court found that the benefits were for iwi (i.e. Māori people) including those who did not have or were unable to establish specific tribal affiliations. It then ruled that the commission's duty extended to 'ensuring that any scheme or legislation proposed by the commission includes equitable and separately administered provision for urban Māori.'[36]

Although urban Māori welcomed the decision, tribal groups were appalled by it. Ngāti Porou described it as 'a judgement whereby a colonial government has made an unwarranted and unwelcome intrusion into indigenous affairs'. Dick Dargaville and Tutekawa Wyllie, previously on opposite sides of the fence, agreed on this occasion that, no matter how the asset was distributed, fisheries ownership should remain with the tribes. And Te Ohu Kaimoana, pleased that the Court of Appeal had confirmed their position about the inability of the Waitangi Tribunal to intervene, was nonetheless concerned about the judgment in favour of urban Māori.[37] Matiu Rata, however, one of the original four Māori fisheries negotiators, welcomed the decision as an affirmation that Sealord was for all Māori, but disagreed that the Waitangi Tribunal had been excluded and was concerned about a separate distribution system for urban Māori. ACT candidate Donna Awatere-Huata wanted the distribution of assets to go even further. 'The best solution would be to give every Māori individual shares in fisheries assets that they could either keep or sell to family trusts, urban authorities or tribal trusts.'[38]

In any event, leave was obtained to have the case heard in the Privy Council in November 1996. The Treaty Tribes and Ngāti Porou wanted to clarify whether the Court of Appeal decision allowed urban groups to claim ownership of fisheries, while the Muriwhenua tribes, together with Tainui Fisheries and Te Waka Hi Ika o Te Arawa, wanted the ban on future Waitangi Tribunal involvement overturned. Other respondents were Te Ohu Kaimoana and Te Iwi Moriori Trust Board.

Two matters worried the Law Lords about the case. Following the general election and during coalition talks between National and New Zealand First, the Māori members of Parliament allegedly pressured the Crown to withdraw its support for the Court of Appeal decision. The government did so, but maintained that it was because they were a caretaker government, not because of Māori pressure. 'In its present caretaker capacity, the Government has decided not to adopt the position as was filed. Accordingly the Government does not support the case. . . .'[39] John Tamihere, in London for the hearing, was critical of the government's backdown but doubted whether the change was related to coalition talks. Instead he blamed 'the old guard who control and hold all the Māori money now—the Sir Tipene O'Regans, the Sir Graham Latimers. . . . National has caved in to political pressure.'[40]

Having clarified the government's new position, the Privy Council then wondered whether it could proceed without deciding on a definition of iwi. Eventually they considered they could, but in the final ruling they did not themselves enter into any debate on the meaning of iwi. Instead they quashed the Court of Appeal decision on the grounds that the court had wrongly approached the resolution of the two main issues—how Māori fisheries assets should be allocated, and whether they could be distributed to individual urban Māori. The appellants considered that the Court of Appeal had answered the wrong question. Rather than confining their judgment to an opinion on whether Te Ohu Kaimoana was required to allocate fisheries assets solely to iwi or iwi-representative bodies, the judges had embarked upon a consideration of what was meant by iwi. The Privy Council concluded that in order to answer the question (the definition of iwi) further evidence should have been made available, and in that respect the Court of Appeal had gone further than it ought.

In referring the matter back to the High Court in New Zealand, the Law Lords framed a new two-part question. Was the Fisheries Commission required by law to allocate fisheries assets solely to iwi, and if so, in this context does iwi mean only traditional Māori tribes? A subsidiary point raised by Tainui, that the matter be referred to Parliament if the commission were unable to resolve the allocation issue, was dismissed by the Privy Council, as was the Tainui contention that the Fisheries Commission should pay for the costs of litigation.

Māori reaction to the Privy Council decision was mixed. Tribal authorities were generally relieved and the Fisheries Commission chairman, Sir Tipene O'Regan, described the decision as 'deeply satisfying.'[41] Urban Māori authorities were disappointed, especially with the prospect of ongoing litigation. But by far the most common reaction was the increased conviction that the court, in New Zealand or abroad, was not the right place to argue the application of traditional understandings to contemporary times. It was a Māori issue which ought to be resolved by Māori. MP Dover Samuels saw it as a task for Māori MPs to address,[42] though others had in mind a forum that was outside Parliament and Te Ohu Kaimoana and the several arms of the state.

The clear fact, however, was that a method for the allocation of pre-settlement assets and, later, of the far greater benefits from Sealord, remained unresolved. Between the proponents of coastline and population models, some progress was made with the establishment of the Taumata Paepae—a joint commission–iwi working group which had attempted to reach agreement about a formula for allocation, though without direct input from urban Māori authorities. Following the Privy Council ruling, the Hon. Tau Henare tried to forge an amicable out-of-court agreement between all four parties (the commission, urban Māori, coastline champions, and population-based tribal advocates). An agreement to wait was more or less obtained.

But it was rudely shattered when the commission announced in April 1997 that a plan to allocate fisheries assets, valued at between $250 million and $350 million, had been decided on. Briefly, the new plan included an allocation of inshore quotas on the basis of actual tribal coastlines (the mana whenua mana moana model). Deepwater quotas, however, would be allocated 60 per cent on the basis of tribal coastline and 40 per cent on the basis of tribal population. Cash and shares would be distributed in proportion to the quota a tribe receives, and distribution of shares in Moana Pacific Fisheries was to be done in a way that would ensure the integrity of the company. In view of its unique situation, a separate proposal for the Chatham Islands was to be considered.

The omission of any reference to urban Māori was seen as deliberately divisive and led to threats of further court action from urban Māori authorities as well as to calls for the Fisheries Commission to resign.[43] In defence, Sir Tipene O'Regan pointed out that the decision was only a proposal and would need to be ratified at the annual meeting of the commission. He also observed that under the terms of the proposal Ngai Tahu would be disadvantaged. Northern Māori, however, were unimpressed, maintaining that O'Regan had again demonstrated his bias. Not persuaded by the plea that Ngai Tahu had been considerably disadvantaged by yielding 40 per cent of deepwater assets to the population formula, Dargaville continued to explain that the new proposal was at the expense of the larger North Island tribes and in that sense was intolerable. And again the Minister of Māori Affairs called for calm discussion and the avoidance of further litigation.

By now, debate about the composition of Te Ohu Kaimoana had resurfaced, and at a conference on 'The Treaty of Waitangi and Political Representation', organised by the New Zealand Institute of Advanced Legal Studies in May 1997, a formal motion was passed by the 200 delegates, the majority of whom were Māori, calling for the next round of appointments to be made by Māori, not the Crown. It was yet another sign that, despite the impact of the Taumata Paepae, decision-making was essentially controlled by a small group whose favoured treatment of tribes far outweighed any consideration of urban Māori. In that sense the commission itself was insufficiently representative of Māori. Nor, being a Crown entity, was it under Māori control.

Somewhat belatedly, after the Court of Appeal had ruled in favour of urban Māori, Te Ohu Kaimoana had also realised that definitive action was needed to encourage greater involvement of all Māori in the settlement. A free phone helpline was established for Māori who did not know what iwi they belonged to.[44] Clearly the commission was keen to render Māori urban authorities unnecessary by boosting iwi registers. And if that gave Māori as individuals and as whānau improved access to the benefits of fishing, then it was a worthwhile goal. Urban Māori, meanwhile, were also keen to create registers of their own. With some publicity they lost little time in launching a campaign to recruit members and to compete with iwi registers by obtaining written consent from city dwellers for the assignment of Treaty representation to urban Māori authorities such as the Manukau Urban Māori Authority.

By 1996, Te Ohu Kaimoana had itself become the major stakeholder in New Zealand's fishing industry, with assets totaling $507.4 million.[45] Its principal commercial company, Sealord, was thriving, with over 630 employees, the largest single quota holder; and the commission was actively promoting Māori entry into fishing through educational programs and quota leasing arrangements. In the first year of the scholarship scheme (1994), 161 Māori men and women received financial assistance to enrol in relevant courses.[46] By 1996 the amount budgeted for scholarships had increased to one million dollars and an iwi fisheries management course was offered from Te Wānanga o Raukawa on behalf of the commission.

Despite its slowness in moving assets on to iwi, the commission has actively sought to involve Māori in the business of fishing and can point to significant successes, summarised in table 6.1. Pending the transfer of assets to their ultimate owners, iwi have had the use of Te Ohu Kaimoana quotas through annual leases. As much as $10 to $15 million per year in potential gross earnings is released in this way. There have also been several disputes, mainly about the commission's leasing decisions; and in one case, involving Te Iwi Moriori from the Chatham Islands, the Court of Appeal ruled that cuts to entitlements for the 1996/97 season had been unfair. Te Ohu Kaimoana was required to make changes which would not disadvantage Moriori people.[47] Ngāti Raukawa similarly won a legal battle regarding the unfair allocations on the west coast of the North Island. By and large, however, the ventures have been profitable, and most iwi have reinvested some of their profits back into the business of fishing, but have also used them for a wide range of customary and social purposes including marae, health, education, and language. In the process communication between iwi has improved.[48]

Table 6.1 Iwi Involvement in Fishing, 1989–1996

Type of Activity	1989	1996
Number of iwi operating fishing businesses	none	> 50
Iwi using iwi fishers to catch all or some of their wetfish/paua quota	nil	almost all iwi (90%)
Iwi/Māori catching TOKM rock lobster quota	nil	> 46
Iwi on-leasing all/some quota to achieve cash profits	nil	many
Iwi directly processing all/some of their quota	nil	10
Iwi actively marketing their own company's fish products	nil	> 5

Source: Te Ohu Kaimoana (TOKM)

As a powerful and wealthy institution, Te Ohu Kaimoana has the potential to drive a Māori agenda for economic recovery and restructuring. Already it has issued criteria for deciding the legitimacy of an iwi and has made progress in formalising a process for the recognition of a tribal mandate. But there remains a wide sense of unease that a commission appointed by the government to decide on a Māori resource should not be answerable to Māori in a more direct manner. Having established Māori entitlement to the resource, governance and control should be more obviously in Māori hands. If nothing else the Privy

Council ruling, and the failure of Te Ohu Kaimoana to reach an acceptable decision, have both served to strengthen Māori opinion against having a Pākehā court or a Crown agency rule on issues of custom and their contemporary application. A Māori Law Commission with power to decide on Māori issues was suggested by Atareta Poananga,[49] though others, including the Māori Congress, were less convinced that a legal body—white or brown—was necessarily required. More important to Congress was the option for a Māori forum within which hapū and iwi disputes, and disputes between Māori organisations and tribes, could be resolved according to the appropriate tikanga. In any case, it appeared rather absurd that a judicial committee on the other side of the earth had been asked to define the nature of Māori society. Almost as ironic was the involvement, largely by default, of a Crown agency, Te Ohu Kaimoana, as an arbiter of tribal altercation and a gatekeeper for Māori access to a distinctly Māori resource.

NOTES FOR CHAPTER 6

1 'When the tail of the fish moves, the rest of the fish is not lacking for direction', quoted in the Preface to the Waitangi Tribunal *Muriwhenua Fishing Report (Wai 22)* to explain the significance of the northern claim (the tail) and its implications for policies and legislation emanating from Wellington (the metaphorical head of the fish).

2 The Treaty of Waitangi, Article 2.

3 Ranginui Walker, (1990), *Ka Whawhai Tonu Matou: Struggle Without End*, Penguin, Auckland, p. 142.

4 Waitangi Tribunal, (1988), *Muriwhenua Fishing Report (Wai 22)*, Waitangi Tribunal, Wellington.

5 *ibid.*, pp. 42–44.

6 *ibid.*, pp. 68–74.

7 *ibid.*, pp. 37–44.

8 *Te Weehi v Regional Fisheries Officer* [1986] 1 NZLR 680 (High Court).

9 Waitangi Tribunal, (1988), *Muriwhenua Fishing Report*, pp. 6–7.

10 *ibid.*, p. 239.

11 New Zealand Law Commission, (1989), *Report on the Treaty of Waitangi and Māori Fisheries*, Wellington.

12 Waitangi Tribunal, (1992), *Ngai Tahu Fishing Report (Wai 27)*, Waitangi Tribunal, Wellington.

13 *Te Rūnanga o Muriwhenua Inc. v Attorney-General and Others*, High Court, Wellington, CP 553/87, October 1987, Greig J.

14 See CP 559/87, 610/87, 614/87, High Court, Wellington, October 1987, Greig J.

15 Whatarangi Winiata, (1992), *Report to the Congress Executive from Fisheries Negotiator*, National Māori Congress, NMC 92/4/10a, p. 2.

16 Ranginui Walker, (1996), *Ngā Pepa a Ranginui: The Walker Papers*, Penguin, Auckland, pp. 105–106.

17 Waitangi Tribunal, (1992), *The Fisheries Settlement Report (Wai 307)*, Tribunals Division, Department of Justice, Wellington.

18 Walker, (1996), *Ngā Pepa a Ranginui*, pp. 102–103.

19 'A Welcome Compromise', Editorial, *The Dominion*, Friday 25 September 1992.

20 Jane Kelsey, (1993), *Rolling Back the State: Privatisation of Power in Aotearoa/New Zealand*, Bridget Williams Books, Wellington, p. 268.

21 Waitangi Tribunal, (1992), *Appointments to the Treaty of Waitangi Fisheries Commission Report (Wai 321)*, Waitangi Tribunal Division, Department of Justice, Wellington.

22 The secretary was referring to the extensive publicity given to the decision by Ngai Tahu to withdraw from the Māori Congress four days earlier.

23 M. H. Durie, (1993), *Submission on Appointment of Treaty of Waitangi Fisheries Commission*, National Māori Congress.

24 'Fisheries commission case dismissed', *The Dominion*, Thursday 3 October 1996.

25 Te Ohu Kaimoana, (1996), 'Chairman's Report' in *Hui-a-tau Report, 29 June 1996*, Treaty of Waitangi Fisheries Commission, Wellington, p. 2.

26 Te Ohu Kaimoana, (1995), *Hui-a-tau Report, 7 July 1995*, Treaty of Waitangi Fisheries Commission, Wellington, pp. 20–21.

27 'Maori fishing rights upheld', *Daily News*, Thursday 20 October 1994.

28 *The Taranaki Fish and Game Council v Kirk McRitchie*, Decision of Judge A. J. Becroft, District Court, Wanganui, 27 February 1997, CRN: 5083006813–14.

29 'Ministers move to avoid split over trout fishing rights', *The Dominion*, Wednesday 26 March 1997.

30 'Others can also fish without a licence, says lawyer', *The Dominion*, Monday 17 March 1997.

31 Winiata, *Report to the Congress Executive from Fisheries Negotiator*, p. 4.

32 Hugh Barlow, (1996), 'Court in the Māori fish net', *The Dominion*, Thursday 30 May 1996.

33 Te Ohu Kaimoana, (1994), *Allocation of Pre-Settlement Assets: Models of Allocation*, Treaty of Waitangi Fisheries Commission, Wellington.

34 'Historic signing opens way for allocation', *Te Reo o te Tini a Tangaroa: The Newsletter of the Treaty of Waitangi Fisheries Commission*, 26, August 1995.

35 Hugh Barlow, (1996), 'Waitangi officials give fisheries plan thumbs down', *The Dominion*, Wednesday 13 March 1996.

36 *Te Rūnanga o Muriwhenua v Treaty of Waitangi Fisheries Commission* [1996] 3 NZLR 10 (Court of Appeal).

37 Te Ohu Kaimoana, (1996), *Hui-a-tau Report, 29 June 1996*, Treaty of Waitangi Fisheries Commission, Wellington, pp. 2–3.

38 *The Dominion*, Friday 3 May 1996.

39 'Privy Council may quash part of iwi appeal', *The Dominion*, Wednesday 27 November 1996.

40 'Pull-out a betrayal of Māori.' *Evening Standard*, Friday 22 November 1996.

41 'Privy Council quashes fisheries appeal ruling', *The Gisborne Herald*, Friday 17 January 1997.

42 'MPs plea on fish row', *The Dominion*, Tuesday 21 January 1997.

43 'O'Regan storms out in TV row', *The Dominion*, Friday 18 April 1997.

44 Te Ohu Kaimoana, (1996), 'Freephone number will help Māori identify Iwi', *Te Reo o te Tini a Tangaroa: The Newsletter of the Treaty of Waitangi Fisheries Commission*, no. 33, p. 3, October 1996.

45 Te Ohu Kaimoana, (1996), *Hui-a-tau Report*, p. 31.

46 Te Ohu Kaimoana, (1994), 'Hundreds get scholarships', *Te Reo o te Tini a Tangaroa: The Newsletter of the Treaty of Waitangi Fisheries Commission*, no. 22, p. 1, December 1994.

47 'Morioris win appeal in fish quota row', *The Dominion*, Saturday 12 October 1996.

48 Whaimutu Dewes, (1995), 'Fisheries—a case study of an outcome', in Geoff McLay (ed.), *Treaty Settlements: The Unfinished Business*, New Zealand Institute of Advanced Legal Studies, Wellington, pp. 129–137.

49 *Mana News*, Radio New Zealand, Wednesday 4 December 1996.

7

MANA TIRITI

APPLICATION OF
THE TREATY OF WAITANGI

Ki oku whakaaro ake mo te Tiriti o Waitangi,
he taonga tapu, he mea tā ki te moko nō o rātou kiri. . . .[1]

In the same year that Whina Cooper led the historic land march from Te Hapua to Parliament, the Treaty of Waitangi Act 1975 became law under the sponsorship of the Minister of Māori Affairs, Matiu Rata. While its significance as a vehicle for reform was to pass unnoticed until the Motunui case in 1983,[2] the Act was a further signal that Māori leadership would not be bound by the agendas of previous governments or the conservative wishes of mainstream New Zealand. Māori were beginning to assert a more open challenge which extended beyond the marae and into areas previously considered the domain of the law, the professions, the farmers, and the politicians. In that process the Waitangi Tribunal, established under the 1975 Act, provided leadership and influence. Quite apart from recommending on the settlement of long-standing Treaty of Waitangi claims, the Tribunal's reports began to sketch an historical backdrop which had been largely hidden from the eyes of ordinary New Zealanders. Case by case, there was an examination of injustices that had never been resolved in the past, nor openly admitted, and again and again it was found that the Crown had failed to meet its obligations under the Treaty. Most New Zealanders were surprised to know that the Crown did have Treaty obligations; and many became anxious lest they be taken seriously.

While there has not been consistent political inclination to act on all of the Waitangi Tribunal recommendations, it would also be misleading to say, as do some commentators, that there is a total absence of goodwill. Results suggest otherwise. But goodwill by itself is an insufficient basis for settling Treaty claims or for recognising the place of the Treaty in New Zealand society. Political whim is even more unsatisfactory. What is missing is a secure understanding, based on both Māori and Crown views, that commits the country to a position on the Treaty so that litigation, protest, alienation, and dispossession fade into history. Although there is a measure of agreement that the Treaty of Waitangi is a foundation of contemporary New Zealand, there is less consensus about how the Treaty's guarantees should be expressed in modern times.

A TREATY IS FORGED

There might have never been a Treaty at all were it not for the Declaration of Independence signed five years earlier in 1835.[3] Having recognised Māori sovereignty and independence then, Britain needed a mechanism to justify imposing its own will on Māori and assuming governance. The report of the Aborigines Committee to Parliament in 1837 provided some guidance, suggesting that indigenous peoples had property rights and that treaties ought to be signed with chiefs to give colonising powers some semblance of right when they occupied other people's territories.[4] Busby's dispatch of 1837, in which he decried Britain's ad hoc policies towards New Zealand, blaming them for the Māori depopulation, recommended a more decisive stand, though not necessarily annexation,[5] and missionaries, especially those from the Church Missionary Society, were similarly anxious for Britain to intervene. Claudia Orange maintains that the situation of Māori in New Zealand was deliberately misrepresented to strengthen the conclusion that colonisation was inevitable and in everyone's best interests, including Māori.[6] For whatever reason, the Colonial Office had itself reached a conclusion that the time for action was nigh. Invasion by force was never seriously entertained by Britain, or other powers, even though ultimately force was used when the sovereignty of the Crown was challenged by Māori during the wars of the 1860s. But in 1839 a treaty was to be the instrument by which the Crown would instigate British rule and rationalise land purchases.

The Treaty of Waitangi had three objectives: the protection of Māori interests, the promotion of settler interests, and the securement of strategic advantage for the Crown.[7] Ironically, the only way the Colonial Office felt it could guarantee the protection of Māori interests was to usurp sovereignty from Māori. Then, it was argued, the way would be clear for British law to be instituted and the unruly settlers controlled. But within a decade the Treaty was used, not to protect Māori, but to separate them from their land and culture and to boost emigration from an overcrowded Britain.

Hobson had the task of implementing the Colonial Office's plans for a formal arrangement with Māori and, once in New Zealand, lost no time in drafting a treaty and arranging a public meeting to launch what was to be a series of signings. Haste and inadequate consultation were hallmarks of the Treaty process, and there was the added complication of linguistic and cultural misunderstanding. In English, the Treaty of Waitangi provided for a transfer of sovereignty to the Crown (Article 1) in exchange for guarantees that tribal properties would be protected, and sold only to the Crown (Article 2), with an additional promise that individual Māori people would acquire the same citizenship rights as British subjects (Article 3). At a relatively late stage, a translation into Māori was undertaken by the Rev. Henry Williams of the Church Missionary Society, who had some fluency in Māori. His translation was a poor rendition and continues to cause conflict and misunderstanding.

It has already been noted in chapter 1 that Williams used the transliteration, 'kāwanatanga', as an equivalent for sovereignty. It failed to capture the concept of absolute power, and the choice of word was in contrast to his use of 'mana' when describing Māori sovereignty in the 1835 Declaration of Independence. On the other hand for 'full exclusive and undisturbed possession' in the second article Williams employed a much more powerful phrase—tino rangatiratanga. Williams' translation had the net effect of converting the Māori version of Article 2 into a statement about continuing Māori authority and negated some of the strength of the English version of Article 1. He introduced an ambiguity. Was kāwanatanga superior to tino rangatiratanga, as Ngata believed,[8] or was the Treaty a prescription for parallel paths of power under a single nation state?

Māori have always placed greater value on the Treaty than the Crown, and relationships between Māori and the state have largely been reflected in their differing attitudes to the Treaty of Waitangi and the varying levels of commitment. When the Treaty was being drafted and then after it had been signed, Māori were relatively uninvolved; they had taken little active part in preparing the texts, and despite efforts to take the Treaty around the country, little notice was actually taken of their views. On the contrary, driven by a fear that the French might assume sovereignty over parts of the country, or that the New Zealand Company might establish an ad hoc republic in the lower North Island, Hobson hastily declared sovereignty over New Zealand on 21 May, months before the Treaty signings were actually completed in October.[9]

Tribes, including Te Arawa and Tuwharetoa, who were opposed to the Treaty were generally ignored, while those who were interested in a treaty but not (yet) committed to it found no opportunity to negotiate further in any meaningful way. Both Tainui and Ngāti Porou, for example, had reservations, and the respective paramount chiefs, Te Wherowhero (later the first Māori king) and Te Kani-a-Takirau, refused to sign but did not prevent others from doing so. It appears that by not signing themselves they believed they were protecting the tribe, while in encouraging others to sign they were not denying the tribe the opportunities that might flow from an alliance with Great Britain. Today their positions might be accommodated through a memorandum of understanding, a signal that the matter was worth further investigation but not ready for any final commitment. Their political strategy was a subtlety lost on the British, who were more interested in collecting signatures without attempting to ascertain the full significance of tribal organisation or the hierarchy of Māori leadership. While they were able to comprehend the authority of the monarch and ministers of the Crown and the limitation of the powers that subalterns possessed, they could not ascribe parallel motivations to Māori. Similarly, 152 years later, the Crown misunderstood the authority which tribal signatories to the Sealord's agreement possessed or, as was frequently the case, did not possess.

By identifying three chronological phases and certain key actions of tribes, the government, and the courts, it is possible to present in a simplified form the differing views and attitudes between Māori and the Crown regarding the Treaty. Table 7.1 provides a summary. In the first phase, Māori enthusiasm was less than British haste. However, after the 1860 Kohimarama Conference, and when the extent of dispossession had become a reality unforeseen by most tribes, Māori recognised the Treaty as a source of rights. By then, the Crown and the courts were uninterested in the Treaty and all but dismissed it.[10] The third phase, dating from the Treaty of Waitangi Act, represents a more serious attempt by the Treaty partners to understand the significance of the Treaty and the mutual obligations to which they are party.

Table 7.1 Relationships Between Māori and the Crown Concerning the Treaty of Waitangi

	Tribes	Parliament	Courts
1840–1859 Cooperation and mutual benefit	Relative indifference to the Treaty did not prevent full participation in the economy.	No specific reference to Treaty and no Māori MPs. But high levels of interaction with Māori.	Symonds case affirmed the importance of the Treaty and its binding implications on the Crown.
1860–1974 Division and disparity	Loss of land and power led to an increasing emphasis on the Treaty as a source of rights.	Dismissive attitude to the Treaty and to Māori property rights.	Prendergast: 'Treaty is a simple nullity.' Privy Council: the Treaty recognisable only if it is in municipal law.
1975–1997 Negotiation and restitution	Treaty the basis for positive Māori development.	Variable recognition of relevance of the Treaty to modern New Zealand. Settlement of claims commences.	Support for Treaty when incorporated in the law. Treaty also used as an aid to interpret the law.

TREATY SETTLEMENT PROCESSES

Although the Treaty of Waitangi was never written as a basis for claims against the Crown, blatant disregard for Treaty principles has led to large numbers of claims, and their settlement has become a major national preoccupation. Table 7.2 summarises the four ways in which a Treaty of Waitangi claim can be settled and the main agencies involved. Mediation is an infrequently used process, and only two cases have been settled that way, though six have been referred. For major claims, mediation has been subsumed by negotiations.[11] Each of the other resolution processes is discussed in greater detail later in this chapter.

Table 7.2 Resolution of Treaty of Waitangi Claims

Process	Agencies with responsibility	Requirements
Litigation	High Court Appeal Court Privy Council	Treaty or Māori values incorporated into domestic law
Formal inquiry	Waitangi Tribunal	Claim must conform to Treaty of Waitangi Act 1975
Mediation	Waitangi Tribunal	Issues delineated and agreement as to the facts
Direct negotiation	Minister in Charge of Treaty Negotiations Office of Treaty Settlements	Acceptance onto the Negotiations Work Program

The Courts

Of the avenues for addressing Treaty grievances, the courts have the longest history but have been uneven in recognising the legal and moral significance of the Treaty. Generally, the court is only able find on the Treaty of Waitangi if the Treaty itself is mentioned in law, though there have been some highly significant exceptions, one in 1847 when the Treaty was seen as binding on the Crown and another in 1987 when it was used as an aid to interpret the law (*Huakina Development Trust v Waikato Valley Authority*). Table 7.3 on page 180 contains a list of some of the relevant cases heard by the courts and the outcomes.[12]

In *R v Symonds*, a Crown challenge regarding the legality of a Crown grant of land to Symonds led the judges (Chief Justice Martin and Justice Chapman) to link the Treaty of Waitangi with notions of aboriginal title, confirming it as a Crown act which could not be lightly dismissed. Although the case was contrived, in the sense that Governor Grey wanted to suspend the 1846 Constitution Act and its provision for the Crown to assume ownership of all 'waste lands', and arranged an illustrative case to force the Treaty into the legal spotlight, it was nonetheless an indication that the Treaty was more than a convenient instrument

Table 7.3 The Treaty in Court

Year	Case	Outcome
1847	R v Symonds	The Treaty is binding on the Crown
1877	Wi Parata v Bishop of Wellington	The Treaty is a simple nullity
1938	Te Heuheu Tukino v Aotea District Maori Land Board	The Treaty can only be recognised if it is incorporated into municipal law
1987	Huakina Development Trust v Waikato Valley Authority	The Treaty is part of the fabric of society (and can be used as an aid to intepret legislation)
1987	NZ Māori Council v Attorney-General (SOE case)	The principles of the Treaty of Waitangi override everything else in the State-Owned Enterprises Act
1990	NZ Māori Council v Attorney-General (FM frequencies)	Broadcasting policy should protect the Māori language
1997	Taranaki Fish & Game Council v Kirk McRitchie	Customary fishing rights need not be restrained by trout licensing requirements

of annexation.[13] The court declared that the right of the Crown to extinguish native title must be consistent with the universal principles of natural law, which recognise the validity of native title and the need for the owners to consent before any transfer of title can take place. A reinstatement of pre-emption and the withdrawal of the 1846 Constitution Act with its claim to Crown ownership over waste land were the immediate results of this court judgment. The wider significance, however, lay in the court's recognition of the Treaty as a solemn document based on the principles of natural law and the doctrine of aboriginal title, and binding on the Crown.

In striking contrast, an opposite conclusion was reached by the Supreme Court in 1877.[14] *Wi Parata v Bishop of Wellington* concerned a block of land in the Porirua area known as Whitireia. It had been gifted by Ngāti Toa to the Anglican Church (through Bishop Selwyn) in 1850 for the purpose of building a church school. The school was never built but the Church continued to manage the land as a Trust.

After the dismissal of a petition from Wi Parata and eighteen other members of Ngāti Toa to the Native Affairs Committee requesting the return of Whitireia, Parata then (1877) applied to the Supreme Court for a declaration that the grant of the Porirua land issued to Bishop Selwyn in 1850 was void and that the land should revert to Ngāti Toa. The case was heard in July 1877 by Chief Justice Prendergast and Justice Richmond, who dismissed the case on the grounds that it had no legal basis. Their findings cast doubt on the capacity of Māori to enter into a treaty since they lacked a national body politic and, in the view of the judges, did not have any consistent system of land law upon which native title could be validated; nor was there any such thing as a legal Māori title to land. They concluded that the Treaty of Waitangi had no bearing on the case since treaties with 'primitive barbarians' lacked legal validity. The Treaty must be regarded as a 'simple nullity'.

It was an unjust decision, and in 1902 Wi Neera brought the case to court again but the Prendergast decision was upheld. The Privy Council, in 1903, did not agree with the principles established in *Wi Parata v Bishop of Wellington*, but their findings were also ignored by the Crown in New Zealand. So the Prendergast view was to prevail for nearly a hundred years. It helped convince successive governments and judges that the Treaty of Waitangi was of little consequence and certainly irrelevant to legal issues. For most purposes the Treaty was then ignored.

However, a small but important step was taken in 1938. When the government decided to extract a payment of £23 000 from Māori land owners to cover a debt incurred by the Egmont Box Company, Ngāti Tuwharetoa challenged the Aotea District Maori Land Board, a quasi-governmental agency which managed the land. Though the situation had arisen through no fault of their own, it was the Tuwharetoa owners who were being asked to make good the debt, and rightly they were incensed. Te Heuheu Tukino, the paramount chief, took the case to court, also alleging that the Crown, acting in loco parentis as trustee, had acquired forests to the value of £1.3 million for a mere £77 000. At the Court of Appeal counsel for Tuwharetoa, H. Hampton, argued that the New Zealand Constitution Act 1852 recognised and affirmed native rights to lands and that any New Zealand legislation violating the Treaty of Waitangi was ultra vires. For the most part Te Heuheu's contentions regarding the Treaty were left unanswered; the view of the Chief Judge appears to have been that the Treaty could not be considered unless it were part of municipal law. Importantly, however, the Treaty was not dismissed as irrelevant, a significant move away from the Prendergast decision.

Not satisfied with the outcome, Te Heuheu successfully applied for leave to have the case heard by the Privy Council where a similar judgment was made: 'It is well settled that any rights purported to be conferred by such a Treaty of cession cannot be enforced by the courts, except in so far as they have been incorporated in municipal law' (Viscount Simon).[15]

That is the position which remains today,[16] even though on two occasions in recent times the Treaty has been used to interpret laws which do not actually contain a reference to the Treaty. In *Huakina Development Trust v Waikato Valley Authority*, 1987, a Tainui group contested decisions of the Planning Tribunal in connection with the Waikato River and the Water and Soil Conservation Act 1967.[17] Justice Chilwell concluded that Māori cultural and spiritual values should be considered when determining 'the interests of the public generally', as the Act required. He went further to describe the Treaty as 'essential to the foundation of New Zealand' and 'there can be no doubt that the Treaty is part of the fabric of New Zealand society'. 'It follows that it is part of the context in which legislation which impinges upon its principles is to be interpreted when it is proper, in accordance with the principles of statutory interpretation, to have resort to extrinsic material.' In effect, the Chilwell decision acknowledged that the law cannot be interpreted in isolation from society's values—even when those values are not named in the law. Identifying the Treaty as 'part of the fabric of New Zealand society', and 'in light of the Treaty of Waitangi Act', he was able to recognise 'the interpretative availability of the Treaty of Waitangi.' It was a major departure from the earlier views, though it was not necessarily consistent with the views of the majority of jurists.[18]

In 1990, however, a similar judgment was made in the Court of Appeal. The New Zealand Māori Council had challenged the Crown in the High Court, seeking assurances that Māori access to FM frequencies would form part of government policy.[19] Justice Heron ruled that Article 2 of the Treaty did cover Māori language and that the Crown had an obligation to devise safeguards, not only to avoid present damage but also to facilitate future revival and development of the language. He made an order that the Crown ought to delay the sale by tender of frequencies for a period of six weeks. The Crown appealed but on a split vote, three to two, the appeal was dismissed.[20] Important to this discussion, however, was the fact that the Treaty had been applied to a statutory scheme established by the Radiocommunications Act, which did not contain a reference to the Treaty.[21]

Of all court cases concerning the status of the Treaty, the most celebrated has been the State-Owned Enterprises case.[22] In 1986 the State-Owned Enterprises Bill was introduced to establish nine state-owned enterprises that would take over major sectors of state trading activity as profitable operations. The policy of the government was that the new corporations would be required to purchase from the Crown the businesses, including the assets transferred to them at prices to be negotiated. In effect the Crown would be able to sell Crown land to the SOEs which, in turn, could dispose of them with few restraints. Of a total of 27 million hectares (the land surface of New Zealand), three million were intended to be transferred to Landcorp, and 880 000 hectares to Forestcorp. While inquiring into the northern Muriwhenua claim (Ngāti Kuri, Te Aupouri, Te Rarawa, Ngai Takato, and Ngāti Kahu), the Waitangi Tribunal was made aware of concern that land transferred by the Crown could compromise a Waitangi Tribunal recommendation for the return of land to Māori owners. A transfer of Crown land to Forestcorp or Landcorp could render that land out of reach of Māori claimants because the Crown might not be able to buy it back or it might have been sold by the SOE.

The Tribunal raised the question whether the bill itself was contrary to the principles of the Treaty and issued an interim report to the Minister of Māori Affairs, dated 8 December 1986.[23] Consequently (though also because of submissions from others including the Māori members of Parliament), changes to the bill were hastily prepared in an attempt to pacify Māori concerns that the bill was inconsistent with Treaty principles and likely to prejudice future Māori claimants seeking to have Crown land returned. The main amendment was the addition of section 9: 'Nothing in this act shall permit the Crown to act in a manner that is inconsistent with the principles of the Treaty of Waitangi.' A further amendment, section 27, was also added, stating that if prior to 18 December 1986 a claim in respect of certain Crown land had been lodged with the Waitangi Tribunal, the land would continue to be subject to the claim—even after transfer to SOE. The SOE could transfer land back to Crown but might not otherwise dispose of it. If no claim had been lodged by 18 December 1986, the land could be transferred to an SOE without any encumbrances.

In March 1987 Sir Graham Latimer and the New Zealand Māori Council made application to the High Court for a judicial review, based on the allegation that 'unless restrained by this Honourable Court it is likely that the Crown will take action consequential on the exercise of statutory powers pursuant to the Act by way of the transfer of the assets the subject of existing and likely future claims before the Waitangi Tribunal in breach of the provisions of section 9 of the Act.' Their concern was based on good information that, regardless of section 9, the transfer of Crown land to SOEs was imminent. In brief, the Māori position was that section 9 and section 27 were contradictory, and there was a need for clarification. Should section 9 take precedence over section 27; and, if so, then in what ways?

The case was heard in May 1987 by five Appeal Court Judges: Sir Robin Cooke (President), Sir Ivor Richardson, Mr Justice Somers, Mr Justice Casey, Mr Justice Bisson. After extensive evidence and the proposition of different sets of principles by the Crown and the New Zealand Māori Council, for its part the Court of Appeal emphasised the principles of partnership (utmost good faith and reasonableness), active protection, and the honour of the Crown. The expectation from the judges was that the Crown would act in good faith and fairly and reasonably towards the Māori people. Any transfer of assets to an SOE without establishing a system to consider consistency with the principles of Treaty of Waitangi would be unlawful. There was a direction that within 21 days the Crown was to prepare a scheme of safeguards so that pre-Act or post-Act Māori claims to the Waitangi Tribunal would not be prejudiced. The scheme was to be submitted to New Zealand Māori Council for agreement or comment within a further 21 days.

Two major conclusions were evident in this case. First, the principles of the Treaty were to override everything else in the SOE Act; and, second, the Treaty partners were to act towards each other reasonably and with the utmost good faith. As ordered by the court, the New Zealand Māori Council and the Crown entered into negotiations. They discussed many issues including, of course, safeguards for Crown land that may be the subject of a Tribunal claim in the future. The negotiations led eventually to the Treaty of Waitangi (State Enterprises) Act 1988—in which safeguards were emphasised and new arrangements made.

The arrangement allowed the Crown to sell all its assets to the SOEs, which could then sell them off again. All the land titles would carry a memorial, warning that the land could be resumed by the government if there were a successful claim before the Waitangi Tribunal, and compensation would be paid. But the SOEs also had the right to ask the Tribunal to order the memorials be lifted. The Tribunal would have to seek out any possible claims. It could order the memorial to be lifted from the title if there were no claims, if the claim was not well founded, or if it was upheld but the Tribunal did not order the land to be returned. In addition, the Tribunal also gained the new power to make binding decisions on the return of SOE land, while its power over other land and resources remained limited to making recommendations. Provision for mediation of claims in place of full hearings was included in the Act, and more funding was made available for researching claims and legal aid.

The Waitangi Tribunal

The preceding section describes the differing approaches taken by the courts over the years to the Treaty of Waitangi. Prior to 1975 there was no effective avenue to contest claims for grievances relating to the Treaty, other than through the courts. But unless the law were in question, and, as earlier discussed, unless the Treaty were incorporated in the law, then recourse to a Treaty argument to settle a Treaty grievance was extremely limited. Because it was established specifically to investigate claims against the Crown for breaches of the principles of the Treaty of Waitangi, the Waitangi Tribunal, Te Rōpu Whakamana i te Tiriti o Waitangi, was the first formal mechanism available to Māori to seek redress on non-statutory Treaty grievances. Initially it attracted little attention, but after the 1983 Motunui case, it was evident that the Tribunal, with or without the powers to make binding recommendations, had the potential to influence the government's attitude and policy. Māori interest escalated; whereas between 1975 and 1986 there were only 36 enquiries, in 1987 there were 88 enquiries in one year, an increase linked mainly to the 1985 amendment to the Treaty of Waitangi Act, extending the jurisdiction of the Tribunal back from 1975 to 1840. In 1988, 56 enquiries were lodged. By August 1991, 224 claims had been registered with the Tribunal, and by March 1993 over 300 claims were on record. By March 1997 the number of claims stood at 633.

Claims lodged with the Tribunal may be described as historical, contemporary, or conceptual. Historical claims relate to the actions of the Crown in the past and are mostly about the way in which land was acquired from Māori owners either through direct purchases from tribes, or through the Māori Land Court, or by confiscation. Contemporary claims cover social and cultural issues as well as the processes used by government—Māori language, resource management, education, immigration. And conceptual claims usually contend for a Māori interest in the use and development of rivers, lakes, foreshores, minerals, and geothermal resources, or in the outputs from the development of those resources.[24] The rapid increase in the number of claims has severely tested the capacity of the Tribunal, calling into question the adequacy of resources and exposing the need for a system of prioritising claims.

Generally claims are considered when all the necessary research has been completed, but this method disadvantages later claims, especially where they will be compromised by remedies suggested for an earlier settlement. To overcome some of these difficulties, the Tribunal has now established a regional approach to historical claims, the Rangahaua Whānui project, by arranging broad historical surveys in each district. It will enable equal weighting to be given to all historic claims, reduce duplication, foster a national overview, and inform the Tribunal about the relative impacts of specific claims *vis-à-vis* other claims.[25] Rangahaua Whānui identified fifteen districts,[26] and within them four criteria were suggested for evaluating the seriousness of Treaty breaches: Crown acts of commission, Crown acts of omission, demography, and the quantity and value of the resource lost.[27]

Nonetheless, the Tribunal, as much as the claimants, is concerned that inevitable time delays in arranging hearings, coupled with costs, reduce access to the process of Treaty hearings and therefore represent an injustice, especially if the range of remedies—or the amount of compensation—is fixed. Of all claims registered, approximately one-third have been cleared.[28] It is apparent that a high proportion of claims have not proceeded past the point of registration, and that the number of registered claims has grown at a faster rate than the number of claims being cleared. And even if, as expected, the Rangahaua Whānui project goes some way to reversing that trend, many claimants will not, themselves, be able to see the fruition of many years of research or the dissipation of intergenerational grievances.

By 31 January 1995, the Tribunal had written 45 reports. On average a single report contains five recommendations, though some have as many as ten. Crown responses to Waitangi Tribunal recommendations have created some Māori scepticism about the Tribunal's lack of power, even though 43 per cent of recommendations have been fully implemented. In 1995 the Controller and Auditor-General reported that more than one third of the recommendations from claims reported in the years ended June 1986, 1987 and 1988 were still not fully implemented. More than half of the recommendations from claims reported in the years ended June 1992 and 1993 had not even been considered by the government and there had been 'no start' on 22 per cent of all recommendations. Only 6 per cent had been totally rejected but less than half had been fully implemented.[29] A further 12 per cent were before Parliament awaiting the final passage of legislation.

Under the leadership of its second chairman, Chief Judge Eddie Durie of Rangitane, Ngāti Kauwhata and Ngāti Raukawa, the Tribunal has earned a reputation for sound judgment and reasoned argument. Not content to accept a jurisprudence shaped only by western custom and practice, the Tribunal has interpreted concepts of justice, fairness, and ownership from Māori perspectives, drawing on the rich evidence from Māori claimants and the knowledge and skills of individual Māori members themselves. Moreover, the Tribunal has been able to conceptualise Māori positions in terms of western law and history and in so doing has contributed greatly to New Zealand's understanding of its heritage. Current (1997) members of the Tribunal are: Bishop Manuhuia Bennett, Sir John Ingram, Brian Corban, Areta Koopu, John Kneebone, Roger Maaka, Judge Richard Kearney, John Clarke, John Turei, Dame Augusta Wallace, Dr Evelyn Stokes, Prof. M. P. K. Sorrenson, the Hon. Dr Michael Bassett, Pamela Ringwood, Keita Walker. Among them is a range of disciplines and qualifications (law, tikanga Māori, historical geography, anthropology, business, agriculture, history, community development) and a mix of Māori and Pākehā, all appointed by the Governor-General on the recommendation of the Minister of Māori Affairs, after consultation with the Minister of Justice. Although the Act requires appointments to recognise the spirit of partnership, and by implication an equal number of Māori and Pākehā members, in the end appointments are political and the current imbalance (six Māori, nine Pākehā) needs to be seen in that light. The Waitangi Tribunal is serviced by the Waitangi Tribunal Division, part of the Department for the Courts, and is responsible for monitoring and maintaining the register of Treaty claims, processing legal aid applications, and managing research.

The Tribunal does not operate in a vacuum and is subject not only to the quality of its research and the constraints of its Act, as well as the legal arguments which may dominate a hearing, but also to prevailing policies—or their absence. On more than one occasion the Chairman of the Tribunal has spoken of the need for a clear claims resolution policy and for Māori participation in the formulation of that policy. 'There is conceivably some danger, when, through lack of structure, important and influential positions in Māori policy formulation, and I presume to include here the Māori Land Court and Waitangi Tribunal, are filled only by state nominees. They become filled according to criteria that the state judges as important for its own policies, crafted not by Māori, but for them.'[30] His warning is a reminder that the Treaty of Waitangi is not only about ways and means of settling Treaty grievances but about a joint (Māori and the Crown) approach to deciding the relative priorities and strategies for resolving grievances. Although consultation with Māori has been of some significance, for the most part the resolution frameworks have not been crafted by Māori.

Five major issues requiring greater clarity have been identified by the Tribunal in the resolution of claims: entitlement, representation, comparative equities, Māori input, and limitations.[31] Some of these relate to the claimants themselves and include questions of entitlement and both customary and modern representation. Who is entitled to benefit from a claim and who is mandated to present a claim and speak on behalf of others? Should the focus be on iwi or hapū or even smaller units? Sir Tipene O'Regan argues that the overlapping claims of hapū and their interrelationships with neighbouring hapū makes it simply impractical to deal with any level of organisation which is less than an iwi, though he does accept that it could be different in the North Island, and he carefully does not use the same argument when discussing the relationships and overlapping claims between neighbouring iwi.[32] Economies of scale are important but frequently leave smaller hapū and some whānau feeling denied a voice, especially if they are not represented, or lack confidence in a broader tribal forum. Māori women, in particular, have been critical of the Māori Treaty negotiators and the iwi approach to settlements. 'Settlement decisions and outcomes should be directed at our core problems and the basic unit of analysis should be Māori individuals and aggregated households.'[33]

The Crown has attempted to deal with the problems of representation through the enactment of section 30(1)(b) of Te Ture Whenua Māori Act 1993. At the request of the Chief Executive of Te Puni Kōkiri or the Chief Judge of the Māori Land Court, the Māori Land Court may determine who are the 'most appropriate representatives of any class or group of Māori affected by the negotiations, consultations, allocation, or other matter.' However, according to Caren Wickliffe, the problem is that the Māori Land Court is only authorised to determine representation issues and allocation. It cannot determine who has the right to settle a claim.[34]

Comparative equities as between claimants have become increasingly important with the government's decision to fix a ceiling to the total budget for settling claims. Claims from tribes differ in both quantity and quality, and it is no easy task to compare one with the other. In the wake of the Waikato (Tainui) settlement, Robert Mahuta was at pains to point out that, at least in the tribe's opinion, Tainui had not set a precedent. 'Other tribes have the responsibility to make up their own minds about settlements and the government policy. This settlement is for Waikato, nobody else.'[35] Within a year, however, negotiating tribes knew that the amount available for claims had been more or less set according to a formula benchmarked against the $170 million awarded to Waikato.

Direct Negotiation

By 1989 when the government published its Treaty of Waitangi principles, it was obvious that the Crown was planning a deliberate strategy to return Treaty issues to the political arena, rather than relying on the Tribunal or a court of law. It was no secret that the government had reservations about the implications of the Waitangi Tribunal recommendations and also about some court cases, including the Tainui Coalcorp case. Early in 1990 the President of the Court of Appeal had been criticised by the Prime Minister, Geoffrey Palmer, for commenting on political matters.[36] Sir Robin Cooke had concluded that it was ultimately for the courts to decide whether the government had met its obligations under the principles of the Treaty of Waitangi. Palmer responded, 'It must be made clear that the roles of Parliament, the government and the courts are understood and certain. It must be made clear that the government will make the final decisions on Treaty issues.'[37]

To increase its capacity to handle Treaty matters, the government established a Crown Task Force consisting of a Cabinet Committee on Treaty of Waitangi issues, a core group of officials from the major government departments and agencies involved with Treaty matters, and a Treaty of Waitangi Policy Unit (now known as the Office of Treaty Settlements). The latter was to provide advice to the Crown on Treaty issues and eventually to arrange and provide leadership in negotiations. Apart from placing the government in the driver's seat, direct negotiations would also be a less costly and less delayed process than litigation. Neither were tribes slow to realise the advantages of talking to the government around the table instead of through lawyers in a court room. A degree of flexibility was now possible. But there were also concerns that direct negotiation would disadvantage smaller claimants who lacked negotiating experience or whose desperate economic conditions would lead them to accept any deal that offered short-term relief. Some of the concerns regarding direct negotiations and the Crown Task Force were raised by the National Māori Congress in a submission to the Ministerial Planning Group that wrote the report, *Ka Awatea* (1991).[38] The appointment of independent mediators, more realistic levels of funding, especially for smaller tribes, and acceptance of Waitangi Tribunal findings (by the Treaty of Waitangi Policy Unit) were recommended.

The Cabinet Committee on Treaty of Waitangi Issues has broad responsibility to develop strategies and policies for the government concerning Treaty matters and especially monitoring and prioritising the claims negotiations register. Several Cabinet ministers make up the committee, including the Minister in Charge of Treaty Negotiations, who chairs the committee, the Deputy Prime Minister, the Attorney-General, the Associate Minister of Finance, the Ministers of Fisheries, the Environment, Agriculture, Conservation, Māori Affairs, and Internal Affairs, and the Parliamentary Under-Secretary for Agriculture and Forestry. In 1995 the functions of the Treaty of Waitangi Policy Unit were assumed by the new Office of Treaty Settlements (OTS) which, though part of the Department of Justice, reports directly to the Minister in Charge of Treaty Negotiations. As direct negotiation has increased, the role of the OTS has become more significant and correspondingly its budget was increased to $8.2 million. The Waitangi Tribunal budget, meanwhile, was also increased (by $500 000 in 1995) but only to $3.7 million.[39]

Direct negotiation has been conducted at several levels, and at least three distinct approaches can be identified: negotiations between the Crown and a group representing all Māori (comprehensive Māori negotiations); negotiations with tribes for tribal interests (tribal negotiations); and negotiations—or more correctly discussions—involving the Crown and particular Māori leaders (leadership summits).[40]

Comprehensive negotiations were employed in the disposal of surplus railways properties and the settlement of Māori fisheries claims. In 1991 the Crown and the National Māori Congress, acting on behalf of all tribes (except three who had already commenced their own negotiations), established a Joint Working Party to negotiate the disposal of surplus railways lands. A combined approach to consultation, research, and decision-making made possible the disposal of major parts of the total portfolio without recourse to litigation or further claims to the Tribunal. All surplus properties were scrutinised by a joint Congress–Crown secretariat, and tribes were invited to indicate any interest in a possible claim. If there were no Māori interest, the land was cleared for sale. If there were a claim, or the potential for a claim, the land was not to be disposed of until the claim had been settled. The advantages of the model have already been discussed in chapter 5, but it was subsequently criticised by the Minister of Justice who thought that the Māori side had misinterpreted their role.[41] In Māori eyes, however, it had worked well, largely because regular contact had been maintained with the tribes and a participatory process was established.

Considerable experience in negotiating was also obtained by the Māori fisheries negotiators in the long lead-up to the Sealord Products agreement.[42] In that case, the negotiation was on behalf of all Māori and for a resource which had only recently been made into a commercial property right. Not only were there concerns about a mandate, but pressures from the fishing industry, tribes, and the government combined to severely test the efficacy of a global settlement process, in which a small group negotiated on behalf of all Māori. A settlement of sorts was the eventual outcome, but the complexities and the Māori misgivings shelved any prospect of a similar approach being used for land settlements.

THE FISCAL ENVELOPE

In December 1994 the government released details of its proposals for the settlement of Treaty of Waitangi claims.[43] Popularly known as the 'fiscal envelope', the proposal was developed over a two-year period with negligible Māori input. It followed close on the heels of the Sealord deal and, like it, was intended to provide durable, full and final settlements for historic claims. But whereas Sealord was a settlement for all Māori, the new proposals were for settlement by direct negotiation on an iwi-by-iwi basis. Simply, a framework for the settlement of claims was proposed. The intention was to settle all claims without utilising natural resources or the conservation estate, and to limit the total value of all claims to a billion dollars. A ten-year period was prescribed, and to ensure durability, legislation would be introduced which removed settled claims from the jurisdiction of the Waitangi Tribunal or the courts.

Before the Proposals for the Settlement of Treaty of Waitangi Claims (as they were called) were officially released, Prime Minister Bolger invited a select group to his house to hear at first hand what was intended. Sir Hepi Te Heuheu publicly declined the invitation on the grounds that acceptance would compromise him and his people. He was opposed to the proposals. Then on 29 January 1995, anxious to avoid the deep divisions which surrounded consultation over the Sealord agreement, he called representatives of all tribes and other Māori organisations to a meeting at the Hirangi marae near Turangi to discuss the proposals.[44] There was a unanimous rejection, which set the stage for the government's planned consultation round. Although the Crown publicly dismissed the Hirangi hui as the work of radicals,[45] it was the conservative Māori element that carried the message back to marae and iwi. Some thirteen hui were then held, and at each the verdict was the same: the proposals were inconsistent with the principles of honour and good faith and should be rejected. Wira Gardiner, who as Chief Executive of Te Puni Kōkiri had the unenviable task of taking the proposals around the country for discussion, reported high levels of tension, misunderstanding, misinformation, and even hostility.[46] His book, *Return to Sender*, contains vivid descriptions of each hui and the stresses imposed on him and his staff as Māori public servants when opposition mounted. Māori fury often boiled over to scald the messengers (Te Puni Kōkiri) as much as the politicians who had drafted the message.

Māori objections to the fiscal envelope proposal, rehearsed at the Turangi hui, revolved around inadequate consultation, the principles used, the government's assumptions and claims of ownership of natural resources and the conservation estate, and of course the billion dollar cap.[47] There was also strong feeling that a more fundamental constitutional point was at stake and should be afforded priority discussion, a matter rejected by the Minister in Charge of Treaty Negotiations. 'Such issues had nothing to do with the proposals.'[48]

Although a consultation round was planned, the government's proposals made it clear that certain key features of the package were not available for discussion—including the conservation estate and the billion dollar cap. Consultation at a relatively late stage, when much of the proposal had already been decided upon, was contrary to the established wisdom on community consultation laid down by the High Court in the Wellington International Airport case.[49] The worst fears, that policy had already been decided and that consultation was merely an exercise in distributing information, were subsequently borne out. Before the 1996 general election, three settlements had been negotiated using the framework contained in the fiscal envelope. Policy or not, it had become the practice.

Surprisingly, in view of the aims of the proposals, the principles of the Treaty of Waitangi were not included among the settlement principles. Reference to the Treaty focused attention on Article 3 and, in particular, on access to mainstream government programs. But the significance of Treaty principles for Māori relationships with the Crown, as defined by the Waitangi Tribunal and the Court of Appeal in 1987, had been omitted. Instead, seven settlement principles were introduced: the Crown explicitly acknowledges historical injustices; one injustice should not create another; the Crown has a duty to act in the best interests of all New Zealanders; if settlements are to be durable they must be fair, sustainable, and remove the sense of grievance; the resolution process must be consistent and equitable between claimant groups; Article 3 rights under the Treaty are not affected; settlements will take into account fiscal and economic constraints. Only two principles gave any indication of fairness to the claimants; the others appeared to provide reassurances for non-claimants. While there was no disagreement that the rights of others should be protected, Māori felt that the resolution of proven claims should be primarily guided by the principles of natural justice, not political expediency, economic affordability, or popular support.

In the proposals, four types of interest in a natural resource were listed: ownership interest, use interest, value interest, regulatory interest. In the context of Treaty claims natural resources comprise water, geothermal energy, river and lake beds, foreshore and seabed, sand and shingle, and minerals including gold, coal, gas, and petroleum; and Māori interests were deemed to be confined to use and value interests. A refusal to contemplate Māori ownership of natural resources, even though acknowledging use and value interests, was described by most tribes as contrary to the Treaty of Waitangi. The courts had recognised Māori interests in natural resources and have never explicitly ruled out Māori ownership. In the proposals, however, the court position had been interpreted as an indication that by implication the courts did not recognise Māori ownership of natural resources. However, 'tino rangatiratanga' in Article 2 conveys a level of interest which goes well beyond 'use and value.' In 1992, for example, as discussed in chapter 2, the Waitangi Tribunal had already found that the Crown had no right to presume control over the Mohaka River, since Ngāti Pāhauwera had never relinquished rangatiratanga.[50] In choosing to ignore this interpretation, the proposals appeared to have prematurely opted for a colonial view of ownership and dismissed global understandings of the ownership rights of indigenous peoples.

The proposals similarly excluded the conservation estate from settlement arrangements. An assumption was made that the estate was owned by the Crown, although Ngai Tahu, Whakatohea, and Ngāti Awa, as well as Tuhoe, made it clear that the acquisition of lands by the Crown for public use had very often contravened the Treaty of Waitangi. Their claims included parts of the estate.

One billion dollars was proposed as the total settlement sum. The amount was non-negotiable and included the assessed value of land and other resources used to settle earlier claims such as the Sealord Products agreement. The proposals did not explain how a sum of one billion dollars had been calculated, but it was justified as a political decision largely on the basis of affordability and acceptability to the wider community. There was an assumption that one billion dollars was fair and affordable. However, neither the methodology used to calculate the amount, nor the basis for deciding affordability was disclosed. The cap was simply stated as a given, even though most claims had not yet received due consideration, while others had yet to be filed. In fact, the amount necessary to ensure a just settlement is not known. Estimates vary, but even highly conservative assessments suggest that the sum of one billion dollars falls well short of a reasonable and fair settlement price by some ten or more billion dollars.

Significant opposition to the proposals also stemmed from the implicit discounting of the Māori version of the Treaty. Nowhere in the proposals were the roles and powers of government fettered by the authority of tino rangatiratanga contained in Article 2 of the Māori version of the Treaty. Similarly, discussion on the conservation estate and natural resources placed no importance on Māori understandings of the meaning of the Treaty as conveyed in the Māori version. Ironically, whereas in 1975 the principles of the Treaty were introduced by the Crown as a tool to enable both versions of the Treaty to be addressed, for the fiscal envelope proposals the government reverted to a literal interpretation of the terms of the Treaty. In so doing it not only relegated the Māori version to an inconsequential position but also began to interpret the Treaty in a fragmented fashion, article by article, rather than as an integrated set of broad understandings.

The effect of the Hirangi hui was to set the stage for a rejection of the proposals at subsequent hui. Opposition was so widespread that by the end of April the future of the fiscal envelope was in doubt. A planned national hui was cancelled, and even though the time for submissions was extended, no analysis of them was ever publicly reported. But just when it seemed that the envelope had quietly disappeared, the billion dollar figure surfaced again in the 1995 budget, and in 1996 the formula was evident in further settlements. Had it always been intended? Was the fiscal envelope still just a proposal, or had it already been accepted as policy? Had it always been policy? And would negotiations to settle claims continue as if there had been substantial Māori acceptance of the government's proposed settlement framework? On all counts the answer appeared to be yes.

It would be misleading to say that Māori could find no good in the fiscal envelope; indeed, the number of tribes who were willing to negotiate within that framework suggests there was some acceptance of the method. Tipene O'Regan, for example, despite earlier assertions that the proposals were largely designed to block Ngai Tahu land claims,[51] said to be worth $200–$300 million, eventually negotiated a $170 million settlement according to the fiscal envelope principles. The idea of putting to rest long-standing grievances as soon as possible made sense; and the advantages of avoiding costly litigation had considerable appeal, especially for tribes who had already spent large sums on court action. The requirement that claimants be able to produce evidence of a mandate was also appealing. Too often, in the past, the wrong group had been negotiating on behalf of others without prior approval. There was also some recognition, perhaps grudging, that the government had taken a courageous step in introducing the settlement of Treaty claims as one of the key elements in the government's strategic policy objectives.

But even after the public outcry had subsided, serious misgivings remained. Among them were concerns about the formula used to settle claims and the lack of transparency as to the wider policy context. The Auditor-General recommended that 'there is a need to complete and make public a comprehensive Treaty settlement policy, including goals for advancing claims through the settlement process.'[52] The Waitangi Tribunal also raised questions about the basis for government settlement policy and, no matter what else had motivated the policy, cast doubts on whether just compensation had been a major consideration. In the *Taranaki Report* the Tribunal estimated that, based on legal principles, the real costs of land confiscation amounted to some billions of dollars. Recognising that for whatever reasons 'a full reparation . . . is unavailable to Māori as a matter of political policy', the Tribunal cautioned against requiring the claimants to sign a full and final release for compensation as though legal principles applied. If a full pay-off for the past on legal lines was impractical, then there should be no pretence that a settlement capped for other reasons was fair.[53]

During negotiations to form a coalition government after the 1996 general election, New Zealand First insisted that the fiscal envelope policy be altered. As a consequence, the two parties agreed to 'discontinue the fiscal envelope on the basis that there is respect for the settlements already effected, which would not be reopened, [that] the parties confirm that the Crown will endeavour to settle claims on their merits using the settlements already effected as benchmarks, [and that they] be fiscally responsible.' In addition there was agreement for a review of government policy on natural resources and funding research and negotiating costs.[54] However, few read into the coalition agreement any real change in policy. Benchmarking claims according to those already settled within the fiscal envelope framework, and the pledge for fiscal responsibility, did little to persuade Māori that there had been any substantial amendments, a view shared by the Minister in Charge of Treaty Negotiations, Doug Graham.[55] A march from Waitangi to Wellington, organised largely by Annette Sykes and Mike Smith, was planned for February 1997, partly to protest against the continuing policy and the coalition government's 'cosmetic attempt to pacify Māori in the face of their betrayal of Māori voters.'[56] Subsequently, the march's destination was changed to Rotorua, and though it failed to achieve impact similar to the 1975 land march, it invited further discussion on the exact meaning of the coalition agreement.

TREATY SETTLEMENTS

Notwithstanding Māori opposition to the fiscal envelope, direct negotiation for the settlement of historic Treaty claims continued within the government's 1994 framework. Doug Graham, as Minister in Charge of Treaty Negotiations, carried much of the burden and in so far as the outcomes have been successful, much of the credit must rest with him. A less than sympathetic Pākehā electorate needed to be persuaded that settlements of this magnitude could be justified and were good for the country as a whole; Māori confidence had to be won over; and Cabinet needed to be committed. But by August 1996, there were signs of progress and a wider public acceptance of the significance of the negotiating process. Mr Graham's advocacy and diplomacy were seen as important ingredients which had the potential to create enduring settlements and position tribes as major corporate players, 'level pegging with Fletcher Challenge and Wattie's.'[57] Among the claimants, Tainui, Whakatohea, Ngai Tahu, Ngāti Awa, northern Taranaki, and Ngāti Whātua appeared eager to talk to the Crown.

Tainui

Tainui, or at least that part of Tainui known as Waikato, settled first. Within one week of the announcement of the government's Proposals for the Settlement of Treaty of Waitangi Claims—and entirely consistent with it—tribal leaders signed a Heads of Agreement. Probably the most significant land claim settlement ever, the Tainui settlement was finally concluded in May 1995 and signed by Te Arikinui Dame Te Atairangikaahu and the Rt. Hon. Jim Bolger. Legislation to finalise the deed of settlement was passed by Parliament, and Queen Elizabeth II gave the Royal Assent personally in Wellington, thus giving immediate effect to the settlement. The Waikato Raupatu Claims Settlement Act 1995 had become the first piece of New Zealand legislation to be signed by the monarch herself.[58]

The settlement related to the confiscation of 486 502 hectares, taken under the New Zealand Settlements Act 1863.[59] After some years of a mutually beneficial relationship between Tainui and the settlers in the Auckland region, colonial authorities became alarmed when Potatau Te Wherowhero, the paramount Waikato chief, was anointed Māori King in 1858. Although the King movement was set up mainly to stop land being sold, by vesting its ownership in a king, the government (in Britain) and the settlers in New Zealand felt threatened. They saw the King as a challenge to the might of Parliament and British rule, but, perhaps more importantly for settlers in Auckland, they feared that access to land purchases in the rich Waikato valley would become difficult.

Concerns were not allayed when some Tainui went to the aid of Te Ati Awa in Taranaki in 1860–61, and took up arms against the colonial forces, apparently against the wishes of Potatau. Governor George Grey, now able to capitalise on a supposed Tainui threat to law and order, and peace, made it known that King movement supporters were preparing to attack Auckland. There was no evidence to back the rumour but it served to justify military action. In 1863 General Duncan Cameron marched with 5 000 soldiers and large numbers of militiamen south from Auckland towards the Waikato.

Grey issued a proclamation on 9 July, requiring all Māori living north of the Mangatawhiri River to take an oath of allegiance to the Crown—or shift to the other side of the river. Then, on 14 July, Grey released another proclamation advising that to preserve law and order it had become necessary to set up military posts beyond the river. Any Māori who resisted would have his land confiscated. In fact, although dated July 11, the second proclamation was not issued until July 14, two days after Grey had actually crossed the river.

Tainui were not prepared to sit back and witness an occupation of their land. They suspected, with good reason, that Cameron's invasion was the first step towards compulsory acquisition of their property—the very reason why all land had been vested in King Potatau. Resistance was met with warfare. In a series of battles, large numbers of lives were lost. Rangiriri, Ngaruawahia, and eventually, after a three-day bombardment, Orakau were taken. The Crown then used the Settlements Act to confiscate the 486 502 hectares. These lands were known as the raupatu lands—the lands taken by force.

The 1927 Sim commission found that an injustice had been done; the actions of the troops and then the confiscation of land were unwarranted. Small compensatory payments were made to some landowners and, in 1946, Te Puea Herangi and Prime Minister Peter Fraser agreed on further payments, £5 000 annually. But no land had been returned. Then in 1991 the Labour government offered a $9 million 'take it or leave it' deal. Tainui, however, never lost sight of the goal of land for land: 'as land was taken so land should be returned', and with the advent of the Waitangi Tribunal a more comprehensive claim had been registered. Meanwhile, court proceedings were filed against the Crown because of the proposed transfer of the Huntly coal mines to Coalcorp, and the Court of Appeal returned a decision favourable to the tribe.[60] With the Tainui legal victory as the leverage, the Crown opted to negotiate directly. The Tribunal hearings never reached reporting stage.

The Tainui settlement included three main components: the return of 15 790 hectares (although the Crown had another 15 000 hectares, the land component was limited to what could be readily returned); an apology from the Queen; and monetary compensation to bring the total value of the package to $170 million. As Tainui would be the new landlord, guarantees were required to protect existing tenants such as the University of Waikato, the Police, the Court. During negotiations, the tribe withdrew its claim over the coal mines and made no claim over the conservation estate, although the deed of settlement provided for a permanent Tainui appointment to the Waikato Conservancy Board. The tribe was also careful to point out that the settlement does not replace their claim over the Waikato River, or other blocks of land. 'The biggest and most expensive claim is yet to be settled—that is the River.'[61] Should Parliament at some stage in the future wish to increase the total amount to be spent on claims, the Waikato settlement is likely to be increased since the settlement was benchmarked at seventeen per cent of all claims. The deed notes that the 'Redress value represents 17 per cent of the value of the redress deemed to have been set aside by the Government for historical claims', an indirect reference to the fiscal envelope cap which was a core feature of the Crown's Proposals for the Settlement of Treaty of Waitangi Claims. However, the bench-marking has a twofold purpose; Parliament would be unlikely to increase the amount of compensation paid to Tainui without also increasing the payments to all other successful claimants; and the prospect of such large scale payouts would reduce the likelihood of changes ever being made by future governments—to Tainui or any tribe. Durability had been strengthened; and was again endorsed in the coalition agreement (settlements already effected were not to be reopened).

Tainui have agreed on the broad principles which will guide the distribution of benefits to the tribe. Individual dividends are unlikely but education will be actively promoted; tribal landholdings will be increased (as an investment for the future) and the thirty or so Waikato hapū will be encouraged towards greater economic independence. As for the land returned, it will be vested in the name of Potatau Te Wherowhero (the first Māori king) and never alienated. On the other hand, land purchased with proceeds from the settlement will be used more flexibly. Thus the tribe will be able to reconcile two often conflicting objectives—to retain land for cultural and customary purposes and to use land for maximum economic advancement. To assist in the post-settlement phase, a new tribal corporate structure has been developed. The Tainui Māori Trust Board had played a key role in negotiating and then developing the agreement, but recognised that it was not the most appropriate vehicle for the next stage, and its demise had been specifically written into the Waikato Raupatu Claims Settlement Act.

Not all Tainui were in favour of the settlement. There were accusations from some of the 33 000 beneficiaries, encouraged by veteran activist Eva Rickard, that the Tainui Trust Board was not sufficiently representative to speak for all hapū; and in any event, they claimed, the settlement should be with each of the 33 hapū individually (those who had had land confiscated), rather than with a body purporting to speak for the wider tribe. That option had been considered by the Board, but because Tainui wanted a settlement based on the return of land, and because the Crown holdings were not evenly distributed among hapū, a collective settlement was seen as both a practical and possible solution. Regardless, two factions sought relief with the Te Whare Ahupiri, the 'justice arm of the Māori Parliament set up by the Confederation of Chiefs of the United Tribes of Ko Huiarau (sometimes called the Confederated Tribes of New Zealand).'[62] Though not widely used as a court of justice, nor recognised by most iwi as a relevant contemporary Māori body, for the two disaffected groups Te Whare Ahupiri represented a source of authority which drew on Māori concepts of justice and tikanga, and in that respect it had appeal. Te Ariki Manahi Kewene alleged that Ngāti Haua and others were being disadvantaged in the settlement process because the Crown was investing their hapū raupatu lands in another body. Te Whare Ahupiri advised that the Crown should 'cease trampling on the mana of the thirty three hapū' and 'should cease to dispossess hapū any further.'[63] Heemi Pene, for the descendants of Maramatutahi of Ngāti Wairere, took a similar action to Te Whare Ahupiri, which in his case recommended Crown compensation for 'trampling on the mana of Maramatutahi and Ngāti Wairere.'[64]

Aware of the vocal opposition, which was to lead to a brief occupation of the marae at Waikato University by a section of Ngāti Wairere, and of Coalcorp land by Te Whaawhaakia, the Tainui Trust Board went to some lengths to explain the agreement to beneficiaries. A series of information hui were held throughout the country and the 11 000 adult beneficiaries were sent written details of the proposals. A postal ballot was then held and beneficiaries had until Friday 28 April to vote in favour or against. The Māori Land Court acted as scrutineer. Though slightly less than half of all beneficiaries responded, of those who did, 75 per cent were in favour of the terms of the settlement. One week before the actual deed was signed, tribal members opposed to the agreement petitioned the High Court to prevent it. However, the court dismissed the case.

The Whakatohea Settlement

The advent of mixed member proportional representation (MMP) and the possibility of a coalition government that might be unable to agree on the terms of future Treaty settlements acted as a catalyst for some tribes to reach agreement with the Crown before the October 1996 general election. A prerequisite of the negotiation process was acceptance onto the Negotiations Work Programme, which in turn presupposed prior agreement between Māori and the Crown that the claims were historically verifiable, the claimant group had a mandate, the Crown's position on the alleged breaches was accepted, and the claim was seen as having sufficient priority. The claimants would also have to agree to negotiate a final settlement and to waive all other avenues of redress.

Whakatohea satisfied these requirements and entered into negotiations in 1995. On 1 October 1996 a draft deed of settlement was signed by Claude Edwards and John Delamere (for Whakatohea) and the Minister in Charge of Treaty Negotiations, the Hon. Doug Graham, for the Crown. At the heart of the matter was 70 000 hectares of highly fertile Bay of Plenty land around Opotiki. Largely in retribution for the 1865 execution of missionary Carl Volkner, an informer who was known to be passing on information to the Governor about the tribe's political and commercial activities, the land had been confiscated. The New Zealand Settlements Act 1863 and the Suppression of Rebellion Act 1863 both allowed the government to take the necessary action. In consequence, the tribe was left poor and despondent. Although in 1992 a Crown pardon was granted to Mokomoko in respect of his alleged complicity in the killing of Volkner, compensation for the land had never been seriously addressed.

Included in the deed of settlement was a Crown apology for the invasion of Whakatohea lands and the wrongful labelling of the tribe as rebels, an act which had led to the unjust confiscation of land, taonga, and other resources. Excluded from the settlement were fishing rights, and there was recognition that Whakatohea would be forgoing a substantial part of its desired redress. The Crown's offer was for $40 million, less the value of any properties transferred from the Crown (estimated at approximately $2 million). Nine small urban properties were involved, including the Post Shop, the Telecom site, the court house, the police station, and the Road Services depot. Critical to the Whakatohea settlement were conservation issues, and the Crown proposed discussions on involving the tribe in the management of Ohiwa Harbour, direct iwi representation on the East Coast Conservation Board, access to specified plants and shrubs, access to whalebone, and the right to identify and have designated sites of special significance, topuni, within the conservation estate. As well, the Crown would grant to Whakatohea deeds of recognition (not ownership) over some riverbeds within the Whakatohea area.

In return, Whakatohea was expected to forgo further court or Waitangi Tribunal action for historic claims (i.e. claims occurring before 21 September 1992) and to establish a trust to receive the money and property from the Crown. As for Tainui, the terms of the Deed needed to be approved by the Whakatohea iwi but also, in the Whakatohea case, by the new government.

Thirteen information hui were arranged by the Māori negotiators to inform iwi members about the proposal. Almost from the outset there were objections, mostly from the young and academic section of the tribe, but also from Professor Ranginui Walker who considered that the process had been too hasty and that the twelve negotiators had 'no control over the offer.' He was critical of John Delamere's 'strong armed' approach. Delamere, now a member of Parliament and Deputy Treasurer, dismissed the opponents of the deed as a 'very vocal and educated minority' who had failed to offer any alternative.[65]

The chief negotiator, Claude Edwards, took a generally pragmatic view. Pushed perhaps by a fear of being dominated by larger tribes, and aware of a rapidly changing political climate, if not oscillating national sympathies, he had decided on a deal which could realise an immediate income for the tribe of $3.6 million a year. Though not a perfect settlement, the $40 million package amounted to approximately one quarter of the $170 million, rumoured to be available to settle all Mātaatua claims. As the smallest of the four Mātaatua tribes, he was not entirely dissatisfied with the proposed terms of the settlement, though he recognised that without sufficient iwi support there could be no progress. In the event hapū opposition was strong, and by July 1997 any prospect of a quick settlement seemed unlikely.

The Ngai Tahu Settlement

Ngai Tahu also successfully completed a draft deed of settlement for their very extensive claim, just one week before the general election. On 5 October 1996 Sir Tipene O'Regan and Charlie Croft (for Ngai Tahu) and the Minister in Charge of Treaty Negotiations, Doug Graham, (for the Crown) signed an agreement which promised Ngai Tahu $170 million in cash and land. Although the same monetary value as the Tainui settlement, the Ngai Tahu settlement was constructed along different lines and came about for different reasons. Whenua raupatu (confiscated lands) played no part in the Ngai Tahu claim.

One of the larger Waitangi Tribunal reports is the 1992 *Ngai Tahu Report*. The three volumes are about dispossession, deceit, broken promises, and inflicted poverty. As in the case of Tainui, a token settlement was made some years ago, and the Ngai Tahu Māori Trust Board had been set up to administer compensatory payments. But it was an inadequate step which failed to satisfy a sense of grievance. The Waitangi Tribunal allowed a more realistic appraisal of the situation, especially in the light of Treaty of Waitangi promises. Though recognising the severity of the injustice and the amount of land alienated, largely by a failure to establish reserves as agreed to before large-scale land sales, the Tribunal did not make specific recommendations for remedies. Instead they adopted the now familiar practice of recommending settlement through negotiation with the Crown.

The Ngai Tahu claim was a major and lengthy claim brought by Ngai Tahu in respect of land, sea fisheries, and mahinga kai (traditional food sources). Claimants maintained that much of the central and southern part of the South Island had never been purchased by the Crown and should therefore be returned to Ngai Tahu, or at least be the subject of compensation. After more than two years of hearings (1987–89), often on marae, the Tribunal report was published in 1991.[66] It covers the 'Nine Tall Trees of Ngai Tahu', i.e. claims arising from eight major land transactions between the tribes and the Crown, made between 1844 and 1864, and the loss of mahinga kai.

One of the transactions (the Otakou Block) had seen 500 000 acres sold to the Crown for £2 400. The Tribunal, emphasising the principle of active protection, considered that in this transaction the Crown had failed to ensure the maintenance of an adequate economic base for Ngai Tahu.

Another transaction, the Kemp purchase, covered about 20 million acres in the middle of the island with less than 6 500 acres set aside as reserves. Again the Tribunal considered that the Crown's actions had shown a lack of good faith and rode roughshod over the rangatiratanga of Ngai Tahu. Grievances relating to the six other land transactions were also examined—Banks Peninsula, Murihiku, North Canterbury, Kaikoura, Arahura, and Rakiura. The mahinga kai grievance concerned the depletion of food sources—such as eels—on land

and inland waters. New management procedures for Lakes Waihora and Wairewa, with greater participation by Ngai Tahu, were proposed.

The main concern during the hearings, however, was not so much the fourteen million hectares which were sold, or the ridiculously low price received as payment, but the failure of the Crown to keep its promise that three million hectares would be set aside as reserves for the tribe. While there were some specific recommendations (relating mainly to pounamu, the West Coast perpetual leases, and Waihora and Wairewa), for the most part the Tribunal advocated that Ngai Tahu and the Crown should negotiate a settlement of any proven grievance. That approach would 'leave the way open for negotiation between the tribe and the Crown and for an overall settlement by agreement between the parties based on the findings of the tribunal.'

Negotiations were anything but smooth. Talks began in 1991 but there were frequent interruptions, walkouts, and mutual accusations of obstruction. It was widely known that the Crown was preparing for a settlement; they had begun purchasing high country properties which would be used to give effect to a settlement and were investigating ways in which Ngai Tahu could enjoy access to the conservation estate. As in the Tainui and Whakatohea claims, conservationists were alarmed, this time because large tracts of South Island high country might be transferred to Ngai Tahu, with possible harmful environmental effects. In addition, recreational groups considered that their access to high country parks and reserves (for tramping, fishing, and hunting) would also be reduced if Ngai Tahu assumed control. Lobby groups made their views known publicly and to the Crown.

Ngai Tahu replied with two observations. First, they dismissed claims that they were less sensitive to environmental protection than anyone else, including the Crown. Second, in assuring sports organisations that access would be maintained, they nonetheless made it clear that they too had rights and that lobby groups appeared to have selectively criticised Ngai Tahu, while appearing to ignore other recreational areas which had passed into overseas ownership.

When eventually in 1995 negotiations became bogged down, Ngai Tahu stopped talking and filed High Court action, also seeking to reverse a Waitangi Tribunal decision not to give the tribe urgency to have another aspect of their claim heard. The Tribunal responded by pointing out that, if Ngai Tahu were afforded priority, it would be at the expense of other tribes. The Crown meanwhile had refused to resume negotiations while court action was pending. Eventually, litigation was adjourned and in 1996, possibly because of uncertainties about the effect of MMP on Treaty settlement processes, talks continued. At the signing of the deed of settlement, Doug Graham apologised for any part he may have played during negotiations when 'goodwill came under scrutiny' but welcomed a new era in the relationship between Ngai Tahu and the Crown.[67]

Although still needing tribal approval, the deed of settlement provided for $170 million, mainly in assets. About 1.38 million hectares (approximately a tenth of the amount originally sold to the government) would be involved in future discussions to be held before the settlement could be concluded. Ngai Tahu would have the right to be offered, at market prices, Crown properties, including those in a Ngai Tahu land bank, and the first right of refusal on much of the surplus Crown properties in the South Island. As for properties of conservation interest, Ngai Tahu would be awarded title to the farmable parts of the Elfin and Routeburn high country stations and title to the non-farmable parts on the understanding that they would be leased back to the Conservation Minister in perpetuity and for a peppercorn rental. Whenua Hou (Codfish Island), of cultural and historic importance to Ngai Tahu and prized by the Department of Conservation, was to remain in Crown ownership, but Ngai Tahu would gain title to the Mutton Bird (Crown Titi) Islands, to be managed as if the islands were a nature reserve (but subject to traditional rights to take mutton birds). Mahinga kai were recognised by awarding the tribe title to Rarotoka (Centre Island); and also granted were the management rights of the adjacent reefs, as well as title to and use of 32 customary fishing areas, and first right of refusal for 30 per cent of the harvest rights to five shellfish species. Restoration of the original Māori names for 78 places, including Aoraki (Mt Cook), was also guaranteed.

Considerable flexibility was retained in the settlement. Ngai Tahu will be able to select Crown properties from an agreed list to the total value of no more than $200 million, less the value of other properties transferred to the tribe under the deed. That means Ngai Tahu can use $30 million on non-settlement money to spend under the deferred selection process. Apart from the Crown Titi Islands, only 630 hectares of New Zealand's five million hectares of conservation estate was earmarked for return, and it will remain free and open to the public.

Media reaction to the settlement was generally favourable, but the Forest and Bird Society had strong reservations and called for public consultation before anything was finalised. Their concern was both about the management of 'publicly owned conservation lands' and the apparent priority of commercial muttonbirding ahead of endangered species conservation. Not all conservation lobbies shared their bias. Chris Laidlaw from the World Wide Fund for Nature called the agreement an exciting new opportunity for conservation management and said it was no threat to conservation. Rather, he saw it as indicative of future co-management of conservation by government and Māori.[68] However, Sir Tipene O'Regan himself described the deed of settlement cautiously as 'acceptable but not fair.' He did not think it reflected justice, and doubted whether justice was achievable anyway. 'But this is an agreement we can live with that gives us a sufficient base, if carefully nurtured, that will restore us over time to the place we aspire to.'[69] Clearly he was not planning to reject the deed.

The task now, however, was to convince the tribe that the deal was a good one. That would not be a foregone conclusion; opposition to the process and to the key Ngai Tahu players had arisen over the preceding two years from hapū on the West Coast and the two Māori women members of Parliament, Whetu Tirikatene-Sullivan and Sandra Lee, both Ngai Tahu, had been opposed to the bill to create the new rūnanga.[70] It was generally known that they had reservations about the proposed settlement and that they could muster support from their own people when it came to seeking tribal approval. In addition, shortly after the deed had been announced, the ancient Waitaha tribe claimed that they had been compromised by the deal. A spokesperson was dismayed that the Crown had resolved to settle when the Waitaha claim, for much of the same land and resources, at least in the lower South Island, had not yet been heard by the Tribunal. Sir Tipene rejected their claim, maintaining that Waitaha had not existed as a distinct entity since the fourteenth century.

Table 7.4 A Comparison of Treaty Claim Settlements, 1994–1996

	Tainui	Whakatohea	Ngai Tahu
Date of Draft Deed	21 December 1994	1 October 1996	5 October 1996
Estimated population	33 000	7 350	29 133
Disputed land	486 439 ha (raupatu lands)	70 000 ha (raupatu lands)	3 000 000 ha (lands promised as reserves)
Crown land available for settlement	15 439 ha	9 small urban properties	1 380 000 ha
Natural resource consessions	Tribal claim to coal withdrawn	Access to plants, whalebone	Pounamu (jade) rights recognised
Conservation estate	Seat on Conservancy Board	Co-management, topuni, deeds of recognition	Ownership of Titi islands; title to some DOC properties with lease-back to Crown; co-management
Total monetary value	$170 million	$40 million	$170 million
% of total settlement budget	17% – benchmarked in the Deed	Not indicated or protected in the Deed	17% – benchmarked in the Deed

TOWARDS A TREATY POLICY

Although after its landslide election in 1984, the fourth Labour government introduced the Treaty of Waitangi into several laws and included it in the terms of reference for the Royal Commission on Social Policy,[71] there has never been clear evidence of a coherent and committed Treaty policy, applicable across all sectors. The broadest and most comprehensive approach came by way of a Cabinet minute in March 1986 requiring government departments to give recognition to the Treaty in all aspects of departmental administration and in the preparation of legislation. The Treaty was to be recognised as if it were part of domestic law and as if 'always speaking', i.e. applicable to all policies, and there was to be consultation with Māori people on all matters relating to the application of the Treaty.

However, a group of officials from various government departments, headed by Treasury, were unhappy with some aspects of the government's Treaty policy and made recommendations for change. Cabinet accepted those changes and a new policy statement was issued in June 1986. Unlike the bold March policy, the revised version dropped reference to the Treaty as domestic law, qualified the Treaty by adding 'principles of the Treaty', required that the Treaty recommendations should include an estimate of financial implications, and modified the clause on consultation to apply only to appropriate Māori people and only on significant matters.[72]

While going much further than any previous government in acknowledging the Treaty's wide application, the policy was more a directive on the processes to be adopted in the formulation of policy than specific policy relating directly to the Treaty. That came later and not always by design. A policy to recognise Māori interests in surplus Crown properties, for example, only came about because of a Court of Appeal ruling after the New Zealand Māori Council challenged the Crown over the State-Owned Enterprises Act in 1987. And a Māori fisheries policy was hammered out at the bargaining table, again in the face of court action. Aware that it was faring poorly in court and in Waitangi Tribunal hearings, the government appears to have decided by 1989 that it would take a more proactive stance on Treaty matters and not be bullied into simply reacting to Māori demands or court rulings. The release of the government's Treaty principles was an early sign of a more determined approach by the Crown to managing and controlling Treaty issues.[73]

Of the five identified Treaty principles, the first, the Principle of Government (Kāwanatanga Principle) was taken more or less directly from Article 1 of the Treaty. It stated that the government had the right to govern and to make laws. That right was, however, fettered by a requirement to accord Māori interests specified in the second Article an appropriate priority. The second principle was the Principle of Self-Management (Rangatiratanga Principle), confirming that iwi should have the right to organise as iwi and, under the law, control the resources they own. Not the same as Māori understandings of rangatiratanga, self-determination, it nonetheless recognised growing Māori interest in tribal development, government interest in devolution, and the move towards greater autonomy with less dependence on the state. Again it was consistent with the broader government policies of a reduced state and greater encouragement for the private sector.

The Principle of Equality, that all New Zealanders are equal before the law, was a reminder that there was little official interest in a separate Māori justice system, as Moana Jackson had proposed in 1988,[74] while the fourth principle, the principle of Reasonable Cooperation, that government and the iwi are obliged to accord each other cooperation on major issues of common concern, owed some of its tenor to the Court of Appeal's direction for good faith. It was never absolutely clear whether the principle of Reasonable Cooperation was intended for a particular target, but it was seen by Māori as a government plea for less ambitious demands. Finally, the fifth principle, the Principle of Redress, stated that the government was responsible for providing effective processes for the resolution of grievances in the expectation that reconciliation could occur.

After the 1990 election, National asked for the principles to be redrafted to accommodate the new policies. The kāwanatanga principle was amended to indicate that the government ought to govern for the common good and the principle of rangatiratanga was extended to reflect self-management within the scope of the law.[75] It is no longer certain that the government's Treaty principles have any official standing or even form the basis of a Treaty policy. The emergence of a coalition government in 1996 was not accompanied by a statement one way or the other, although direct negotiation continued, supporting the principle of redress, and any hint of self-governance by Māori brought swift assertions of Crown authority, the point of the first principle. Government departments have never been told to disregard the five principles; nor have they been reminded to enforce them. And although they were never intended for Māori, rather for the government and its departments, Māori have largely forgotten them anyway. Importantly the principles were not referred to in the Crown's Proposals for the Settlement of Treaty of Waitangi Claims, nor have they been mentioned in settlement documents.

Inconsistent Policies

Insofar as some statutes contain a Treaty clause, there is a Treaty policy, or more correctly a series of policies, since the Treaty reference in legislation is not identical. However, the ten or so Acts which do refer to the Treaty are all linked to physical resources such as land, the environment, or Treaty settlements; there is no reference to the Treaty in any social policy legislation.[76] That does not mean there is no policy. Indeed, when briefing audiences on the health reforms, the Hon. Simon Upton was at pains to assure Māori audiences that the Treaty formed an important part of government health policy and that it would be reflected in regulations and purchasing guidelines. He also drew the distinction between Article 2 and Article 3 matters, identifying health (and education, employment, housing) as Article 3 matters which would be recognised through policies other than Treaty settlement policies.[77] The separation of the two (economic and social policies), and a concern to unhook settlements from broader Treaty issues, is consistent with the wider macro-policies of the government and its free market orientation, but makes little sense in Māori communities where economic and social circumstances are inextricably inter-twined and where economic goals, including self-sufficiency, are part (only) of tribal concepts of self-determination and autonomy.

One of the few indications that there might be a broad Treaty policy, however, is contained in *Path to 2010*, the National government's 1993 strategic objectives document. It notes that the government will 'continue to work towards an agreed understanding of the place of the Treaty of Waitangi in New Zealand society.'[78] But the outcomes from that objective have not yet materialised apart from polices for the settlement of Treaty claims, a pressing matter though scarcely the same as a broader Treaty policy. Māori objection to the fiscal envelope was sometimes traced to the failure to construct claims policy on any broader Treaty policy. 'Rather than first formulating a mutually acceptable Treaty policy, the govern-ment has opted instead to tackle one aspect of the Treaty of Waitangi but in isolation from either Treaty principles or Treaty provisions. The government urgently needs to declare its position on the Treaty of Waitangi. Are both the Māori and English versions of the Treaty to be afforded equal standing? Are the principles of the Treaty to be used in deciding the relevance of the Treaty or are the strict terms of the Treaty, the provisions, to form the basis for discussion?'[79]

There are several sources of confusion about Treaty policy. First, there is a difference between Treaty policy and government Māori policy. Second, as already noted, Treaty policy needs to be distinguished from Treaty claims settlement practices and policies. Third, there is a fundamental difference between a Treaty policy and a policy of total Māori independence.

Māori Policy and Treaty Policy

Government Māori policy differs from Treaty of Waitangi policy in several important respects. Perhaps most significantly, government policy for Māori since 1840 has largely been contrary to the spirit of the Treaty. Māori land policy for example not only flew in the face of the intentions of Article 2, but also flouted Lord Normanby's instruction that the Crown had a responsibility to ensure that Māori retained a sufficient economic base for future needs. Alienation of land from Māori owners was the more pressing goal. Education policy discouraged (rather than encouraged) the retention of the Māori language, while fisheries policy presumed that Māori fishing interests were of a subsistence rather than a commercial nature. Māori people are the targets of Māori policy; and some Māori policies favour Māori interests over non-Māori, not necessarily for Treaty of Waitangi reasons as much as for social equity. Treaty policy, however, has a broader national context. Moreover, it is pan-sectoral and, unlike Māori policy, includes a Crown fiduciary obligation. Current distinctions between a possible Treaty policy and Māori polices are shown in table 7.5. Government policy for Māori is an indication of government objectives for Māori. Treaty policy is more about the government's relationship to Māori.

Table 7.5 Treaty of Waitangi Policy and Current Māori Policy

	Treaty Policy	Government Māori Policy
Broad aims	National development	Māori development
Benefits/costs	All New Zealanders	Māori
Justification	Terms of colonisation	Māori are a significant part of the population
Focus	Pan-sectoral	Sectoral
Time	Past and future	Present and future
Obligation	Mutual respect	Meeting Māori needs
Emphasis	Māori–Crown relationships	Government objectives for Māori

Claims Policy and Treaty Policy

If the framework proposed in the fiscal envelope is indeed Treaty claims settlement policy, then it also differs from Treaty policy in several important ways. Most obviously, and not surprisingly, claims policy is focused on historical events. Treaty policy, however, is about future development. Claims policy does not ignore the contribution a settlement will make to the future and tribes who have completed settlements, or are about to, recognise the importance of investing for future generations. But settlements generally use a formula of past loss rather than current circumstances to reach a conclusion about need. Not that the underlying basis for claims policy is at all clear. Affordability plays a large role, too large according to most Māori commentators, and acceptability to the electorates may receive more prominence than Māori would wish. A sense of urgency has played an inappropriately large role. While the year 2000 has some appeal as a target for a new start, there is no good reason why claims should be settled by then or even within a decade; neither is the threat that MMP might slow claims settlements an adequate cause for precipitate action. Much is also made of finality and durability at a time when society generally is caught in the midst of change.

Since the announcement of the fiscal envelope proposal, new reasons for fixing the size of settlements have emerged that did not appear to be factored into the original documents. Demography, for example, has become a rationale. After the announcement of the Whakatohea and Ngai Tahu settlements, the minister commented that for a population of only 6000 (in the case of Whakatohea) and 20000 (Ngai Tahu), the settlements were fiscally generous. Emeritus Professor Gould took a similar line, decrying the level of the Ngai Tahu deal because the population was so small.[80] He also took the opportunity to introduce another rationale, by questioning whether a fair skin altered the notion of what constituted a fair settlement. His somewhat tortuous point was that tribes which were 'more' Māori had a more deserving case.

There is no question that some or possibly all (except the last) of these factors should be considered in a claims policy, but a more explicit underpinning is needed to counter political expediency, which is devoid of a robust philosophy or methodology or which allows spurious academic argument along the lines pursued by Gould. Pragmatism appears to guide decisions of 'fairness' to a degree that adds to the confusion about what is actually being settled. On the one hand, settlements recognise the desire to 'right a wrong', but it would be misleading to describe them as providing economic restoration or the end of negotiations between tribes and the Crown. Essentially, the settlement of claims refers only to the historical subset of a broader Treaty of Waitangi relationship and, in that sense, concepts of durability and full and final settlement apply to the removal of past grievances, but do not reduce the Crown's guarantees to Māori. While historical claims have taxed both claimants and the Crown, it is highly likely that contemporary and contextual claims, which will be ongoing, will be infinitely more demanding. Table 7.6 compares Treaty claims policy with a possible Treaty policy and, among other things, highlights the uncertainty about the basis for claims policies—a mix of pragmatism and principles, coupled with expediency and confused with the parallel need to consider ongoing Treaty relationships. As well, in current claims policy there is no real provision for the joint participation of the Crown and Māori in formulating policy, rather than negotiating within the terms of policy preordained by the Crown.

Table 7.6 Treaty Policy and Treaty Claims Policy

	Treaty Policy (proposed)	Government Treaty Claims Policy
Broad aim	Future development	Resolution of historical injustices
Benefits	All New Zealanders Tribes and Māori	Claimants but not at the expense of others
Basis for policy	The Treaty of Waitangi (principles and/or provisions)	Legal principles and/or: national economic policy; future needs; demography; acceptability; cultural identity
Timeframe	The future Ongoing	Sense of urgency Time limited
Policy Formulation	Māori–Crown partnership	Negotiated settlements based on government framework

Māori Independence and a Treaty Policy

One of the main sources of confusion in the Treaty of Waitangi is the discrepancy between the English and Māori versions. That is one reason why the use of Treaty principles has been favoured rather than a strict adherence to the words of the Treaty. Of particular concern is whether sovereignty was ceded to the Crown. The Māori version suggests something less than sovereignty was ceded, governance perhaps, the tribes retaining their own authority and independence (tino rangatiratanga in Article 2). Regardless, it is difficult not to conclude that the Treaty of Waitangi was about the establishment of a single nation state and provision for a degree of Māori autonomy, along the lines suggested in section 71 of the New Zealand Constitution Act 1852 (though never implemented). Continuing debate about the level and terms of that autonomy characterise interaction between Māori and the Crown and form much of the substance of this book. Māori often claim that independence is a right and sometimes seek support from the Treaty.

Māori independence requires quite a different policy approach from a Treaty driven one. It would be much stronger if based on the Declaration of Independence, which was explicitly about a Māori nation state and Māori political and national independence. The Declaration was also about a Māori nation, rather than a series of independent tribal domains. Though the Congress proposed in the Declaration did not eventuate, and Māori did not establish a formal legislature or national assembly, the prospect of independence was not lost and surfaced again in 1990 with the formation of the National Māori Congress.[81] It was a similar theme at the Pakaitore occupation in 1995 and at several hui to discuss the fiscal envelope. Unlike a Treaty policy, a policy for total Māori independence would leave little room for the Crown to intervene in Māori affairs or to pass legislation to limit Māori. Some of these differences are shown in table 7.7.

Table 7.7 Treaty Policy and Policies for Total Māori Independence

	Treaty Policy	Policies for Total Māori Independence
Broad Aim	Future development of New Zealand as a unified nation state	Establishment of a Māori nation state
Benefits	All New Zealanders	Māori
Basis for Policy	The Treaty of Waitangi	Declaration of Independence
Crown/Māori Relationship	Parliament (Māori seats) Tribal discussions Māori lobbying	Formal links between the two nation states
Policy Formulation	Māori-Crown partnership	Māori policy decided by Māori

A Treaty of Waitangi Policy Framework

Tables 7.5, 7.6, and 7.7 suggest some elements for a possible Treaty of Waitangi policy framework. Furthermore they underline the need for one, so that claims policy, Māori policy and even discussion on policies for total Māori independence can proceed from a clearer starting point. At least in respect of claims policy, it is uncertain whether the strategy adopted by the Crown is economic, or jurisprudential, or compensatory, or all three. Without a broader reference point, such as a constitution, there is a danger that so-called full and final settlements will not be able to stand up to the demands of future generations; nor should they, if settlements are seen as synonymous with the discharge of total Treaty obligations rather than settling an historical injustice. A Treaty policy as a framework to inform claims policy will have a greater capacity to provide a rational and enduring basis for settlements and to offer a signpost for future development, outside the ambit of claims.

Although there is no comprehensive Treaty of Waitangi policy framework, considerable progress has been made, both in New Zealand and abroad, to at least recognise the issues. More difficult has been the creation of a climate for addressing the wider policy matter, and agreeing on the terms and partners to discussions. Certainly, it appears that the Crown's total Treaty energies have been diverted into historical claims with little attention to the wider policy framework. In table 7.8 a five-part Treaty policy framework is proposed.

Table 7.8 A Treaty of Waitangi Policy Framework

Foundations	Key Goals	Applications	Processes	Outcomes
• Treaty of Waitangi • Draft Declaration of Rights of Indigenous Peoples • a New Zealand Constitution • Declaration of Independence	• national advancement • mutual benefits • active protection of Māori interests • mutual respect and good faith between Treaty partners	• social, cultural and economic well-being • future development • resolution of past injustices • human resources • physical resources • arrangements for partnership at regional and national levels	• joint formulation of policies • Māori/Crown participation in policy formulation • legislative enforcement • provision for review • agreement as to measures and audits	• balance between a fair and just society and a strong economy • full Māori participation in society and in the economy • affirmation of Māori as indigenous people of New Zealand • clear Māori structures and processes for implementation of policy

The foundations of a Treaty policy framework include, of course, the Treaty of Waitangi though, as already discussed, there is a need for clarity on the relative advantages of using principles as against articles or provisions. Consistency is needed to avoid a series of disconnected policies. In a submission to the Royal Commission on Social Policy in 1987, Mira Szaszy decried the principles approach,[82] and it appears that the government also found them of limited value in the fiscal envelope proposals, when, without adequate explanation, a shift to the articles of the Treaty (rather than the principles) was used to rationalise distinctions between physical and human resource development. The Waitangi Tribunal, meanwhile, focuses on the principles rather than the provisions,[83] and in some eight or so Acts legislation refers to Treaty principles, not the articles of the Treaty. Principles are said to 'avoid the pedantry of textual literalism.'[84]

Apart from the Treaty itself, the Declaration of the Rights of Indigenous Peoples is a relevant supporting document. Though basically different in several respects, it can be regarded as the modern equivalent of the 1837 report of the Aborigines Committee which contributed to the Treaty. British constitutional arrangements were also integral to the Treaty; indeed, the transfer of sovereignty to the Crown specifically recognised Britain's inability to contemplate any form of shared sovereignty. Finally, as a precursor to the Treaty, the Declaration of Independence could be regarded as a further foundation for the development of a broad Treaty policy.

The Treaty was intended to deliver benefits to both Māori and the Crown and was primarily a guide for future development. As the modern nation evolved, it was recognised that active protection of Māori interests would be necessary, and that good relationships between the tribes and the Crown were essential. And it appears that there was no restriction on the application of the Treaty to cover the range of developmental concerns and the opportunities for Māori involvement in society and the economy. What was missing in 1840, however, were guidelines for Māori participation in decision-making. The 1867 provision for four Māori seats in Parliament was a start, but because it did little to establish a sense of partnership a variety of other approaches were also used to consult with Māori— rūnanga and councils, commissions, party political favouritism, and select committee hearings. Māori are still searching for a more systematic solution, which does not depend on goodwill alone, nor on political patronage. The MMP Parliament with fifteen Māori members may hold promise, though in formal relationships with the Crown it is likely that Māori will seek to give a mandate to a more representative body, which might include Māori parliamentarians but not be confined to them.

Benefits for Māori and for the nation as a whole should be evident in the outcomes of Treaty policies, not only through improved economic opportunities for Māori but also through more effective Māori participation in society and the economy.[85] New Zealand is a small country and cannot afford to have any section of society not taking part. Full Māori participation in society has a double meaning. On the one hand Māori might reasonably expect to share all the benefits of society, including standards of health, education, housing similar to those of other New Zealanders but, as well, and having regard both to the Treaty and to the greater recognition of the rights of indigenous peoples, they should expect to be able to exercise their own preferences for political organisation, cultural expression, and relationships with the environment. Sometimes Māori will wish to organise as tribes, or as communities, or at other times, as a united Māori nation.

Table 7.9 Impediments to a Comprehensive Treaty of Waitangi Policy

Issue	Māori Position	Crown Position	Remedies
Principles or provisions of the Treaty?	Words of the Treaty are important. The Waitangi Tribunal has shown the value of using principles.	Not clear. Principles are included in legislation. But Crown claims terminology refers to articles.	Debate between Māori and the Crown needed to resolve the issues or to decide on indications for each approach.
The absence of a New Zealand Constitution	Interest in a Māori nation and/or nation state. But greater confidence in Parliament since 1996 general election.	Reduced ties with Britain and a possible move towards a republic.	Position of Treaty not clear. Constitutional debate required which includes Māori and the Crown.
Māori mandate	No clear mandate exists for a national Māori group to negotiate macro-policy with the Crown.	Te Puni Kōkiri plays a leading role in formulating Māori policy.	Māori agreement about processes for shaping Māori policy needed. Role of Māori MPs needs discussion by Māori.
Māori beneficiaries	Tribal versus Māori interests.	Uncertainty about who is entitled.	Māori agreement about entitlements.
Conservation estate and natural resources	Ownership has never been forfeited.	Crown owns natural resources and will retain conservation estate.	Joint Māori/Crown Commission to consider options.
Settlement of Treaty Claims	Terms of settlements do not reflect justice or future needs.	Crown's proposals will guide negotiations. Political expediency.	Joint Māori/Crown policy is needed which is consistent with broad Treaty policy.
Misinformation and prejudice	Māori have carried the burden of the Treaty.	Treaty awareness is important but active promotion of awareness is limited.	Active steps to inform the public about the Treaty and its relevance for future development.

The fact that there is no broad Treaty policy can be attributed to many causes, including the difficulty of the task, the perceived fiscal risks, and the apparent unwillingness to commit to a macro-policy which will have wide implications. Other practical and process impediments, shown in table 7.9 on the previous page, also contribute.

Because there are several obstacles to developing a comprehensive Treaty policy for New Zealand, it might be argued that dealing with more manageable and tangible problems, such as claims, is a more practical step. At the same time, however, the areas which need further clarification are of critical importance to future constitutional, economic, and social development, and should not be avoided because they seem too difficult. It is a matter of some importance that they be addressed and that the Crown and Māori agree to an appropriate forum for reaching consensus. A recurring Treaty principle expressed by Māori, the courts, the Waitangi Tribunal, and communities, is partnership. Although partnership is difficult to define or to arrange, it has generated enough positive experiences to warrant continuing enthusiasm and a commitment to the principle, not only in negotiating durable solutions within already determined frameworks, but also in crafting national philosophies and substrates for broad policies, and eventually for a New Zealand constitution.

What is less apparent, however, is whether Māori futures will be well served by the Treaty of Waitangi or whether other options, such as indigenous rights, should be given greater priority. Once settlements have been effected, will the Crown still want to recognise the force of the Treaty for future development, or will it seek to relegate the Treaty to an historical context? Māori scepticism about the fiscal envelope was fuelled by a nagging doubt that the exercise was aimed at settling not just historical claims but the Treaty itself. Despite reassurances to the contrary in the deeds of settlement, the absence of a broad Treaty of Waitangi policy, or a clearer statement about the constitutional position of the Treaty, has fuelled the concern. Neither has it been helped by a citizens initiated referendum referred to Parliament by Mark Whyte in 1997.[86] In its original form it asked 'Should the Treaty of Waitangi, being an outdated document, be set aside and replaced with a national constitution which guarantees the equal rights of all New Zealanders without favour or discrimination?' Apart from unmasked bias and the lack of understanding about the Treaty and the New Zealand constitution, the question was as much a challenge to Parliament and the courts as to Māori. In the face of this modern colonising zeal and a citizens' desire for the assimilation of Māori, it is time for the Crown to join Māori and affirm the constitutional inviolability of the Treaty of Waitangi.

NOTES FOR CHAPTER 7

1 An extract from an address by Sir James Henare to the Rūnanga Waitangi, a national hui to discuss the Treaty of Waitangi held at Ngaruawahia, in September 1984. He emphasises that by signing with symbols from their own personal facial tattoos, the Māori signatories regarded the Treaty as a sacred document; in Te Rūnanga o Waitangi Planning Committee, (1984), *He Kōrero mo Waitangi*, Te Rūnanga o Waitangi.

2 P. Temm, (1990), *The Waitangi Tribunal: The Conscience of the Nation*, Random Century, Auckland, p. 48.

3 See Appendix 1.

4 Peter Adams, (1977), *Fatal Necessity: British Intervention in New Zealand 1830–1847*, Auckland University Press and Oxford University Press, Auckland, pp. 91–93.

5 Adams, *Fatal Necessity*, pp. 165–167.

6 Claudia Orange, (1987), *The Treaty of Waitangi*, Allen and Unwin/Port Nicholson Press, Wellington, pp. 30–31.

7 Adams, pp. 87–88.

8 Peter Cleave, (1989), *The Sovereignty Game: Power, Knowledge and Reading the Treaty*, Victoria University Press, Wellington, p. 45.

9 Orange, *The Treaty of Waitangi*, pp. 84–85.

10 Arohia Durie, (1994), 'The Treaty in the Life of the Nation', in P. Green (ed.), *Studies in New Zealand Social Problems*, 2nd edition, Dunmore Press, Palmerston North, p. 117.

11 E. T. Durie, (1996), *A Judge's Eye View of the Waitangi Tribunal*, a paper presented at a Conference on Indigenous Peoples: Rights, Lands, Resources, Autonomy International and Trade Show, Vancouver.

12 *Taranaki Fish and Game Council v Kirk McRitchie* is discussed in chapter 6.

13 Frederika Hackshaw, (1989), 'Nineteenth Century Notions of Aboriginal Title', in I. H. Kawharu (ed.), *Waitangi: Māori and Pakeha Perspectives of the Treaty of Waitangi*, Oxford University Press, Auckland, pp. 102–108.

14 Paul McHugh, (1991), *The Māori Magna Carta: New Zealand Law and the Treaty of Waitangi*, Oxford University Press, Oxford, pp. 113–117.

15 *Hoani Te Heuheu Tukino v Aotea District Māori Land Board* [1941] AC 308 (Privy Council).

16 Mai Chen, Geoffrey Palmer, (1993), *Public Law in New Zealand*, Oxford University Press, Auckland, p. 342.

17 *Huakina Development Trust v Waikato Valley Authority* [1987] 2 NZLR 188 (High Court).

18 McHugh, *The Māori Magna Carta*, pp. 270–273.

19 This case is discussed in more detail in chapter 3.

20 *Attorney-General v New Zealand Māori Council* [1991] 2 NZLR 129 (Court of Appeal).

21 McHugh, *The Māori Magna Carta*, p. 274.

22 *New Zealand Māori Council v Attorney-General* [1987] 1 NZLR 641 (Court of Appeal).

23 Waitangi Tribunal, (1988), *Muriwhenua Fishing Report,* Appendix A 3.4.1.

24 E. T. Durie, (1995), 'Background Paper', in Geoff McLay (ed.), *Treaty Settlements: The Unfinished Business,* New Zealand Institute of Advanced Legal Studies and Victoria University of Wellington Law Review, Wellington, pp. 8–10.

25 *ibid.,* p. 11–12.

26 Auckland, Hauraki, Bay of Plenty, Urewera, Poverty Bay and the East Coast, Waikato, the volcanic plateau, the King Country, Whanganui, Taranaki, Hawke's Bay–Wairarapa, Wellington, the northern South Island, the southern South Island, the Chatham Islands.

27 Alan Ward, (1997), *National Overview Waitangi Tribunal Rangahaua Whanui Series,* vol. 1, Waitangi Tribunal, Wellington, p.12.

28 Controller and Auditor-General, (1995), *The Settlement of Claims Under the Treaty of Waitangi,* Second Report for 1995, Wellington, p. 35.

29 *ibid.,* pp. 38–39.

30 E. T. Durie, (1994), 'Keynote Address', in *Kia Pūmau Tonu: Proceedings of the Hui Whakapūmau,* Department of Māori Studies, Massey University, p. 19.

31 E. T. Durie (1995), 'Background Paper', pp. 15–18.

32 Tipene O'Regan, (1995), 'A Ngai Tahu Perspective on Some Treaty Questions', in Geoff McLay (ed.), *Treaty Settlements,* pp. 93–94.

33 Tania Rangiheuea, (1995), 'The Role of Māori Women in Treaty Negotiations and Settlements', in Geoff McLay (ed.), *Treaty Settlements,* p. 109.

34 Caren Wickliffe, (1995), 'Issues for Indigenous Claims Settlement Policies Arising in Other Jurisdictions', in Geoff McLay (ed.), *Treaty Settlements,* pp. 125–126.

35 Robert Mahuta, (1995), 'Tainui: a case study of direct negotiation', in Geoff McLay (ed.), *Treaty Settlements,* p. 85.

36 Jane Kelsey, (1993), *Rolling Back the State: Privatisation of Power in Aotearoa/New Zealand,* Bridget Williams Books, Wellington, pp. 213–216.

37 Geoffrey Palmer, (1990), 'Treaty of Waitangi Issues Demand Clarity, Certainty', *New Zealand Herald,* 2 January 1990.

38 Ministerial Planning Group, *Ka Awatea,* Ministry of Māori Development, Wellington, pp. 90–91.

39 Controller and Auditor-General, *The Settlement of Claims Under the Treaty of Waitangi,* p. 29.

40 M. H. Durie, (1997), 'Mana Motuhake The State of the Māori Nation', in Raymond Miller (ed.), *New Zealand Politics in Transition,* Oxford University Press, Auckland.

41 Carol Archie, (1995), 'Doug Graham', in *Maori Sovereignty: The Pakeha Perspective,* Hodder Moa Beckett, Auckland, p. 118.

42 The experience of the fisheries negotiators is discussed in detail in Chapter 6.

43 New Zealand Government (1994), *Crown Proposals for the Settlement of Treaty of Waitangi Claims: Detailed Proposals,* Office of Treaty Settlements, Wellington.

44 John Roberts, (1996), *Alternative Vision He Moemoea Ano: The Significance of the Hirangi Hui,* Joint Public Questions Committee of the Methodist Church of New Zealand and the Presbyterian Church of Aotearoa New Zealand, Wellington, pp. 3–7.

45 Ranginui Walker, (1995), *Ngā Pepa a Ranginui: The Walker Papers,* Penguin, Auckland, p. 122.

46 Wira Gardiner, (1995), *Return to Sender: What Really Happened at the Fiscal Envelope Hui,* Reed, Wellington.

47 M. H. Durie, (1995), 'Proceedings of a Hui held at Hirangi Marae Turangi', in Geoff McLay (ed.), *Treaty Settlements: The Unfinished Business,* Victoria University of Wellington Law Review, Wellington, pp. 19–27.

48 Catriona MacLennan, (1995), 'Radicals stirring against fiscal deal—Graham', *The Dominion,* 31 January 1995.

49 *Wellington International Airport Ltd. v Air NZ* [1991] 1 NZLR 671.

50 Waitangi Tribunal, (1992), *Mohaka River Report (Wai 119),* GP Publications, Wellington, pp. 65–66.

51 Marta Steeman, (1995), 'What's wrong with the fiscal envelope', *MG Business Mercantile Gazette,* vol. 118, no. 5226, pp. 5–6.

52 Controller and Auditor-General, *The Settlement of Claims Under the Treaty of Waitangi,* p. 43.

53 Waitangi Tribunal, (1996), *The Taranaki Report: Kaupapa Tuatahi (Wai 143),* Waitangi Tribunal Report 1996, GP Publications, Wellington, p. 314.

54 Agreement between New Zealand First and the New Zealand National Party (1996).

55 'Lifting of treaty cap largely symbolic—Graham,' *The Dominion,* Wednesday 18 December 1996.

56 Mike Smith, Katie Murray, Sam Fu, Annette Sykes, (1996), *Hikoi Waitangi ki Te Puku o te Ika,* (brochure).

57 Ian Templeton, (1996), 'Envelope may carry its promise through', Sunday Star-Times, August 25 1996.

58 Tainui Māori Trust Board, (1996), *Tainui Māori Trust Board Annual Report 1995,* Tainui Māori Trust Board, Ngaruawahia, pp. 12–16.

59 'Grey's move led to Tainui payout', *The Dominion,* Friday May 26 1995.

60 *Tainui Māori Trust Board v Attorney-General* [1989] 2 NZLR 513 (Court of Appeal).

61 Shane Solomon, (1995), *The Waikato Raupatu Claims Settlement Act: A Draft User's Guide to the Act as at 28 October 1995,* Tainui Māori Trust Board, Ngaruawahia.

62 The Whare Ahupiri is the judicial arm of the Confederation of United Tribes who signed the Declaration of Independence in 1835. Headed by the Taiopuru, the 'Sovereign Head of the United Tribes,' emphasis is placed on dispute resolution between Māori and the Crown and between tribes and hapū.

63 Mary Forbes, (1995), *In the Matter of the Crown's Fiscal Settlement on Raupatu Claims with Ngati Haua me ngā Hapū o Ngati Maniapoto,* circular to all hapū/Iwi, Te Whare Ahupiri o Ngā Ko Here, Auckland.

64 Mary Forbes, (1996), *In the Matter of a Submission by the Descendants of Maramatu-tahi, Eldest Son of Wairere of Ngati Wairere, A Mana Tupuna of the Te Rapa Lands, Against the Crown*, circular to all hapū/Iwi, Te Whare Ahupiri o Ngā Ko Here, Auckland.

65 'Bay Māori to reject $140m settlement', *New Zealand Herald*, Monday December 30 1996.

66 Waitangi Tribunal, (1991), *The Ngai Tahu Report 1991*, Brooker and Friend, Wellington.

67 Hugh Barlow, (1996a), 'Freeing the future from grievances', *The Dominion*, Wednesday 9 October 1996.

68 Hugh Barlow, (1996b), 'Sir Tipene rejects Waitaha claims', *The Dominion*, Tuesday 8 October 1996.

69 Barlow (1996a).

70 Gabrielle Huria, (1996), 'The Bill', in *Te Karaka: The Ngai Tahu Magazine*, Raumati/Summer 1966, pp. 4–6.

71 The Terms of Reference for the Royal Commission on Social Policy described 'the principles of the Treaty' as one of the 'foundations of our society and economy.'

72 Geoffrey Palmer, (1992), *New Zealand's Constitution in Crisis: Reforming Our Political System*, John McIndoe, Dunedin, pp. 82–83.

73 Department of Justice, (1989), *Principles for Crown Action on the Treaty of Waitangi*, Wellington.

74 Moana Jackson, (1988), *The Māori and the Criminal Justice System A New Perspective: He Whaipaanga Hou, Part 2*, Department of Justice, Wellington.

75 Jane Kelsey, (1993), *Rolling Back the State*, pp. 257–258.

76 M. H. Durie, (1991), 'The Treaty of Waitangi Perspectives for Social Policy', in I. H. Kawharu (ed.), *Waitangi*, pp. 280–299.

77 Department of Health, (1992), *Whaia te Ora mo te Iwi—Strive for the Good Health of the People*, Department of Health, Wellington.

78 New Zealand Government, (1993), *Path to 2010*, p. 6.

79 M. H. Durie, (1995), 'Proceedings of a Hui held at Hirangi Marae Turangi', p. 24–25.

80 J. D. Gould, (1996), 'Favoured Status for Ngai Tahu', *The Dominion*, Thursday 24 October 1966.

81 Lindsay Cox, (1993), *Kotahitanga: The Search for Māori Political Unity*, Oxford University Press, Auckland, pp. 155–158.

82 Royal Commission on Social Policy, (1988), *The April Report*, Vol. II, Royal Commission on Social Policy, Wellington, p. 48.

83 William Renwick, *The Treaty Now*, GP Publications, Wellington, pp. 28–31.

84 McHugh, *The Māori Magna Carta*, p. 268.

85 Hon. D. Graham, 'Address by the Minister in Charge of Treaty of Waitangi Negotiations', in Geoff McLay (ed.), *Treaty Settlements*, p. 142.

86 *Parliamentary Gazette*, March 1997.

8

MANA MOTUHAKE

AUTONOMY, GOVERNANCE, AND NATIONHOOD

Ka torona atu toku ringaringa ki nga pito e whā o te ao,
a, e kore tetahi ringa e kaha ki te peehi.[1]

Te Kooti Arikirangi, Aorangi Marae, 1892

DEFINING THE TERMS

Māori aspiration for greater control over their own destinies and resources is variously described as a search for sovereignty, autonomy, independence, self-governance, self-determination, tino rangatiratanga, and mana motuhake. There are important distinctions between those terms, though they all capture an underlying commitment to the advancement of Māori people as Māori, and the protection of the environment for future generations. And all reject any notion of an assimilated future.

However, the debate is complicated by the semantic confusion associated with concepts which are themselves outdated or so subject to international variation in meaning that their use in New Zealand raises more cloud than clarity. Sovereignty is a good example. The equation of Māori self-determination with sovereignty disturbs the government the most, essentially (and despite the final constitutional separation from Britain in 1986) because New Zealand retains a British view that sovereignty is an indivisible attribute of the sovereign vested in Parliament. The notion of sovereignty is, however, not as meaningful as might be assumed, and constitutional experts in New Zealand have warned against the use of the word, not because it is the prerogative of the Crown but because its significance in a global society is tending to diminish. According to Sir Kenneth Keith, 'In the present world, made even smaller by technology and many other human and natural forces, no State is fully sovereign in its external relations . . . no politician or government has real internal sovereignty. What we are seeing is the dispersal of power from so-called sovereign States in at least three directions—to the international community, to the private sector, and to public bodies and communities within the State.' [2] Former Prime Minister Geoffrey Palmer had similar misgivings: '. . . notions of sovereignty are collapsing all over the world. . . . Far from being the indivisible omnipresent concept that Hobbes made it in *Leviathan*, sovereignty is more like a piece of chewing gum. It can be stretched and pulled in many directions to do almost anything. Sovereignty is not a word that is useful and it should be banished from political debate.'[3] The former chief executive of Te Puni Kōkiri, Wira Gardiner, on the other hand, accepts sovereignty as a broad concept within which Māori control over assets, resources and lives can be supreme, though he also recognises the potential for confusion and misunderstanding largely because the term itself is not well understood.[4]

More to the point, if any term carries with it the force of colonial presumption, it is sovereignty.[5] It did not arise from Māori concepts of power, governance, or territorial right nor, since it ascribes sovereign power to a supreme source, does it reflect Māori decision-making, which favours consensus rather than decree. In advocating Māori sovereignty, the focus inevitably shifts away from the advancement of Māori as Māori to the relationship of Māori with the Crown and presumes that the fundamental issue is one of Parliamentary control. Since 1854, parliamentary decisions have certainly impacted on Māori, often cruelly, but there is also a growing conviction by many Māori that cultural and economic survival is not necessarily to be found in a duplication of colonial arrangements for power or governance. Ironically, by encoding Māori aspirations in demands for sovereignty, Māori society itself could be undermined through the adoption of systems and processes which, though sanctioned in British law and custom, are the antithesis of Māori aspirations for a fair society.

Many Māori prefer other expressions to convey the message of Māori autonomy and control and often favour tino rangatiratanga. Mike Smith, for example, although not dismissing Māori sovereignty, slips more comfortably into the concept of tino rangatiratanga to describe Māori aspirations for independence and self-sufficiency and introduces dimensions not readily incorporated into the usual understandings of sovereignty—mana atua, mana tangata, and mana whenua.[6] Sir Tipene O'Regan goes further, dismissing sovereignty as a Pākehā concept which, if applied to Māori, would limit endeavours. Instead, like many Māori leaders and writers he favours tino rangatiratanga as a more fitting description of iwi control over people and assets in a particular region.[7] Peter Tapsell, the former Speaker of the House of Representatives, agrees with O'Regan that sovereignty is an English word which does not suit Māori beliefs, and he also finds tino rangatiratanga a more relevant term.[8]

Difficulties in explaining the precise meaning of tino rangatiratanga, however, have led to further confusion. As an English equivalent, self-determination captures a sense of Māori ownership and active control over the future and is less dependent on the narrow constructs of colonial assumptions. Even the expression self-determination, however, is not without its own problems, especially when it is applied in the international arena. The expression is contained in Article 3 of the Draft Declaration of the Rights of Indigenous Peoples 1993: 'Indigenous peoples have the right of self-determination. By virtue of that right they freely determine their political status and freely pursue their economic, social and cultural development.' In that context, self-determination has prompted some protest on the part of several states, including New Zealand, especially if it were used to imply a secession from a colonial rule. The New Zealand government appears to be more comfortable with 'self-management' rather than self-determination.[9]

Mana motuhake is another expression used to describe power and control. Last century it was adopted by the King movement as a motto,[10] and more recently it has been used as the name for a political party, as well as a catch cry for Māori autonomy and separate development. But, in addition, mana motuhake embodies a link with customary Māori systems of authority, especially in the face of colonising forces. Distinctions between mana motuhake and tino rangatiratanga are contextual rather than categorical, but while they have much in common, mana motuhake more strongly emphasises independence from state and Crown and implies a measure of defiance.

Although there is no single definition of tino rangatiratanga or mana motuhake, it is nonetheless possible to identify two contemporary dimensions to the themes they provoke: the way in which control and authority is distributed within Māori society and the demarcation of power between Māori and the Crown. The essential tasks are for Māori to reach agreement about decision-making within Māori society and for Māori and the Crown to agree on the most appropriate constitutional arrangements that will enhance the standing of both.[11]

Table 8.1 Arrangements for Tino Rangatiratanga

Arrangements Within the Māori Nation	Arrangements Between Māori and the Crown
Iwi	Political sovereignty
Hapū	Legal sovereignty
Māori as individuals	Parliamentary representation
Māori communities of interest	Partnership at tribal, regional, and national levels
National Māori confederations	

The first point, agreement by Māori about the political nature of Māori society and the desirable structures necessary to advance tino rangatiratanga, is probably the more important. Hekia Parata articulates a not uncommon Māori view that tino rangatiratanga, or, in her terms, sovereignty, can only make sense at tribal levels rather at the generic Māori level.[12] O'Regan agrees with her but Smith and Tapsell have different views. Smith contends that, because of the mobility of modern Māori society, it has become impossible to revive an exclusively tribal society and sees the development of a national Māori identity as a challenge if 'we are seriously going to assert ourselves in our own country.'[13] Tapsell is even more convinced that tribalism will serve contemporary Māori less well than a sense of Māori nationalism and considers that 'it has suited pakeha people to leave us with a spirit of tribalism.'[14]

MARAE AUTONOMY AND AUTHORITY

In fact, there are many facets to the expression of Māori autonomy and authority, though probably the most illustrative is the marae. As a centre for both formal and informal meetings, the marae is the most enduring forum for debate and decision-making and, more often than not, the most authentic in terms of Māori cultural values and symbolism. Most marae centre on whānau or hapū, and reflect the culture and history of its members, their shared ancestors, common journeys, and joint fortunes and misfortunes. Decisions made on a marae tend to carry more authority than those made in other arenas, insofar as they relate directly to the affairs of a group, and this is one reason why the marae is a preferred venue for hui, especially when binding decisions are needed. A marae is one of the few places where the agenda is controlled by tangata whenua (those who belong because of their descent from a common ancestor), and if self-determination has any meaning at all, then it finds fuller expression in the politics, procedures, and leadership of the marae. No two marae are the same, and despite efforts in many regions to observe more standard practices, in the end each retains its own style. In that sense the marae is autonomous.

Although most ancestral marae (marae tupuna) are located within tribal areas, and have origins dating back decades or, in some cases, centuries, new marae have sometimes developed around a new hapū. In 1996, for example, the Taumata o te Ra marae was opened at Halcombe, near Feilding. It was established by Ngāti Manomano, a new hapū based on the large Kereama whānau and though the principal house, Manomano, was decorated in both classical and contemporary styles, the marae observes all the customs of the neighbouring Ngāti Raukawa marae with adherence to the Tainui tradition.[15]

Generally marae are governed by trustees, usually representing the whānau who are the key stakeholders, and often appointed by tacit approval rather than formal election. Increasingly, however, greater transparency is demanded and many marae have adopted the practice of electing trustees from the floor. In the process there is often confusion and sometimes conflict between the proponents of customary leadership and the champions of the ballot box. A more frequent practice is to appoint trustees according to whānau tradition and to vote for a committee to manage the marae on a day-to-day basis.

Marae jealously guard their independence, and outside interference is not well received. During the Decade of Māori Development employment schemes were often located on marae, but as they came to encroach on marae priorities and usages they were less well tolerated; all too often marae were being regarded as if the prime purpose was to provide a venue for government programs. Of course, the autonomy of a marae is never absolute. All developments must conform with local by-laws and the Resource Management Act, while trustees must be appointed by the Māori Land Court under Te Ture Whenua Māori, and may be challenged in the court. Marae are also expected to conform with the custom of a particular tribe, and although there is a certain amount of leeway, major departures from the norm will not be tolerated by neighbouring marae and hapū.

Not all marae operate under similar conditions or understandings and table 8.2 shows the differences between three types of marae. In several urban centres marae (marae-a-rohe) have been established to meet the needs of Māori people living in the vicinity, regardless of tribal origins. So-called urban marae may not be gazetted by the Māori Land Court and may not have trustees appointed by the court. Instead their governance may resemble that of a community facility, without regard for historical associations or custom. They will be subject to local city by-laws and, as well, must have some accountability to tangata whenua if disputes and conflict are to be avoided.

Other marae may be part of an institution and have a supportive role according to the nature of the institution (marae tautoko kaupapa). Many schools, universities, polytechnics, hospitals, churches, and even the New Zealand Army have marae, so that appropriate Māori custom can be observed. Their development has been an important part of reconfiguring public institutions to reflect the nation's dual heritage and to create user-friendly facilities in otherwise alienating environments. But the emergence of marae as a feature of government institutions has not been welcomed by all Māori. Two concerns have surfaced. The first is a fear that the cultural activities usually practised on a marae could be distorted and undervalued if they are rehearsed on an institutional marae without the necessary expertise or spiritual under-pinnings, and if they are subject to the more pressing demands of the institution. The second concern is that a marae in a school or university does not belong to Māori but to the governing body of the parent institution. Māori may well manage the operation on behalf of the institution, but ultimately the Board of Trustees or University Council provides the governance. In those cases, what was often thought to be the impregnable bastion of Māori autonomy, the marae, has been appropriated to support the state. The dilemma is a very real one. On the one hand, Māori students or participants in an institution may demand a marae so that they can have a sense of belonging and a safe place in which to be Māori. On the other hand, the act of establishing a marae within the orbit of a non-Māori institution can undermine the meaning of a marae as an autonomous Māori institution and also undermine the significance of neighbouring marae tupuna.

Table 8.2 Three Categories of Marae Governance

	Marae tupuna	Marae-a-rohe	Marae tautoko kaupapa
Key stakeholders	Whānau sharing a common ancestor	Māori people living in a particular locality (often urban)	Māori participants in a non-Māori institution
Governing body	Marae trustees	Marae management committee	Governors of the parent institution
Limits to autonomy	Māori Land Court Ture Whenua Māori Tribal custom	Local bylaws Relationship with tangata whenua	Institutional rules and priorities
Main purpose	A focus for tribal activities and planning	Cultural enforcement for Māori urban dwellers	Support for Māori (and others) who use the institution

The autonomy of marae has been discussed in some detail because in many ways the ensuing issues can be generalised to other situations and usefully illustrate the wider ambiguities surrounding tino rangatiratanga. There are three levels to the debate. First, just as marae autonomy is sometimes contested by the expectations of the wider tribe, so collective tribal authority (confederations of tribes) is often similarly perceived by individual tribes as a threat to tribal autonomy. Second, the distinctions between marae tupuna and marae-a-rohe parallel the debate about tribal systems of governance and the relative rights and merits of urban Māori governing bodies. Third, the imposition of institutional rules over marae that are established in schools or hospitals or government institutions provokes Māori concern about the intrusion of the state into the control, management, and disposal of Māori resources and culture. There is also a fourth point: marae autonomy, even in optimal circumstances, is relative and subject to the laws of the land.

IWI GOVERNANCE

Puao-te-ata-tu, a report released in 1986 by John Rangihau and his review team, claimed that the Department of Social Welfare practised institutional racism, at least in its dealings with Māori children.[16] The resulting impact was strong, especially as the Labour government at the time was seeking to give greater recognition of the Treaty of Waitangi. One of the outcomes was the establishment of the Matua Whāngai program which sought to maintain difficult children within the whānau rather than under departmental control.[17] Though poorly resourced, the innovative approach was an attempt to recognise Māori values and practices and to acknowledge the importance of whānau, hapū, and iwi to the nurturance of children.[18] A tribal approach was integral, both in the implementation of the program and also in cementing the underlying philosophy that blood ties are, in the end, more appropriate and more dependable than the goodwill of the state or foster parents. Iwi development had also been a product of the Hui Taumata in 1984 and was incorporated into the fourth Labour government's Māori policy alongside devolution. In a discussion document, *Tirohanga Rangapū*, the demise of the large and by now inefficient Department of Māori Affairs was proposed, with many of its functions being subsumed by iwi.[19] 'They [iwi] are strong, enduring, sophisticated systems of cooperation and community effort and as such it has been advocated that they provide an appropriate means of delivering government programmes to Māori people.'[20] The subsequent policy statement, *Te Urupare Rangapū*, went further, prescribing a role for iwi, and in particular iwi authorities, in policy advice and the delivery of government programmes.[21]

While the policy was eventually well received by Māori, tribes were not prepared for the battles that would follow. Two issues were to become significant challenges for iwi governance. Of prime importance were the questions of mandate and the type of legal identity an iwi would adopt in order to trade with the government and other bodies. Prior to *Urupare Rangapū*, some tribes were organised around Māori Trust Boards, established under the Māori Trusts Board Act 1955 primarily to receive and distribute compensatory payments from the government for various injustices. Other iwi had no clear tribal structure apart from customary networks and informal alliances between hapū, while in a few areas, existing District Māori Councils approximated iwi structures, though more correctly they were formed from regional rather than iwi considerations. Under the leadership of Apirana Mahuika, Ngāti Porou was one of the first tribes to adopt a new structure, Te Rūnanga o Ngāti Porou, and specific legislation was passed in 1987.[22] Several other iwi followed, although many opted to retain existing Trust Boards to act as iwi authorities and some formed incorporated societies for the same purpose. For most tribes prolonged and heated debate was the rule. What constituted an iwi? How did a hapū differ from an iwi? Who had the power to make decisions on behalf of an iwi? To whom would an iwi authority be accountable? Why was it necessary to adopt a legal identity at all?

For the Crown the issues were quite different. Given the new policy contained in *Urupare Rangapū* government agencies were now required to consult with iwi, form partnerships with them, and devolve services and resources to them. It was important to know who should be approached and which, of several organisations, could presume to speak for the tribe as a whole. The Rūnanga Iwi Bill introduced in 1990 was to provide the answer. It proposed criteria for gazetting iwi organisations as authorised voices and required those authorities to be registered through the Māori Land Court, where they could be challenged by their own tribal members or by neighbouring tribes disputing an assertion of boundaries or even status as a legitimate iwi. The National Māori Congress spent some time debating the bill and concluded that it was an unnecessary imposition which could lead the Crown to dictate the terms under which iwi organised themselves, and in the process remove from tribes their autonomy and any semblance of power which remained. A delegation of kaumātua, led by Sir Hepi Te Heuheu, advised the Prime Minister accordingly. Relatively minor amendments were subsequently made to the bill before it was enacted in August 1990.

However, the Rūnanga Iwi Act, the first piece of legislation to recognise the status of tribes, had a short life. Almost as soon as the National government assumed office later in 1990, Winston Peters, the Minister of Māori Affairs who was opposed to the bill from the outset, had it repealed. He argued that there were already mechanisms (such as tribal trust boards and incorporated societies) for giving recognition to iwi. Ironically, by 1995 Peters was highly critical of government Treaty settlement proposals and made much of the need for clear mandates before the Crown entered into any discussions with tribal authorities.[23] The Rūnanga Iwi Act was intended to provide just that. With its repeal, a mandating process was lost that might have circumvented many of the difficulties associated with the negotiations between Māori and the Crown, including the Sealord agreement.

The question of mandated iwi authorities arose again both in connection with the distribution of the pre-settlement fisheries assets and also the negotiated settlement of historic Treaty of Waitangi claims. Tribes negotiating Treaty claims with the Crown were expected to demonstrate that they had an appropriate infrastructure to manage settlement packages and that they could count on a mandate before signing any settlement. In the case of the first three negotiated settlements, Tainui, Whakatohea, and Ngai Tahu, negotiations were handled on behalf of the tribe by tribal trust boards. But in all cases it was clear that the trust board structure was an inappropriate vehicle for tribal governance, partly because it was a creature of statute and members were appointed, on advice, by the Minister of Māori Affairs, but also because it required ministerial approval in order to conduct business and gave accountability to the Crown rather than to the tribe itself. Dissatisfied with that outdated arrangement, Ngai Tahu has created a new structure, Te Rūnanga o Ngai Tahu, which makes the tribe accountable to itself and provides a body to represent the tribe in its dealings with the Crown and with local government.[24] Now enshrined in statute,[25] the bill was in the select committee stage for nearly three years, partly because some of the tribe, including the two Ngai Tahu members of Parliament (Whetu Tirikatene-Sullivan and Sandra Lee) were opposed to it, claiming that the rights of hapū would be undermined. However, most of the tribe supported the bill, which was passed by Parliament in 1996, before the deed of settlement was announced.

As required in the Waikato Raupatu Claims Settlement Act 1995, Tainui also took steps to establish a representative body which would be more appropriate as a governing body for the tribe. A three-year consultation process commenced in 1996 and registered beneficiaries will be asked to help shape the new structure. Among the options being studied are a marae-based rūnanga with representatives from each of the 61 beneficiary marae, a hapū-based rūnanga with representation from each of the 33 hapū, and an iwi electorate model where any registered beneficiary can stand for election to the rūnanga (or board) and the elected board is responsible to all 33 000 beneficiaries rather than to hapū or marae.[26] The Whakatohea tribe has embarked on a similar process and is consulting its people to determine the best governing structure. A representative body with elected members which distributes income from the settlement and develops a relationship with the Crown is one possibility.[27]

Impetus for more transparent tribal governance also came from the Office of Treaty Settlements as part of the pre-settlement process and from Te Ohu Kaimoana when attention turned to the distribution of assets to iwi. Largely by default, Te Ohu Kaimoana had to devise its own list of iwi entitled to benefit from Sealord's and in the process developed certain criteria for iwi status, including recognition by neighbouring iwi, a network of marae and hapū, and descent from a common ancestor. Furthermore, organisations purporting to represent those tribes were required to show that they had been elected at an advertised hui, that the constitution of the organisation enabled continued participation in decision-making by iwi members, and the executive represented across-the-board membership. Early in 1997, out of about 50 iwi, only a handful had provided the necessary information.[28] Concerns about the composition of iwi trust boards and rūnanga executives were voiced by several speakers at the Hui Whakapūmau in 1994. 'When leadership of one generation considers it their inalienable right to make binding decisions affecting the lives of future generations, and without even tokenistic attempts to consult with them, the loss of respect must be an obvious and predictable outcome.'[29]

Different concerns about modern tribal governance structures have also been raised in connection with the emphasis on business models, which appear to corporatise iwi. Tribal members are aware of the corporations in Alaska which have all but ousted traditional tribal structures and are keen to avoid creating economically oriented organisations which fail to capture the essential cultural basis of the tribe. On the other hand, tribal leaders have been at pains to retain an iwi identity but have also pointed out that economic self-sufficiency is critical to self-determination; tino rangatiratanga cannot be achieved without a sound economic base that enables financial independence from the government. According to Bob Mahuta, powerlessness does not come about simply by being a minority but from a lack of capital.[30]

IWI AND URBAN MĀORI

Apart from iwi governance and tribal structures, including marae, there are many other Māori organisations at local, regional, and national levels, exercising the right of Māori people to organise as whānau, communities, interest groups, and political parties. Over the past one hundred or so years, there has been a proliferation of organisations, created largely in response to the changing nature of Māori society. Church-based groups, councils, committees, educational trusts, and urban authorities have been formed, and although they have often failed to gain total formal acceptance either by the Crown or by Māori, their emergence has been a reflection of the diversity of Māori society and changes in affiliations and aspirations. District Māori Councils represent a Māori community focus at regional levels today, as do local branches of the Māori Women's Welfare League and in some communities kōhanga reo and urban Māori authorities.

While there is a distinction between iwi interests and rights, and the rights of a more generic Māori community to seek control and authority through other means, the two sets are not incompatible. Māori society is complex and it is both simplistic and misleading to suggest that Māori interests can be totally accommodated within one constitutional framework only. Importantly, however, the rights and obligations of each must be respected and the relationships between them agreed upon. Too frequently, debate centres on whether the case for tribes (as the fundamental constitutional element of Māori society) outweighs the case for other Māori communities of interest. A dual focused approach, however, regards both elements as legitimate and places greater emphasis on the relationship between them.

The debate about the role of tribes, iwi, and Māori people generally surfaced at the Privy Council in 1996 in response to the Court of Appeal ruling in favour of urban Māori that iwi did not have exclusive rights to fishing quota.[31] Representing two urban Māori authorities, Te Whānau o Waipareira and the Manukau Urban Māori Authority, John Tamihere and June Jackson had claimed that a focus on iwi structures alone would bypass those Māori living in urban centres who were divorced from tribal networks. The Privy Council quashed the appeal but, rightly, did not themselves decide on the relative merits of either claimants, nor attempt to define iwi. Instead they referred the matter back to New Zealand. It is a matter which Māori themselves need to resolve, though not necessarily through adversarial court proceedings. The question is not so much whether the iwi system is the only form of tino rangatiratanga, but how tribal independence and autonomy relate to decision-making within the collective Māori world. At times, tribal authority and rights are more significant than the rights of Māori people generally. But for other purposes Māori authority makes more sense and is more significant when it moves beyond the disparate domains of tribes to embrace all Māori.

Sympathetic to both the autonomy of each iwi and at the same time the creation of a collective Māori voice, the Māori Congress has often been challenged to meet those apparently contradictory expectations. By 1995, however, it had agreed that the two need not be incompatible and resolved to move towards some formal recognition of both, within a Māori nation.

THE MĀORI NATION

The concept of a Māori nation may seem at odds with the popular conception of a single New Zealand nation, though it need not be. In describing aboriginal nations as the nations within, Fleras and Elliot[32] maintain that aboriginal people assume the status of nationhood when they assert a special relationship with the state based on a unique set of entitlements. It is a step beyond simply identifying themselves as the original inhabitants of a land who wish to preserve their cultural heritage towards claiming some form of self-government based on a principle of self-determination. Insofar as an ethnic core is a foundation for nationhood,[33] the concept of a Māori nation is well founded on a shared cultural heritage, physical distinctiveness, a history which pre-dates colonisation, aspirations towards self-determination, and a non-acceptance of the state as the appropriate author of Māori destiny. The fact that there is no established Māori nation state does little to diminish the reality of a Māori nation; it simply highlights the absence of a Māori body politic. Nations without states are by no means infrequent—the Scots, the Welsh, and the Canadian Indians claim nationhood although they do not control states of their own.

Nor does the notion of a Māori nation mean that tribal authority ceases to have meaning. While many tribes describe themselves as iwi nations, seldom are tribes insulated from the commonalties which all Māori share. A Māori nation incorporates tribes but goes further to encompass other dimensions. 'The exercise of tino rangatiratanga for future Māori advancement must be able to include the total Māori population, not only those operating from an iwi base.'[34]

There is, at least among Māori, a reasonable level of agreement that the four fundamental foundations of tino rangatiratanga are: mana wairua—a spiritual dimension relevant to all aspects of Māori life and organisation; mana whenua—the security of relationships with land and other physical resources and the authority of tribes to exercise control over their own resources; mana tangata—individual well-being, citizenship rights, and freedom from financial dependence on governments; mana ariki—the authority of ariki to lead and guide their own and other peoples. These foundations make up the four essential constitutional elements of the Māori nation and provide some guidance as to the meaning of tino rangatiratanga. They are summarised in table 8.3. Mana whenua has comparable connotations to Article 2 of the Treaty of Waitangi, while mana tangata recognises the citizenship rights inherent in Article 3.

Table 8.3 Constitutional Elements of the Māori Nation

Mana Wairua	Mana Whenua	Mana Ariki	Mana Tangata
Spiritual and cultural values, beliefs, practises	Iwi and hapū ownership and control over tribal resources, including land, forests, rivers, the sea	The authority of paramount leaders within their own tribes and as leaders for all Māori	The rights of individual Māori to organise as Māori and to assert citizenship rights

Source: M. H. Durie, 'Tino Rangatiratanga: Māori Self-Determination'

The Māori nation can also be represented as a complex system of interacting organisations at local, regional, and national levels. Table 8.4 on the following page summarises seven organisational dimensions which together make up the Māori nation. Tribal organisations include marae tupuna, whānau, hapū, and iwi. At a national level, the Federation of Māori Authorities and Māori Congress are tribally based collectives at both hapū and iwi levels. In contrast, community organisations are not based on descent from common ancestors so much as on interests derived from living in the same (usually urban) locality. Māori committees and branches of the Māori Women's Welfare League are good examples. At a national level, they are represented by the League itself and the New Zealand Māori Council. Māori church organisations are strong and cover the range of mainstream denominations as well as distinctly Māori religions such as Ratana and Ringatu. Cultural organisations hinge on participation in Māori cultural pursuits, including language, and are epitomised by the kōhanga reo networks, as well as kapa haka groups and groups for the promotion of the arts, weaving, and carving.

Contemporary Māori society contains a number of organisations which are formed on particular interests, or sectoral groups: Tino Rangatiratanga in secondary education, the Women's Health League in health, Nga Ringa Whakahaere o te Iwi Māori in traditional healing, He Puna Waihanga in the arts, Matawhānui for university staff, and Te Huarahi in post-primary teaching. There are also political groups committed to the advancement of Māori, including Māori party political organisations and activist groups, such as Te Ahi Kaa and Te Kawariki. Finally, a number of organisations are part of the machinery of the state but nonetheless are closely aligned to Māori aspirations and resources and in that sense form part of the Māori nation. The Māori Land Court, Te Ohu Kaimoana, the Waitangi Tribunal, Te Ohu Whakatipu (in the Ministry of Women's Affairs), and Te Puni Kōkiri are essentially agencies of the state but their links, programs, and cultural orientation are strongly attuned to the wider Māori community.

Table 8.4 Examples of Organisational Networks in the Māori Nation

Tribal	Community	Church	Cultural	Sectoral	Political	State
iwi, marae	Māori committees, Māori Women's Welfare League, sports	Māori sections of mainstream churches & Māori churches	kōhanga reo, kapa haka, Māori artists	Te Huarahi, Matawha- nui	Mana Motuhake, Ahi Kaa	Waitangi Tribunal, Māori Language Commission, Te Ohu Kaimoana

At a meeting of the Executive in Hawera in May 1995, the Māori Congress agreed to promote a Māori body politic which at the very least would play a role in shaping Māori policy at a national level. A national Māori body politic has long been an aspiration of Māori. It was, for example, one of the objectives in the 1835 Declaration of Independence (a 'Congress'), was similarly advanced by the Kotahitanga movement in 1890 (leading to the 1892 Paremata Māori), and was again evident in 1990 when tribes established the National Māori Congress. There have been many other national Māori organisations, including the New Zealand Māori Council and the Māori Women's Welfare League, which have displayed some features of a Māori body politic though without necessarily seeing themselves as a governing body.

Several models for more effective Māori participation in policy making and shaping the law have been advocated.[35] Some, such as a Māori assembly, would lead on to parallel structures which worked in partnership with the Crown, not unlike the Saami Parliament with the Norwegian government or the Assembly of First Nations with the Canadian government. Others, including the model proposed by the Bishopric of Aotearoa, urge a radical restructuring of Parliament to include a Māori House within the House of Representatives and a Senate within which Māori participation is determined according to the Treaty of Waitangi. All models have common features and envisage structures which in effect will provide for a more consistent Māori voice at a national level and in discussions with the Crown.

The essential functions of a national Māori body politic should be consistent with the principles of tino rangatiratanga. They might include the formulation of Māori policy, the management and implementation of Māori policies, active participation in the development and interpretation of law, planning for the needs of future generations, auditing national policies and legislation, making appointments to national Māori institutions and Māori appointments to Crown agencies, control and management of public spending for and on behalf of Māori, the development of foreign policy for Māori, and the pursuit of Māori interests abroad.[36]

However, even if there is a measure of agreement about the existence of a Māori nation, there is not unanimity among Māori about the need for a national Māori body. Many tribes, for example, fear that a national organisation could undermine tribal authority and compromise the right of tribes to negotiate their own affairs. Others, such as Tainui, are sympathetic to Māori nationalism and a Māori organisation under which Māori might unite, but see economic development at a tribal level as the first priority.[37] Ngai Tahu are less convinced and reject any suggestion of a national Māori body in favour of 'a series of Māori nations subsisting in a wider society.'[38] For different reasons, many urban Māori are worried that a national Māori body will be seriously biased in favour of tribes at the expense of urban Māori.

Yet despite these concerns, there is much wider agreement that macro-policies for Māori should be decided by Māori, because the government is unable to bring a distinctive Māori approach necessary for effective social, cultural, and economic development. That was one motivation for the establishment of the National Māori Congress (later known simply as the Māori Congress) in 1990. Concerned about conflicts between iwi, and worried by the imposition of policies by the state, three distinguished Māori leaders were instrumental in forming a loose alliance of iwi, and some other Māori bodies, as a counter to government haste in prescribing Māori pathways. Sir Hepi Te Heuheu, the Māori Queen Te Arikinui Dame Te Atairangikaahu, and Mrs Reo Hura, the leader of the Ratana Church, were sufficiently respected by all tribes to launch the movement under the banner of whakakotahitanga (unification) and under the chairmanship of Apirana Mahuika. The Congress was a powerful force in balancing govern-ment impatience with Māori aspirations and played a major role in the disposal of surplus railways properties, as well as strengthening the resolve of iwi to achieve the goals of tino rangatiratanga. Although by the end of the Sealord debate several iwi had opted out, the Congress continued to advocate greater Māori autonomy and, under the leadership of Te Atawhai Tairoa, championed the Māori option case and the prospect of a national Māori body politic.

Non-Māori have other concerns about the recognition of a Māori nation and Māori nationalism. The emergence of a national Māori body politic based on ethnic characteristics challenges the New Zealand belief in a single nation, which allows some recognition of ethnicity but no real opportunity for shared power or shared decision-making. Though not opposed to a fair deal for Māori, many feel that there are limits to autonomy and that the sovereignty of Parliament should not be challenged.[39] At the same time, the exercise of authority by groups other than Parliament is possible within existing constitutional arrangements. This can be done by passive sanctions (a decision by Parliament not to concern itself with the exercise of power and authority by a particular group), formal recognition of existing arrangements through legislation, and delegation of authority to an entity which did not previously exercise it. The government argues that these provisions are sufficient for Māori empowerment, including the establishment of a national Māori body, without challenging the ultimate sovereignty of Parliament.[40]

Māori interest, however, while allowing that some views are extreme, generally emphasises the principle of partnership, whereby Māori control over things Māori can occur alongside the elected government. Increasingly, legal debate is centring on the constraints which the Māori nation imposes on parliamentary supremacy, rather than the establishment of a Māori challenge to national sovereignty.[41] Tino rangatiratanga, Māori self-determination, has become the aim, and autonomy is the goal. Leaving aside the need to strike a balance between tribal independence and collective Māori authority, the question is whether Māori aspirations for greater autonomy can be met within the existing frameworks or whether fresh constitutional arrangements are needed. Policy advice, as distinct from actual decision-making, is a minimal position, and unlikely to satisfy all Māori. The government, on the other hand, is unhappy about any notion of shared sovereignty and views with some alarm the escalating calls for self-determination. Self-management, they argue, would require little if any constitutional change and would be consistent with overall economic and social goals. But self-determination, if it hinged on the development of a Māori nation state, would be unacceptable to the government. For that reason it appears there would be support for a national Māori body which provided advice to the government but was not itself seen as a government.

In the *Taranaki Report*, the Waitangi Tribunal discussed Māori disempowerment and the determination of Taranaki Māori to retain autonomy. Not only was extensive land deprivation seen as a foundation for the Taranaki claim but also the Tribunal considered that the destruction of autonomy and self-government was an equal injustice and went on to illustrate how Māori governance had been progressively undermined by the imposition of government-inspired policy and systems of administration. Aboriginal autonomy or aboriginal self-government was described in the report as a 'right of indigenes to constitutional status as first peoples and their rights to manage their own policy, resources, and affairs within minimum parameters necessary for the proper operation of the State.' Equivalent Māori words are tino ranga-tiratanga and mana motuhake. According to the Tribunal, 'The single thread that most illuminates the historical fabric of Māori and Pakeha contact has been Māori determination to maintain Māori autonomy and the Government's desire to destroy it. . . . [A]n endowment that provides adequately for tribal autonomy in the future is important, not payments for individual benefit.'[42]

A CHANGING NEW ZEALAND CONSTITUTION

There is every sign that New Zealand's constitutional arrangements will change over the next decade. The New Zealand Constitution Act 1986 formally cleared the way for greater independence from Britain, and since then other funda-mental constitutional changes have occurred. The adoption of mixed member proportional representation is an obvious example. According to a UMR Insight survey, wide acceptance of a referendum to adopt the MMP parliamentary system was not necessarily based on a clear understanding of the system so much as a desire for constitutional change.[43] Constitutional change has also been reflected in a restructuring of the state sector and greater recognition of international conventions for domestic law and practice. Other changes are imminent or rumoured, including the abolition of recourse to the Privy Council and the establishment of a republic.

Dispensing with the Privy Council was contained in the New Zealand Courts Structure Bill, introduced into Parliament in 1996 despite considerable Māori opposition. Submissions had been called for by the government and, among others, the Māori Committee of the Law Commission prepared a lengthy argument in favour of retaining the Council. The committee made two main points: there was a need for more extensive consultation with Māori, and the matter was linked with the wider issues of the constitutional position of Māori in New Zealand. Removing the right of appeal to the Privy Council ought not to be considered out of the broader context of constitutional reform. It was argued that Māori regard the Privy Council as important because it is technically a means of access to the Sovereign. The Treaty of Waitangi was viewed as a pact with the Queen as much as with the Crown, and therefore dismissal of the Council removes a significant protection. Though the link might have been more symbolic than actual, it was nonetheless of constitutional significance.[44] The Solicitor-General dismissed the importance of the symbolic link with the Sovereign, and the Attorney-General, Paul East, in his paper to government, rejected the constitutional link. 'The issue of appeals is separate from wider Māori constitutional issues.' The government had also dismissed any link between the Proposals for the Settlement of Treaty of Waitangi Claims and a New Zealand constitution and were clearly unwilling to enter into discussions of that sort.

After the 1996 general election and the formation of a coalition between National and New Zealand First, however, the government changed its mind about the Privy Council. Early in 1997 the Minister of Justice announced that plans to sever links with the Privy Council were 'dead in the water.' Māori welcomed the about-turn, and so did the Law Society, which was concerned that the alternative would have allowed for only one right of appeal from the High Court when two rights of appeal are available in most other countries with similar legal systems.[45] The Māori position was vindicated to some extent in January 1997, when the Privy Council quashed the Court of Appeal decision regarding the allocation of benefits to urban Māori and sent the matter back to the High Court for further evidence.

Republicanism is another constitutional issue which has attracted a wide range of opinion. On more than one occasion, most strongly in 1994, Prime Minister Jim Bolger has suggested that New Zealand should become a republic. Māori reaction has been mixed. As with the Privy Council, the link with the Crown and the Sovereign has long-standing significance and offers some prospect of protection against unilateral action by government. Though symbolic only, it is a reminder that the Treaty was signed not with a settler government but with the British Crown, and is further evidence of a lack of complete trust in the government in New Zealand to act fairly and in a manner consistent with the Treaty of Waitangi. However, many Māori also feel that the move towards a republic is inevitable and that it would present an opportunity to develop a written constitution within which the Treaty of Waitangi was entrenched and the position of Māori as tangata whenua enhanced.

Before any definite steps to form a republic were taken, a clear constitutional framework would be necessary. Predictably, Māori would insist that the promise of the Treaty be retained and that they be fully involved in any constitutional conferences. There is support for the inclusion of the Treaty in a modern New Zealand constitution from many quarters. In an editorial for the *New Zealand Political Review*, Chris Trotter proposed a constitution for a New Zealand republic based on the provisions of the Treaty. 'In trying to describe the process of de-colonisation, I encountered a much more frightening process: recolonisation. Pakeha New Zealanders are themselves becoming the victims of a "second wave" of colonialism; not at the behest of an imperial nation state, . . . but in the interests of imperious transnational corporations. The struggle for sovereignty has become the struggle to preserve the freedom of both Māori and Pakeha.'[46] And he considered that the Treaty of Waitangi was the best safeguard.

Neither has the Crown rejected the significance of the Treaty of Waitangi as a constitutional foundation. Quite the reverse. In a briefing paper to the Minister of Justice after the 1996 general election, the Department of Justice described the Treaty as 'New Zealand's founding document': 'The Treaty calls for inter-pretation of its underlying principles. These questions are so important to our nationhood that they need to be the subject of informed and well-intentioned discussions involving, first and foremost, the Treaty partners and all other members of society wishing to participate.'[47]

The Hon. Matiu Rata, believing that it was only a matter of time before a republic was formed, promoted the idea of a constitutional commission to collate opinion and report back prior to a referendum.[48] Other Māori calls for constitutional change have been voiced on many marae and in numerous meetings. Moana Jackson's report in 1988, calling for a Māori justice system, was an indication that Māori were not only dissatisfied with the delivery of social services (including legal services) by the state, but were concerned about fundamental constitutional conventions and processes.[49] The three Hirangi hui were also about an appropriate constitution that would facilitate tino rangatiratanga.[50] The first hui was called by Sir Hepi Te Heuheu in January 1995 in response to the release of the Government's proposals for the settlement of Treaty of Waitangi claims. A unanimous resolution was passed by the 1 000 or more participants calling for the Treaty of Waitangi to be entrenched as the constitution for New Zealand. In reply, the government rejected the suggestion that the settlement process was in any way a constitutional matter. The second hui was held in September 1995 and was dominated by rangatahi, youth, who again reaffirmed the need for constitutional changes that would enable tino rangatiratanga to be realised. Decolonisation was emphasised as an important prerequisite. By the third hui, in April 1996, the agenda revolved around the recognition of mana Māori as the basis for constitutional change. Any change was to be centred on Māori values and identity and the twin pillars of mana motuhake and tino rangatiratanga. The rhetoric was strong and the aim more or less understood, but by the third hui it was apparent that there was some ambivalence about constitutional reform for New Zealand as opposed to the development of a constitution for the Māori nation. Three options were identified: continue under the Westminster system; form a partnership with the Crown; Māori govern themselves.[51]

An opportunity to seriously address the position of Māori within New Zealand and to force a constitutional debate along the lines suggested by Matiu Rata may have been lost, at least for the time being. It is unlikely that most Māori would subscribe to a separate Māori nation-state today, even though there would be some enthusiasm about recognising the existence of a Māori nation. The Mana Māori vote in the 1996 General Election might have been considerably higher if Māori seriously wished to move towards the realisation of Māori sovereignty and an independent state, and despite the sovereignty march to Rotorua from Waitangi after the 1997 Waitangi Day celebrations, greater attention was focused on Parliament and the performance of the fifteen Māori members than on the message of the marchers. The key question, however, is whether there is room for sharing and partnership between kāwanatanga and rangatiratanga. The Waitangi Tribunal has developed a considerable jurisprudence based on rangatiratanga and has argued convincingly that as sovereignty is legally unchallengeable, so is rangatiratanga unchallengeable as a matter of Treaty principle.[52]

THE FORMULATION OF MĀORI POLICY

Most policies for Māori are decided through the Crown either by Cabinet or by state departments and Crown entities. Policies for Treaty settlements, for example, are not formulated by iwi but by the Treaty of Waitangi Fisheries Commission, the Crown Forest Rental Trust, the Māori Land Court (especially in deciding on custom law), the Waitangi Tribunal, the Office of Treaty Settlements, and ministers of the Crown. Iwi have little opportunity for direct input into settlement policies. Nor do they have consistent say over appointments to the Māori Land Court, the Tribunal, Commissions, or Trusts and while they are able to make submissions on major issues, the decisions are taken elsewhere. Too often iwi are asked to react to proposals and policies which others have formulated on their behalf.

The same is true for national social and economic policies. Even though most departments of state have Māori advisers and Māori policy analysts, and despite the presence of Te Puni Kōkiri, policies for Māori are, in the end, shaped by the state and approved by the executive without needing to incorporate Māori priorities. Usually the emphasis is on developing sectoral policies (health policies, education policies, welfare policies, employment policies, etc.) and then adding a Māori view—the so-called mainstreaming approach.

Māori, however, are seeking a mechanism for an integrated approach to policy development which has Māori development as the central focus, sectoral perspectives being added as necessary. Te Puni Kōkiri has the potential to do that, but it is not called on to provide policy leadership on a consistent basis. More often, it is simply required to respond to sectoral policies developed in other ministries and departments. Even then Te Puni Kōkiri may only be asked to comment on selected areas of policy (as in the fiscal envelope proposals).

If for no other reason, a national Māori body could provide the necessary basis for actively developing Māori policy. It would, however, be important that any national Māori body politic had defined relationships with other Māori organisations and with the Crown. A clear division of responsibilities would be needed, so that the national organisation did not determine policies which should be decided by iwi and hapū within their own structures. Not only should there be an open relationship with iwi, but the relative prerogatives would need to be agreed upon. In general terms, the national body could focus on national policies while iwi would continue to exercise authority over their own particular areas; no national Māori organisation could presume to speak for iwi or for hapū. Though supportive of the Māori Congress and convinced of the spiritual and material basis for a Māori identity, Sir Hugh Kawharu cautions against any encroachment on hapū rights. 'Congress must not derogate the right of hapū to deal with the Crown on hapū defined issues or allow the Crown to deal only with the tribe. As the Treaty itself affirms, rangatiratanga resides in the hapū not in the tribe.'[53]

In addition to establishing defined relationships with iwi, a national Māori body would need to develop formal mechanisms for interacting with the Crown. One link could be with Parliament, and Māori members of Parliament who represent Māori electorates might have particular responsibilities to support policy decisions arising from the national Māori organisation when they went to Parliament. If the Māori body were to play a serious role in developing Māori policy, then agreed understandings with Parliament would be required, along with opportunity for liaison between the national Māori organisation and departments of state. Agreements would be necessary so that departments, ministries, and Crown entities would be required to take account of Māori policies developed by the national Māori organisation when offering their own advice to cabinet ministers.

At present, the exercise of tino rangatiratanga at national and international levels is compromised because there is no Māori body politic. In its absence, policy making for and on behalf of Māori is assumed by the Crown, with irregular Māori input and, inevitably, increasing Māori discontent. Even policy decisions about Māori resources rest with the state, not Māori. Te Ohu Kaimoana, Te Taura Whiri i te Reo Māori, the Māori Land Court, Ngā Whenua Rāhui, despite having high Māori membership, are not Māori-owned or Māori-governed yet all make major decisions on cultural and physical resources. While the key participants are Māori, the accountabilities, reporting lines, and appointment processes lie with the state.

Current Māori interest in a body politic is high, despite the reservation of some iwi that their own autonomy could be undermined, and despite the lack of agreement about the structure of a national body. In fact, the promotion of several models for a national body politic has not masked their common features, including the capacity to make policy for and on behalf of Māori, and a partnership with the Crown. To advance matters further, Māori will wish to first determine the relationship between their own constitutional elements within the Māori nation, and then adopt a structure which best expresses the nature of the Māori nation and a capacity to develop appropriate Māori policy. Once agreements have been reached between Māori, the relationship between the Māori nation and the Crown might be more readily defined. Even then, however, it will be necessary to overcome the dogma of unitary Crown sovereignty so that self-determination can be expressed in a manner which is consistent with the political and constitutional rights of indigenous peoples.

The establishment of a national Māori body politic will not by itself achieve tino rangatiratanga; Māori society is too complex to have its total authority vested in a single institution. But a national body, even if not the sum total of tino rangatiratanga, will serve to create an avenue for an active Māori role in policy making and a central base upon which the wide range of Māori interests can be advanced.

THE GOALS OF SELF-DETERMINATION

Self-governance at local or national levels requires a level of organisation which incorporates both customary Māori practises and the application of democratic principles. The two are not incompatible, nor should their juxtaposition be discounted. Māori can be strengthened by the past and can learn from it. But the challenges of tomorrow will require a canopy of skills and wisdoms many of which will come from other cultures and nations. In that respect much of the emphasis on decolonisation is overstated. The task is not so much to shed the vestiges of western civilisation, or to dismantle the past 150 years as if it were all a mistake, but to draw on the past, good and bad, in order to reconstruct a pathway for future generations.

Structural arrangements for self-determination are important and the promotion of absolute Māori independence (as if it were a possibility) has been seized upon by the media to illustrate how unrealistic Māori can be. A media image of Māori bent only on separate development and anti-Pākehā sentiment is as misleading as the picture of a racially harmonious nation within which Māori are happy to blend with an otherwise colourless society. Central to the debate is whether Māori aspirations for fairness and the chance to remain Māori can be fostered within a single nation-state or whether other arrangements are necessary. Views change. A decade ago, Māori might have been less inclined to have any confidence in the courts or in Parliament. Now, with significant rulings on Treaty issues from the High Court and the Court of Appeal, and with the emergence of a bicultural jurisprudence, as well as a strategically placed presence in Parliament, Māori appear to be searching for a place within the nation state of Aotearoa New Zealand—rather than apart from it.

But tino rangatiratanga, mana motuhake, Māori self-determination, cannot be measured simply by the constitutional arrangements for governance or the level of Māori autonomy. More important is whether the goals of self-determination are being realised. The broad aims of self-determination are the advancement of Māori people as Māori and the protection of the environment for future generations. Economic self-sufficiency, social equity, cultural affirmation, and political power, stand alongside a firm Māori identity strengthened by access to whānau, hapū, and iwi and confirmation that future generations of Māori will be able to enjoy their lands and forests, rivers and lakes, harbours and the sea and the air. Those goals underlie the significance of Māori self-determination. The extent to which they can be achieved will likely determine the way in which Māori self-determination will be pursued. Though not unmindful of progress—efforts to revitalise language and culture, improved standards of health and education, mechanisms for the resolution of Treaty grievances, recognition of te ao Māori in legislation, strong Māori Parliamentary representation—Māori are not entirely convinced that their right to advance as Māori in Aotearoa is secure.

A five-point approach is needed to consolidate Māori advancement (see table 8.5 on the following page). First, opportunities for dialogue between Māori and the Crown should not hinge on crises or claims. While avenues for redress of grievances are now identifiable, and through them economic development stands to gain, Māori advancement should be more strategically aligned with forward planning rather than the resolution of historical injustices. A forum for joint planning is necessary. Second, and related to the first point, it is time for the Crown and Māori to develop a comprehensive Treaty of Waitangi policy, distinct from a settlement policy and focused on the future rather than the past. Third, a shift in emphasis from Māori representation to Māori governance will be required if Māori are to retain autonomy at least over their own resources. It is no longer acceptable for the Crown or Crown agencies such as Te Ohu Kaimoana or even the Māori Land Court to act as gatekeepers for resources which belong to Māori. Fourth, Māori need to find a greater measure of agreement on the nature of modern Māori society and the arrangements which will best serve cultural development, social equity and economic security. Iwi, hapū, urban Māori, whānau are all part of the Māori nation and their relationships should be celebrated, not severed. An assembly which can give expression to Māori aspirations, and provide convergence for Māori diversity, will create a focus for the future and a national identity for interaction with the Crown and other nations. Fifth, a deliberate strategy for constitutional change in New Zealand is now needed. Ad hoc and piecemeal reform, fired by political whim and rhetoric as much as need or purpose, prevents a coordinated and reasoned approach. Māori and the Crown, and all New Zealanders, should be invited to participate in the development of a New Zealand constitution which reflects the country's heritage and positions it for the next century as a power in the Pacific, if not the globe.

Table 8.5 A Five-Point Plan for Māori Self-Determination

1	Forward planning
2	A comprehensive Treaty of Waitangi policy
3	Māori governance over Māori resources
4	A Māori assembly
5	Deliberate strategies for constitutional change

At the end of the nineteenth century, Māori morale was low and the population was decimated. Into the twenty-first century, the numbers are high but resources are largely depleted and all too often identity is insecure. To the extent that an evolving New Zealand constitution might celebrate rather than contest rangatiratanga, Māori goals for self-determination and governance will be enhanced. Otherwise litigation, confrontation, occupation and protest will continue, cementing mistrust and suspicion and in the process exacerbating the divisions which already exist within society. Māori self-determination is not primarily about a divided country or two nation-states, or the rejection of other cultures. Fundamentally, it is about the realisation of collective Māori aspirations. And despite the many faces of contemporary Māori society and the wide range of views which exist, there is nonetheless a high level of agreement that the central goal of tino rangatiratanga is for Māori to govern and enjoy their own resources and to participate fully in the life of the country. Māori want to advance, as Māori, and as citizens of the world.

NOTES FOR CHAPTER 8

1 'I shall stretch forth my hand to the four corners of the world, and no hand will be able to suppress me,' a prophecy made by Te Kooti at Aorangi marae, 31 December 1892, in Judith Binney, (1995), *Redemption Songs: A Life of Te Kooti Arikirangi Te Turuki*, Auckland University Press/Bridget Williams Books, Auckland, p. 459.

2 Kenneth Keith, (1995), 'The Roles of the Tribunal, the Courts and the Legislature', in G. McLay (ed.), *Treaty Settlements: The Unfinished Business*, New Zealand Institute of Advanced Legal Studies and Victoria University of Wellington Law Review, Wellington, p. 47.

3 Geoffrey Palmer, (1995), 'Where To from Here', in Geoff McLay (ed.), *Treaty Settlements*, pp. 153–154.

4 Hineani Melbourne, (1995), 'Wira Gardiner', in *Māori Sovereignty: The Māori Perspective*, Hodder Moa Beckett, Auckland, pp. 83–84.

5 Menno Boldt, (1993), *Surviving as Indians: The Challenge of Self-Government*, University of Toronto Press, Toronto, pp. 133–137.

6 Hineani Melbourne, (1995), 'Mike Smith', in *Māori Sovereignty*, pp. 101–103.

7 Hineani Melbourne, (1995), 'Sir Tipene O'Regan', in *Māori Sovereignty*, p. 158.

8 Hineani Melbourne, (1995), 'Peter Tapsell', in *Māori Sovereignty*, p. 67.

9 Te Puni Kōkiri, (1994), *Mana Tangata: Draft Declaration on the Rights of Indigenous Peoples 1993: Background and Discussion on Key Issues*, Ministry of Māori Development, Wellington, p. 13.

10 Lindsay Cox, (1993), *Kotahitanga: The Search for Māori Political Unity*, Oxford University Press, Auckland, pp. 59–60.

11 M. H. Durie, (1995), 'Tino Rangatiratanga: Māori Self-Determination', *He Pukenga Kōrero*, vol. 1, no. 1, pp. 44–53.

12 Hineani Melbourne, (1995), 'Hekia Parata', in *Māori Sovereignty*, pp. 38–39.

13 Hineani Melbourne, (1995), 'Mike Smith', in *Māori Sovereignty*, p. 105.

14 Hineani Melbourne, (1995), 'Peter Tapsell', in *Māori Sovereignty*, pp. 65–66.

15 Taumata o te Ra Marae Committee, (1996), *Taumata o te Ra Marae*, a souvenir booklet to commemorate the opening of Taumata o te Ra, Marae Committee, Halcombe.

16 Ministerial Advisory Committee on a Māori Perspective for the Department of Social Welfare, (1986), *Puao-te-ata-tu*, A Report to the Minister of Social Welfare, Wellington.

17 Joan Metge, (1995), *New Growth from Old: The Whānau in the Modern World*, Victoria University Press, Wellington, pp. 58–59.

18 John Cody, (1990), 'Devolution, Disengagement and Control in the Statutory Social Services', in Peter McKinley (ed.), *Redistribution of Power? Devolution in New Zealand*, Victoria University Press, Wellington, pp. 167–169.

19 Rauru Kirikiri and Tipene O'Regan, (1988), 'Māori Development and Devolution',

in John Martin and Jim Harper (eds), *Devolution and Accountability*, Studies in Public Administration No. 34, GP Books, Wellington, pp. 116–120.

20 Hon. K. T. Wetere, (1988), *Tirohanga Rangapū: Partnership Perspectives*, Office of the Minister of Māori Affairs, Wellington.

21 Hon. K. T. Wetere, (1988), *Te Urupare Rangapū Partnership Response Policy Statement*, Office of the Minister of Māori Affairs, Wellington.

22 Te Runanga o Ngati Porou Act 1988.

23 Hon. Winston Peters, (1995), 'A Time for Leadership', in Geoff McLay (ed), *Treaty Settlements*, pp. 28–34.

24 Gabrielle Huria, (1996), 'The Bill', in *Te Karaka: The Ngai Tahu magazine*, Summer 1996, pp. 4–6.

25 Te Rūnanga o Ngai Tahu Act 1996.

26 Tainui Maaori Trust Board, (1996), *Annual Report 1996*, Ngaruawahia.

27 Whakatohea Settlement Negotiators, (1996), *Whakatohea Settlement Offer* Information Hui papers.

28 'TOKM seeks mandate information from iwi groups', *Kia Hiwa Ra*, December–January 1996–97.

29 Aroha Mead, (1994), 'Māori Leadership: The Waka Tradition: The Crews Were the Real Heroes', in Department of Māori Studies (ed.), *Kia Pūmau Tonu: Proceedings of the Hui Whakapūmau Māori Development Conference* August 1994, Massey University, p. 112.

30 Hineani Melbourne, (1995), 'Bob Mahuta', *in Māori Sovereignty*, p. 151.

31 See chapter 6, Mana Moana.

32 A. Fleras, J. L. Elliott, (1992), *The Nations Within: Aboriginal–State Relations in Canada, the United States, and New Zealand*, Oxford University Press, Toronto.

33 A. D. Smith, (1989), 'The Origins of Nations', *Ethnic and Racial Studies*, vol. 12, no. 3, pp. 340–367.

34 Arohia Durie, (1994), 'The Treaty of Waitangi in the Life of the Nation', in P. F. Green (ed.), *Studies in New Zealand Social Problems*, Dunmore Press, Palmerston North, p. 294.

35 M. H. Durie, (1995), 'Tino Rangatiratanga: Māori Self-Determination'.

36 M. H. Durie, (1995), 'Tino Rangatiratanga, a discussion paper', in *Report for the Congress Executive 13 May 1995*, Māori Congress, Wellington.

37 Melbourne, *Māori Sovereignty*, pp. 143–152.

38 Melbourne, *Māori Sovereignty*, pp. 153–165.

39 Carol Archie, (1995), 'Doug Graham' in *Māori Sovereignty*, pp. 118–120.

40 Minister of Māori Affairs, (1995), *Crown/Māori Governance Strategy, Draft 7*, Te Puni Kōkiri, Wellington.

41 E. T. Durie, (1995), 'Justice, Biculturalism and the Politics of Law', in M. Wilson, A. Yeatman (eds), *Justice and Identity: Antipodean Practices*, Bridget Williams Books, Wellington, pp. 31–44.

42 Waitangi Tribunal, (1996), *The Taranaki Report Kaupapa Tuatahi (Wai 143)*, GP Publications, Wellington, pp. 5–15.

43 'Kiwis still in dark over MMP', *The Dominion*, Wednesday September 14 1994.

44 Māori Committee, (1995), *Appeals to the Privy Council: Submission made on behalf of the Māori Committee to the Law Commission and the New Zealand Māori Council*, Law Commission, Wellington.

45 'Law Society applauds U-turn on Privy Council', *The Dominion*, Thursday January 23 1997.

46 Chris Trotter, (1995), 'Talking About Sovereignty', Editorial, *New Zealand Political Review*, April/May 1995, p. 4.

47 Ministry of Justice, (1996), *Briefing Paper for the Minister of Justice*, Department of Justice, Wellington.

48 Hon. Matiu Rata, (1995), *Self Reliance – Tino Rangatiratanga*, paper presented at the Conference on Treaty of Waitangi Settlement Methods, Institute for International Research, Wellington.

49 M. Jackson (1988), *The Māori and the Criminal Justice System: A New Perspective: He Whaipaanga Hou*, Policy and Research Division, Department of Justice, Wellington.

50 Māori Congress, (1996), *Post Hirangi Discussion Paper*, Māori Congress, Wellington.

51 John Roberts, (1996), *Alternative Vision He Moemoea Ano: The Significance of the Hirangi Hui*, Joint Public Questions Committee of the Methodist Church of New Zealand and the Presbyterian Church of Aotearoa New Zealand, pp. 21–22.

52 Andrew Sharp (1997), 'The Waitangi Tribunal 1984–1996', in R. Miller (ed.), *New Zealand Politics in Transition*, Oxford University Press, Auckland, p. 392.

53 I. H. Kawharu, (1996), 'Rangatiratanga and Sovereignty by 2040', *He Pukenga Kōrero*, vol. 1, no. 2, pp. 11–20.

APPENDICES

APPENDIX 1
THE DECLARATION OF INDEPENDENCE
(ENGLISH AND MĀORI TEXTS)

APPENDIX 2
THE TREATY OF WAITANGI
(ENGLISH AND MĀORI TEXTS)

APPENDIX 1
THE DECLARATION OF
INDEPENDENCE

HE WAKAPUTANGA O TE RANGATIRATANGA O NU TIRENE

1   KO MATOU, ko nga tino Rangatira o nga iwi o NU TIRENE i raro mai o Haurake, kua oti nei te huihui i Waitangi, i Tokerau, i te ra 28 o Oketopa, 1835. Ka wakaputa i te Rangatiratanga o to matou wenua; a ka meatia ka wakaputaia e matou he Wenua Rangatira, kia huaina, "Ko te Wakaminenga o nga Hapu o Nu Tirene".

2   Ko te Kingitanga, ko te mana i te wenua o te wakaminenga o Nu Tirene, ka meatia nei kei nga tino Rangatira anake i to matou huihuinga; a ka mea hoki, ekore e tukua e matou te wakarite ture ki tetahi hunga ke atu, me tetahi Kawanatanga hoki kia meatia i te wenua o te wakaminenga o Nu Tirene, ko nga tangata anake e meatia nei e matou, e wakarite ana ki te ritenga o o matou ture e meatia nei e matou i to matou huihuinga.

3   Ko matou, ko nga tino Rangatira, ka mea nei, kia huihui ki te runanga ki Waitangi a te Ngahuru i tenei tau i tenei tau, ki te wakarite ture, kia tika ai te wakawakanga, kia mau pu te rongo, kia mutu te he, kia tika te hokohoko. A ka mea hoki ki nga tauiwi o runga, kia wakarerea te wawai, kia mahara ai ki te wakaoranga o to matou wenua, a kia uru ratou ki te wakaminenga o Nu Tirene.

4   Ka mea matou, kia tuhituhia he pukapuka, ki te ritenga o tenei o to matou wakaputanga nei, ki te Kingi o Ingarani, hei kawe atu i to matou aroha; nana hoki i wakaae ki te Kara mo matou. A no te mea ka atawai matou, ka tiaki i nga Pakeha e noho nei uta, e rere mai ana ki te hokohoko, koia ka mea ai matou ki te Kingi kia waiho hei Matua ki a matou i to matou tamarikitanga, kei wakakahoretia to matou Rangatiratanga.

Kua wakaaetia katoatia e matou i tenei ra, i te 28 o Oketopa 1835, ki te aroaro o te Rehirenete o te Kingi o Ingarani.

DECLARATION OF INDEPENDENCE
OF NEW ZEALAND

1 We the hereditary chiefs and heads of the tribes of the Northern parts of New Zealand, being assembled at Waitangi, in the Bay of Islands, on this 28th day of October 1835, declare the Independence of our country, which is hereby constituted and declared to be an Independent State, under the designation of the United Tribes of New Zealand.

2 All sovereign power and authority within the territories of the United Tribes of New Zealand is hereby declared to reside entirely and exclusively in the hereditary chiefs and heads of tribes in their collective capacity, who also declare that they will not permit any legislative authority separate from themselves in their collective capacity to exist, nor any function of government to be exercised within the said territories, unless by persons appointed by them, and acting under the authority of laws regularly enacted by them in Congress assembled.

3 The hereditary chiefs and heads of tribes agree to meet in Congress at Waitangi in the autumn of each year, for the purpose of framing laws for the dispensation of justice, the preservation of peace and good order, and the regulation of trade; and they cordially invite the Southern tribes to lay aside their private animosities and to consult the safety and welfare of our common country, by joining the Confederation of the United Tribes.

4 They also agree to send a copy of this Declaration to His Majesty the King of England, to thank him for his acknowledgement of their flag, and in return for the friendship and protection they have shown, and are prepared to show, to such of his subjects as have settled in their country, or resorted to its shores for the purposes of trade, they entreat that he will continue to be the parent of their infant State, and that he will become its Protector from all attempts upon its independence.

Agreed to unanimously on this 28th day of October, 1835, in the presence of His Britannic Majesty's Resident.

(Here follow the signatures or marks of thirty-five hereditary chiefs or Heads of tribes, which form a fair representation of the tribes of New Zealand from the North Cape to the latitude of the River Thames.)

English witnesses

(Signed) Henry Williams, Missionary, CMS
George Clarke, CMS
James C Clendon, Merchant
Gilbert Mair, Merchant

APPENDIX 2
THE TREATY OF WAITANGI

(ENGLISH VERSION)

Her Majesty Victoria Queen of the United Kingdom of Great Britain and Ireland regarding with Her Royal Favour the Native Chiefs and Tribes of New Zealand and anxious to protect their just Rights and Property and to secure to them the enjoyment of Peace and Good Order has deemed it necessary in consequence of the great number of Her Majesty's Subjects who have already settled in New Zealand and the rapid extension of Emigration both from Europe and Australia which is still in progress to constitute and appoint a functionary properly authorised to treat with the Aborigines of New Zealand for the recognition of Her Majesty's Sovereign authority over the whole or any part of those islands—Her Majesty therefore being desirous to establish a settled form of Civil Government with a view to avert the evil consequences which must result from the absence of the necessary Laws and Institutions alike to the native population and to Her subjects has been graciously pleased to empower and to authorise me William Hobson a Captain in Her Majesty's Royal Navy Consul and Lieutenant Governor of such parts of New Zealand as may be or hereafter shall be ceded to her Majesty to invite the confederated and independent Chiefs of New Zealand to concur in the following Articles and Conditions.

Article The First
The Chiefs of the Confederation of the United Tribes of New Zealand and the separate and independent Chiefs who have not become members of the Confederation cede to Her Majesty the Queen of England absolutely and without reservation all the rights and powers of Sovereignty which the said Confederation or Individual Chiefs respectively exercise or possess, or may be supposed to exercise or to possess over their respective Territories as the sole Sovereigns thereof.

Article The Second
Her Majesty the Queen of England confirms and guarantees to the Chiefs and Tribes of New Zealand and to the respective families and individuals thereof the full exclusive and undisturbed possession of their Lands and Estates Forests Fisheries and other properties which they may collectively or individually possess so long as it is their wish and desire to retain the same in their possession; but the chiefs of the United Tribes and the individual Chiefs yield to Her Majesty the exclusive right of pre-emption over such lands as the proprietors thereof may be disposed to alienate—at such prices as may be agreed between the respective

Proprietors and persons appointed by Her Majesty to treat with them in that behalf.

Article The Third
In consideration thereof Her Majesty the Queen of England extends to the Natives of New Zealand Her royal protection and imparts to them all the Rights and Privileges of British subjects.

William Hobson, Lieutenant Governor

Now therefore We the Chiefs of the Confederation of the United Tribes of New Zealand being assembled in Congress at Victoria in Waitangi and We the Separate and Independent Chiefs of New Zealand claiming authority over the Tribes and Territories which are specified after our respective names, having been made fully to understand the Provisions of the foregoing Treaty, accept and enter into the same in the full spirit and meaning thereof: in witness of which we have attached our signatures or marks at the places and the dates respectively specified.

Done at Waitangi this Sixth day of February in the year of Our Lord one thousand eight hundred and forty.

(Here follow the 512 signatures, dates, and locations.)

TE TIRITI O WAITANGI

(MĀORI VERSION)

Ko Wikitoria, te Kuini o Ingarani, i tana mahara atawai ki nga Rangatira me Nga Hapu o Nu Tirani, i tana hiahia hoki kia tohungia ki a ratou o ratou rangati-ratanga, me to ratou wenua, a kia mau tonu hoki te Rongo ki a ratou me te ata noho hoki, kua wakaaro ia he mea tika kia tukua mai tetahi Rangatira hei kai wakarite ki nga tangata Maori o Nu Tirani. Kia wakaaetia e nga Rangatira Maori te Kawanatanga o te Kuini, ki nga wahi katoa o te wenua nei me nga motu. Na te mea hoki he to komaha ke nga tangata o tona iwi kua noho ki tenei wenua, a e haere mai nei.

Na, ko te Kuini e hiahia ana kia wakaritea te Kawanatanga, kia kaua ai nga kino e puta mai ki te tangata Maori ki te pakeha e noho ture kore ana.

Na, kua pai te Kuini kia tukua a hau, a Wiremu Hopihona, he Kapitana i te Roiara Nawa, hei Kawana mo nga wahi katoa o Nu Tirani, e tukua aianei amua atu ki te Kuini; e mea atu ana ia ki nga Rangatira o te Wakaminenga o nga Hapu o Nu Tirani, me era Rangatira atu, enei ture ka korerotia nei.

Ko Te Tuatahi
Ko nga Rangatira o te Wakaminenga, me nga Rangatira katoa hoki, kihai i uru ki taua Wakaminenga, ka tuku rawa atu ki te Kuini o Ingarani ake tonu atu te Kawanatanga katoa o o ratou wenua.

Ko Te Tuarua
Ko te Kuini o Ingarani ka wakarite ka whakaae ki nga Rangatira, ki nga Hapu, ki nga tangata katoa o Nu Tirani, te tino Rangitiratanga o o ratou wenua o ratou kainga me o ratou taonga katoa. Otiia ko nga Rangatira o te Wakaminenga, me nga Rangatira katoa atu, ka tuku ki te Kuini te hokonga o era wahi wenua e pai ai te tangata nona te wenua, ki te ritenga o te utu e wakaritea ai e ratou ko te kai hoko e meatia nei i te Kuini hei kai hoko mona.

Ko Te Tuatoru
He wakaritenga mai hoki tenei mo te wakaaetanga ki te Kawanatanga o te Kuini. Ka tiakina e te Kuini o Ingarani nga tangata Maori katoa o Nu Tirani. Ka tukua ki a ratou nga tikanga katoa rite tahi ki ana mea ki nga tangata o Ingarani.

(Signed) William Hobson,
Consul and Lieutenant-Governor

Na, ko matou, ko nga Rangatira o te Wakaminenga o nga Hapu o Nu Tirani, ka huihui nei ki Waitangi. Ko matou hoki ko nga Rangatira o Nu Tirani, ka kite nei i te ritenga o enei kupu, ka tangohia, ka wakaaetia katoatia e matou. Koia ka tohungia ai o matou ingoa o matou tohu.

Ka meatia tenei ki Waitangi, i te ono o nga ra o Pepuere, i te tau kotahi mano, e waru rau, e wa tekau, o to tatou Ariki.

SELECT BIBLIOGRAPHY

Adams, Peter, (1977), *Fatal Necessity: British Intervention in New Zealand 1830–1847*, Auckland University Press/Oxford University Press, Auckland.

Aotearoa Broadcasting Systems Inc., (1988), *Report to Members*, ABS, Wellington.

Archie, Carol, (1995), *Maori Sovereignty: The Pakeha Perspective*, Hodder Moa Beckett, Auckland.

Asher, George; Naulls, David, (1987), *Māori Land*, Planning Paper No. 29, New Zealand Planning Council, Wellington.

Aspin, C., (1994), *A Study of the Mathematics Achievement in a Kura Kaupapa Māori*, MA thesis, Victoria University, Wellington.

Baird, Deborah; Geering, Lloyd; Saville-Smith, Kay; Thompson, Linda; Tuhipa, Tose, (1995), *Whose Genes Are They Anyway? Report from the HRC Conference on Human Genetic Information*, Health Research Council, Auckland.

Benton, R. A., (1987), 'From the Treaty of Waitangi to the Waitangi Tribunal', in Walter Hirsh (ed.), *Living Languages*.

Benton, R. A., (1991), *The Māori Language: Dying or Reviving*, New Zealand Council for Educational Research, Wellington.

Biggs, Bruce, (1989), 'Humpty Dumpty and the Treaty of Waitangi', in I. H. Kawharu (ed.), *Waitangi*.

Binney, Judith, (1995), *Redemption Songs: A Life of Te Kooti Arikirangi Te Turuki*, Auckland University Press/Bridget Williams Books, Auckland.

Boldt, Menno, (1993), *Surviving as Indians: The Challenge of Self-Government*, University of Toronto Press, Toronto.

Butterworth, G. V., (1990), *Māori Affairs*, GP Books, Wellington.

Chen, Mai; Palmer, Geoffrey, (1993), *Public Law in New Zealand*, Oxford University Press, Auckland.

Christensen, Ian, (1996), 'Māori Mathematics', *He Pukenga Kōrero*, vol. 1, no. 2, pp. 42–47.

Cleave, Peter, (1989), *The Sovereignty Game: Power, Knowledge and Reading the Treaty*, Victoria University Press, Wellington.

Cloher, Dorothy Urlich; Hohepa, Margie, (1996), 'Te Tū a te Kōhanga Reo i Waenga i te Whānau me te Tikanga Poipoi Tamariki: Māori Families, Child Socialisation and the Role of the Kohanga Reo', *He Pukenga Kōrero*, vol. 1, no. 2, pp. 33–41.

Cody, John, (1990), 'Devolution, Disengagement and Control in the Statutory Social Services', in Peter McKinley (ed.), *Redistribution of Power? Devolution in New Zealand*, Victoria University Press, Wellington.

Commissioner for the Environment, (1988), *Environmental Management and the Principles of the Treaty of Waitangi*, Parliamentary Commissioner for the Environment, Wellington.

Conference Steering Committee, (1984), *A Briefing on Māori Economic Affairs*, Māori Economic Development Summit Conference, Dunmore Press, Palmerston North.

Congress Executive, (1991), *Waitangi Tribunal Claim: The Native Flora and Fauna of Aotearoa, A Resume of the Issues*, National Māori Congress, Wellington.

Conservation Authority, (1994), *Māori Customary Use of Native Birds, Plants and Other Traditional Materials: A Discussion Paper*, New Zealand Conservation Authority, Te Whakahaere Matua o Aotearoa, Wellington.

Controller and Auditor-General, (1995), *The Settlement of Claims Under the Treaty of Waitangi*, Second Report for 1995, Wellington.

Core Services Committee, (1994), *Core Services for 1995/96*, National Advisory Committee on Core Health and Disability Support Services, Wellington.

Cox, Lindsay, (1993), *Kotahitanga: The Search for Māori Political Unity*, Oxford University Press, Auckland.

Crengle, Diane, (1993), *Taking Into Account the Principles of the Treaty of Waitangi: Ideas for the Implementation of Section 8 Resource Management Act 1991*, Ministry for the Environment, Wellington.

Crown Congress Joint Working Party, (1991), *Information Brief for Iwi Arrangements in Respect of Surplus Crown Railway Properties and Treaty of Waitangi Claims*, Crown Congress Joint Working Party, Wellington.

Dahlberg, Tina (1996), 'Māori Representation in Parliament and Tino Rangatiratanga', *He Pukenga Kōrero*, vol. 2, no. 1, pp. 62–72.

Dalziel, Raewyn, (1981), 'The Politics of Settlement', in W. H. Oliver (ed.), *The Oxford History of New Zealand*.

Davey, J., (1993), *From Birth to Death iii*, Institute of Policy Studies, Victoria University of Wellington.

Department of Conservation, (1994), *Conservation Action: Department of Conservation Achievements and Plans*, Department of Conservation, Wellington.

Department of Conservation, (1996), *Conservation Action: Department of Conservation Achievements and Plans 1995/1996–1996/1997*, Wellington.

Department of Health, (1992), *Whaia te Ora mo te Iwi—Strive for the Good Health of the People*, Department of Health, Wellington.

Department of Justice, (1989), *Principles for Crown Action on the Treaty of Waitangi*, Wellington.

Department of Māori Studies (ed.), (1994), *Kia Pūmau Tonu: Proceedings of the Hui Whakapūmau*, Department of Māori Studies, Massey University.

Department of Marketing, (1996), *National Identity International Social Survey Programme*, Massey University.

Dewes, Whaimutu, (1995), 'Fisheries—a case study of an outcome', in Geoff McLay (ed.), *Treaty Settlements*.

Douglas, Edward Te Kohu, (1994), 'Demographic Changes and their Social Consequences for Māori', in Department of Māori Studies (ed.), *Kia Pūmau Tonu*.

Durie, Arohia, (1994), 'The Treaty of Waitangi in the Life of the Nation', in P. F. Green (ed.), *Studies in New Zealand Social Problems*, 2nd edition, Dunmore Press, Palmerston North.

Durie, Arohia, (1995), 'Kia Hiwa Ra: Challenges for Māori Academics in Changing Times', *He Pukenga Kōrero*, vol. 1, no. 1, pp. 1–9.

Durie, E. T., (1979), *Submission to the Royal Commission on Māori Land Courts*, No. 11, Wellington.

Durie, E. T., (1994), *Custom Law, A Discussion Paper*, Waitangi Tribunal, Wellington.

Durie, E. T., (1994), 'Keynote Address', in Department of Māori Studies (ed.), *Kia Pūmau Tonu*.

Durie, E. T., (1995), 'Background Paper', in Geoff McLay (ed.), *Treaty Settlements*.

Durie, E. T., (1995), 'Justice, Biculturalism and the Politics of Law', in M. Wilson, A. Yeatman (eds), *Justice and Identity*.

Durie, E. T., (1996), *A Judge's Eye View of the Waitangi Tribunal*, a paper presented at a Conference on Indigenous Peoples: Rights, Lands, Resources, Autonomy International and Trade Show, Vancouver.

Durie, M. H., (1991), 'The Treaty of Waitangi Perspectives for Social Policy', in I. H. Kawharu (ed.), *Waitangi*.

Durie, M. H., (1993), 'Māori and the State: Professional and Ethical Implications for the Public Service', in *Proceedings of the Public Service Senior Management Conference*, Wellington.

Durie, M. H., (1993), *Submission on Appointment of Treaty of Waitangi Fisheries Commission*, National Māori Congress, Wellington.

Durie, M. H., (1994), 'An Introduction to the Hui Whakapuumau', in Department of Māori Studies (ed.), *Kia Pūmau Tonu*.

Durie, M. H., (1994), 'Kaupapa Hauora Māori: Policies for Māori Health', in *Te Ara Ahu Whakamua: Proceedings of the Māori Health Decade Hui*, Te Puni Kōkiri, Wellington.

Durie, M. H., (1994), *Whaiora: Māori Health Development*, Oxford University Press, Auckland.

Durie, M. H., (1995), 'Beyond 1852: Māori, the State and a New Zealand Constitution', *Sites*, no. 30, pp. 31–47.

Durie, M. H., (1995), *Ngā Matatini Māori Diverse Māori Realities*, paper prepared for the Ministry of Health, Wellington.

Durie, M. H., (1995), *Principles for the Development of Māori Policy*, paper presented at the Māori Policy Development AIC Conference, Wellington.

Durie, M. H., (1995), 'Proceedings of a Hui held at Hirangi Marae Turangi', in Geoff McLay (ed.), *Treaty Settlements*.

Durie, M. H., (1995), 'Te Hoe Nuku Roa Framework: A Māori Identity Measure', *Journal of the Polynesian Society*, vol. 104, no. 4, pp. 461–470.

Durie, M. H., (1995), 'Tino Rangatiratanga Māori Self-Determination', *He Pukenga Kōrero*, vol. 1, no. 1, pp. 44–53.

Durie, M. H., (1995), 'Tino Rangatiratanga, a discussion paper', in *Report for the Congress Executive 13 May 1995*, Māori Congress, Wellington.

Durie, M. H., (1996), *A Framework For Purchasing Traditional Healing Services*, a paper prepared for the Ministry of Health, Wellington.

Durie, M. H., (1996), *Mātauranga Māori: Iwi and the Crown: A Discussion Paper*, Department of Māori Studies, Massey University.

Durie, M. H., (1997), 'Mana Motuhake: The State of the Māori Nation', in Raymond Miller (ed.), *New Zealand Politics in Transition*.

Dyall, Lorna; Bridgman, Geoff, (1996), *Ngā Ia o te Oranga Hinengaro Māori 1984–1993: Māori Mental Health Trends*, Mental Health Foundation, Auckland.

Federation of Māori Authorities, (1996), *Report of the Executive to the 9th Annual General Meeting of the Federation, Whanganui*, Federation of Māori Authorities, Wellington.

Fleras, A.; Elliott, J. L., (1992), *The Nations Within: Aboriginal–State Relations in Canada, the United States, and New Zealand*, Oxford University Press, Toronto.

Forbes, Mary (1995), *In the Matter of the Crown's Fiscal Settlement on Raupatu Claims with Ngati Haua me ngā Hapū o Ngati Maniapoto*, circular to all hapū/Iwi, Te Whare Ahupiri o Ngā Ko Here, Auckland.

Forbes, Mary, (1996), *In the Matter of a Submission by the Descendants of Maramatutahi, Eldest Son of Wairere of Ngati Wairere, A Mana Tupuna of the Te Rapa Lands, Against the Crown*, circular to all hapū/Iwi, Te Whare Ahupiri o Ngā Ko Here, Auckland.

Fox, Derek, (1988), 'The Mass Media: A Māori Perspective', in Royal Commission on Social Policy, *The April Report, Vol. IV*, Royal Commission on Social Policy, Wellington, pp. 487–494.

Full Employment Committee, (1994), *Employment: An Iwi Perspective*, Māori Congress, Wellington.

Gardiner, Wira, (1994), 'Marae to Global Village: 1000 Years of Māori Development', in Department of Māori Studies (ed.), *Kia Pūmau Tonu*.

Gardiner, Wira, (1995), *Return to Sender: What Really Happened at the Fiscal Envelope Hui*, Reed, Wellington.

Graham, Hon. D., 'Address by the Minister in Charge of Treaty of Waitangi Negotiations', in Geoff McLay (ed.), *Treaty Settlements*.

Green, P. F. (ed.), (1994), *Studies in New Zealand Social Problems*, 2nd edition, Dunmore Press, Palmerston North.

Hackshaw, Frederika, (1989), 'Nineteenth Century Notions of Aboriginal Title', in I. H. Kawharu (ed.), *Waitangi*.

Hay, D. R., (1991), *Ko te Whakaata Irirangi Tikanga Māori—Nga whakaritenga: Tikanga Māori Television—the requirements*, Wellington Māori Language Board and the New Zealand Māori Council, Wellington.

Hemi, M. A., (1995), 'Tino Rangatiratanga: Assessing the Resource Management Act', Masterate thesis, Lincoln University.

Henare, Denese, (1994), 'Social Policy Outcomes Since the Hui Taumati', in Department of Māori Studies (ed.), *Kia Pūmau Tonu*.

Henare, Denese, (1995), 'The Ka Awatea Report: Reflections on its Process and Vision', in Margaret Wilson and Anna Yeatman (eds.), *Justice & Identity*.

Henderson, J., (1963), *Ratana: The Man, the Church, the Political Movement*, The Polynesian Society, Wellington.

Hirsh, Walter (ed.), (1987), *Living Languages: Bilingualism and Community Languages in New Zealand*, Heinemann, Auckland.

Hohepa, Margie, (1990), *Te Kōhanga Reo Hei Tikanga Ako i te Reo Māori: Te Kōhanga Reo as a Context for Language Learning*, MA thesis, University of Auckland, Auckland.

Hunn, J. K., (1961), *Report on the Department of Maori Affairs, Appendix to the Journals of the House of Representatives, 1960*, Wellington.

Huria, Gabrielle, (1996), 'The Bill', in *Te Karaka: The Ngai Tahu Magazine,* Raumati/Summer 1966, pp. 4–6.

Ihimaera, Witi; Long, D. S. (eds), *Into the World of Light: An Anthology of Māori Writing,* Heinemann, Auckland.

Jackson, Moana, (1988), *The Māori and the Criminal Justice System: A New Perspective: He Whaipaanga Hou,* Policy and Research Division, Department of Justice, Wellington.

Jahnke, Robert, (1996), 'Voices Beyond the Pale', *He Pukenga Kōrero,* vol. 2, no. 1, pp. 12–19.

Joint Māori/Crown Working Group, (1996), *Report of the Joint Māori/Crown Working Group on Māori Broadcasting Policy,* Wellington.

Justice Committee, (1992), *Electricity Sector Reforms Trans Power, a Report to the Congress Executive,* National Māori Congress, Wellington.

Justice Committee, (1993), *The Treaty of Waitangi and Constitutional Implications of the Electoral Reform Bill, A Discussion Paper,* National Māori Congress, Wellington.

Kaa, Wiremu, (1987), 'Policy and Planning: Strategies of the Department of Education in Providing for Māori Language Revival', in Walter Hirsh (ed.), *Living Languages.*

Kame'eleihiwa, Lilikalā, (1992), *Native Land and Foreign Desires,* Bishop Museum Press, Honolulu.

Karetu, Timoti, (1990), 'The Clue to Identity', *New Zealand Geographic,* no. 5, pp. 112–117.

Karetu, Timoti, (1995), 'Te Tau o te Reo Māori', *He Pukenga Kōrero,* vol. 1, no. 1, pp. i–ii.

Kawharu, I. H. (ed.), (1989), *Waitangi: Maori and Pakeha Perspectives of the Treaty of Waitangi,* Oxford University Press, Auckland.

Kawharu, I. H., (1996), 'Rangatiratanga and Sovereignty by 2040', *He Pukenga Kōrero,* vol. 1, no. 2, pp. 11–20.

Keegan, Peter J., (1996), *The Benefits of Immersion Education: A Review of the New Zealand and Overseas Literature,* NZCER, Wellington.

Keegan, Peter J., (1997), *1996 Survey of the Provision of Te Reo Māori,* New Zealand Council for Educational Research and Te Puni Kōkiri, Wellington.

Keenan, Danny, (1996), 'A Permanent Expedient?', *He Pukenga Kōrero,* vol. 2, no. 1, pp. 58–61.

Keith, Kenneth, (1995), 'The Roles of the Tribunal, the Courts and the Legislature', in Geoff McLay (ed.), *Treaty Settlements.*

Kelsey, Jane, (1990), *A Question of Honour,* Allen and Unwin, Wellington.

Kelsey, Jane, (1993), *Rolling Back the State: Privatisation of Power in Aotearoa/New Zealand,* Bridget Williams Books, Wellington.

Kerr, Beatrice, (1987), 'Te Kōhanga Reo He Kakano i Ruia Mai i Rangiatea', in Walter Hirsh (ed.), *Living Languages.*

King, M. (ed.), (1975), *Te Ao Hurihuri: The World Moves On*, Hicks Smith, Wellington.

King, Michael, (1983), *Whina: A Biography of Whina Cooper*, Penguin Books, Auckland.

Kirikiri, Rauru; O'Regan, Tipene (1988), 'Māori Development and Devolution', in John Martin and Jim Harper (eds), *Devolution and Accountability*, Studies in Public Administration No. 34, GP Books, Wellington, pp. 116–120.

Love, Ngātata, (1994), 'The Hui Taumata and the Decade of Māori Development in Perspective', in Department of Māori Studies (ed.), *Kia Pūmau Tonu.*

Luiten, Jane, (1992), *An Exploratory Report Commissioned by the Waitangi Tribunal on Early Crown Purchases Whanganui ki Porirua, Wai 52, 88, 108, 113, 182, 207, 287, 265*, Waitangi Tribunal, Wellington.

Luxton, Hon. John; Marshall, Hon. Dennis, (1994), *Toitū te Mana Toitū te Whenua Māori Reserved Lands: Government Policy Decisions 1994*, Te Puni Kōkiri, Wellington.

Macdonald, D. J. D., (1995), *The Settlement of Claims Under the Treaty of Waitangi*, Second report for 1995, Controller and Auditor-General, Wellington.

MacLennan, Catriona, (1995), 'Radicals stirring against fiscal deal—Graham', *The Dominion*, 31 January 1995.

Mahuta, Robert, (1995), 'Tainui: a case study of direct negotiation', in Geoff McLay, *Treaty Settlements.*

Manatu Māori, (1991), *Māori and Work: The Position of Māori in the New Zealand Labour Market*, Manatu Māori Ministry of Māori Affairs, Wellington.

Manatu Māori, (1991), *Wāhi Tapu: Protection of Māori Sacred Sites*, Ministry of Māori Affairs, Wellington.

Māori Committee, (1995), *Appeals to the Privy Council: Submission made on Behalf of the Māori Committee to the Law Commission and the New Zealand Māori Council*, Law Commission, Wellington.

Māori Congress, (1996), *Post Hirangi Discussion Paper*, Māori Congress, Wellington.

Māori Health Committee, (1987), *Tribal Authorities as Advocates for Māori Health*, New Zealand Board of Health, Wellington.

Māori Land Investment Group, (1996), *Securing Finance on Multiple-owned Māori Land*, Te Puni Kōkiri, Wellington.

Mātaatua Tribes, (1993), *The Mātaatua Declaration on Cultural Property Rights of Indigenous Peoples*, presented at the First International Conference on the Cultural and Intellectual Property Rights of Indigenous Peoples, Whakatane.

Matunga, Hirini P., (1994), *The Resource Management Act 1991 and Māori Perspectives*, Centre for Māori Studies and Research, Lincoln University.

McEwen, J. M., (1986), *Rangitane: A Tribal History*, Reed Methuen, Auckland.

McHugh, Paul, (1991), *The Māori Magna Carta: New Zealand Law and the Treaty of Waitangi*, Oxford University Press, Oxford.

McKinley, S.; Black, T.; Christensen, I.; Richardson, P., (1996), 'Toi te Kupu: A Framework for Māori Language Resource Materials', *He Pukenga Kōrero*, vol. 2, no. 1, pp. 26–33.

McLay, Geoff (ed.), (1995), *Treaty Settlements: The Unfinished Business*, New Zealand Institute of Advanced Legal Studies, Wellington.

Mead, Aroha, (1994), 'Māori Leadership: The Waka Tradition: The Crews Were the Real Heroes', in Department of Māori Studies (ed.), *Kia Pūmau Tonu*.

Melbourne, Hineani, (1995), *Māori Sovereignty: The Maori Perspective*, Hodder Moa Beckett, Auckland.

Metge, Joan, (1995), *New Growth from Old: The Whānau in the Modern World*, Victoria University Press, Wellington.

Mikaere, Buddy, (1997), 'What's Wrong with Maori Broadcasting?' *The Dominion*, Saturday 8 February 1997.

Miller, Harold, (1966), *Race Conflict in New Zealand 1814–1865*, Blackwood & Janet Paul, Auckland.

Miller, J., (1958), *Early Victorian New Zealand*, Oxford University Press, London.

Miller, Raymond (ed.), (1997), *New Zealand Politics in Transition*, Oxford University Press, Auckland.

Minister of Finance, (1995), *Proposed Restructuring of ECNZ into Two SOEs*, Circular letter, Office of the Minister of Finance, Wellington.

Minister of Māori Affairs, (1995), *Crown/Māori Governance Strategy, Draft 7*, Te Puni Kōkiri, Wellington.

Ministerial Advisory Committee on a Māori Perspective for the Department of Social Welfare, (1986), *Puao-te-ata-tu*, A Report to the Minister of Social Welfare, Wellington.

Ministerial Planning Group, (1991), *Ka Awatea: Report of the Ministerial Planning Group*, Office of the Minister of Māori Affairs, Wellington.

Ministry for the Environment (1994), *Resource Management Consultation with Tangata Whenua*, Ministry for the Environment, Wellington.

Ministry of Commerce, (1991), *Māori Television: Options for Development Te Pouaka Whakaata Māori: me pehea—he aha ngā tikanga*, Ministry of Commerce, Wellington.

Ministry of Education, (1994), Maori in Education, *Education Trends Reports*, vol. 6, no. 1.

Ministry of Education, (1995), *Ngā Haeata Mātauranga: Annual Report on Māori Education 1994/95 and Strategic Direction for 1995/96*, Ministry of Education, Wellington.

Ministry of Education, (1997), *Ngā Haeta Mātauranga: Annual Report on Māori Education 1995/96 and Strategic Directions for 1997*, Te Tāhuhu o te Mātauranga, Ministry of Education, Wellington.

Ministry of Justice, (1996), *Briefing Paper for the Minister of Justice*, Department of Justice, Wellington.

Munn, Shane, (1995), 'Exploring Relationships Between Knowledge, Science and Technology', *Proceedings of the Inaugural NAMMSAT Conference*, Te Puni Kōkiri, Ministry of Māori Development, Wellington, pp. 64–69.

Mutu, Margaret, (1994), *The Use and Meaning of Māori Words Borrowed into English for Discussing Resource Management and Conservation in Aotearoa/New Zealand: A Discussion Paper Prepared for the Conservation Board Chairpersons Conference*, New Zealand Conservation Authority, Wellington.

Mutu, Margaret, (1995), *Report to the Minister of Māori Affairs on the New Zealand Conservation Authority*, Department of Māori Studies, University of Auckland, Auckland.

National Māori Congress, (1991), *Submission to Ngā Whenua Rahui from the National Māori Congress*, NMC 91/2/12, National Māori Congress, Wellington.

National Māori Congress, (1992), *Submission on the Energy Sector Reform Bill to the Planning and Development Select Committee*, National Māori Congress, Wellington.

National Māori Congress, NZ Māori Council, Māori Women's Welfare League, (1991), *A Collective Submission on Supplementary Order Paper No. 22 Resource Management Bill*, National Māori Congress, Wellington.

New Zealand Government, (1993), *Path to 2010*, Wellington.

New Zealand Government, (1994), *Crown Proposals for the Settlement of Treaty of Waitangi Claims: Detailed Proposals*, Office of Treaty Settlements, Wellington.

New Zealand Government, (1994), *Report Submitted by the New Zealand Government to the United Nations World Summit for Social Development*, Wellington.

New Zealand Law Commission, (1989), *Report on the Treaty of Waitangi and Māori Fisheries*, Wellington.

New Zealand Māori Council, (1983), *Te Wahanga Tuatahi—Kaupapa*, NZMC, Wellington.

Ngā Kaiwhakamarama i Ngā Ture, (1994), *Detailed Scoping Paper on the Protection of Māori Intellectual Property in the Reform of the Industrial Statutes and Plant Varieties Act: A Submission to Te Puni Kōkiri*, Wellington.

Ngāti Hauiti, (1996), *Kaupapa Taiao: Environmental Policy Statement*, Te Rūnanga o Ngāti Hauiti, Hunterville.

Nicholson, Rangi; Garland, Ron, (1991), 'New Zealanders' Attitudes to the Revitalisation of the Māori Language', *Journal of Multilingual and Multicultural Development*, vol. 12, no. 5, pp. 393–410.

Nuttall, P., Ritchie, J. (1995), *Maaori Participation in the Resource Management Act: An Analysis of Provision Made for Maaori Participation in Regional Policy Statements and District Plans Produced under the Resource Management Act 1991*, Tainui Maaori Trust Board and Centre for Maaori Studies and Research, University of Waikato, Hamilton.

Officials Committee, (1991), *Report on the Officials Committee on Māori Television*, Ministry of Commerce, Wellington.

Ohia, Monty, (1993), *Bilingualism and Bilingual Education: Their Scope, Advantages, Disadvantages, and the Implications for Māori Learners*, MEdAdmin thesis, Massey University, Palmerston North.

Oliver, W. H. (ed.), (1981), *The Oxford History of New Zealand*, Oxford University Press, Wellington.

Oliver, W. H., (1988), 'Social Policy in New Zealand: An Historical Overview', in *The April Report*, Vol. 1, Royal Commission on Social Policy, Wellington.

Oliver, W. H., (1991), *Claims to the Waitangi Tribunal*, Waitangi Tribunal Division, Department of Justice, Wellington.

Orange, Claudia, (1987), *The Treaty of Waitangi*, Allen and Unwin/Port Nicholson Press, Wellington.

O'Regan, Tipene, (1995), 'A Ngai Tahu Perspective on Some Treaty Questions', in Geoff McLay (ed.), *Treaty Settlements*.

Palmer, Geoffrey, (1990), 'Treaty of Waitangi Issues Demand Clarity, Certainty', *New Zealand Herald*, 2 January 1990.

Palmer, Geoffrey, (1992), *New Zealand's Constitution in Crisis: Reforming Our Political System*, John McIndoe, Dunedin.

Palmer, Geoffrey, (1995), 'Where To from Here', in Geoff McLay (ed.), *Treaty Settlements*.

Patterson, John, (1992), *Exploring Māori Values*, Dunmore Press, Palmerston North.

Patuwai, Nguha, (1994), 'Kia Tu Kia Ora: A Māori Perspective on Ethnodevelopment', MPhil thesis, Department of Māori Studies, Massey University.

Peters, Hon. Winston, (1995), 'A Time for Leadership', in Geoff McLay (ed), *Treaty Settlements*.

Pomare, Eru; Keefe-Ormsby, Vera; Ormsby, Clint; Pearce, Neil; Reid, Paparangi; Robson, Bridget; Wātene-Haydon, Naina, (1995), *Hauora Māori Standards of Health III: A Study of the Years 1970–1991*, Te Roopu Rangahau Hauora a Eru Pomare, Wellington.

Pomare, M., (1908), 'The Māori', in *Transactions of the Eighth Session of the Australasian Medical Congress*, Government Printer, Melbourne.

Poole, Ian, (1991), *Te Iwi Māori: A New Zealand Population Past, Present and Projected*, Auckland University Press, Auckland.

Puketapu, B., (1994), 'Hokia ki te Kopae a ngā Pāheke: The Classical Māori Journey', in Department of Māori Studies (ed.), *Kia Pūmau Tonu*.

Ramsden, I., (1994), 'Māori Policy', in Department of Māori Studies (ed.), *Kia Pūmau Tonu*.

Rangihau, John, (1975), 'Being Māori', in M. King (ed.), *Te Ao Hurihuri*.

Rangiheuea, Tania, (1995), 'The Role of Māori Women in Treaty Negotiations and Settlements', in Geoff McLay (ed.), *Treaty Settlements*.

Rata, Hon. Matiu, (1995), *Self Reliance—Tino Rangatiratanga*, paper presented at the Conference on Treaty of Waitangi Settlement Methods, Institute for International Research, Wellington.

Reedy, T., (1992), *Kura Kaupapa Māori Research and Development Project Final Report*, Ministry of Education, Wellington.

Renwick, William, *The Treaty Now*, GP Publications, Wellington.

Review Team, (1993), *A Framework for Negotiation Toitū te Whenua*, Te Puni Kōkiri, Wellington.

Roberts, John, (1996), *Alternative Vision He Moemoea Ano: The Significance of the Hirangi Hui*, Joint Public Questions Committee of the Methodist Church of New Zealand and the Presbyterian Church of Aotearoa New Zealand, Wellington.

Ross, H., (1980), 'Busby and the Declaration of Independence', *New Zealand Journal of History*, vol. 14, no. 1, pp. 83–89.

Royal Commission on Social Policy, (1988), *The April Report*, Royal Commission on Social Policy, Wellington.

Royal Commission on the Electoral System, (1986), *Towards a Better Democracy: Report of the Royal Commission on the Electoral System*, Wellington.

Royal, Turoa, (1987), 'A Bi-lingual Model for Secondary Schools', in Walter Hirsh (ed.), *Living Languages*.

Saunders, John, (1996), 'View Point: Only high-paid experts benefiting', *Evening Standard*, Friday 25 October 1996.

Sharp, Andrew, (1997), 'The Waitangi Tribunal 1984–1996', in R. Miller (ed.), *New Zealand Politics in Transition*.

Shipley, Hon. Jenny, (1995), *Policy Guidelines for Māori Health: Ngā Aratohu Kaupapahere Hauora Māori*, Parliament, Wellington.

Sinclair, Douglas, (1975), 'Land: Māori View and European Response', in Michael King (ed.), *Te Ao Hurihuri*.

Smith, A. D., (1989), 'The Origins of Nations', *Ethnic and Racial Studies*, vol. 12, no. 3, pp. 340–367.

Smith, Graham, (1995), 'Whakaoho Whanau: New Formations of Whanau as Innovative Intervention into Māori Cultural and Educational Crises', *He Pukenga Kōrero*, vol. 1, no. 1, pp. 18–36.

Sole, Tony, (1991), *Protection of Indigenous Sacred Sites: The New Zealand Experience*, Manatu Māori Ministry of Māori Affairs, Wellington.

Solomon, Shane, (1995), *The Waikato Raupatu Claims Settlement Act: A Draft User's Guide to the Act as at 28 October 1995*, Tainui Māori Trust Board, Ngaruawahia.

Sorrenson, M. P. K., (1965), 'The Politics of Land', in J. G. A. Pocock (ed.), *The Māori and New Zealand Politics*, Blackwood and Janet Paul, Auckland.

Sorrenson, M. P. K., (1981), 'Maori and Pakeha', in W. H. Oliver (ed.), *The Oxford History of New Zealand*.

Sorrenson, M. P. K., (1986), 'A History of Māori Representation in Parliament', in Royal Commission on the Electoral System, *Towards a Better Democracy*.

Soutar, Monty, (1996), 'A Framework for Analysing Written Iwi Histories', *He Pukenga Kōrero*, vol. 2, no. 1, pp. 43–57.

Statistics New Zealand, (1994), *New Zealand Now Māori*, Department of Statistics, Wellington.

Statistics New Zealand, (1994), *Population Issues for New Zealand: New Zealand National Report on Population*, Department of Statistics, Wellington.

Statistics New Zealand, (1994), *Statistical Standards for Iwi*, Department of Statistics, Wellington.

Statistics New Zealand, (1996), *Household Labour Force Survey September 1996*, Department of Statistics, New Zealand.

Statistics New Zealand, (1997), *1996 Census of Populations and Dwellings: Iwi Populations and Dwellings*, Department of Statistics, Wellington.

Statistics New Zealand, (1997), *1996 Population Census Iwi Affiliation*, Statistics New Zealand Te Tai Tatau, Wellington.

Steeman, Marta, (1995), 'What's wrong with the fiscal envelope', *MG Business Mercantile Gazette*, vol. 118, no. 5226, pp. 5–6.

Sullivan, Ann, (1997), 'Māori Politics and Government Policies', in R. Miller (ed.), *New Zealand Politics in Transition*.

Tainui Māori Trust Board, (1996), *Annual Report 1996*, Ngaruawahia.

Tainui Māori Trust Board, (1996), *Tainui Māori Trust Board Annual Report 1995*, Tainui Māori Trust Board, Ngaruawahia.

Taitoko, Wayne, (1996), *Preparation is Everything Information is Power: A Tainui Perspective*, Maaori Geographic Informations Systems Conference, Wellington.

Tamihere, J., (1994), 'Management of Māori Health Programmes', in *Te Ara Ahu Whakamua: Proceedings of the Māori Health Decade Hui*, Te Puni Kōkiri, Wellington.

Taumata o te Ra Marae Committee, (1996), *Taumata o te Ra Marae*, a souvenir booklet to commemorate the opening of Taumata o te Ra, Marae Committee, Halcombe.

Taura Whiri i te Reo Māori, (1995), *Te Matatiki: Contemporary Māori Words*, Oxford University Press, Auckland.

Te Hoe Nuku Roa, (1996), *A Report and Analysis on the Initial Findings Regarding Māori Language in the Manawatu Whanaganui Region*, Department of Māori Studies, Massey University, Palmerston North.

Te Hoe Nuku Roa, (1996), *Māori Profiles: An Integrated Approach to Policy and Planning: A Report Prepared for the Ministry of Māori Development*, Department of Māori Studies, Massey University, Palmerston North.

Te Hoe Nuku Roa, (1996), *Report on the Baseline Manawatu–Whanganui Survey*, Department of Māori Studies, Massey University, Palmerston North.

Te Hoe Nuku Roa, (1996), *Reports on the Manawatu–Whanganui, Tairawhiti, Wellington Regional Baseline Surveys*, Department of Māori Studies, Massey University.

Te Māngai Pāho, (1994), *Māori Television Hui 29–30 September Proceedings*, Te Managi Pāho Māori Broadcasting Funding Agency, Wellington.

Te Māngai Pāho, (1996), *Annual Report 1995/96*, Māori Broadcasting Funding Agency, Wellington.

Te Ohu Kaimoana, (1994), *Allocation of Pre-Settlement Assets: Models of Allocation*, Treaty of Waitangi Fisheries Commission, Wellington.

Te Ohu Kaimoana, (1995), *Hui-a-tau Report, 7 July 1995*, Treaty of Waitangi Fisheries Commission, Wellington.

Te Ohu Kaimoana, (1996), *Hui-a-tau Report, 29 June 1996*, Treaty of Waitangi Fisheries Commission, Wellington.

Te Pūmanawa Hauora, (1996), *Oranga Kaumātua: The Health and Wellbeing of Older Māori, A Report Prepared for the Ministry of Health and Te Puni Kōkiri*, Department of Māori Studies, Massey University.

Te Puni Kōkiri, (1993), *Mauriora ki te Ao: An Introduction to Environmental and Resource Management Planning*, Ministry of Māori Development, Wellington.

Te Puni Kōkiri, (1993), *Newsletter Special*, March 1993, Ministry of Māori Development, Wellington.

Te Puni Kōkiri, (1994), *Mana Tangata: Draft Declaration on the Rights of Indigenous Peoples 1993: Background and Discussion on Key Issues*, Ministry of Māori Development, Wellington.

Te Puni Kōkiri, (1994), *Ngā Taonga Tuku Iho Nō Ngā Tūpuna: Māori Genetic, Cultural and Intellectual Property Rights*, Submission to Commerce Select Committee, Wellington.

Te Puni Kōkiri, (1996), *Briefing Papers to the Incoming Government*, Ministry of Māori Development, Wellington.

Te Rangihiroa (Peter Buck), (1949), *The Coming of the Māori*, Māori Purposes Fund Board, Whitcombe and Tombs, Wellington.

Te Rūnanga o Waitangi Planning Committee, (1984), *He Kōrero mo Waitangi*, Te Runanga o Waitangi.

Te Whānau o Waipareira (1995), *Claim to the Waitangi Tribunal*, Waitangi Tribunal, Department of Justice, Wellington.

Temm, P. (1990), *The Waitangi Tribunal: The Conscience of the Nation*, Random Century, Auckland.

Trotter, Chris, (1995), 'Talking About Sovereignty', Editorial, *New Zealand Political Review*, April/May 1995, p. 4.

Waitangi Tribunal, (1983), *Report Findings and Recommendations of the Waitangi Tribunal on an Application by Aila Taylor for and on Behalf of Te Atiawa Tribe in Relation to Fishing Grounds in the Waitara District (Wai 6)*, Waitangi Tribunal, Department of Justice, Wellington.

Waitangi Tribunal, (1984), *Kaituna River (Wai 4)*, Waitangi Tribunal, Department of Justice, Wellington.

Waitangi Tribunal, (1985), *Finding of the Waitangi Tribunal on the Manukau Claim (Wai 8)*, Waitangi Tribunal, Department of Justice, Wellington.

Waitangi Tribunal, (1986), *Report of the Waitangi Tribunal on the te Reo Māori Claim (Wai 11)*, Department of Justice, Wellington.

Waitangi Tribunal, (1987), *Orakei Report (Wai 9)*, Department of Justice, Wellington.

Waitangi Tribunal, (1987), *The Waiheke Claim (Wai 10)*, Waitangi Tribunal, Wellington.

Waitangi Tribunal, (1988), *Muriwhenua Fishing Report (Wai 22)*, Waitangi Tribunal, Wellington.

Waitangi Tribunal, (1988), *Report of the Waitangi Tribunal on the Mangonui Sewerage Claim (Wai 17)*, Waitangi Tribunal, Department of Justice, Wellington.

Waitangi Tribunal, (1990), *Report of the Waitangi Tribunal on Claims Concerning the Allocation of Radio Frequencies (Wai 26 and Wai 150)*, Brooker and Friend, Wellington.

Waitangi Tribunal, (1990), *Te Manutukutuku*, Newsletter of the Waitangi Tribunal, Wellington.

Waitangi Tribunal, (1991), *Ngai Tahu Report 1991 (Wai 27)*, vol. 1, Brooker and Friend, Wellington.

Waitangi Tribunal, (1992), *Appointments to the Treaty of Waitangi Fisheries Commission Report (Wai 321)*, Waitangi Tribunal Division, Department of Justice, Wellington.

Waitangi Tribunal, (1992), *Mohaka River Report (Wai 119)*, GP Publications, Wellington.

Waitangi Tribunal, (1992), *Ngai Tahu Fishing Report (Wai 27)*, Waitangi Tribunal, Wellington.

Waitangi Tribunal, (1992), *Te Roroa Report (Wai 38)*, Waitangi Tribunal, Wellington.

Waitangi Tribunal, (1992), *The Fisheries Settlement Report (Wai 307)*, Tribunals Division, Department of Justice, Wellington.

Waitangi Tribunal, (1993), *Māori Development Corporation Claim (Wai 350)*, Waitangi Tribunal, Wellington.

Waitangi Tribunal, (1993), *Ngawha Geothermal Resource Report (Wai 304)*, Waitangi Tribunal, Wellington.

Waitangi Tribunal, (1993), *Te Arawa Representative Geothermal Claims (Wai 32)*, Waitangi Tribunal, Wellington.

Waitangi Tribunal, (1994), *Report of the Waitangi Tribunal on the Maori Electoral Option Claim (Wai 413)*, Waitangi Tribunal, Wellington.

Waitangi Tribunal, (1996), *The Taranaki Report: Kaupapa Tuatahi (Wai 143)*, GP Publications, Wellington.

Waitangi Tribunal, (1997), *Muriwhenua Land Report (Wai 45)*, GP Publication, Wellington.

Walker, Ranginui, (1978), *Ngā Tau Tohetohe: Years of Anger*, Penguin Books, Auckland.

Walker, Ranginui, (1987), 'Maori Myth Tradition and Philosophic Beliefs', in Jock Phillips (ed.), *Te Whenua te Iwi: The Land and the People*, Allen and Unwin, Wellington.

Walker, Ranginui, (1990), *Ka Whawhai Tonu Matou: Struggle Without End*, Penguin, Auckland.

Walker, Ranginui, (1996), *Ngā Pepa a Ranginui: The Walker Papers*, Penguin, Auckland.

Ward, Alan, (1973), *A Show of Justice: Racial Amalgamation in Nineteenth Century New Zealand*, Auckland University Press/Oxford University Press, Auckland.

Ward, Alan, (1997), *National Overview Waitangi Tribunal Rangahaua Whanui Series*, vol. 1, Waitangi Tribunal, Wellington.

Wereta, W., (1994), 'Māori Demographic Trends', in Department of Māori Studies (ed.), *Kia Pūmau Tonu*.

Wetere, Hon. K. T., (1988), *Te Urupare Rangapū: Partnership Response*, Office of the Minister of Māori Affairs, Wellington.

Wetere, Hon. K. T., (1988), *Tirohanga Rangapū: Partnership Perspectives*, Office of the Minister of Māori Affairs, Wellington.

Wetere, Hon. K. T., (1994), 'Opening Address: Hui Taumata–Hui Whakapūmau—Ten Years of Māori Development', in Department of Māori Studies (ed.), *Kia Pūmau Tonu*.

Wetere, Hon. K. T., Minister of Māori Affairs, (1984), in Department of Māori Affairs, *Māori Economic Summit Conference, Conference Proceedings*, Wellington.

Whakatohea Settlement Negotiators, (1996), *Whakatohea Settlement Offer* Information Hui papers.

White, John, (1887–90), *The Ancient History of the Māori*, 6 vols., George Didsbury, Government Printer, Wellington.

White, Te Taru; Webber, Glenn, (1996), *A National Māori Land Data Base*, paper presented at the Maaori Geographic Information Systems Conference, Wellington.

Wickliffe, Caren, (1995), 'Issues for Indigenous Claims Settlement Policies Arising in Other Jurisdictions', in Geoff McLay (ed.), *Treaty Settlements*.

Williams, Haare, (1987), 'Broadcasting and the Māori Language', in Walter Hirsh (ed.), *Living Languages*.

Wilson, M.; Yeatman, A. (eds), (1995), *Justice and Identity: Antipodean Practices*, Bridget Williams Books, Wellington.

Winiata, Whatarangi, (1992), *Report to the Congress Executive from Fisheries Negotiator*, National Māori Congress, NMC 92/4/10a.

Wiri, Rapata, (1966), 'Land Alienation at Waikaremoana', *He Pukenga Kōrero*, vol. 1, no. 2, pp. 48–60.

Working Group on Indigenous Populations, (1993), *Draft Declaration on the Rights of Indigenous Peoples: Report on the Eleventh Session of the United*

Nations Working Group on Indigenous Populations, United Nations, Geneva.

Working Party, (1996), *Matters of Importance to Tangata Whenua,* Horowhenua District Council.

INDEX